THE SACRED BOOKS OF THE EAST

F. MAX MULLER (ED.)

LIST OF THE 50 VOLUMES

1. Upanishads.
2. Sacred Laws of Aryas.
3. Texts of Confucianism.
4. Zend-Avesta.
5. Pahlavi Texts.
6. Qur'an.
7. Institutes of Vishnu.
8. Bhagavadgita, & c.
9. Qur'an.
10. (i) Dhammapada.
10. (ii) Sutta-Nipata.
11. Buddhist Suttas.
12. Satapatha-Brahmana.
13. Vinaya Texts.
14. Sacred Laws of Aryas.
15. Upanishads.
16. Texts of Confucianism.
17. Vinaya Texts.
18. Pahlavi Texts.
19. Fo-sho-hing-tsanking.
20. Vinaya Texts.
21. Saddharma Pundarika.
22. Gaina-Sutras.
23. Zend-Avesta.
24. Pahlavi Texts.
25. Laws of Manu.
26. Satapatha-Brahmana.
27. Texts of Confucianism (Li Ki).
28. Texts of Confucianism (Li Ki).
29. Grihya-Sutras.
30 Grihya-Sutras.
31. Zend-Avesta.
32. Vedic Hymns.
33. Minor Law-Books.
34. Vedanta-Sutras.
35. Milinda.
36. Milinda.
37. Pahlavi Texts.
38. Vedanta-Sutras.
39. Texts of Taoism
40. Texts of Taoism
41. Satapatha-Brahmana
42. Atharva-veda.
43. Satapatha-Brahmana.
44. Satapatha-Brahmana.
45. Gaina-Sutras.
46. Vedic Hymns.
47. Pahlavi Texts.
48. Vedanta-Sutras.
49. (i) Buddhakarita.
49. (ii) Mahayana Texts.
50. A General Index

The Sacred Books of the East, Vol. 19

THE FO-SHO-HING-TSAN-KING

A LIFE OF BUDDHA

by

ASVAGHOSHA BODHISATTVA

Edited by

F. MAX MULLER

Translated from Sanskrit into Chinese

by

DHARMARAKSHA, A. D. 420

AND FROM CHINESE INTO ENGLISH

by

SAMUEL BEAL

GYAN

Published by

Gyan Publishing House
5, Ansari Road
Daryaganj, New Delhi-110002
Phone: 011-47034999, 9811692060
E-mail: books@gyanbooks.com

Distribution Network
gyanbooks.com
India, USA, Canada, UK, Australia, France

ISBN : 978-81-212-2937-1 (Set)
ISBN : 978-81-212-2394-2 (PB)
First Published, 1883

2nd Impression 2021

Printed at: Gyan Press, Delhi.

The Sacred Books of the East, Vol. 19

The Fo-Sho-Hing-Tsan-King
Edited by: F. Max Muller, Author: Asvaghosha Bodhisattva,
Translated by: Dharmaraksha, Samuel Beal

THE

FO-SHO-HING-TSAN-KING

A LIFE OF BUDDHA

BY

ASVAGHOSHA BODHISATTVA

TRANSLATED FROM SANSKRIT INTO CHINESE

BY

DHARMARAKSHA, A.D. 420

AND FROM CHINESE INTO ENGLISH

BY

SAMUEL BEAL

Oxford

AT THE CLARENDON PRESS

1883

CONTENTS

PAGE

INTRODUCTION ix

BOOK I.

SECT.

1. The Birth 1
2. Living in the Palace 20
3. Disgust at Sorrow 29
4. Putting away Desire 38
5. Leaving the City 47

BOOK II.

6. The Return of *Kh*andaka 59
7. Entering the Place (Wood) of Austerities 70
8. The General Grief of the Palace 81
9. The Mission to seek the Prince 94

BOOK III.

10. Bimbisâra Râ*g*a invites the Prince 111
11. The Reply to Bimbisâra Râ*g*a 119
12. Visit to Ârâ*d*a Udrarâma 131
13. Defeats Mâra 147
14. O-wei-san-pou-ti (Abhisambodhi) 156
15. Turning the Law-wheel 168

BOOK IV.

16. Bimbisâra Râ*g*a becomes a Disciple 180
17. The Great Disciple becomes a Hermit 192
18. Conversion of the 'Supporter of the Orphans and Destitute' (Anâthapi*nd*ada) 201
19. Interview between Father and Son 218

SECT. PAGE

20. Receiving the *G*etavana Vihâra 230
21. Escaping the Drunken Elephant and Devadatta . . 241
22. The Lady Âmrâ (Âmrapâlî) sees Buddha . . . 249

BOOK V.

23. By Spiritual Power fixing his (Term of) Years . . 257
24. The Differences of the Li*kkh*avis 268
25. Parinirvâ*n*a 277
26. Mahâparinirvâ*n*a 290
27. Praising Nirvâ*n*a 309
28. Division of the *S*arîras 325

NOTES.

I. Comparative List of 17 Chapters of the Sanskrit and Chinese Copies of the Buddha*k*arita 340
II. Example of the Style of the Expanded Sûtras, as translated into Chinese 344
III. The same Title given to different Works 365

INDEX 373

Transliteration of Oriental Alphabets adopted for the Translations of the Sacred Books of the East . . 377

INTRODUCTION.

HAVING been asked by the Editor of 'the Sacred Books of the East' to contribute to the series a volume from the Buddhist literature of China, I undertook, with some distrust, to translate from that language the Phû-yau-king, which is the second version of the Lalita Vistara, known in China, and dated A. D. 308.

After some months of rather disappointing work I found the text so corrupt and imperfect, and the style of the composition so inflated, that I gave up my task, having completed the translation of six chapters (kiouen) of the text, out of eight.

The editor being still desirous to have one book at least from the Chinese Tripi*t*aka in his collection of translations (and more especially a translation of some Life of Buddha, the date of which could be fixed), kindly renewed his request, and proposed that the Fo-sho-hing-tsan-king, which professed to be a translation of A*s*vaghosha's Buddha*k*arita, made by an Indian priest called Dharmaraksha (or Dharmâkshara), about the year 420 A. D., should be substituted for the work first selected.

This is the work here translated. The difficulties have been many, and the result can only be regarded as tentative. The text itself, and I have had only one Chinese text to work on, is in many places corrupt, and the style of the composition, especially in the metaphysical portions of it, is abstruse and technical. The original Sanskrit, I am told, differs considerably from the Chinese translation, and except in the restoration of proper names, in which the editor of these books has most readily helped me, the assistance derived from it has been very little. I offer the result of my work, therefore, with some mistrust, and yet with this confidence, that due allowance will be made for imperfections in the preparation of a first translation of a text comprising nearly 10,000 lines of poetry, printed in the original without stops or notes of any sort, and in a difficult style of Chinese composition.

NORTHERN BUDDHISM.

This term is now well recognised. It is used to denote the Buddhism of Nepal, Thibet, China, Japan, and Mongolia, as distinguished from the Buddhism of Ceylon, Burmah, and Siam. The radical difference between the two schools is this, that Northern Buddhism is the system developed after contact with Northern tribes settled on the Indus, while the Southern school, on the contrary, represents the primitive form of the Buddhist faith as it came (presumably) from the hands of its founder and his immediate successors. We might, without being far wrong, denote the developed school as the Buddhism of the valley of the Indus, whilst the earlier school is the Buddhism of the valley of the Ganges. In China there is a curious mixture of the teaching of both schools. The books of the contemplative sect in Southern China are translations or accommodations from the teaching of men belonging to the South of India, whilst in the North we find the books principally followed are those brought by priests from the countries bordering on the Indus, and therefore representing the developed school of the later complex system.

Northern Buddhism, again, may be divided into two, if not three, distinct periods of development, or epochs. The earliest includes in it the period during which the teaching of the immediate followers of Buddha, who brought their books or traditions northward and there disseminated them, generally prevailed; this is called the teaching of the 'little vehicle' (Hînayâna), or 'imperfect means of conveyance' (across the sea of sense). The second period is that during which the expanded form of belief denoted as the 'great vehicle' (Mahâyâna) was accepted; here the radical idea is that the teaching of Buddha provides 'universal salvation' for the world. Thirdly, the 'indefinitely expanded' form, known as Vaipulya, which is founded on the idea of a universal nature, to which all living things belong, and which, by recovering itself in each case, secures for the subject complete restoration to the one nature from which all living things have wandered. This is evidently a form of pure Pantheism, and denotes the period when the distinctive belief of Buddhism merged into later Brahmanism, if indeed it did not originate it.

We cannot lay down any sharp line of division (either as to time or minute difference of doctrine) between these forms of thought as they are found in the books; but they may be traced back, through the teaching of the sects into which the system became separated, to the great schism of the primitive Buddhist church at Vaisâlî, 100 years after the Nirvâna.

With respect to this schism the statement made in the Dîpavamsa[1] is this: 'The wicked Bhikkus, the Vaggiputtakas (i.e. the Vaisâlî Buddhists), who had been excommunicated by the Theras, gained another party; and many people, holding a wrong doctrine, ten thousand, assembled and (also) held a council. Therefore this Dhamma Council is called the Great Council (Mahâsaṅgîti),' (Oldenberg's translation, p. 140.) Turning now to the Mahâsaṅghika version of the Vinaya, which was translated into Chinese by Fa-hien (circ. 420 A.D.), who brought it from Pâtaliputra (chap. XXXVI), we read (K. 40, fol. 23 b), 'After the Nirvâna (Ni-pan, i. e. Nibbâna) of Buddha the Great Kâsyapa, collecting the Vinaya Pitaka, was the (first) Great Master (Mahâsthavira), and his collection of the Dharmapitaka was in 80,000 divisions. After the death (mih to, destruction) of the great Kâsyapa the next master (lord) was Ânanda, who also held the Dharmapitaka in 80,000 (divisions). After him the honourable (lord) Mo-yan-tin (Madhyântika) was chief, and he also held the Dharmapitaka in 80,000 (divisions). After him came

[1] The Dîpavamsa, an early historical record of Buddhism compiled in Ceylon between the beginning of the fourth and the first third of the fifth century A.D.

*S*anavâsa (she-na-po-sa), who also held the Dharmapi*t*aka in 80,000 (divisions). After him came Upagupta, of whom the lord of the world (Buddha) predicted that as "a Buddha without marks" (alakshana*n*ako Buddha*h*; see Burnouf, Introd. p. 378, note 1) he should overcome Mâra, which is related in the Avadânas (yin ün). This (master) could not hold the 80,000 divisions of the Dharmapi*t*aka. After him there were five schools (the school of the "Great Assembly" being the first of the five) to which the following names were given: (1) Dharmaguptas, (2) Mahî*s*âsakas, (3) Kâ*s*yapîyas, (4) Sarvâstivâdas. This last is also called the school "that holds the existence of all," because it maintains the distinct nature of (things existing in) past, present, and future time. Each of these schools had its own president and distinctive doctrine. Because of this in the time of A*s*okarâ*g*a, when the king was in doubt what was right and what was wrong, he consulted the priests as to what should be done to settle the matter. They replied, "The law (dharma) ought to be settled by the majority." The king said, "If it be so, let the matter be put to the vote (by lots or tokens of wood), and so let it be seen who is right (in the majority)." On this they cast lots, and our sect (i.e. the Mahâsaṅghikas) was in great preponderance. Therefore it is called the Mahâsaṅgîti or Great Assembly.'

From this it appears that the Mahâsaṅghikas, on their part, claimed to be the original portion of the Buddhist church, and that they regarded the four sects, whose names are given, to be heretical. The same colophon has a further notice respecting this subject. It states that 'There was in former times in Mid-India a wicked king who ruled the world. From him all the *S*rama*n*as fled, and the sacred books were scattered far and wide. This wicked king having died, there was a good king who in his turn requested the *S*rama*n*as to come back to their country to receive his protection (nurture). At this time in Pâ*t*aliputra there were 500 priests who wished to decide (matters of faith), but there was no copy of the Vinaya, or teacher who knew the Vinaya, to be found. They therefore sent forthwith to the *G*etavana Vihâra to copy out the Vinaya in its original character, as it had been handed down to that period. Fa-hien, when he was in the country of Magadha, in the town of Pâ*t*aliputra, in the temple of A*s*okarâ*g*a, in the Vihâra of the Southern Devarâ*g*a (Virûdhaka), copied out the Sanskrit (Fan) original and brought it back with him to P'ing *k*au, and in the twelfth year of the title I-hi (417 A. D.) [416 according to the cyclical characters] and the tenth month, he translated it.' Here we seem to have an obscure allusion to a first and second A*s*oka. Is it possible that the reference is to an actual council held at Pâ*t*aliputra in opposition to the orthodox assembly under Moggaliputta? The 500 priests who were sent to the *G*etavana might have represented the popular party, and being without a copy of their version of the Vinaya, they procured one from *S*râvastî. This may or may not be so, and in the absence of further details we cannot give it much weight.

On examining the copy of the Vinaya alluded to by Fa-hien, viz. that belonging to the Mahâsaṅghikas, we find ample reason for adhering to the statement of the Dîpava*m*sa, viz. 'that the members of the great congregation proclaimed a doctrine against the faith' (p. 139 op. cit.) The sections illustrating the Parâ*g*ika and other rules are of a gross and offensive character. The rules are illustrated by an abundance of tales or *g*âtakas introduced in the text (this seems to favour the presence of a Northern element in the redaction). The account of the two councils differs from that found in the other copies of the Vinaya, and in the history of the second council at Vai*s*âlî there is mention made only of one of the sins of the 'Va*gg*iputtakas,' viz. receiving money; but the council itself is called, according to this account, for the purpose of revising the canon. Now this seems to show that the Mahâsaṅghika school took its rise at this time, and that a redaction of the canon was prepared by that school distinct from that in common use. According to the statement found in the Dîpava*m*sa, 'they composed other Suttas and another Vinaya' (p. 141, § 36). This is confirmed by an account which we have given us in a work belonging to the Vinaya class in the Chinese Tripi*t*aka, called 'The Questions of *S*âriputra' (Catalogue, case 48, miscellaneous). I thought this might be the work referred to in the edict of A*s*oka as the 'Questions of Upatissa,' but on examination it appears to be a production of the Mahâsanghika school, and not exclusively bearing on questions of the Vinaya. Perhaps it was written and named in opposition to the orthodox text alluded to in the edict. To exhibit the teaching of the school to which it belongs I will briefly allude to the earlier portion of this Sûtra. The scene is laid in Râ*g*a*gri*ha, the question proposed by *S*âriputra is, 'Who is the true disciple of Buddha, and who not?' Buddha replies, 'The true disciple is one who attends to and obeys the precepts, as the Bhikshu Pao-sse, i. e. precious thing (Yasa), who hearing the statement of Buddha that all things (sa*m*skârâ) were impermanent, immediately perceived the whole truth. The disciple who attends to the tradition of the church is also a true one, as the Bhikshu who attended to *S*âriputra's statement respecting Kâludâyi's drinking wine. Those, on the other hand, who neglect either the direct instruction of Buddha, or that of his successors—these are not true disciples.' *S*âriputra then proceeds to ask what are the permissions and what the prohibitions made by Buddha in the rules of the Vinaya, especially in respect of food, as, for example, where Buddha forbids an early meal at the invitation of a villager, or where he permits the use of fish and other condiments. Buddha replies that these things must depend on circumstances, and that the rule of the true disciple is to follow the directions of the president of the church. For instance, after my Nirvâ*n*a (he proceeds) the great Kâ*s*yapa will have authority equal to mine; after Kâ*s*yapa, Ânanda; after Ânanda, Madhyântika; after Madhyântika, *S*anakavâsa; after *S*anakavâsa, Upagupta; after Upagupta there will be a Maurya (king) *K*u-ko (A*s*oka), who will rule the world and extend the Scriptures (Dharmavinaya). His grandson will be called Pushyamitra (Fu-sha-mih-to-lo), who will succeed to the empire of the righteous king (or who will succeed directly to the empire of the king, or the royal estate). This one will ask his ministers what he must do to gain an undying fame; and being told he must either patronise religion as his predecessor or persecute it, he will adopt the latter course, overthrow the pagodas (dâgobas), destroy the Scriptures, murder the people. Five hundred Arhats, however, will escape the persecution. Meantime the Scriptures being taken up to Maitreya, he will preserve them. At last the king and his army being destroyed (by a mountain cast on them), this line of kings will perish. Afterwards a righteous king will succeed, and Maitreya will send down 300 youths, born apparitionally among men, who will recover the law from the 500 Arhats, and go amongst men instructing them, so that once more the Scriptures, which had been taken to heaven by Maitreya, will be disseminated in the world. At this time the king of the country will divide the Dharmavinaya into many parts, and will build a stronghold in which to preserve them, and so make it difficult for those wishing to consult them, to do so. Then an old Bhikshu of good repute will write a remonstrance, and selecting such passages of the Vinaya as are in accordance with Kâ*s*yapa's council, and known as the Vinaya of the 'Great Congregation' (will make them known); the other party will, on their part, include with these the false additions that have been since made. Thus will begin the contention and wrangling. At length the king will order the two schools to assemble, and the matter to be put to the vote, in this way,—taking a number of slips of wood, some black, the others white, he will say, 'let the adherents of the old school take the black slips, and the new school the white slips.' Then those taking the black slips will be myriads in number, those taking the white only hundreds. Thus there will be a separation. The old school will be called 'the Mahâsaṅghikas,' the new 'the school of the elders,' and hence also named 'the Ta-pi-lo' (Sthâvira (school)).

This obscure account tends at any rate to show that the original separation of the church, from which resulted the later schisms, began at the time of the Great Assembly at Vai*s*âlî. Whether we are to gather that a second and final separation took place afterwards when the good king was reigning (Dharma-Asoka?) is not certain, but it seems to be implied in this and the former record, and is in every respect probable. This would therefore account for the silence of the Northern school respecting the Council at Pâtaliputra, and would fully explain why the Sthâvira school insists on that council as the charter, so to speak, of their orthodoxy.

LIVES OF BUDDHA.

There is no life of Buddha in the Southern school. Facts connected with his life are found in the different canonical books, and these being put together give an outline of his career, though there is no single work devoted to the account of his life. But there are many such works in the Chinese collection of books. Some of them still exist, others have been lost. The earliest of which we have any record was translated by *K*u-fa-lan (Gobharana) between A.D. 68 and A.D. 70. It was called the

(1) Fo-pen-hing-king
佛本行經

in five chapters. It is lost, but there are quotations from it found in Chinese Buddhist books which indicate its character. In the commentary, for example, of Taou-shih, who edited a life of Buddha by Wong pûh, there is frequent reference to a work, Pen-hing-king, which in all probability is the book under our present consideration. This we gather from a comparison of these quotations with the text of other works that bear a similar title. For instance, there is a book called Fo-pen-hing-tsih-king, which is stated to be a Chinese version of the Abhinishkramana Sûtra, that is sometimes quoted as the Pen-hing-king, but the passages given by Taou-shih are not to be found in this work. Neither are they taken from the Pen-hing-king, written by Paou-Yun, nor are they to be found in the Pen-hing-king by Asvaghosha. We may justly argue therefore that the commentator, Taou-shih, in quoting from the Pen-hing-king, refers to the work translated by *K*u-fa-lan, which is now lost. If so, the book can have differed in no material point from the common legendary account of Buddha's early career. In § 8 the Pen-hing is quoted in reference to the selection of Buddha's birth-place; in § 11 the dream of Mâyâ at the conception of the child is referred to. In § 23 there is the history of Asita and his horoscope. In § 27 the trial in athletic sports. In § 29 the enjoyment of the prince in his palace for ten years. In § 31 the account of the excursion beyond the walls and the sights of suffering. In § 33 the interview with his father before his flight from the palace. In § 38 the act of cutting his hair with his sword and the intervention of *S*akra. In § 39 his exchange of garments with the hunter. In § 40 his visit to the *R*ishis in the snowy mountains. In § 41 the account of his six years' fast at Gayâ. In § 44 there is allusion to the Nâgas Kalika and Mu*k*ilinda. In § 46 the rice milk given by the two daughters of Su*g*âta. Here the quotations from the Pen-hing come to an end. We can scarcely doubt therefore that this work ended with the account of the supreme enlightenment of Buddha. It is said that the Fo-pen-hing was in five kiouen; it could not therefore have been a short abstract, but must have been a complete history of Buddha from his birth to the period of his victory over Mâra. It would thus correspond with what is termed the 'intermediate epoch,' in the Southern records. We may conclude therefore that such a life of Buddha was in circulation in India in a written form at or before the beginning of our era. It was brought thence by *K*u-fa-lan, and translated into Chinese A.D. 67–70. M. Stanislas Julien, in the well-known communication found on p. xvii n. of the translation of the Lalita Vistara from Tibetan by M. Foucaux, speaks of this work as the first version of the Lalita Vistara into Chinese.

We have next to consider a work translated into Chinese by two *S*rama*n*as from India in the year A.D. 194, and named

(2) Siu-hing-pen-k'i-king.

修行本起經

This work belongs to case lxviii in my Catalogue of the Buddhist Tripi*t*aka, and is numbered 664 by Mr. Bunyiu Nanjio. It was translated by *K*u-ta-lih (Mahâbâla) and Kong-mang-tsiang. As the title indicates, it is a brief memoir of Buddha's preparatory career (i. e. preparatory to his enlightenment), in two parts[1] and seven vargas. It is stated in the work, Kao-săng-fu, K. i, fol. $\frac{8}{1}$, that this book was brought from Kapilavastu by the *S*rama*n*a Dharmaphala (Tan-kwo). This is also repeated in the work Lai-tai-san-pao, K. iv, fol. 18. The opening scene therefore lies in Kapilavastu. Its language is sufficiently exaggerated, but not to that wearisome degree found in the later Sûtras. It begins with the nomination of Buddha by Dîpankara, and ends with the defeat of Mâra under the tree of knowledge. It therefore includes both the distant and the intermediate epochs. I shall give the headings of the seven vargas, with some remarks on the character of the narrative.

Varga 1 (pp. 1–9). 'Exhibiting change.' The scene is laid in Kapilavastu, in the Nyagrodha Vihâra. Surrounded by a vast assembly of disciples, Buddha enquires of Maudgalyâyana, 'Can you for the sake of all living things[2] declare the origin of my career (pen k'i)?' On this Maudgalyâyana, addressing Buddha in the usual orthodox way, asks him to recite the history in virtue of his own inherent spiritual power. On this Buddha declares how he had been born during innumerable kalpas in every character of life for the sake of stemming the tide of lust and covetousness which engulphed the world, and by a life of continual progress through the exercise of the virtues of wisdom, patience, charity, &c. had arrived at the final condition of enlightenment. He then gives the history of his nomination when Dîpankara was Buddha, and of his successive births until finally, after having been born as Vessantara, he occupied the Tushita heaven, and thence descended to be

[1] Abstract of Four Lectures, p. 10.

[2] This is given in Chinese Ta-sa-ho-kie, which can only be restored to Tasâ. See Childers, sub voce.

born in Kapilavastu as the Bodhisattva about to accomplish his career as Buddha.

Varga 2. Bodhisattva descends as a spirit. In this section we find an account of Bodhisattva's conception. He descends under the form[1] of a white elephant, and is seen by Mâyâ in a dream: 'She beholds in the middle of heaven a white elephant resplendent with glory, and lighting up the world, accompanied by music and sounds of rejoicing, and whilst accompanying Devas scatter flowers and incense, the elephant approaches her, and for a moment hovers above the spot and disappears.' The dream is interpreted by the soothsayers as an exceedingly fortunate one, because 'it indicated the descent of a holy spirit (Shing-shin) into the womb.' The child born therefore would be either a wheel-turning flying-as-he-goes (fi-hing), universal monarch, or a Buddha 'born to save the world.' The queen from that moment leads a pure, uncontaminate life.

'Now on account of this conception,
Bearing as I do a Mahâsattva,
I give up all false, polluting ways,
And both in heart and body rest in purity.'

The kings of neighbouring countries bring their presents of gold, silver, jewels, and robes, and on the eighth day of the fourth month the child is born under an Asoka tree. The angels sing for joy, and thirty-two supernatural events indicate the nativity. We need not enumerate all these events; the first, however, is that the earth was greatly shaken, and all rough and hilly places became smooth. The fifteenth is, the star Pushya came down and appeared waiting on the prince. The last is that the tree spirit (i. e. the spirit residing in the tree under which the Bodhisattva was born) appearing from it as a man bowed his head in worship[2]. We then have an account of Asita's visit and prediction. The

[1] Or, riding on a white elephant. The phrase in the Chinese is ambiguous. There is reason to suppose that the original thought was that the Bodhisattva was riding on an elephant, but was invisible as a spirit.

[2] Tree and Serpent Worship, plate xci, fig. 4.

varga concludes with the account of his superiority over his teachers.

Varga 3. The athletic contest. This section contains an account of the prince's marriage with Ku-i (Gopî) after the exhibition of his strength in fighting, wrestling, and archery. The prince in this account restores the elephant to life which Devadatta had killed, and is charged by Devadatta and his followers as being strengthened by Mâra (the devil) in doing the wonders he did. He marries Gopî, and with 60,000 attendant women dwells in his palace. But his heart is not at rest.

Varga 4. The excursion for observation. This is the usual account of the prince's visit to the garden and the sights he beheld. The charioteer is accompanied by 1000 other chariots and 10,000 cavalry. A *S*uddha Deva called Nandahara assumes the form of an old man, a sick man, a corpse, and a *S*rama*n*a successively, and thus determines the prince to leave the world (worldly life) and become an ascetic. In order to distract his mind the king requests the prince to attend a ploughing festival. Whilst thus engaged he beholds the suffering of the oxen, and the heat and toil of the men, and the countless insects being destroyed and devoured by the birds. Retiring under the shadow of a *G*ambu tree[1] he enters Dhyâna (profound meditation). The king hearing where he was proceeds to the spot, and observes the branches of the trees bent down[2] over the prince, and on approaching the horses bend their knees in reverence. The king and his retinue then return to the city. On entering the gate he is met by countless thousands of people with flowers and incense, whilst the soothsayers shout with joy, 'O king! live for ever!' The king enquiring the reason, the Brahmans tell him that to-morrow the seven treasures would appear, and the king would become a 'holy ruler' (a *K*akravartin).

Varga 5. Leaving his home. The prince without ceasing

[1] Tree and Serpent Worship, plate xxv, fig. 1, where the three buildings represent the three palaces built for the prince.

[2] The leaves are bent down in the plate (op. cit.)

meditated on the joy of a contemplative life in the desert. Being now nineteen years old, he vowed on the seventh day of the fourth month to leave his home. In the middle of the night he was addressed by Ku-i his wife, who had been troubled by five dreams. Having appeased her, the gods determined, ere he composed himself again, to induce him to leave his home. They sent Ou-suh-man [is this Wésamuna? (Manual of Buddhism, p. 51)] to lull the people to sleep, whilst the Deva Nandahara causes all the women of the palace to appear in loathsome attitudes, &c. The prince beholding the sight, and regarding all things that exist 'as a phantom, a vision, a dream, an echo,' called his coachman to bring his horse, and accompanied by countless divine beings left the city. Leaving the city they fled on their way, till at morning light they had gone 480 lis, and arrived at the A-nu-ma country (the river Anavamâ or Anomâ; a Chinese note explains it as the 'ever-full'). Here he dismisses his attendant and sends him back with the horse and his jewels to Kapilavastu. Having cut off his hair, he proceeded to the Magadha country, and there has an interview with Bimbisâra râ*g*a. To the enquiry whence he came and what his title was, he replies, 'I come from Ka-wei (Kapila or Kavila) to the east of the fragrant mountains and north of the snowy mountains.' On this Bimbisâra asks him in haste, 'Surely you are not that celebrated Siddhârtha?' On his replying in the affirmative, the king bows down at his feet, and asks why one so richly endowed and so distinguished in his person was not a universal monarch, and why he had left his home. The prince replies that he had gone forth to seek deliverance from old age, disease, and death. On this follows a long series of lines (geyas), beginning, 'Suppose we could.' Finally Bodhisattva leaves the king and encounters Arâta and Kâlâma (i. e. Ârâla Kâlâma), but not satisfied with their teaching he again departs.

Varga 6. Six years' austerities. Bodhisattva goes forward and arrives at the valley (river-valley (*k*uen)) of Se-na. This valley was level and full of fruit trees, with no noxious insects or snakes. Here dwelt the *R*ishi (Taosse) Se-na, with 500 followers. Here Bodhisattva took his residence under a *S*âla tree. The gods offer him nectar (sweet dew), but he receives it not, but vows to take one grain of millet (hemp) a day. When he had continued thus for six years, and reduced himself to the verge of death, the two daughters of Se-na have a dream, in which they see a lily having seven colours wither away; there comes a man who waters it, and it revives, whilst other buds spring up on the face of the water. Awaking they ask their father to explain the dream, but neither he nor his followers can do so. On this *S*akra descends under the form of a Brahma*k*ârin, who explains the dream. The girls having prepared a dish of cream convey it to Bodhisattva; he receives it, and his strength revives. Having washed his hands and flung the dish into the river, whence it is carried by a golden-winged bird to heaven, he proceeds to the Bodhi tree.

Varga 7. Defeats Mâra. Seated under the tree he causes a stream of light to proceed from between his eyes and to enter the dwelling of Mâra. Mâra, greatly disconcerted, knowing that the Bodhisattva if he fulfils his purpose will overthrow his power, resolves to oppose him. His son Sumati warns him against such an attempt, but Mâra, summoning his three daughters, acquaints them with his design. They robe themselves in their choicest attire, and with 500 attendants go to the spot where Bodhisattva was. They proceed to tempt him with lascivious offers. Bodhisattva with a word changes their appearance into that of old women. On this Mâra, enraged, summons the king of the demon spirits (kwei-shin) to assemble with eighteen myriads of others. They surround the tree for a distance of thirty-six yo*g*anas, and assuming every shape (lions, bears, tigers, elephants, oxen, horses, dogs, monkeys, &c.) they belch forth smoke and fire. Bodhisattva sits unmoved. Mâra then advances and endeavours to induce him to give up his purpose. Bodhisattva replies in loving words, and finally the entire host is dispersed. Buddha then arrives at perfect wisdom, the condition which neither Brahma nor any other being had yet attained, and so completes his purpose.

The following life of Buddha, although named in the catalogues, has not come under my notice:

(3) Siau-pen-k'i-king

小本起經

in two kiouen; translated by the *S*rama*n*a *K*i-yau, A. D. 196.

The next history of Buddha in point of the date of its translation is the

(4) Ta-tseu-sui-ying-pen-k'i-king.

太子瑞應本起經

This is the work of an Upâsaka belonging to the Wu dynasty (222–264 A.D.), who came to China towards the end of the After-Han dynasty, and was a diligent translator. The work before us is a brief one, divided into two parts, without any subdivision into sections. The first part, which resembles the translation last noticed, takes us to the defeat of Mâra. The second includes in it a description of Buddha's condition as the 'fully enlightened,' and also the conversion of the fire-worshipping Kâ*s*yapas. With respect to his work of preaching, this book has the peculiarity of excluding all mention of the journey to Benares after the enlightenment. It makes the conversion of the five men take place near the Bodhi tree in Magadha, and omits all mention of Yasa, *S*âriputra, or Maudgalyâyana. The account of the conversion of the Kâ*s*yapas is full and circumstantial. It agrees in a marked way with the particulars given in the Manual of Buddhism (Spence Hardy, pp. 188–191). The illustrations of this event, given in the Sanchi Sculptures (plates xxiv, xxxi, xxxii, 1st ed.), show that it was a popular episode in the history of Buddha at the time of the completion of the Sanchi Stûpa. It is also given in the following pages in A*s*vaghosha's work, so that we cannot doubt this event formed part of the recognised work of Buddha as a teacher. This short life therefore includes in it the three portions known in the South as the distant, intermediate, and proximate epochs. The last named, however, differs materially from the more expanded account found in other books, and is in fact confined to the labour of the conversion of the five men and the three Kâ*s*yapa brothers.

We now come to the consideration of the life of Buddha known as the

(5) *K*ung-pen-k'i-king.

中本起經

This translation was made by the *S*rama*n*a Dharmaphala in conjunction with Kong-mang-tsiang, about the year 208 A.D. It was brought by Dharmaphala from Kapilavastu, and it is said to be extracted from the Dîrghâgama (the long Âgama), which is undoubtedly a primitive and, as we should say, a canonical work. This translation is in two parts, divided into 15 vargas.

Varga 1. Turning the wheel of the law. This section begins with Buddha's interview with Upaka, after he had attained enlightenment, and gives an account of the conversion of the five men.

Varga 2. Indicating changes. Contains the history of Yasa, and the conversion of his four friends (Fu-nai, Pu*n*ya-*g*it; Vimala; Kiu-yen-pih, Gavâmpati; Su-to, Subâhu).

Varga 3. The conversion of Kâ*s*yapa.

Varga 4. Converts Bimbisâra râ*g*a.

Varga 5. Conversion of *S*âriputra and Maudgalyâyana.

Varga 6. Returns to his own country.

Varga 7. The history of Su-ta (i. e. Sudatta or Anâthapi*nd*ada).

Varga 8. The history of the queen of Udyâna, king of Kau*s*âmbî. She would not comply with the king's wishes, because it was a fast day.

Varga 9. Gautamî becomes a Bhikshu*n*î.

Varga 10. Inconstancy. Contains the history of Prasena*g*it's interview with Buddha, and of the minister who had lost his child.

Varga 11. Self-love. Contains the history of an interview with Prasena*g*it, and a sermon preached by Buddha on self-love.

Varga 12. Conversion of Mahâkâ*s*yapa (Agnidatta).

Varga 13. Conversion of Ambapâlî.

Varga 14. Discussion with the Nirgranthas.

Varga 15. Buddha eats the food fit for horses[1].

It will be seen from the above summary, that so early at least as the end of the second century A. D. a life of Buddha, with the details above named, was in circulation in Kapilavastu.

The next life of Buddha, in point of date, is the second version of the Lalita Vistara, known in China as the

(6) Phû-yau-king.

普曜經

This was translated by the Indian priest Dharmaraksha, during the Western Tsin dynasty, about A.D. 300. It is in eight chapters, and belongs to the expanded class of Buddhist literature. The story of Buddha's life is here told from his birth to his death, but in the exaggerated and wearisome form peculiar to the works of this (expanded) school. It would seem as if the idea of merit attaching to the reproduction of every word of the sacred books had led the later writers, not only to reproduce the original, but to introduce, by an easy but tiresome method, the repetition of a simple idea under a multitude of verbal forms, and so secure additional merit[2].

There is another life of Buddha named in the Chinese Catalogues, translated A. D. 420 by Buddhabhadra, who was a descendant of Am*ri*todana, the uncle of Buddha. This life is named

(7) Kwo-hu-yin-ko-king.

過去因果經

It is in four kiouen. It has not come under my notice; but another translation of the same text, likewise in four kiouen, and made shortly after Buddhabhadra by a native of Mid-India called Gu*n*abhadra (A. D. 436), is before me. This work is called

[1] See Abstract of Four Lectures, p. 52.

[2] To show the character of this style of composition we give at the end (Note II) a section from this Sûtra relating to the birth of Bodhisattva.

(8) Kwo-hu-hien-tsai-yin-ko-king.

過去現在因果經

It is not divided into sections, but each kiouen embraces a distinct portion of the history.

Kiouen I contains an account of Sumedhas and his nomination by Dîpaṅkara Buddha. It then proceeds to narrate the events attending the conception, incarnation, and early years of the Bodhisattva until his tenth year, and his superiority at school (p. 26).

Kiouen II begins with the martial contest and victory of Bodhisattva over his compeers, and ends with the flight from his palace at nineteen years of age (p. 27).

Kiouen III begins with Bodhisattva's interview with the different *R*ishis, and concludes with the conversion of the five men after Buddha's enlightenment (p. 34).

Kiouen IV begins with the conversion of Yasa and his father, and afterwards his fifty friends. It then gives in great detail the history of the Kâ*s*yapas, and ends with an account of the gift of the *G*etavana. This life of Buddha is of a circumstantial character, and is full of interesting episodes.

The next memoir in point of time of translation is the history of Buddha as it occurs in the Vinaya Pi*t*aka. I shall take as my example the Vinaya according to the Mahî*s*âsaka school. In the 15th and 16th chapters of this work is a brief life of Buddha. This copy of the Vinaya was brought from Ceylon by Fa-hien at the beginning of the fifth century (A.D. 414); it was not translated by him, but by Buddha*g*iva, a native of Cophene, A.D. 423 (see Abstract of Four Lectures, p. 21), with the assistance of Tao-sing (*K*u-tao-sing), a *S*rama*n*a of Khoten.

In this life the order of events (and the precise words occasionally) agree with the Pâli of the Mahâvagga, as published by Oldenberg. It begins, however, with the history of the origin of the *S*âkyas, and in this it resembles the account in the Manual of Buddhism[1], except that in the Chinese the

[1] Spence Hardy, p. 130.

description of *G*anta, the son of Ambâ, is that he was contemptible and ugly, whilst in the Singhalese account he is described as lovely and well-favoured. After the complete enlightenment, Buddha sits in contemplation at the foot of different trees. Here there occurs a divergence from the Pâli, as it is in the interval of his remaining thus in contemplation that he visits the village of Senâpati, and gives to his daughter Su*g*âtâ the two refuges in Buddha and the law. This is a curious statement, as it seems to imply that at that time the triple refuge was not known; in other words, that there was no Saṅgha, or Church.

The interview with Upaka is identical with the Pâli. The sermon at Benares and the conversion of the five men, the visit to and conversion of Bimbisâra, the conversion of Yasa and his friends, the visit to Uruvilva and the Kâ*s*yapas, the conversion of Upatishya and Kolita—all this is as in the Southern account. The narrative then breaks off suddenly, and the rules of the Vinaya with respect to teacher and pupil &c. are introduced. This notice of Buddha's life, although not translated in China before the fifth century, must date back from the time when the Southern copy of the Vinaya, which Fa-hien brought from China, was first put together. The Mahî*s*âsika school was an offshoot from the Âryasthâvira branch of the Buddhist church, and in all probability was regarded in Ceylon as orthodox, in opposition to the Mahâsaṅghikas. It is curious that in the Mahâsaṅghika copy of the Vinaya which Fa-hien brought from Patna, and which he himself translated into Chinese, there is no section corresponding to the one just adduced, that is, this copy of the Vinaya contains no record of Buddha's life. This may be accounted for on the ground that the two redactions were made at different times and at places far apart. But yet it is curious that a copy of the Vinaya brought from Patna, and said to have been copied from an authentic original, should differ so widely from a copy found by the same person at the same time in Ceylon[1]. This circumstance at any rate will

[1] Fa-hien, p. 144.

show the mixed character of Buddhist books in China, and the difficulty of classifying them in any distinct order.

We come now to notice a life of Buddha translated by a native Chinese priest. It is called the

(9) Fo-pen-hing-king

佛本行經

and was translated by Pao-yun, a companion of Fa-hien in his travels in India, about A.D. 420. It is in seven chapters, and composed in varying measures or verses of 4, 5 or 7 symbols to the line. We have no means of determining the name of the original work from which Pao-yun translated his book, but it evidently was not the Buddha-*k*arita-kâvya of A*s*vaghosha. It resembles it in no particular, except that it is in verse. The contents of this work I have already given elsewhere (Abstract of Four Lectures, p. 100); so that there is no need to allude to it here at any length.

Nor need I refer, except to name it, to the Chinese version of the Lalita Vistara. This translation was made by the *S*rama*n*a Divâkara during the Tang dynasty. He was a native of Mid-India, and flourished in China A.D. 676. It is in 12 chapters and 27 sections. The headings of these chapters have been given elsewhere (Catalogue, pp. 18, 19). The contents of the Chinese version agree in the main with the Tibetan. It is named

(10) Fang-kwang-tai-*k*wang-yan-king.

方廣大莊嚴經

There is a life of Buddha translated by an Indian priest of Cophene, about A.D. 445, which is called

(11) Săng-kia-lo-c'ha-sho-tsih-fo-hing-king.

僧伽羅剎所集佛行經

This appears to have been written by a priest called Sañgharaksha, who was born in the kingdom of Su-lai, and came to Gandhâra when Kanishka flourished. This monarch is called in the text Kien-to-ki-ni-wang. The symbols Kien-to correspond with the family title given elsewhere to Kanishka, viz. *K*an-tan, i.e. *K*andana or sandalwood (see the work Tsah-pao-tsang-king in the Indian Office Collection of Buddhist Books, kiouen vi, fol. 12 [Catalogue, case lxvi]). This Chinese title may probably correspond with the tribal name of Gushan, or perhaps (according to Oldenberg) with the title Koiranos, of the coins. But in any case Saṅgharaksha is said to have lived during the time of this monarch, and to have written the life of Buddha, which was afterwards translated into Chinese by Saṅghabhadanta (?). This work is in 5 kiouen; it comprises the usual stories from the birth of Buddha to the distribution of his relics after his death. There is at the end a curious story about A*s*oka, who reigned 100 years after the Nirvâ*n*a. He is said to have had a dream which induced him to assemble the Bhikshus in a convocation. He was told by them that there was in Râ*g*agr*i*ha a casket on which there was a record enshrined, or a gold plate, which had been delivered by Buddha. On opening the casket a prophecy was found stating that in Magadha, in the city of Râ*g*agr*i*ha, there were two householders whose two sons were called Vi*g*ayamitra and Vasudatta; of these the former, in consequence of his merit in giving a ball of earth to Buddha, should be born 100 years after as A*s*oka râ*g*a of the Maurya family. In consequence of this prophecy A*s*oka built 84,000 shrines for the relics of Buddha, obeying in this the direction of his dream, that he should cause the *s*arîras of the holy one to be everywhere diffused.

Another life of Buddha is one I have partly translated in the Romantic History of Buddha. It is called

(12) Fo-pen-hing-tsih-king

佛本行集經

and was translated by *G*ñânagupta or *G*ñânakûta of the Tsui dynasty (circ. A.D. 588). It is said to be the same as the Abhinishkrama*n*a Sûtra, but of this there is no positive evidence. It is in 60 kiouen, and embraces Buddha's history from the beginning to the time of the conversion of the Kâ*s*yapas and others.

The following is the title of a life of Buddha, translated by Fă-khin of the Sung dynasty (began 960 A.D.), and named

(13) Fo-shwo-*k*ung-hu-mo-ho-ti-king
佛說衆許摩訶帝經

which is, as it appears, a work of the Sammatiya school of Buddhism, corresponding with the Mahâvastu. The phrase 衆許 is used in the introductory chapter to denote Sammata, who was 'chosen by all' to be the first king; and 摩訶帝 is the Chinese form of Mahâvastu, 'the great (thing).' This memoir is in 2 vols. and 13 kiouen; it is very complete, agreeing in its details with the notices found in the Manual of Buddhism, and in Bigandet's Life of Godama. It was probably in the original a Pâli work.

The last version of the Lalita Vistara, known as the

(14) Shin-t'ung-yaou-hi-king,
神童遊戲經

has not come under my notice.

A*s*VAGHOSHA.

The most reliable of the lives of Buddha known in China is that translated in the present volume, the Buddha-*k*arita-kâvya. It was no doubt written by the Bodhisattva A*s*vaghosha, who was the twelfth Buddhist patriarch, and a contemporary of Kanishka[1]. Translators in China attribute both this book and the work which I have called the 'Sermons of A*s*vaghosha' (ta *k*wang yăn king lun) to him, and there is no reason to question it. Kumâra*g*îva, who translated the latter work, was too familiar with Indian subjects to be mistaken in this particular, and Dharmaraksha (we will employ this restoration of his name) was also a native of Mid-India, and deeply versed in Buddhist

[1] There is no absolute certainty about the date of Kanishka; it may probably be referred to the beginning of the latter half of the first century A.D. (see next page).

literature (he became a disciple at six years of age). Both these translators lived about A.D. 400.

I am told, however, by Mr. Rockhill, that Târânâtha, the Tibetan author, mentions three writers of the name of A*s*vaghosha, the 'great one,' the younger, and one who lived in the eighth century A.D. This latter, who was also called Çura, could not be the A*s*vaghosha of our text, as the translation of the work dates from the fifth century. And as of the other two, one was called 'the great' and the other 'the younger,' it admits of little question that the Bodhisattva would be the former. But in the Chinese Catalogues, so far as I have searched, there is no mention made of more than one writer called by this name, and he is ever affirmed to have been a contemporary of Kanishka. In the book Tsah-pao-tsang-king, for instance (kiouen vi), there are several tales told of the *K*andan 'Kanika' or 'Kanishka,' in one of which (fol. 13) A*s*vaghosha is distinctly named as his religious adviser, and he is there called 'the Bodhisattva;' so that, according to evidence derived from Chinese sources, there seems no reason to doubt that the author of the book I have here translated was living at and before the time of the Scythian invasion of Magadha under the *K*andan king Kanishka. With respect to the date of this monarch we have no positive evidence; the weight of authority sides with those who place him at the beginning of the *S*aka period, i.e. A.D. 78. It is therefore possible that the emissaries who left China A.D. 64 and returned A.D. 67 may have brought back with them some knowledge of the work of A*s*vaghosha called Fo-pen-hing, or of the original then circulating in India, on which A*s*vaghosha founded his poem. It is singular at least that the work of A*s*vaghosha is in five chapters as well as that translated by *K*u-fa-lan. In any case we may conclude that as early as about A.D. 70, if not before, there was in India a work known as Buddha*k*arita (Fo-pen-hing).

As to the origin of such a work, it seems likely to have sprung from an enlargement of the Mahâparinirvâ*n*a Sûtra. We know that the record of the history of Buddha's last days was extant under this title from early times, and nothing would be simpler than the gradual enlargement of such a record, so as to include in it not only his last days, but his work throughout his life. Each district in which Buddha taught had probably its own recollections on this point, and to any zealous writer the task of connecting these several histories would be an easy one. Such a man was A*s*vaghosha. Brought up in Central India, travelling throughout his life as a preacher and musician, and finally a follower of Kanishka through his Northern campaigns; such a man would naturally be led to put together the various tales or traditions he had gathered as to the birth and life of his great master, and connect them with the already recognised account of his end or last days on earth. The detailed account of Buddha's death, recorded in the Mahâparinirvâ*n*a Sûtra, finds a place at the end of the present work; this account being well known to A*s*vaghosha, there can be no difficulty in understanding how he came to write an entire poem on the subject of the master's life and death.

I am told by Professor Max Müller that the Sanskrit versions of the Buddha*k*arita break off at the end of varga 17, that is, after the account of the conversion of the great Kâ*s*yapa. Whether this is accidental, or whether it indicates the original extent of the poem, I have no means of judging. One thing is certain, that at the time when the translation was made by Dharmaraksha (viz. about A.D. 420), the work was of the size of the present volume. There is no à priori reason for supposing the later portion to have been added by a writer subsequent to A*s*vaghosha. A poem does not easily admit of 'a continuation' by another author; nor can we think that a distinguished writer like A*s*vaghosha would omit in his biography the account of the death of his hero, especially as the materials were at hand, and the dramatic effect of the poem would be undoubtedly increased by the addition of such a popular record. It seems therefore more natural to suppose that the Sanskrit MSS. are incomplete copies of the original, and that the Chinese version before us is in fact a translation of the entire poem as it came from its author's hands.

There is little to add, with respect to the history of A*s*vaghosha, to the few notices I have given elsewhere (Abstract, &c., p. 95 sqq.) One or two allusions to him will be found in the work of Wong pûh (Shing tau ki, §§ 186 and 190). These only confirm the general tradition that he was originally a distinguished Brahman and became a convert to Buddhism[1]. The Buddha*k*arita contains sufficient proof of his acquaintance with and hostility to Brahmanical teaching, and the frequent discussions found therein relative to the non-existence of 'I' (an individual self) illustrate the record contained in § 190 of the work (Shing tau) named above, 'that Vîra, a writer of *S*âstras (Lun sse), a disciple of A*s*vaghosha Bodhisattva, wrote a treatise in 100 gâthâs on the subject of "non-individuality" (wou 'ngo luñ), which the heretics were unable to gainsay.' With reference to this doctrine of the non-existence of the individual subject, it is not possible in such a work as this to say much. I shall be glad to place on record, however, my belief that in Buddhism this question is much more than a speculative question of philosophy. It touches the skirt of the highest moral truth. For the individual self in Buddhism is the evil or carnal self, the origin of sorrow. This, the Buddhist says (at least as I read his confession of faith), does not exist; the evil self is not a separate reality, it is the delusion of 'sense;' it is 'nothing.' Destroy this idea of self and there will be light. If we regard the question thus, it assumes a form more interesting and vital than that of any philosophical enquiry. As I said above, it touches the skirt of the highest truth; and in this approach to truth lies the power of the Buddhist doctrine.

THE FAITHFULNESS OF CHINESE TRANSLATIONS.

It is wonderful to look through the large collection of Buddhist books translated into Chinese from the dialects

[1] Mr. Rockhill has kindly given me an extract from a Tibetan work, Mañgusrîmûlatantra, in which Asvaghosha is identified with Mât*rig*âta or Mât*rig*ita, concerning whom, see Abstract, &c., p. 141.

of India, principally by Indian or Indo-Scythian priests. I use this last expression to indicate the nationality of those translators who came to China from Cabul and regions north of the Indus. For 600 years and more a succession of Buddhist teachers and preachers followed one another from India and Central Asia towards China with little interruption. The result is, that the Buddhist Tripi*t*aka (canon) as we have it in that country is a collection of translations without connection of parts, denoting the Buddhism of India and neighbouring countries, in every period of its development. Hence side by side with the early teaching of the faith found in such books as the Dharmapada (Tan poh), we have the gross form of Tantra worship contained in the 'Dhâra*n*î of *K*a*nd*â,' *K*a*nd*â being in fact the same as Kâlî or Durgâ or *G*agatmât*ri*. Nevertheless this collection of translations is a most important one. Its importance has yet to be realised. To the student of Buddhism it is an inexhaustible mine of wealth. And to the student of history some knowledge of it is indispensable.

The question presents itself, therefore, can we rely on the truthfulness of the work done by these men in China? To this question only a qualified answer can be given ; we may rely on the work of men of known ability. And in other cases we may test the work done by comparison with the originals. We should have no reluctance, I think, in accepting the translations of men like Kumâra*g*îva, to whom both Chinese and Sanskrit must have been familiar, and whose work may be tested by comparison with Sanskrit texts. And if he may be trusted, so may others also who worked with him or in his time. Amongst these was Dharmaraksha, the translator of the Buddha*k*arita of this volume. He was a man of Mid-India, and became a disciple at six years of age, and daily recited 10.000 words of Scripture. At first he belonged to the school of the lesser development, and was well acquainted with the discourses of the five Vidyâs. Afterwards he became a follower of the greater development. He arrived in China in the year 412 A.D. and worked at translations till A.D. 454. Now we can hardly suppose that a man of such natural gifts as Dharmaraksha could have laboured for forty-two years at translations, without being worthy of trust. Moreover we find that Kumâragîva was working at this period in China, and that he translated the work of Asvaghosha called Ta-kwang-yan-king-lun, which appears to be related to the Ta-kwang-yan-king, another name for the Life of Buddha (Lalita Vistara). Is it likely that the two translators were unknown to one another?

It is true, indeed, that I have not been able to test the translation of Dharmaraksha by comparison with the Sanskrit. As I understand Professor Max Müller, the Sanskrit text is not always easy to interpret, and differs in many places from the Chinese version. Sometimes it is possible to see how it happened that the Chinese translator misunderstood the text before him. Sometimes it would seem that he omitted intentionally whole passages which would be either unintelligible or uninteresting to Chinese readers. As there is some prospect of the Sanskrit text of Asvaghosha's work being published, we may hope to arrive in time at something like certainty on the point under consideration.

But with respect to the trustworthiness of Chinese translations in general, it depends, as I said before, on the character of the individual scholar. There is no reason at all why a Brahman should not have become familiar with Chinese, and when we add to this the extraordinary facilities afforded the Buddhist missionaries in China for executing their work, in the way I mean of royal patronage and able coadjutors, there is no reason to suspect the result of their labours. Yet doubtless there are many unreliable versions of sacred texts to be found. Every zealous Upâsaka who came to China was not thereby duly qualified for the work of translation; and as a rule we should be cautious in attaching entire credence to the literary labours of such persons.

Asvaghosha's Style.

The Chinese priest I-tsing says that the hymns used in the Buddhist church during his visit to India were composed and arranged by A*s*vaghosha (Nan-hae, § 32). There can be little doubt that he was a musician as well as poet. He travelled about, we are told, with a body of musicians, and was the means of converting many persons of distinction by his skill (Abstract, &c., p. 97). The work before us gives proof of his poetical talent. In translating his verses, even from the Chinese, an impulse to follow in his poetical vein has been felt. But the requirements of a literal translation forbad any such diversion. Nevertheless the reader will observe many passages that would have easily allowed a more 'flowery diction.' The passage in verse 629 and following verses is very touching—the consuming grief of Ya*s*odharâ until 'her breath grew less and sinking thus, she fell upon the dusty ground.' The account of Buddha's enlightenment in verse 1166 and following is also striking: 'Thus did he complete the end of self, as fire goes out for want of grass; thus he had done what he would have men do; he first had found the way of perfect knowledge. He finished thus the first great lesson; entering the great *Ri*shi's house, the darkness disappeared, light burst upon him; perfectly silent and at rest, he reached the last exhaustless source of truth; lustrous with all wisdom the great *Ri*shi sat, perfect in gifts, whilst one convulsive throe shook the wide earth.'

There are many passages throughout the poem of great beauty; there is much also that is dry and abstruse, yet we cannot doubt that in that day and among these people the 'great poem' of A*s*vaghosha must have had considerable popularity. Hence the translations of it are numerous; it must have tested Dharmaraksha's powers to have turned it into Chinese. There is also a Tibetan copy of it; and whether it was originally composed in Sanskrit or not, we know that there are now various editions of it in that language. I do not pretend to have found the author's meaning in all cases; the Chinese is not easy; but in the main drift of the poem I have followed my text as faithfully and literally as possible. The concluding portion of the last section, as it seems to support the idea of only one A*s*oka, first fierce and then gentle, or religious, is, to say the least, a curious passage. But we may not attach too much weight to an isolated statement of this sort; there may have been reasons more than we know of why the orthodox tradition of the Dharma-A*s*oka, the patron of the Theravâdi school, should have been ignored by a friend of Kanishka. But in any case the evidence is too slight to build upon; we can only say that in A*s*vaghosha's time it had become usual to put the Council of Pâ*t*aliputra out of sight, and to regard the Theravâdi school as one opposed to the generally received traditions of the North.

I cannot conclude this Introduction without expressing my thanks to Mr. Bunyiu Nanjio, who kindly suggested emendations of my translation of some passages at the beginning of the work, and also to Professor Max Müller, to whom I am indebted for the restoration of many of the proper names that occur throughout the text.

S. BEAL.

THE RECTORY, WARK,
NORTHUMBERLAND,
Feb. 4, 1883.

FO-SHO-HING-TSAN-KING.

FO-SHO-HING-TSAN-KING.

A METRICAL VERSION

OF THE

LIFE OF BUDDHA BY MA-MENG-PU-SA.

(ASVAGHOSHA BODHISATTVA.)

KIOUEN I.

VARGA 1. THE BIRTH.

(There was) a descendant of the Ikshvâku[1] (family), an invincible[2] Sâkya monarch, pure in mind (mental gifts) and of unspotted virtue, called therefore 'Pure-rice' (Suddhodana). 1

Joyously reverenced by all men (or, 'beings'), as the new moon (is welcomed by the world), the king indeed (was) like the heaven-ruler Sakra[3], his queen like (the divine) Sakî. 2

Strong and calm of purpose as the earth, pure in mind as the water-lily, her name, figuratively assumed, Mâyâ, she was in truth incapable of class-comparison. 3

---

[1] The Ikshvâku (sugar-cane) family of Potala. Suddhodana was the father of the Bodhisattva.

[2] Wou-shing; this is the equivalent for the Agitavatî (river). But it here refers to the Sâkyas, as a race of Kakravartin monarchs.

[3] Or, like Sakra, king of Devas, the husband of Sakî.

On her in likeness as the heavenly queen descended the spirit and entered her womb. A mother, but free from grief or pain, (she was) without any false or illusory[1] mind. 4

Disliking the clamorous ways of the world, (she remembered) the excellent garden of Lumbinî, a pleasant spot, a quiet forest retreat, (with its) trickling fountains, and blooming flowers and fruits. 5

Quiet and peaceful, delighting in meditation, respectfully she asked the king for liberty to roam therein; the king, understanding her earnest desire, was seized with a seldom-felt anxiety (to grant her request). 6

He commanded his kinsfolk, within and without (the palace), to repair with her to that garden shade; and now the queen Mâyâ knew that her time for child-bearing was come. 7

She rested calmly on a beautiful couch, (surrounded by) a hundred thousand female attendants; (it was) the eighth day of the fourth moon, a season of serene and agreeable character. 8

Whilst she (thus) religiously observed[2] the rules of a pure discipline, Bodhisattva was born from her right side, (come) to deliver the world, constrained by great pity, without causing his mother pain or anguish. 9

As king Yu-liu[3] was born from the thigh, as king Pi-t'au[4] was born from the hand, as king Man-to[5]

---

[1] Here there seems to be a play on the word wan 幻, which is the equivalent for Mâyâ or illusion. The Sanskrit text reads Mâyâpagatâ-iva Mâyâ, i. e. Mâyâ without deceit.

[2] Or, (the season for) religiously observing the rules of abstinence.

[3] Aurva.

[4] P*ri*thu, born from the arm of Ve*n*a.

[5] Mândhât*ri*.

was born from the top of the head, as king Kia-*k'h*a[1] was born from the arm-pit, 10

So also was Bodhisattva on the day of his birth produced from the right side; gradually emerging from the womb, he shed in every direction the rays of his glory. 11

As one (born) from recumbent space[2], and not through the gates of life, through countless kalpas, practising virtue, self-conscious he came forth to life, without confusion. 12

Calm and collected, not falling headlong (was he born), gloriously manifested, perfectly adorned, sparkling with light he came from the womb[3], as when the sun first rises (from the East). 13

(Men) indeed regarded[4] his exceeding great glory, yet their sight remained uninjured: he allowed them to gaze, the brightness of his person concealed for the time, as when we look upon the moon in the heavens. 14

His body, nevertheless, was effulgent with light, and like the sun which eclipses the shining of the lamp, so the true gold-like beauty of Bodhisattva shone forth and was diffused everywhere. 15

Upright and firm and unconfused in mind, he deliberately took seven steps[5], the soles of his feet

---

[1] Kakshîvat. These names are supplied from the Sanskrit text.

[2] This may also be translated 'as one who falls from space,' i. e. miraculously born from space.

[3] He passed from the womb to be born. The idea seems to be that though conceived in the womb, he was born supernaturally from the side.

[4] Kwan-tsai, weighed and considered.

[5] These seven steps are frequently figured by seven lotus-marks. I-tsing refers to such marks at Nâlanda, where Buddha walked seven steps, forward and backward; they are also figured on the

resting evenly upon the ground as he went, his footmarks remained bright as seven stars. 16

Moving like the lion, king of beasts, and looking earnestly towards the four quarters, penetrating to the centre the principles of truth, he spake thus with the fullest assurance: 17

'This birth is in the condition of a Buddha[1]; after this I have done with renewed birth; now only am I born this once, for the purpose of saving all the world.' 18

And now from the midst of heaven there descended two streams of pure water, one warm, the other cold, and baptized his head[2], causing refreshment to his body. 19

And now he is placed in the precious palace hall, a jewelled couch for him to sleep upon, and the heavenly kings with their golden flowery hands hold fast the four feet of the bed. 20

Meanwhile the Devas in space, seizing their jewelled canopies, attending, raise in responsive harmony their heavenly songs, to encourage him to accomplish his perfect purpose[3]. 21

Then the Nâga-râ*g*as filled with joy, earnestly desiring to show their reverence for the most excellent law[4], as they had paid honour to the former Buddhas, now went to meet Bodhisattva; 22

---

cloth held by the attendants at the birth of Bodhisattva. See Tree and Serpent Worship, plate lxv, figure 2, middle scene.

[1] This birth is a Buddha-birth.

[2] He was thus consecrated to be a king; see Childers, Pâli Dict., sub Abhisiñ*k*ati; also Eitel, Handbook, sub Mûrddhâbhishikta.

[3] Inviting him to perfect the way of Buddha.

[4] That is, 'to advance the cause of true religion.'

They scattered before him Mandâra flowers, rejoicing with heartfelt joy to pay such religious homage; (and so, again,) Tathâgata having appeared in the world, the *S*uddha[1] angels rejoiced with gladness; 23

With no selfish or partial joy, but for the sake of religion they rejoiced, because creation[2], engulfed in the ocean of pain, was now to obtain perfect release. 24

Then the precious Mountain-râ*g*a, Sume(ru)[3], firmly holding this great earth[4] when Bodhisattva appeared in the world, was swayed by the wind of his perfected merit. 25

On every hand the world was greatly shaken, as the wind drives the tossing boat; so also the minutest atoms of sandal perfume, and the hidden sweetness of precious lilies, 26

Floated on the air and rose through space and then commingling came back to earth; so again the garments of Devas descending from heaven touching the body, caused delightful thrills of joy; 27

The sun and moon with constant course redoubled the brilliancy of their light, whilst in the world the

[1] The *S*uddha-vâsas, 'beings dressed in pure garments.' A class of heavenly beings, supposed to take peculiar interest in the religious welfare of men.

[2] 'Creation,' in the sense of 'all that lives.'

[3] Sumeru, written also Sumĕ and Meru. The primeval mountain; the Alborz, Atlas, or Olympus of other tribes. It is explained as 'the high, or resplendent, mountain.' On it was the heaven of the gods (the thirty-three gods).

[4] It would seem from this that the original idea of Sumeru was 'the mountain of Heaven;' the visible heaven, or firmament, which 'firmly holds the earth.'

fire's gleam of itself prevailed without the use of fuel. 28

Pure water, cool and refreshing from the springs, flowed here and there, self-caused; in the palace all the waiting women were filled with joy at such an unprecedented event. 29

Proceeding all in company, they drink and bathe themselves; in all arose calm and delightful thoughts; countless inferior Devas (bhûtas), delighting in religion, like clouds assembled. 30

In the garden of Lumbinî, filling the spaces between the trees, rare and special flowers, in great abundance, bloomed out of season. 31

All cruel and malevolent kinds of beings, together conceived a loving heart; all diseases and afflictions among men without a cure applied, of themselves were healed. 32

The various cries and confused sounds of beasts were hushed and silence reigned; the stagnant water of the river-courses flowed apace, whilst the polluted streams became clear and pure. 33

No clouds gathered throughout the heavens, whilst angelic music, self-caused, was heard around; the whole world of sentient creatures enjoyed peace and universal tranquillity. 34

Just as when a country visited by desolation, suddenly obtains an enlightened ruler, so when Bodhisattva was born, he came to remove the sorrows of all living things. 35

Mâra[1], the heavenly monarch, alone was grieved and rejoiced not. The Royal Father (*S*uddhodana)

[1] Mâra, the king of the world of desire. According to the Buddhist theogony he is the god of sensual love. He holds the

beholding his son[1], strange and miraculous[2], as to his birth, 36

Though self-possessed and assured in his soul, was yet moved with astonishment and his countenance changed, whilst he alternately weighed with himself the meaning (of such an event), now rejoiced and now distressed. 37

The queen-mother beholding her child, born thus contrary to laws of nature, her timorous woman's heart was doubtful; her mind through fear, swayed between extremes: 38

Not distinguishing the happy from the sad portents, again and again she gave way to grief[3]; and now the aged women of the world, (of the 'long night[4]') in a confused way supplicating heavenly guidance, 39

Implored the gods to whom their rites were paid, to bless the child; (cause peace to rest upon the royal child.) Now there was at this time in the grove, a certain soothsayer[5], a Brahman, 40

Of dignified mien and wide-spread renown, famed for his skill and scholarship: beholding the signs[6], his

world in sin. He was the enemy of Buddha, and endeavoured in every way to defeat him. He is also described as the king of death.

[1] Beholding his 'born son,' or 'begotten son.'

[2] K'i-teh, truly unique (Williams' Dict.) Mi tsang yau, unseen before, miraculous.

[3] The text seems to point to alternately recurring hope and grief.

[4] The text here is difficult. I take *Kh*ang-suh to be equal to *Kh*ang-yê, which is a frequent expression to denote the 'long night' of transmigration or ignorance. If this be not so, then *Kh*ang-suh may be simply 'aged.'

[5] *Kh*i Siang, a discerner of signs or portents.

[6] That is, either the signs on the child's body, or the occurrences attending his birth.

heart rejoiced, and he exulted at the miraculous event. 41

Knowing the king's mind to be somewhat perplexed, he addressed him (thus) with truth and earnestness, 'Men born in the world, chiefly desire to have a son the most renowned[1]; 42

'But now the king, like the moon when full, should feel in himself a perfect joy, having begotten an unequalled[2] son, (for by this the king) will become illustrious among his race; 43

'Let then his heart be joyful and glad, banish all anxiety and doubt, the spiritual omens that are everywhere manifested indicate for your house and dominion a course of continued prosperity[3]. 44

'The most excellently endowed child now born will bring deliverance to the entire world[4], none but a heavenly teacher has a body such as this[5], golden colour'd, gloriously resplendent. 45

'One endowed with such transcendent marks, must reach the state of "Samyak[6]-Sambodhi," or if he be induced to engage in worldly delights, then he must become a universal monarch[7]; 46

---

[1] Or, a most victorious son; or, a son most renowned.

[2] K'i-teh, truly unique; strange or wonderful; (p. 7, n. 2.)

[3] Increasing or advancing prosperity.

[4] Must assuredly save the world.

[5] A body, such a masterpiece.

[6] *Kh*ing-hsio, perfect illumination, Samyak-Sambuddha; or, as in the text.

[7] A wheel-turning monarch. A monarch like the sun 'that flies as he goes;' the old conceit of a king of the age of gold[a]; the expectation of peace and prosperity resulting from the universal authority of such a righteous king, is an old, perhaps a primitive, one. The *K*akravartin is the eastern form of the myth.

[a] That is, probably, 'a golden (wheel) king.'

'Everywhere recognised as the ruler of the great earth, mighty in his righteous government, as a monarch ruling the four empires[1], uniting under his sway all other rulers; 47

'As among all lesser lights, the sun's brightness is by far the most excellent. But if he seek a dwelling among the mountain forests, with single heart searching for deliverance[2], 48

'Having arrived at the perfection of true wisdom, he will become illustrious[3] throughout the world; for as mount Sumeru is monarch among all mountains, 49

'Or, as gold is chief among all precious things, or, as the ocean is supreme among all streams[4], or, as the moon is first among the stars, or, as the sun is brightest of all luminaries, 50

'So Tathâgata, born in the world, is the most eminent[5] of men; his eyes clear and expanding[6], the lashes both above and below moving with the lid, 51

'The iris of the eye of a clear blue colour[7], in shape like the moon when half full, such characteristics as these, without contradiction, foreshadow the most excellent condition of perfect (wisdom).' 52.

---

[1] The four empires, that is, the four continents or quarters of the world.

[2] Deliverance, that is, from sin; or sorrow the result of sin (moksha).

[3] Shine universally; as the light of the sun.

[4] The ocean is always in Buddhist works, as in Homer, associated with 'flowings.' The expression in the Chinese, liu-hai, corresponds exactly with 'Ωκεανοῖο ῥέεθρα.

[5] The most worshipful.

[6] Widening more and more.

[7] Of a deep purple or violet colour.

At this time the king addressed the twice-born[1], 'If it be as you say, with respect to these miraculous signs, that they indicate such consequences, 53

'Then no such case has happened with former kings, nor down to our time has such a thing occurred.' The Brahman addressed the king thus, 'Say not so; for it is not right; 54

'For with regard to renown and wisdom, personal celebrity, and worldly substance, these four things indeed are not to be considered according to precedent or subsequence; 55

'But whatever is produced according to nature[2], such things are liable to the law of cause and effect: but now whilst I recount some parallels let the king attentively listen; 56

'Bh*ri*gu, Aṅgira[3] (Aṅgiras?), these two of *Ri*shi family[4], having passed many years apart from men, each begat an excellently-endowed son, 57

'B*ri*haspati with *S*ukra, skilful in making royal treatises, not derived from former families (or, tribes); 58

'Sârasvata, the *Ri*shi, whose works[5] have long disappeared, begat a son, Po-lo-sa[6], who compiled illustrious Sûtras[7] and Shâstras; 59

---

[1] That is, the Brahman; wearing the twice-born thread.

[2] Or, whatever is born according to the nature of things.

[3] I restore these names according to the Sanskrit text, supplied by Professor Max Müller.

[4] That is, belonging to the *Ri*shi tribe; in other words, 'these two *Ri*shis.'

[5] Or, it may, perhaps more correctly, be rendered 'separated by a long period from Sûtras or Shâstras,' or, when these works had long been lost.

[6] Is this Parâ*s*ara, the reputed father of Vyâsa? (see Max Müller's Ancient Sanskrit Literature, p. 479.)

[7] Illustrious Sûtras (Ming King) may possibly refer to the Vedas, but the five vidyâs are also called by this name (Jul. II, 73).

'That which now we know and see, is not therefore dependent on previous connection; Vyâsa, the *Ri*shi, the author of numerous treatises, 60

'After his death had among his descendants, Poh-mi (Vâlmîki), who extensively collected Gâthâ sections; Atri, the *Ri*shi, not understanding the sectional treatise on medicine, 61

'Afterwards begat Âtreya, who was able to control diseases; the twice-born *Ri*shi Kusi (Ku*s*ika), not occupied with heretical treatises, 62

'Afterwards (begat) Kia-ti-na râ*g*a, who thoroughly understood heretical systems; the sugar-cane monarch[1], who began his line, could not restrain the tide of the sea, 63

'But Sagara-râ*g*a, his descendant, who begat a thousand royal sons, he could control the tide of the great sea so that it should come no further. 64

'*G*anaka, the *Ri*shi, without a teacher acquired power of abstraction. All these, who obtained such renown, acquired powers of themselves[2]; 65

'Those distinguished before, were afterwards forgotten; those before forgotten, became afterwards distinguished[3]; kings like these and godlike *Ri*shis have no need of family inheritance, 66

'And therefore the world need not regard those going before or following. So, mighty king! is it with you, you should experience true joy of heart, 67

'And because of this joy should banish for ever doubt or anxiety.' The king hearing the words

[1] That is, the first of the Ikshvâku monarchs who reigned at Potala (Tatta) at the mouth of the Indus.

[2] Or, were born by their own power.

[3] Or, the former were better, the later inferior; the former inferior, the later better.

of the seer was glad, and offered him increased gifts[1]. 68

'Now have I begotten a valiant (excellent) son (he said), who will establish a wheel authority, whilst I, when old and grey-headed, will go forth to lead a hermit's life[2], 69

'So that my holy king-like son may not give up the world and wander through mountain forests.' And now near the spot within the garden, there was a *R*ishi, leading the life of an ascetic[3]; 70

His name was Asita, wonderfully skilful in the interpretation of signs; he approached the gate of the palace; the king (beholding him) exclaimed, 'This is none other but Brahmadeva, 71

'Himself enduring penance from love of true religion, these two characteristics[4] so plainly visible as marks of his austerities.' Then the king was much rejoiced; 72

And forthwith he invited him within the palace, and with reverence set before him entertainment, whilst he, entering the inner palace, rejoiced only (in prospect of) seeing the royal child. 73

Although surrounded by the crowd of court-ladies, yet still he was as if in desert solitude; and now they place a preaching throne and pay him increased honour and religious reverence, 74

As Antideva râ*g*a reverenced the priest Vasish*th*a. Then the king addressing the *R*ishi, said, 'Most fortunate am I, 75

'Great *R*ishi! that you have condescended to

[1] Or, extended his religious offerings.

[2] Leaving my home will practise a pure (Brahman) life.

[3] Practising austerities.

[4] That is, 'purity' and 'penance.'

come here to receive from me becoming gifts and reverence; I pray you therefore enter on your exhortation.' 76

Thus requested and invited the *R*ishi felt unutterable joy, and said, 'All hail, ever victorious monarch! possessed of all noble (virtuous) qualities[1], 77

'Loving to meet the desires of those who seek, nobly generous in honouring the true law, conspicuous as a race for wisdom and humanity, with humble mind you pay me homage, as you are bound. 78

'Because of your righteous deeds in former lives[2], now are manifested these excellent fruits; listen to me, then, whilst I declare the reason of the present meeting. 79

'As I was coming on the sun's way[3], I heard the Devas in space declare that the king had born to him (begotten) a royal son, who would arrive at perfect intelligence[4]; 80

'Moreover I beheld such other portents[5], as have

---

[1] The Chinese symbol 'teh' properly means 'virtue,' as in the title of Laou Tseu's work, Tau-teh-king. But in Buddhist books it generally corresponds with the Sanskrit gu*n*a, in the sense of a 'quality' or 'characteristic.'

[2] The expression suh *kh*ih points to conduct in former conditions of existence. It properly means 'a night's rest' or 'a lodging one night' (Williams), but in Buddhist books it commonly refers to abodes or conditions of life, occupied during the night (long night) of transmigration.

[3] Following the way of the sun.

[4] Complete the way of true wisdom (Sambodhi or Sambuddha).

[5] Such miraculous portents going before. It would seem from Asita's description that he came from the East following the sun, and as he came he saw before him miraculous portents.

constrained me now to seek your presence; desiring to see the *S*âkya monarch who will erect the standard of the true law.' 81

The king hearing the *Ri*shi's words was fully assured; escaping from the net of doubt, he ordered an attendant to bring the prince, to exhibit him to the *Ri*shi. 82

The *Ri*shi, beholding the prince, the thousand-rayed wheel on the soles of his feet, the web-like filament between his fingers [1], between his eyebrows the white [2] wool-like prominence, 83

His privy parts hidden as those of the horse, his complexion bright and lustrous; seeing these wonderful birth-portents, the seer wept and sighed deeply. 84

The king beholding the tears of the *Ri*shi, thinking of his son, his soul was overcome, and his breath fast held his swelling heart. Thus alarmed and ill at ease, 85

Unconsciously he arose from his seat, and bowing his head at the *Ri*shi's feet he addressed him in these words, 'This son of mine, born thus wonderfully, 86

'Beautiful in face, and surpassingly graceful, little different from the gods in form, giving promise of superiority in the world, ah! why has he caused thee grief and pain? 87

'Forbid it, that my son should die! (should be short-lived!)—(the thought) creates in me grief and

[1] Or, his fingers and his toes.

[2] That is, the ûr*n*â. This white wool-like mark seems to have been derived in the first instance from the circle of hair on the forehead of the bull. Moschus describes the bull that carried off Europa as having this 'silver white circle' on his forehead.

anxiety; that one athirst, within reach of the eternal draught[1], should after all reject and lose it! sad indeed! 88

'Forbid it, he should lose his wealth and treasure! dead to his house! lost to his country! for he who has[2] a prosperous son in life, gives pledge that his country's weal is well secured; 89

'And then, coming to die, my heart will rest content, rejoicing in the thought of offspring surviving me; even as a man possessed of two eyes, one of which keeps watch, while the other sleeps; 90

'Not like the frost-flower of autumn, which though it seems to bloom, is not a reality. A man who, midst his tribe and kindred, deeply loves a spotless son, 91

'At every proper time in recollection of it has joy; O! that you would cause me to revive[3]!' The *Ri*shi, knowing the king-sire to be thus greatly afflicted at heart, 92

Immediately addressed the Mahârâ*g*a: 'Let not the king be for a moment anxious! the words I have spoken to the king, let him ponder these, and not permit himself to doubt; 93

'The portents now are as they were before, cherish

---

[1] The 'eternal draught' or 'sweet dew' of Ambrosia. This expression is constantly used in Buddhist writings. It corresponds with the Pâli amata*m*, which Childers explains as the 'drink of the gods.'

[2] Or, if I have.

[3] This *s*loka may be translated otherwise thus: 'A man among all his kindred loves deeply a spotless[a] son; at this time, in recollection thereof, speaking, cause me to revive;' or the latter lines may still be rendered, 'in memory of what you said before, cause me now, by speaking as before, to revive.'

[a] Wou-kwo-tseu; either 'a faultless son' or 'nothing beyond his son.'

then no other thoughts! But recollecting I myself am old, on that account I could not hold my tears; 94

'For now my end is coming on. But this son of thine will rule the world, born for the sake of all that lives[1]! this is indeed one difficult to meet with; 95

'He shall give up his royal estate, escape from the domain of the five desires[2], with resolution and with diligence practise austerities, and then awakening, grasp the truth. 96

'Then constantly, for the world's sake (all living things), destroying the impediments of ignorance and darkness, he shall give to all enduring light, the brightness of the sun of perfect wisdom. 97

'All flesh submerged in the sea of sorrow; all diseases collected as the bubbling froth; decay and age like the wild billows; death like the engulfing ocean; 98

'Embarking lightly in the boat of wisdom he will save the world from all these perils, by wisdom stemming back the flood. His pure teaching like to the neighbouring shore, 99

'The power of meditation, like a cool lake, will be enough for all the unexpected birds; thus deep and full and wide is the great river of the true law; 100

'All creatures parched by the drought of lust may freely drink thereof, without stint; those

[1] This line may be also rendered 'because he has done with birth, therefore he is born.' The text is full of such double-meanings.

[2] The five desires, or five appetites of sight, smell, taste, hearing, and touch.

enchained in the domain of the five desires, those driven along by many sorrows, 101

'And deceived amid the wilderness of birth and death, in ignorance of the way of escape, for these Bodhisattva has been born in the world, to open out a way of salvation[1]. 102

'The fire of lust and covetousness, burning with the fuel of the objects of sense, (on the flames) he has caused the cloud of his mercy to rise, so that the rain of the law may extinguish them. 103

'The heavy gates of gloomy unbelief, fast kept by covetousness and lust, within which are confined all living things, he opens and gives free deliverance. 104

'With the tweezers of his diamond wisdom he plucks out the opposing principles of lustful desire. In the self-twined meshes of folly and ignorance all flesh poor and in misery, helplessly (lying), 105

'The king of the law has come forth, to rescue these from bondage. Let not the king in respect of this his son encourage in himself one thought of doubt or pain; 106

'But rather let him grieve on account of the world, led captive by desire, opposed to truth; but I, indeed, amid the ruins of old age and death, am far removed from the meritorious condition of the holy one[2], 107

'Possessed indeed of powers of abstraction, yet

[1] The word 'salvation' corresponds to the Sanskrit moksha, deliverance or escape. The garden of Lumbinî is sometimes called the 'garden of deliverance,' because Mâyâ was there delivered of her child.

[2] Or, removed from an opportunity of reaping merit by the teaching of the holy one.

not within reach of the gain he will give, to be derived from his teaching as the Bodhisattva; not permitted to hear his righteous law, 108

'My body worn out, after death, alas! (destined) to be born as a Deva[1] still liable to the three calamities (old age, decay, and death), (therefore I weep).' The king and all his household attendants, hearing the words of the *Ri*shi, 109

Knowing the cause of his regretful sorrow, banished from their minds all further anxiety: 'And now (the king said) to have begotten this excellent son, gives me rest at heart; 110

'But that he should leave his kingdom and home, and practise the life of an ascetic, not anxious to ensure the stability of the kingdom, the thought of this still brings with it pain.' 111

At this time the *Ri*shi, turning to the king with true words, said, 'It must be even as the king anticipates, he will surely arrive at perfect enlightenment.' 112

Thus having appeased every anxious heart among the king's household, (the *Ri*shi) by his own inherent spiritual power ascended into space and disappeared. 113

At this time *S*uddhodana râ*g*a, seeing the excellent marks (predictive signs) of his son, and, moreover, hearing the words of Asita, certifying that which would surely happen, 114

Was greatly affected with reverence to the child, he redoubled measures for its protection, and (was

[1] The condition of the highest Deva, according to Buddhism, does not exempt him from re-birth; subject to the calamities incident on such a renewal of life.

filled) with constant thought; (moreover) he issued decrees through the empire, to liberate all captives in prison, 115.

According to the custom when a (royal) son was born, giving the usual largess, in agreement with the directions of the Sacred Books, and extending his gifts to all; (or, all these things he did completely). 116

The child[1] when ten days old, (his father's) mind being now quite tranquil, he announced a sacrifice to all the gods, and prepared to give liberal offerings to all the religious bodies; 117

*S*râma*n*as and Brâhma*n*as invoked by their prayers a blessing from the gods, whilst he bestowed gifts on the royal kinspeople and the ministers and the poor within the country; 118

The women who dwelt in the city or the villages, (all those who needed) cattle or horses or elephants or money, each, according to his necessities, was liberally supplied; 119

Then selecting by divination a lucky time, they took the child back to his own palace, with a double-feeding white-pure-tooth[2], carried in a richly-adorned chariot (cradle), 120

With ornaments of every kind and colour round his neck; shining with beauty, exceedingly resplendent with unguents. The queen embracing

[1] 'Shing-tseu,' the born or begotten child.

[2] I am unable to translate this line except literally, 'two-feeding white pure ivory (or, tooth),' 'rh fan pih tsing 'nga. [I am informed, however, by Professor Max Müller that it refers to the 'elephant.' The elephant is called dvipa, the twice-drinker, corresponding to 'rh fan (for 'rh yin), the double-feeder (drinker), in the Chinese.]

him in her arms, going around, worshipped the heavenly spirits. 121

Afterwards she remounted her precious chariot, surrounded by her waiting women; the king, with his ministers and people, and all the crowd of attendants, leading the way and following, 122

Even as the ruler of heaven, *S*akra, is surrounded by crowds of Devas; as Mahe*s*vara, when suddenly his six-faced child was born, 123

Arranging every kind of present, gave gifts, and asked for blessings; so now the king, when his royal son was born, made all his arrangements in like manner; 124

So Vai*s*rava*n*a, the heavenly king, when Nalakûvara[1] was born, surrounded by a concourse of Devas, was filled with joy and much gladness; 125

So the king, now the royal prince was born, in the kingdom of Kapila, his people and all his subjects were likewise filled with joy. 126

VARGA 2. LIVING IN THE PALACE.

And now in the household of *S*uddhodana râ*g*a, because of the birth of the royal prince, his clansmen and younger brethren (namesakes), with his ministers, were all generously disposed, 127

Whilst elephants, horses and chariots and the wealth of the country and precious[2] vessels, daily increased and abounded, being produced wherever requisite[3]; 128

---

[1] Na-lo-kiu-po. Nalakûvara was the son of Vai*s*rava*n*a.

[2] Vessels of the seven precious (substances).

[3] According to occasion in abundance produced. The expression 'tsah' may either refer to variety or number. Thus the

So too countless hidden treasures came of themselves from the earth. From the midst of the pure snowy mountains, a wild herd of white elephants, 129

Without noise, of themselves, came; not curbed by any, self-subdued, every kind of colour'd[1] horse, in shape and quality surpassingly excellent, 130

With sparkling jewelled manes and flowing tails, came prancing round, as if with wings; these too, born in the desert, came at the right time, of themselves. 131

A (herd of) pure-colour'd, well-proportioned cows, fat and fleshy, and remarkable for beauty, giving fragrant and pure milk with equal flow, came together in great number[2] at this propitious time: 132

Enmity and envy gave way to peace; content and rest prevailed on every side, whilst there was closer union amongst the true of heart, discord and variance were entirely appeased; 133

The gentle air distilled a seasonable rain, no crash of storm or tempest was heard, the springing seeds, not waiting for their time, grew up apace and yielded abundant increase; 134

The five cereals grew ripe with scented grain, soft and glutinous, easy of digestion; all creatures big with young, possessed their bodies in ease and their frames well-gathered; 135

All men, even those who had not received the seeds of instruction derived from the four holy

convocation of the Arhats at Vaiśâlî is called 'tsah;' a miscellaneous collection of anecdotes or tales is called by the same name.

[1] Or, every kind of party-colour'd horse.

[2] Like the clouds.

ones[1]; all these, throughout the world, born under the control of selfish appetite, without any thought for others' goods, 136

Had no proud, envious longings; no angry, hateful thoughts. All men and women[2] were grave (profound) as the first man of the age (kalpa). 137

All the temples of the gods and sacred shrines, the gardens, wells, and fountains, all these like things in heaven, produced of themselves, at the proper time, (their several adornments). 138

There was no famishing hunger, the soldiers' weapons were at rest, all diseases disappeared; throughout the kingdom all the people were bound close in family love and friendship; 139

Piously affectioned they indulged in mutual pleasures, there were no impure or polluting desires, they sought their daily gain righteously, no covetous money-loving spirit prevailed, 140

But with religious purpose they gave liberally; there was no thought of any reward (return), but all practised the four rules of purity; and every hateful thought was suppressed and destroyed. 141

Even as in days gone by, Manu râ*g*a begat a child (called) 'Brilliancy of the Sun,' on which there prevailed through the country great prosperity, and all wickedness came to an end; 142

---

[1] This seems to mean that those who had not received benefit from the teaching of the four previous Buddhas, that even these were placable and well-disposed.

[2] This is a difficult verse, it may be translated literally thus, 'All learned women (or, all the wives of sages) were profoundly grave as the first man of the kalpa.' Whether it refers to the docility of the otherwise quarrelsome women, or to their gravity and learning, it is not easy to say.

So now the king having begotten a royal prince, these marks of prosperity were seen; and because of such a concourse of propitious signs, the child was named Siddhârtha[1]. 143

And now his royal mother, the queen Mâyâ, beholding her son born under such circumstances, beautiful as a child of heaven, adorned with every excellent distinction, 144

From excessive joy which could not be controlled died, and was born in heaven[2]. Then Pragâpatî Gautamî, beholding the prince, like an angel, 145

With beauty seldom seen on earth, seeing him thus born and now his mother dead, loved and nourished him as her own child; and the child regarded her as his mother. 146

So as the light of the sun or the moon, little by little increases, the royal child also increased each day in every mental excellency and beauty of person; 147

(His body exhaled) the perfume of priceless sandal wood, (decorated with) the famed *G*ambunada gold (gems); divine medicines (there were) to preserve him in health, glittering necklaces upon his person; 148

The members of tributary states, hearing that

---

[1] The description here given of the peace and content prevailing in the world on the birth of Bodhisattva (and his name given to him in consequence) resembles the account of the golden age in classic authors.

[2] Mâyâ is generally stated to have died after seven days from the birth of her child. But here the context seems to require a longer interval, as he was ten days old when taken to the temple. Mâyâ was born in the Trayastri*ms*as Heaven, or the Heaven of the Thirty-three Gods. The legend states that Buddha after his enlightenment proceeded there to convert her.

the king had an heir born to him, sent their presents and gifts of various kinds, oxen, sheep, deer, horses, and chariots, 149

Precious vessels and elegant ornaments, fit to delight the heart of the prince; but though presented with such pleasing trifles, the necklaces and other pretty ornaments, 150

The mind (nature) of the prince was unmoved, his bodily frame small indeed, but his heart established; his mind at rest within its own high purposes[1], was not to be disturbed by glittering baubles. 151

And now he was brought to learn the useful arts, when lo! once instructed (at one hearing) he surpassed his teachers. His father, the king, seeing his exceeding talent, and his deep purpose to have done with the world and its allurements, 152

Began to enquire as to the names of those in his tribe who were renowned for elegance and refinement. Elegant and graceful, and a lovely maiden, was she whom they called Yasodharâ; 153

In every way fitting to become a consort for the prince; and to allure by pleasant wiles his heart. The prince with a mind so far removed (from the world), with qualities so distinguished, and with so charming an appearance, 154

Like the elder son of Brahmadeva, Sanatkumâra (She-na Kiu-ma-lo); the virtuous damsel, lovely and refined, gentle and subdued in manner; 155

Majestic like the queen of heaven, constant ever,

[1] His mind resting on its high and excellent purpose; so at least the expression K'ai, domain or precinct, may sometimes be rendered. It means, 'within the limits of its own high excellent (purpose).'

cheerful night and day, establishing the palace in purity and quiet, full of dignity and exceeding grace, 156

Like a lofty hill rising up in space[1]; or as a white autumn cloud; warm or cool according to the season; choosing a proper dwelling according to the year, 157

Surrounded by a return of singing women, who join (their voices) in harmonious heavenly concord, without any jarring or unpleasant sound, exciting (in the hearers) forgetfulness of worldly cares. 158

As the heavenly Gandharvas[2] of themselves in their beauteous palaces (cause) the singing women to raise heavenly strains, the sounds of which and their beauty ravish both eyes and heart; 159

(So) Bodhisattva dwelt in his lofty palace, with music such as this. The king his father, for the prince's sake, dwelt purely in his palace, practising every virtue; 160

Delighting[3] in the teaching of the true law, he[4] put away from him every evil companion, (that) his heart might not be polluted by lust; regarding inordinate desire as poison, 161

Keeping his passion and his body in due control, destroying and repressing all trivial thoughts, desiring to enjoy virtuous conversation, loving[5] instruction (fit) to subdue the hearts of men, 162

---

[1] That is, rising from the earth above other hills.

[2] Gandharvas, heavenly musicians; muses.

[3] With nobleness of purpose (*gin*) loving the transforming power of the true law. That is, leading a religious life.

[4] That is, as I understand it, the king himself, for his son's sake, devoted himself to piety.

[5] Or, by means of loving instruction subduing men's hearts; or, by love, teaching to subdue men's hearts.

Aiming to accomplish the conversion of unbelievers; removing all schemes of opposition[1] (from whatever source they came), by the enlightening power of his doctrine, aiming to save the entire world; (thus he desired) that the body of people should obtain rest; 163

Even as we desire to give peace to our children, so did he long to give rest to the world[2]. He also attended to his religious duties (sacrificing by fire to all the spirits), with clasped hands adoring the moon (drinking the moon's brightness); 164

Bathing his body in the waters of the Ganges; cleansing his heart in the waters of religion, performing his duties with no private aim, but regarding his child and the people at large, 165

Loving righteous conversation[3], righteous words with loving (aim), loving words with no mixture of falsehood, true words imbued by love, 166

And yet withal so modest and self-distrustful, unable on that account to speak as confident of truth; loving to all, and yet not loving the world, with no thought of selfishness or covetous desire, 167

Aiming to restrain the tongue and in quietness to find rest from wordy contentions, not seeking in the

---

[1] Or, every kind of doctrine (magical art) that opposed religion.

[2] Or, (he said) like as I desire rest for my child, so &c.

[3] This and the whole of the context is obscure; the account evidently refers to *S*uddhodana; the line which I have translated 'loving righteous conversation' may be rendered 'loving conversation (or, converse), opposing a want of truth or righteousness (i),' or, 'loving an absence of all unrighteousness in conversation.' The next line, which is evidently in contrast with the previous one, may be translated, 'Righteous words, opposed to an absence of love.' The next line is, 'Loving words, opposed to that which is not true.' And then follows, 'Truthful words, opposed to that which is not love.'

multitude of religious duties to condone for a worldly principle in action[1]; 168

But aiming to benefit the world, by a liberal and unostentatious charity; the heart without any contentious thought, but resolved by goodness to subdue the contentious, 169

Composing the one[2], whilst protecting the seven, removing the seven, guarding and adjusting the five, reaching to the three, by having learned the three, knowing the two, and removing the two; 170

Desiring to mortify the passions, and to destroy every enemy of virtue, not multiplying coarse or unseemly words, but exhorting to virtue in the use of courteous language, 171

Full of sympathy and ready charity, pointing out and practising the way of mutual dependence, receiving and understanding the wisdom of spirits and *Ri*shis, crushing and destroying every cruel and hateful thought; 172

Thus his fame and virtue were widely renowned, (and yet himself) finally (or, for ever) separate from the ties of the world, showing the ability of a master builder, laying a good foundation of virtue, an example for all the earth; 173

So a man's heart composed and at rest, his limbs and all his members will also be at ease. And now

---

[1] I would rather translate these two lines thus, 'Not regarding so much the assemblies convoked for sacrificing to the gods, as excelling in the merit (happiness) of separation from worldly things;' or the word 'sse' may mean 'sacrifice' itself (as ποιέω in Greek), and then it would be 'excelling in merit without sacrifice.'

[2] These four lines are enigmatical. They perhaps have some reference to the teaching of the seven *Ri*shis, or the number seven may refer to the 'seven passions.'

the son of *S*uddhodana, and his virtuous wife Ya*s*odharâ, 174

As time went on, growing to full estate, their child Râhula was born; and then *S*uddhodana râ*g*a considered thus, 'My son, the prince, having a son born to him, 175

'The affairs of the empire will be handed down in succession, and there will be no end to its righteous government; the prince having begotten a son, will love his son as I love him[1], 176

'And no longer think about leaving his home as an ascetic, but devote himself to the practice of virtue; I now have found complete rest of heart, like one just born to heavenly joys.' 177

Like as in the first days of the kalpa, *Ri*shi-kings by the way in which (they walked), practising pure and spotless deeds, offered up religious offerings, without harm to living thing, 178

And illustriously prepared an excellent karma, so the king excelling in the excellence of purity[2], in family and excellency of wealth, excelling in strength and every exhibition of prowess, 179

Reflected the glory of his name through the world, as the sun sheds abroad his thousand rays. But now, being the king of men (or, a king among men), he deemed it right to exhibit his son's (prowess), 180

For the sake of his family and kin, to exhibit him; to increase his family's renown, his glory spread so high as even to obtain the name of 'God begotten;' and having partaken of these heavenly joys, 181

---

[1] Or, loving his son, and loving me also.

[2] We have here a succession of lines in which there is a play on the word 'excellency' (shing), or 'victorious' (*g*ina).

Enjoying the happiness of increased wisdom; understanding the truth, by his own righteousness derived from previous hearing of the truth; the reward of previous acts, widely known[1]. 182

Would that this might lead my son (he prayed) to love his child and not forsake his home; the kings of all countries, whose sons have not yet grown up, 183

Have prevented them exercising authority in the empire, in order to give their minds relaxation, and for this purpose have provided them with worldly indulgences, so that they may perpetuate the royal seed; 184

So now the king, having begotten a royal son, indulged him in every sort of pleasure; desiring that he might enjoy these worldly delights, and not wish to wander from his home in search of wisdom; 185

In former times the Bodhisattva kings, although their way (life) has been restrained (severe), have yet enjoyed the pleasures of the world, and when they have begotten a son, then separating themselves from family ties, 186

Have afterwards entered the solitude of the mountains, to prepare themselves in the way of a silent recluse. 187

Varga 3. Disgust at Sorrow[2].

Without are pleasant garden glades, flowing fountains, pure refreshing lakes, with every kind of

[1] These verses are very obscure, and can only be understood by comparison with the Sanskrit.

[2] In this section we have an account of the excursion of the royal prince without the precincts of the palace, and the sights which affected his mind with a desire to leave the world.

flower, and trees with fruit, arranged in rows, deep shade beneath. 188

There, too, are various kinds of wondrous birds, flying and sporting in the midst, and on the surface of the water the four kinds of flowers, bright colour'd, giving out their floating scent; 189

Minstrel maidens[1] cause their songs, and chorded music, to invite the prince. He, hearing the sounds of singing, sighs for the pleasures of the garden shades, 190

And cherishing within these happy thoughts[2], he dwelt upon the joys of an outside excursion; even as the chained elephant ever longs for the free desert wilds. 191

The royal father, hearing that the prince would enjoy to wander through the gardens, first ordered all his attendant officers to adorn and arrange them, after their several offices: 192

To make level and smooth the king's highway, to remove from the path all offensive matter, all old persons, diseased or deformed, all those suffering through poverty or great grief, 193

So that his son in his present humour might see nothing likely to afflict his heart. The adornments being duly made, the prince was invited to an audience; 194

The king seeing his son approach, patted his head and looking at the colour of his face, feelings of sorrow and joy intermingled, bound him. His mouth willing to speak, his heart restrained. 195

(Now see) the jewel-fronted gaudy chariot; the four equally-pacing, stately horses; good-tempered

[1] Otherwise, singing-women. [2] Or, thoughts of happiness.

and well-trained; young and of graceful appearance; 196

Perfectly pure and white, and draped with flowery coverings. In the same chariot stands the (stately) driver; the streets were scattered over with flowers; precious drapery fixed on either side of the way, 197

With dwarfed trees lining the road, costly vessels employed for decoration, hanging canopies and variegated banners, silken curtains, moved by the rustling breeze, 198

Spectators arranged on either side of the path. With bodies bent and glistening eyes, eagerly gazing, but not rudely staring, as the blue lotus flower (they bent) drooping in the air, 199

Ministers and attendants flocking round him, as stars following the chief of the constellation[1]; all uttering the same suppressed whisper of admiration, at a sight so seldom seen in the world; 200

Rich and poor, humble and exalted, old and young and middle-aged, all paid the greatest respect, and invoked blessings on the occasion: 201

So the country-folk and the town-folk, hearing that the prince was coming forth, the well-to-do not waiting for their servants, those asleep and awake not mutually calling to one another, 202

The six kinds of creatures not gathered together and penned, the money not collected and locked up, the doors and gates not fastened, all went pouring along the way on foot; 203

The towers were filled and the mounds by the trees, the windows and the terraces along the streets; with bent body fearing to lift their eyes, carefully

[1] As stars following the constellation-king.

seeing that there was nothing about them to offend, 204

Those seated on high addressing those seated on the ground, those going on the road addressing those passing on high, the mind intent on one object alone; so that if a heavenly form had flown past, 205

Or a form entitled to highest respect, there would have been no distraction visible, so intent was the body and so immovable the limbs. And now beautiful as the opening lily, 206

He advances towards the garden glades, wishing to accomplish the words of the holy prophet (*Ri*shi). The prince seeing the ways prepared and watered, and the joyous holiday appearance of the people, 207

(Seeing too) the drapery and the chariot pure, bright, shining, his heart exulted greatly and rejoiced. The people (on their part) gazed at the prince, so beautifully adorned, with all his retinue, 208

Like an assembled company of kings (gathered) to see a heaven-born prince. And now a Deva-râ*g*a of the Pure abode, suddenly appears by the side of the road; 209

His form changed into that of an old man, struggling for life, his heart weak and oppressed. The prince seeing the old man, filled with apprehension, asked his charioteer, 210

'What kind of man is this? his head white and his shoulders bent, his eyes bleared and his body withered, holding a stick to support him along the way. 211

'Is his body suddenly dried up by the heat, or has he been born in this way?' The charioteer, his heart much embarrassed, scarcely dared to answer truly, 212

Till the pure-born (Deva) added his spiritual power, and caused him to frame a reply in true words: 'His appearance changed, his vital powers decayed, filled with sorrow, with little pleasure, 213

'His spirits gone, his members nerveless, these are the indications of what is called "old age." This man was once a sucking child, brought up and nourished at his mother's breast, 214

'And as a youth full of sportive life, handsome, and in enjoyment of the five pleasures; as years passed on, his frame decaying, he is brought now to the waste of age.' 215

The prince greatly agitated and moved, asked his charioteer another question and said, 'Is yonder man the only one afflicted with age, or shall I, and others also, be such as he?' 216

The charioteer again replied and said, 'Your highness also inherits this lot, as time goes on, the form itself is changed, and this must doubtless come, beyond all hindrance: 217

'The youthful form must wear the garb of age, throughout the world, this is the common lot.' Bodhisattva, who had long prepared the foundation of pure and spotless wisdom, 218

Broadly setting the root of every high quality, with a view to gather large fruit in his present life, hearing these words respecting the sorrow of age, was afflicted in mind, and his hair stood upright. 219

Just as the roll of the thunder and the storm alarm and put to flight the cattle; so was Bodhisattva affected by the words; shaking with apprehension, he deeply sighed; 220

Constrained at heart because of the pain of 'age;'

with shaking head and constant gaze, he thought upon this misery of decay; what joy or pleasure can men take (he thought), 221

In that which soon must wither, stricken by the marks of age; affecting all without exception; though gifted now with youth and strength, yet not one but soon must change and pine away. 222

The eye beholding such signs as these before it, how can it not be oppressed by a desire to escape[1]? Bodhisattva then addressed his charioteer, 'Quickly turn your chariot and go back, 223

'Ever thinking on this subject of old age approaching, what pleasures now can these gardens afford, the years of my life like the fast-flying wind; turn your chariot, and with speedy wheels take me to my palace.' 224

And so his heart keeping in the same sad tone, (he was) as one who returns to a place of entombment; unaffected by any engagement or employment, so he found no rest in anything within his home. 225

The king hearing of his son's sadness urged (his companions) to induce him again to go abroad, and forthwith incited his ministers and attendants to decorate the gardens even more than before. 226

The Deva then caused himself to appear as a sick man; struggling for life, he stood by the wayside, his body swollen and disfigured, sighing with deep-drawn groans, 227

His hands and knees contracted and sore with disease, his tears flowing as he piteously muttered (his petition). The prince asked his charioteer, 'What sort of man, again, is this?' 228

[1] How can a man not (desire) to remove it (i.e. old age) as a hateful thing?

Replying he said, 'This is a sick man. The four elements all confused and disordered, worn and feeble, with no remaining strength, bent down with weakness, looking to his fellow-men for help.' 229

The prince hearing the words thus spoken, immediately became sad and depressed in heart, and asked, 'Is this the only man afflicted thus, or are others liable to the same (calamity)?' 230

In reply he said, 'Through all the world, men are subject to the same condition; those who have bodies must endure affliction, the poor and ignorant, as well as the rich and great.' 231

The prince, when these words met his ears, was oppressed with anxious thought and grief; his body and his mind were moved throughout, just as the moon upon the ruffled tide. 232

'Placed thus in the great furnace of affliction, say! what rest or quiet can there be! Alas! that worldly men, (blinded by) ignorance and oppressed with dark delusion, 233

'Though the robber sickness may appear at any time, yet live with blithe and joyous hearts!' On this, turning his chariot back again, he grieved to think upon the pain of sickness. 234

As a man beaten and wounded sore, with body weakened, leans upon his staff, so dwelt he in the seclusion of his palace, lone-seeking, hating worldly pleasures. 235

The king hearing once more of his son's return, asked anxiously the reason why, and in reply was told—'he saw the pain of sickness.' The king in fear like one beside himself, 236

Roundly blamed the keepers of the way; his heart constrained, his lips spoke not; again he increased the crowd of music women, the sounds of merriment twice louder than aforetime, 237

If by these sounds and sights (the prince) might be gratified; and indulging worldly feelings, might not hate his home. Night and day the charm of melody increased, but his heart was still unmoved by it. 238

The king himself then went forth to observe everything successively, and to make the gardens even yet more attractive, selecting with care the attendant women, that they might excel in every point of personal beauty; 239

Quick in wit and able to arrange matters well, fit to ensnare men by their winning looks; he placed additional keepers along the king's way, he strictly ordered every offensive sight to be removed, 240

And earnestly exhorted the illustrious coachman, to look well and pick out the road as he went. And now that Deva of the pure abode, again caused the appearance of a dead man; 241

Four persons carrying the corpse lifted it on high, and appeared (to be going on) in front of Bodhisattva; the surrounding people saw it not, but only Bodhisattva and the charioteer; 242

(Once more) he asked, 'What is this they carry? with streamers and flowers of every choice description, whilst the followers are overwhelmed with grief, tearing their hair and wailing piteously.' 243

And now the gods instructing the coachman, he replied and said, 'This is a "dead man," all his powers of body destroyed, life departed; his heart without thought, his intellect dispersed; 244

'His spirit gone, his form withered and decayed; stretched out as a dead log; family ties broken

—all his friends who once loved him, clad in white cerements, 245

'Now no longer delighting to behold him, remove him to lie in some hollow ditch (tomb).' The prince hearing the name of DEATH, his heart constrained by painful thoughts, 246

He asked, 'Is this the only dead man, or does the world contain like instances?' Replying thus he said, 'All, everywhere, the same; he who begins his life must end it likewise; 247

'The strong and lusty and the middle-aged, having a body, cannot but decay (and die).' The prince now harassed and perplexed in mind; his body bent upon the chariot leaning-board, 248

With bated breath and struggling accents, stammered thus, 'Oh worldly men! how fatally deluded! beholding everywhere the body brought to dust, yet everywhere the more carelessly living; 249

'The heart is neither lifeless wood nor stone, and yet it thinks not "all is vanishing!"' Then turning, he directed his chariot to go back, and no longer waste his time in wandering. 250

How could he, whilst in fear of instant death, go wandering here and there with lightened heart! The charioteer remembering the king's exhortation feared much nor dared go back; 251

Straightforward then he pressed his panting steeds, passed onward to the gardens, (came to) the groves and babbling streams of crystal water, the pleasant trees, spread out with gaudy verdure, 252

The noble living things and varied beasts so wonderful, the flying creatures and their notes melodious, all charming and delightful to the eye and ear, even as the heavenly Nandavana. 253

VARGA 4. PUTTING AWAY DESIRE.

The prince on entering the garden, the women came around to pay him court; and to arouse in him thoughts frivolous; with ogling ways and deep design, 254

Each one setting herself off to best advantage; or joining together in harmonious concert, clapping their hands, or moving their feet in unison, or joining close, body to body, limb to limb; 255

Or indulging in smart repartees, and mutual smiles; or assuming a thoughtful saddened countenance, and so by sympathy to please the prince, and provoke in him a heart affected by love. 256

But all the women beheld the prince, clouded in brow, and his godlike body not exhibiting its wonted signs of beauty; fair in bodily appearance, surpassingly lovely[1], 257

All looked upwards as they gazed, as when we call upon the moon Deva to come[2]; but all their subtle devices[3] were ineffectual to move Bodhisattva's heart. 258

At last commingling together they join and look astonished and in fear, silent without a word. Then there was a Brahmaputra, whose name was called Udâyi[4] (Yau-to-i). 259

(He) addressing the women, said, 'Now all of

---

[1] Surpassingly adorned or magnificent.

[2] Or, as when the moon Deva (first) comes.

[3] In every way practising subtle devices (upâya).

[4] There is mention of Udâyi in the Fo-pen-hing-tsah-king, chap. XIV. See also note 1, p. 124, Romantic History of Buddha.

you, so graceful and fair, (see if you cannot) by your combined power hit on some device; for beauty's power is not for ever. 260

'Still it holds the world in bondage, by secret ways and lustful arts; but no such loveliness in all the world (as yours), equal to that of heavenly nymphs[1]; 261

'The gods beholding it would leave their queens, spirits and *Ri*shis would be misled by it; why not then the prince, the son of an earthly king[2]? why should not his feelings be aroused? 262

'This prince indeed, though he restrains his heart and holds it fixed[3], pure-minded, with virtue uncontaminated, not to be overcome by power of women; 263

'(Yet) of old there was Sundarî (Su-to-li) able to destroy the great *Ri*shi, and to lead him to indulge in love, and so degrade his boasted eminence[4]; 264

'Undergoing long penance, Gautama fell likewise (by the arts of) a heavenly queen; Shing-kü, a *Ri*shi putra, practising lustful indulgences according to fancy[5], (was lost). 265

'The Brahman *Ri*shi Vi*s*vâmitra (Pi-she-po), living religiously[6] for ten thousand years, deeply

[1] In appearance equal to Devîs.

[2] Or, what then is man (to do), though son of a king, that his feelings should not be aroused?

[3] Holding his will, though firmly fixed.

[4] And bend his head beneath her feet.

[5] The phrase which ends this line is obscure. It may be rendered thus, 'Shing-kü, the *Ri*shi putra, practised lustful ways, beside the flowings of the fountain.' [See a similar case, Catena of Buddhist Scriptures, p. 259.] The Sanskrit text is as follows: '*Ri*shya*sri*ṅga, the son of a Muni, unlearned with women.'

[6] Practising religious rules, or, preparing a religious life.

ensnared by a heavenly queen, in one day was completely shipwreck'd in faith [1]; 266

'Thus those enticing women, by their power, overcame the Brahman ascetics; how much more may ye, by your arts, overpower (the resolves) of the king's son; 267

'Strive therefore after new devices [2], let not the king fail in a successor to the throne; women, altho' naturally weak [3], are high and potent in the way of ruling men. 268

'What may not their arts accomplish in promoting in men a lustful (impure) desire?' At this time all the attendant women, hearing throughout the words of Udâyi, 269

Increasing their powers of pleasing, as the quiet horse when touched by the whip, went into the presence of the royal prince, and each one strove in the practice of every kind of art, 270

(They) joined in music and in smiling conversation, raising their eyebrows, showing their white teeth, with ogling looks, glancing one at the other, their light drapery exhibiting their white bodies, 271

Daintily moving with mincing gait, acting the part of a bride as if coming gradually nearer [4], desiring to promote in him a feeling of love, remembering the words of the great king [5], 272

---

[1] Completely ruined. The name of the queen was Gh*ri*tâ*k*î.

[2] The Chinese 'fong pien' denotes the use of 'means to an end;' generally it can be rendered 'expedients.'

[3] Or, the nature of women although weak.

[4] So I understand the passage, as if a coy wife gradually approached her husband.

[5] Who the great king is I do not find, but I take the two lines following to be a quotation. [The great king was probably the father of Buddha.]

'With dissolute form and slightly clad, forgetful of modesty and womanly reserve.' The prince with resolute heart was silent and still, with unmoved face (he sat); 273

Even as the great elephant-dragon, whilst the entire herd moves round him[1]; so nothing could disturb or move his heart, dwelling in their midst as in a confined room[2]. 274

Like the divine *S*akra, around whom all the Devîs assemble, so was the prince as he dwelt in the gardens; (the maidens) encircling him thus; 275

Some arranging their dress, others washing their hands or feet, others perfuming their bodies with scent, others twining flowers for decoration, 276

Others making strings for jewelled necklets, others rubbing or striking their bodies, others resting, or lying, one beside the other, others, with head inclined, whispering secret words, 277

Others engaged in common sports, others talking of amorous things, others assuming lustful attitudes, striving thus to move his heart; 278

But Bodhisattva, peaceful and collected, firm as a rock, difficult to move, hearing all these women's talk, unaffected either to joy or sorrow, 279

Was driven still more to serious thought, sighing to witness such strange conduct, and beginning to understand the women's design, by these means to disconcert his mind, 280

'Not knowing that youthful beauty soon falls, destroyed by old age and death, fading and perishing! This is the great distress! What ignor-

[1] Or, surrounded by the entire herd.

[2] That is, cramped in the midst of the encircling crowd of girls.

ance and delusion (he reflected) overshadow their minds, 281

'Surely they ought to consider old age, disease, and death, and day and night stir themselves up to exertion, whilst this sharp double-edged sword hangs over the neck. What room for sport or laughter, 282

'Beholding those (monsters) old age, disease, and death? A man who is unable to resort to this inward knowledge, what is he but a wooden or a plaster man, what heart-consideration in such a case! 283

'Like the double tree that appears in the desert, with leaves and fruit all perfect and ripe, the first cut down and destroyed, the other unmoved by apprehension, 284

'So it is in the case of the mass of men, they have no understanding either!' At this time Udâyi came to the place where the prince was, 285

And observing his silent and thoughtful mien, unmoved by any desire for indulgence (the five desires), he forthwith addressed the prince, and said, 'The Mahârâ*g*a, by his former appointment[1], 286

'Has selected me to act as friend to his son; may I therefore speak some friendly words? an enlightened friendship (or, friend) is of three sorts, that which removes things unprofitable, 287

'Promotes that which is real gain, and stands by a friend in adversity. I claim the name of

[1] This passage is obscure; literally it is 'former—seeing—command.'

"enlightened friend," and would renounce all that is magisterial, 288

'But yet not speak lightly or with indifference. What then are the three sources of advantage? listen, and I will now utter true words, and prove myself a true and sincere adviser. 289

'When the years are fresh and ripening, beauty and pleasing qualities in bloom, not to give proper weight to woman's influence, this is a weak man's policy (body)[1]. 290

'It is right sometimes to be of a crafty mind, submitting to those little subterfuges, which find a place in the heart's undercurrents, and obeying what those thoughts suggest, 291

'In way of pleasures to be got from dalliance, this is no wrong in woman's (eye)! even if now the heart has no desire, yet it is fair to follow such devices; 292

'Agreement (acquiescence) is the joy of woman's heart, acquiescence is the substance (the full) of true adornment; but if a man reject these overtures, he's like a tree deprived of leaves and fruits; 293

'Why then ought you to yield and acquiesce? that you may share in all these things. Because in taking, there's an end of trouble—no light and changeful thoughts then worry us— 294

'For pleasure is the first and foremost thought of all, the gods themselves cannot dispense with it. Lord *S*akra was drawn by it to love the wife of Gautama the *Ri*shi; 295

'So likewise the *Ri*shi Agastya, through a long

[1] 'This is the character of non-victorious men.' Again there is a play on the word 'Shing' a *G*ina. The Sanskrit renders it 'rudeness.' The Chinese fi-shing-*g*in may also mean coarse or unpolished.

period of discipline[1], practising austerities, from hankering after a heavenly queen (Devî), lost all reward of his religious endeavours, 296

'The *R*ishi B*ri*haspati, and *K*andradeva putra; the *R*ishi Parâ*s*ara, and Kava*ñg*ara (Kia-pin-*k*e-lo)[2]: 297

'All these, out of many others, were overcome by woman's love. How much more then, in your case, should you partake in such pleasant joys; 298

'Nor refuse, with wilful heart, to participate in the worldly delights, which your present station, possessed of such advantages, offers you, in the presence of these attendants.' 299

At this time the royal prince, hearing the words of his friend Udâyi, so skilfully put, with such fine distinction, cleverly citing worldly instances, 300

Answered thus to Udâyi: 'Thank you for having spoken sincerely to me, let me likewise answer you in the same way, and let your heart suspend its judgment whilst you listen; 301

'It is not that I am careless about beauty, or am ignorant of (the power of) human joys, but only that I see on all the impress of change; therefore my heart is sad and heavy; 302

'If these things were sure of lasting, without the ills of age, disease, and death, then would I too take my fill of love; and to the end find no disgust or sadness; 303

'If you will undertake to cause these women's beauty not after-while to change or wither, then, though the joy of love may have its evil, still it might hold the mind in thraldom; 304

('To know that other) men grow old, sicken, and

[1] '*K*ang-yê,' the long night.

[2] The Sanskrit text has, 'Vasish*th*a begat Kapi*ñg*alâda.'

die, would be enough to rob such joys of satisfaction; yet how much more in their own case (knowing this) would discontentment fill the mind; 305

'(To know) such pleasures hasten to decay, and their bodies likewise; if, notwithstanding this, men yield to the power of love, their case indeed is like the very beasts. 306

'And now you cite the names of many *Ri*shis, who practised lustful ways in life; their cases likewise cause me sorrow, for in that they did these things, they perished. 307

'Again, you cite the name of that illustrious king, who freely gratified his passions, but he, in like way, perished in the act; know, then, that he was not a conqueror (*G*ina); 308

'With smooth words to conceal an intrigue, and to persuade one's neighbour to consent, and by consenting to defile his mind; how can this be called a just device? 309

'It is but to seduce one with a hollow lie,—such ways are not for me to practise; or, for those who love the truth and honesty; for they are, forsooth, unrighteous ways, 310

'And such a disposition is hard to reverence; shaping one's conduct after one's likings, liking this or that, and seeing no harm in it, what method of experience is this! 311

'A hollow compliance, and a protesting heart, such method is not for me to follow; but this I know, old age, disease, and death, these are the great afflictions which accumulate, 312

'And overwhelm me with their presence; on these I find no friend to speak, alas! alas! Udâyi! these, after all, are the great concerns; 313

'The pain of birth, old age, disease, and death; this grief is that we have to fear; the eyes see all things falling to decay, and yet the heart finds joy in following them; 314

'But I have little strength of purpose, or command; this heart of mine is feeble and distraught, reflecting thus on age, disease, and death. Distracted, as I never was before; 315

'Sleepless by night and day, how can I then indulge in pleasure? Old age, disease, and death consuming me, their certainty beyond a doubt, 316

'And still to have no heavy thoughts, in truth my heart would be a log or stone.' Thus the prince, for Uda's sake, used every kind of skilful argument, 317

Describing all the pains of pleasure; and not perceiving that the day declined. And now the waiting women all, with music and their various attractions, 318

Seeing that all were useless for the end, with shame began to flock back to the city; the prince beholding all the gardens, bereft of their gaudy ornaments, 319

The women all returning home, the place becoming silent and deserted, felt with twofold strength the thought of impermanence. With saddened mien going back, he entered his palace; 320

The king, his father, hearing of the prince, his heart estranged from thoughts of pleasure, was greatly overcome with sorrow, and like a sword it pierced his heart. 321

Forthwith assembling all his council, he sought of them some means to gain his end; they all replied, 'These sources of desire are not enough to hold and captivate his heart.' 322

Varga 5. Leaving the City.

And so the king increased the means for gratifying the appetite for pleasure; both night and day the joys of music wore out the prince, opposed to pleasure; 323

Disgusted with them, he desired their absence, his mind was weaned from all such thoughts, he only thought of age, disease, and death; as the lion wounded by an arrow. 324

The king then sent his chief ministers, and the most distinguished of his family, young in years and eminent for beauty, as well as for wisdom and dignity of manners, 325

To accompany, and rest with him, both night and day, in order to influence the prince's mind. And now within a little interval, the prince again requested the king that he might go abroad. 326

Once more the chariot and the well-paced horses were prepared, adorned with precious substances and every gem; and then with all the nobles, his associates, surrounding him, he left the city gates: 327

Just as the four kinds of flower[1], when the sun shines, open out their leaves, so was the prince in all his spiritual splendour; effulgent in the beauty of his youth time; 328

As he proceeded to the gardens from the city, the road was well prepared, smooth, and wide, the trees were bright with flowers and fruit, his heart was joyous, and forgetful of its care. 329

---

[1] It may be a description of some particular flower, 'four-seed (kind)-flower.'

Now by the roadside as he beheld the ploughmen, plodding along the furrows, and the writhing worms, his heart again was moved with piteous feeling, and anguish pierced his soul afresh; 330

To see those labourers at their toil, struggling with painful work, their bodies bent, their hair dishevelled, the dripping sweat upon their faces, their persons fouled with mud and dust; 331

The ploughing oxen, too, bent by the yokes, their lolling tongues and gaping mouths; the nature of the prince, loving, compassionate, his mind conceived most poignant sorrow, 332

And nobly moved to sympathy, he groaned with pain; then stooping down he sat upon the ground, and watched this painful scene of suffering; reflecting on the ways of birth and death! 333

'Alas! he cried, for all the world! how dark and ignorant, void of understanding!' And then to give his followers chance of rest, he bade them each repose where'er they list; 334

Whilst he beneath the shadow of a *G*ambu tree, gracefully seated, gave himself to thought. He pondered on the fact of life and death, inconstancy, and endless progress to decay. 335

His heart thus fixed without confusion, the five desires (senses) covered and clouded over, lost in possession of enlightenment and insight, he entered on the first pure state of ecstacy. 336

All low desire removed, most perfect peace ensued; and fully now in Samâdhi (he saw) the misery and utter sorrow of the world; the ruin wrought by age, disease, and death; 337

The great misery following on the body's death; and yet men not awakened to the truth! oppressed with others' suffering (age, disease, and death), this load of sorrow weigh'd his mind; 338

'I now will seek (he said) a noble law, unlike the worldly methods known to men, I will oppose disease and age and death, and strive against the mischief wrought by these on men.' 339

Thus lost in tranquil contemplation, (he considered that) youth, vigour, and strength of life, constantly renewing themselves, without long stay, in the end fulfil the rule of ultimate destruction; 340

(Thus he pondered) without excessive joy or grief, without hesitation or confusion of thought, without dreaminess or extreme longing, without aversion or discontent, 341

But perfectly at peace, with no hindrance, radiant with the beams of increased illumination. At this time a Deva of the Pure abode, transforming himself into the shape of a Bhikshu, 342

Came to the place where the prince was seated; the prince with due consideration rose to meet him, and asked him who he was. In reply he said, 'I am a Shâman, 343

'Depressed and sad at thought of age, disease, and death, I have left my home to seek some way of rescue, but everywhere I find old age, disease, and death, all (things) hasten to decay and there is no permanency; 344

'Therefore I search for the happiness of something that decays not, that never perishes, that never knows beginning, that looks with equal mind on enemy and friend, that heeds not wealth nor beauty, 345

'The happiness of one who finds repose alone in

solitude, in some unfrequented dell, free from molestation, all thoughts about the world destroyed, dwelling in some lonely hermitage, 346

'Untouched by any worldly source of pollution, begging for food sufficient for the body.' And forthwith as he stood before the prince, gradually rising up he disappeared in space. 347

The prince with joyful mind, considering, recollected former Buddhas, established thus in perfect dignity of manner; with noble mien and presence, as this visitor. 348

Thus calling things to mind with perfect self-possession, he reached the thought of righteousness, and by what means it can be gained. Indulging thus for length of time in thoughts of religious solitude, 349

He now suppressed his feelings and controlled his members, and rising turned again towards the city. His followers all flocked after him, calling him to stop and not go far from them, 350

But in his mind these secret thoughts so held him, devising means by which to escape from the world, that tho' his body moved along the road, his heart was far away among the mountains; 351

Even as the bound and captive elephant, ever thinks about his desert wilds. The prince now entering the city, there met him men and women, earnest for their several ends; 352

The old besought him for their children, the young sought something for the wife, others sought something for their brethren; all those allied by kinship or by family, 353

Aimed to obtain their several suits, all of them joined in relationship dreading the pain (expectation) of separation. And now the prince's heart was filled with joy, as he suddenly heard those words 'separation and association.' 354

'These are joyful sounds to me,' he said, 'they assure me that my vow shall be accomplished.' Then deeply pondering the joy of 'snapped relationship,' the idea of Nirvâ*n*a, deepened and widened in him[1], 355

His body as a peak of the Golden Mount, his shoulder like the elephant's, his voice like the spring-thunder, his deep-blue eye like that of the king of oxen, 356

His mind full of religious thoughts (aims), his face bright as the full moon, his step like that of the lion king, thus he entered his palace, 357

Even as the son of Lord *S*akra (or, *S*akra-putra) his mind reverential, his person dignified, he went straight to his father's presence, and with head inclined, enquired, 'Is the king well?' 358

Then he explained his dread of age, disease, and death, and sought respectfully permission to become a hermit. 'For all things in the world' (he said), 'though now united, tend to separation;' 359

Therefore he prayed to leave the world; desiring to find 'true deliverance.' His royal father hearing the words 'leave the world,' was forthwith seized with great heart-trembling, 360

Even as the strong wild elephant shakes with his weight the boughs of some young sapling; going forward, seizing the prince's hands, with falling tears, he spake as follows: 361

[1] Literally, 'deeply widened the mind of Nirvâ*n*a (Ni-pan).'

'Stop! nor speak such words, the time is not yet come for "a religious life," you are young and strong, your heart beats full, to lead a religious life frequently involves trouble, 362

'It is rarely possible to hold the desires in check, the heart not yet estranged from their enjoyment; to leave your home and lead a painful ascetic life, your heart can hardly yet resolve on such a course; 363

'To dwell amidst the desert wilds or lonely dells, this heart of yours would not be perfectly at rest, for though you love religious matters, you are not yet like me in years; 364

'You should undertake the kingdom's government, and let me first adopt ascetic life; but to give up your father and your sacred duties, this is not to act religiously; 365

'You should suppress this thought of "leaving home," and undertake your worldly duties, find your delight in getting an illustrious name, and after this give up your home and family.' 366

The prince, with proper reverence and respectful feelings, again besought his royal father; but promised if he could be saved from four calamities, that he would give up the thought of 'leaving home;' 367

If he would grant him life without end, no disease, nor undesirable old age, and no decay of earthly possessions; then he would obey and give up the thought of 'leaving home.' 368

The royal father then addressed the prince, 'Speak not such words as these, for with respect to these four things, who is there able to prevent them, or say nay to their approach; 369

'Asking such things as these (four things), you would provoke men's laughter! But put away this thought of "leaving home," and once more take yourself to pleasure.' 370

The prince again besought his father, 'If you may not grant me these four prayers, then let me go I pray, and leave my home. O! place no difficulties in my path; 371

'Your son is dwelling in a burning house, would you indeed prevent his leaving it! To solve a doubt is only reasonable, who could forbid a man to seek its explanation? 372

'Or if he were forbidden, then by self-destruction he might solve the difficulty, in an unrighteous way: and if he were to do so, who could restrain him after death?' 373

The royal father, seeing his son's mind so firmly fixed that it could not be turned, and that it would be waste of strength to bandy further words or arguments, 374

Forthwith commanded more attendant women, to provoke still more his mind to pleasure; day and night (he ordered them) to keep the roads and ways, to the end that he might not leave his palace; 375

(He moreover ordered) all the ministers of the country to come to the place where dwelt the prince, to quote and illustrate the rules of filial piety, hoping to cause him to obey the wishes of the king. 376

The prince, beholding his royal father bathed with tears and o'erwhelmed with grief, forthwith returned to his abode, and sat himself in silence to consider; 377

All the women of the palace, coming towards him, waited as they circled him, and gazed in silence on his beauteous form. They gazed upon him not with furtive glance, 378

But like the deer in autumn brake looks wistfully at the hunter; around the prince's straight and handsome form, (bright) as the mountain of true gold (Sumeru), 379

The dancing women gathered doubtingly, waiting to hear him bid them sound their music; repressing every feeling of the heart through fear, even as the deer within the brake; 380

Now gradually the day began to wane, the prince still sitting in the evening light, his glory streaming forth in splendour, as the sun lights up Mount Sumeru; 381

Thus seated on his jewelled couch, surrounded by the fumes of sandal-wood, the dancing women took their places round; then sounded forth their heavenly (Gandharva) music, 382

Even as Vaisaman (Vaisravana) produces every kind of rare and heavenly sounds. The thoughts which dwelt within the prince's mind entirely drove from him desire for music, 383

And tho' the sounds filled all the place, they fell upon his ear unnoticed. At this time the Deva of the Pure abode, knowing the prince's time was come, 384

The destined time for quitting home, suddenly assumed a form and came to earth, to make the shapes of all the women unattractive, so that they might create disgust, 385

And no desire arise from thought of beauty. Their half-clad forms bent in ungainly attitudes, forgetful in their sleep, their bodies crooked or supine, the instruments of music lying scattered in disorder; 386

Leaning and facing one another, or with back to back, or like those beings thrown into the abyss, their jewelled necklets bound about like chains, their clothes and undergarments swathed around their persons; 387

Grasping their instruments, stretched along the earth, even as those undergoing punishment at the hands of keepers (eunuchs), their garments in confusion, or like the broken kani flower (poppy?); 388

Or some with bodies leaning in sleep against the wall, in fashion like a hanging bow or horn, or with their hands holding to the window-frames, and looking like an outstretched corpse; 389

Their mouths half opened or else gaping wide, the loathsome dribble trickling forth, their heads uncovered and in wild disorder, like some unreasoning madman's; 390

The flower wreaths torn and hanging across their face, or slipping off the face upon the ground; others with body raised as if in fearful dread, just like the lonely desert (?) bird; 391

Or others pillowed on their neighbour's lap, their hands and feet entwined together, whilst others smiled or knit their brows in turn, some with eyes closed and open mouth, 392

Their bodies lying in wild disorder, stretched here and there, like corpses thrown together. And now the prince seated, in his beauty, looked with thought on all the waiting women; 393

Before, they had appeared exceeding lovely, their laughing words, their hearts so light and gay, their forms so plump and young, their looks so bright; but now, how changed! so uninviting and repulsive. 394

And such is woman's disposition! how can they, then, be ever dear, or closely trusted; such false appearances! and unreal pretences; they only madden and delude the minds of men. 395

And now (he said), 'I have awakened to the truth! Resolved am I to leave such false society.' At this time the Deva of the Pure abode descended and approached, unfastening the doors. 396

The prince, too, at this time rose and walked along, amid the prostrate forms of all the women; with difficulty reaching to the inner hall, he called to *K*andaka, in these words, 397

'My mind is now athirst and longing for the draught of the fountain of sweet dew, saddle then my horse, and quickly bring it here. I wish to reach the deathless city; 398

'My heart is fixed beyond all change, resolved I am and bound by sacred oath; these women, once so charming and enticing, now behold I altogether loathsome; 399

'The gates, which were before fast-barred and locked, now stand free and open! these evidences of something supernatural, point to a climax of my life.' 400

Then *K*andaka stood reflecting inwardly, whether to obey or not the prince's order, without informing his royal father of it, and so incur the heaviest punishment. 401

The Devas then gave spiritual strength; and unperceived the horse equipped came round, with even pace; a gallant steed, with all his jewelled trappings for a rider; 402

High-maned, with flowing tail, broad-backed, short-haired and ear'd, with belly like the deer's, head like the king of parrots, wide forehead, round and claw-shaped nostrils, 403

Breath like the dragon's, with breast and shoulders square, true and sufficient marks of his high breed. The royal prince, stroking the horse's neck, and rubbing down his body, said, 404

'My royal father ever rode on thee, and found thee brave in fight and fearless of the foe; now I desire to rely on thee alike! to carry me far off to the stream (ford) of endless life, 405

'To fight against and overcome the opposing force of men, the men who associate in search of pleasure, the men who engage in the search after wealth, the crowds who follow and flatter such persons; 406

'In opposing sorrow, friendly help is difficult (to find), in seeking religious truth there must be rare enlightenment, let us then be knit together thus as friends; then, at last, there will be rest from sorrow. 407

'But now I wish to go abroad, to give deliverance from pain; now then, for your own sake it is, and for the sake of all your kind, 408

'That you should exert your strength, with noble pace, without lagging or weariness.' Having thus exhorted him, he bestrode his horse, and grasping the reins, proceeded forth; 409

The man like the sun shining forth from his tabernacle (sun-palace-streams), the horse like the white floating cloud (the white cloud-pile), exerting himself but without exciting haste, his breath concealed and without snorting; 410

Four spirits (Devas) accompanying him, held up

his feet, heedfully concealing (his advance), silently and without noise; the heavy gates fastened and barred (locked), the heavenly spirits of themselves caused to open; 411

Reverencing deeply the virtuous (sinless) father, loving deeply the unequalled son, equally affected with love towards all the members of his family (these Devas took their place). 412

Suppressing his feelings, but not extinguishing his memory, lightly he advanced and proceeded beyond the city, pure and spotless as the lily flowers which spring from the mud; 413

Looking up with earnestness at his father's palace, he announced his purpose—unwitnessed and unwritten—'If I escape not birth, old age, and death, for evermore I pass not thus along;' 414

All the concourse of Devas, the space-filling Nâgas and spirits followed joyfully and exclaimed Well! well! (sâdhu), in confirmation of the true words (he spoke); 415

The Nâgas and the company of Devas acquired a condition of heart difficult to obtain, and each with his own inherent light led on the way shedding forth their brightness. 416

Thus man and horse both strong of heart went onwards, lost to sight, like streaming stars, but ere the eastern quarter flashed with light, they had advanced three yoganas. 417

KIOUEN II.

VARGA 6. THE RETURN OF *K*ANDAKA[1].

And now the night was in a moment gone, and sight restored to all created things, (when the royal prince) looked thro' the wood, and saw the abode of Po-ka, the *R*ishi ; [the hermitage of the Bhârgavides, see Burnouf, Introduction to Ind. Bud. p. 385]; 418

The purling streams so exquisitely pure and sparkling, and the wild beasts all unalarmed at man, caused the royal prince's heart to exult. Tired, the horse[2] stopped of his own will, to breathe. 419

'This, then,' he thought, 'is a good sign and fortunate, and doubtless indicates divine approval[3].' And now he saw belonging to the *R*ishi, the various vessels[4] used for (asking) charity; 420

And (other things) arranged by him in order, without the slightest trace of negligence. Dismounting then he stroked his horse's head, and cried, 'You now have borne me (well)!' 421

---

[1] There was a tower erected on the spot where Bodhisattva dismissed his coachman. See Fah-hien, p. 92. The distance given by A*s*vaghosha, viz. three yo*g*anas, or about twenty miles, is much more probable than the eight hundred lis, given in later accounts as the length of Bodhisattva's journey. Compare Fah-hien p. 92, note 2.

The name '*K*anna' may perhaps be more properly restored to '*K*andaka.'

[2] The text here seems to require the alteration of 形 into 馬.

[3] Mi-tsang-li, not-yet-advantage; or, unheard of, or miraculous, profit.

[4] 'Ying' is often used for 'a proper measure vessel,' i. e. an alms dish.

With loving eyes he looked at *K*andaka, (eyes) like the pure cool surface of a placid lake (and said), 'Swift-footed! like a horse in pace, yea! swift as any light-winged bird, 422

'Ever have you followed after me when riding, and deeply have I felt my debt of thanks, but not yet had you been tried in other ways; I only knew you as a man true-hearted, 423

'My mind now wonders at your active powers of body; these two I now begin to see (are yours); a man may have a heart most true and faithful, but strength of body may not too be his; 424

'Bodily strength and perfect honesty of heart, I now have proof enough are yours. (To be content) to leave[1] the tinselled world, and with swift foot to follow me, 425

'Who would do this but for some profit, if without profit to his kin[2], who would not shun it? but you, with no private aim, have followed me, not seeking any present recompense; 426

'As we nourish and bring up a child, to bind together and bring honour to a family; so we also reverence and obey a father, to gain (obedience and attention) from a begotten son; 427

'In this way all think of their own advantage; but you have come with me disdaining profit; with many words I cannot hold you here, so let me say in brief to you, 428

'We have now ended our relationship; take, then, my horse and ride back again; for me, during the

---

[1] To reject and leave. 捨 for 捐.

[2] It may also be, 'to himself and kin.'

long night past[1], that place I sought to reach now I have obtained.' 429

Then taking off his precious neck-chain, he handed it to *K*andaka, 'Take this,' he said, 'I give it you, let it console you in your sorrow;' 430

The precious[2] jewel in the tire that bound his head, bright-shining, lighting up his person, taking off and placing in his extended palm, like the sun which lights up Sumeru, 431

He said, 'O *K*andaka! take this gem, and going back to where my father is, take the jewel and lay it reverently[3] before him, to signify my heart's relation to him; 432

'And then, for me, request the king to stifle every fickle feeling of affection, and say that I, to escape from birth and age and death, have entered on the wild (forest)[4] of painful discipline, 433

'Not that I may get a heavenly birth, much less because I have no tenderness of heart, or that I

---

[1] The long night is the dark passage of continued transmigration, or change; the sense is, that Bodhisattva having sought for the condition of being, or life, he now has reached through a succession of previous births, the relationship or connection with his charioteer as master and man, is at an end.

[2] The head-jewel, or *k*û*d*â-mâ*n*i. This crest-jewel is figured in various ways in Buddhist art; as a rule it may be taken to indicate 'the highest' (the head), and in this form it is placed on the head of the figures of Buddha (in Ceylon); and is found at Sanchi and Amarâvati as an object of reverence; it symbolises the supreme authority of Buddha, Dharma, Saṅgha.

[3] Or, holding the jewel, worship reverently at the king's feet.

[4] The 'forest of mortification,' i.e. the place where mortification was to be endured. For an account of Bodhisattva's penance (six years' penance [Sha*d*varshika-vrata]), see Râjendralâla Mitra's Buddha Gayâ, p. 26.

cherish any cause of bitterness, but only that I may escape this weight of sorrow; 434

'The accumulated long-night[1] weight of covetous desire (love), I now desire to ease the load (cause a break), so that it may be overthrown for ever; therefore I seek the way (cause) of ultimate escape; 435

'If I should obtain emancipation, then shall I never need to put away my kindred[2], to leave my home, to sever ties of love. O! grieve not for your son! 436

'The five desires of sense beget the sorrow[3]; those held by lust themselves induce the sorrow; my very ancestors, victorious kings, thinking (their throne) established and immovable, 437

'Have handed down to me their kingly wealth; I, thinking only on religion, put it all away; the royal mothers at the end of life their cherished treasures leave for their sons, 438

'Those sons who covet much such worldly profit; but I rejoice to have acquired religious wealth; if you say that I am young and tender, and that the time for seeking wisdom is not come, 439

'You ought to know that to seek true religion, there never is a time not fit; impermanence and fickleness[4], the hate of death, these ever follow us, 440

'And therefore I (embrace) the present day, con-

---

[1] The 'long night' of previous life.

[2] As, for instance, in the Vessantara *G*âtaka (birth), in which Bodhisattva gave up home, children, and wife, in pursuance of religious perfection.

[3] The five desires are the root of sorrow.

[4] This line may also be rendered, 'impermanence, no fixed condition, this!'

vinced that now is time to seek religion[1]. With such entreaties as the above, you must make matters plain on my behalf; 441

'But, pray you, cause my father not to think longingly after me; let him destroy all recollection of me[2], and cut out from his soul the ties of love; 442

'And you, grieve not[3] because of what I say, but recollect to give the king my message.' *K*andaka hearing respectfully the words of exhortation, blinded and confused through choking sorrow, 443

With hands outstretched did worship; and answering the prince, he spoke, 'The orders that you give me, will, I fear, add grief to grief, 444

'And sorrow thus increased will deepen, as the elephant who struggles into deeper mire. When the ties of love are rudely snapped, who, that has any heart, would not grieve! 445

'The golden ore may still by stamping be broken up, how much more the feelings choked with sorrow[4]! the prince has grown up in a palace[5], with every care bestowed upon his tender person, 446

'And now he gives his body to the rough and thorny forest; how will he be able to bear a life of privation[6]? When first you ordered me to equip your steed, my mind was indeed sorely troubled, 447

---

[1] Convinced (resolved) that this is the time to seek the practice of the law, i. e. to engage in the work of religion.

[2] Let him destroy all recollection of me as a form, or, a living person: this does not forbid him to recollect the office and dignity of Bodhisattva.

[3] Or, let not slip my words.

[4] How much rather, may the heart be broken, choked with sorrow!

[5] Concealed or kept securely in his palace.

[6] Fu-hing; the practice of austerities, or mortification.

'But the heavenly powers urged me on, causing me to hasten the preparation (of the horse[1]), but what is the intention that urges the prince, to resolve thus to leave his secure palace? 448

'The people of Kapilavastu, and all the country afflicted with grief; your father, now an old man, mindful of his son, loving him moreover tenderly[2]; 449

'Surely this determination to leave your home, this is not according to duty; it is wrong, surely, to disregard father and mother,—we cannot speak of such a thing with propriety! 450

'Gotamî, too, who has nourished you so long, fed you with milk when a helpless child, such love as hers cannot easily be forgotten; it is impossible surely to turn the back on a benefactor; 451

'The highly gifted (virtuous) mother of a child, is ever respected by the most distinguished families[3]; to inherit distinction[4] and then to turn round, is not the mark of a distinguished man: 452

'The illustrious child of Ya*s*odharâ, who has inherited a kingdom, rightly governed, his years now gradually ripening, should not thus go away from and forsake his home; 453

'But though he has gone away from his royal father, and forsaken his family and his kin, forbid it

---

[1] To hasten on the decoration, i.e. the harnessing, of the horse.

[2] Or, thinking his son beloved and in security.

[3] Illustrious families or tribes are strong, or able, to wait upon or respect. There seems to be a play here on two words: first, shing, illustrious or distinguished, alluding to the *S*âkyas as a race of *G*inas or conquerors; secondly, neng, able, alluding to the origin of the word *S*âkya, i.e. able.

[4] To obtain 'distinction;' still referring to the word shing; also in the next lines. Consult also p. 28, note 2 supra.

he should still drive me away, let me not depart from the feet of my master; 454

'My heart is bound to thee, as the heat is (bound up[1]) in the boiling water; I cannot return without thee to my country; to return and leave the prince thus, in the midst of the solitude of the desert[2], 455

'Then should I be like Sumanta[3] (Sumantra), who left and forsook Râma; and now if I return alone to the palace, what words can I address to the king? 456

'How can I reply to the reproaches of all the dwellers in the palace with suitable words? Therefore let the prince rather tell me, how I may truly[4] describe, 457

'And with what device, the disfigured body, and the merit-seeking condition of the hermit! I am full of fear and alarm, my tongue can utter no words; 458

'Tell me then what words to speak; but who is there in the empire will believe me? If I say that the moon's rays are scorching, there are men, perhaps, who may believe me; 459

'But they will not believe that the prince, in his conduct, will act without piety; (for) the prince's heart is sincere and refined, always actuated with pity and love to men. 460

'To be deeply affected with love, and yet to

---

[1] Or, my heart is bound to thee, or cherishes thee, as the fire embraces the vessel set over it.

[2] I have here inverted the order of the lines, to bring out the sense.

[3] Sumantra, the minister and charioteer of Da*s*aratha (Râmâya*n*a II, 14, 30).

[4] The order of these lines is again inverted, as they are complicated in the original. The word 'hu,' which I have translated 'truly,' may mean 'dumbly,' or, 'unfeelingly.'

forsake (the object of love), this surely is opposed to a constant mind. O then, for pity's sake! return to your home, and thus appease my foolish longings.' 461

The prince having listened to *K*andaka, pitying his grief expressed in so many words, with heart resolved and strong in its determination, spoke thus to him once more, and said: 462

'Why thus on my account do you feel the pain of separation? you should overcome this sorrowful mood, it is for you to comfort yourself; 463

'All creatures, each in its way, foolishly arguing that all things are constant, would influence me to-day not to forsake my kin and relatives; 464

'But when dead and come to be a ghost, how then, let them say, can I be kept? My loving mother when she bore me, with deep affection painfully carried me, 465

'And then when born she died, not permitted to nourish me. One alive, the other dead, gone by different roads, where now shall she be found? 466

'Like as in a wilderness on some high tree all the birds living with their mates assemble in the evening and at dawn disperse, so are the separations of the world; 467

'The floating clouds rise (like) a high mountain, from the four quarters they fill the void, in a moment again they are separated and disappear; so is it with the habitations of men; 468

'People from the beginning have erred thus, binding themselves in society and by the ties of love, and then, as after a dream, all is dispersed; do not then recount the names of my relatives; 469

'For like the wood which is produced in spring,

gradually grows and brings forth its leaves, which again fall in the autumn-chilly-dews—if the different parts of the same body are thus divided— 470

'How much more men who are united in society! and how shall the ties of relationship escape rending? Cease therefore your grief and expostulation, obey my commands and return home; 471

'The thought of your return alone will save me, and perhaps after your return I also may come back. The men of Kapilavastu, hearing that my heart is fixed, 472

'Will dismiss from their minds all thought of me, but you may make known my words, "when I have escaped from the sad ocean of birth and death, then afterwards I will come back again; 473

'"But I am resolved, if I obtain not my quest, my body shall perish in the mountain wilds."' The white horse hearing the prince, as he uttered these true and earnest words, 474

Bent his knee and licked his foot, whilst he sighed deeply and wept. Then the prince with his soft and glossy palm, (fondly) stroking the head of the white horse, 475

(Said), 'Do not let sorrow rise (within), I grieve indeed at losing you, my gallant steed[1]—so strong and active, your merit now has gained its end[2]; 476

'You shall enjoy for long a respite from an evil birth[3], but for the present take as your reward[4]

[1] Or, my gentle horse!

[2] This merit, or, meritorious deed, is now completed.

[3] The idea is, that the horse, in consequence of the merit he has acquired by bearing the prince from his home, shall enjoy henceforward a higher state of existence.

[4] 'A superior reward now, for the present,' or, 'a better reward than that I now bestow,' viz. the jewels &c.

these precious jewels and this glittering sword, and with them follow closely after *K*andaka.' 477

The prince then drawing forth his sword, glancing in the light as the dragon's eye, (cut off) the knot of hair with its jewelled stud[1], and forthwith cast it into space; 478

Ascending upwards to the firmament, it floated there as the wings of the phœnix; then all the Devas of the Trayastri*ms*a[2] heavens seizing the hair, returned with it to their heavenly abodes; 479

Desiring always to adore the feet (offer religious service), how much rather now possessed of the crowning locks, with unfeigned piety do they increase their adoration, and shall do till the true law has died away. 480

Then the royal prince thought thus, 'My adornments now are gone for ever, there only now remain these silken garments, which are not in keeping with a hermit's life.' 481

Then the Deva of the Pure abode, knowing the heart-ponderings of the prince, transformed himself into a hunter's likeness, holding his bow, his arrows in his girdle, 482

His body girded with a Kashâya[3]-colour'd robe, thus he advanced in front of the prince. The prince

---

[1] That is, the '*k*û*d*â ma*n*i,' or hair ornament. This ornament is represented at Sanchi and Bharhut (plates xxx and xvi respectively ['Tree and Serpent Worship' and 'The Stûpa of Bharhut']. In the former plate the figure on the upper floor with the women is probably Mâra seeing Bodhisattva fulfilling his purpose).

[2] That is, the heaven of the thirty-three gods supposed to be on the top of Sumeru.

[3] Kashâya, the dark colour of the ground, adopted as the colour for their robes by the Buddhists.

considering this garment of his, the colour of the ground, a fitting pure attire, 483

Becoming to the utmost the person of a *Ri*shi, not fit for[1] a hunter's dress, forthwith called to the hunter, as he stood before him, in accents soft, and thus addressed him: 484

'That dress of thine belikes me much, as if it were not foul[2], and this my dress I'll give thee in exchange, so please thee.' 485

The hunter then addressed the prince, 'Although I ill can spare (am not unattached to) this garment, which I use as a disguise among the deer, that alluring them within reach I may kill them, 486

'Notwithstanding, as it so pleases you, I am now willing to bestow it in exchange for yours.' The hunter having received the sumptuous dress, took again his heavenly body. 487

The prince and *K*andaka, the coachman, seeing this, thought deeply[3] thus, 'This garment is of no common character, it is not what a worldly man has worn;' 488

And in (the prince's) heart great joy arose, as he regarded the coat with double reverence, and forthwith giving all the other things[4] to *K*andaka, he himself was clad in it, of Kashâya colour; 489

---

[1] This may also be translated, 'a suitable colour for one who is the opposite of, i.e. opposed to the occupation of, a hunter.'

[2] That is, as if it were pure; there is a play on the expression 'not foul' or 'impure,' meaning that the dress was itself of a dark or impure colour, and that the occupation of the hunter made it more so.

[3] Thought 'deeply;' the expression 奇特想 means 'rare,' or, 'seldom-felt thought.'

[4] That is, as I understand it, giving the remaining articles of his dress to *K*andaka.

Then like the dark and lowering cloud[1], that surrounds the disc of the sun or moon, he for a moment gazed, scanning his steps (way), then entered on the hermit's grot; 490

*K*andaka following him with (wistful) eyes, his body disappeared, nor was it seen again. 'My lord and master now has left his father's house, his kinsfolk and myself (he cried), 491

'He now has clothed himself in hermit's garb[2], and entered the painful[3] forest;' raising his hands he called on Heaven, o'erpowered with grief he could not move; 492

Till holding by the white steed's neck, he tottered forward on the homeward road, turning again and often looking back, his steps (body) going on, his heart back-hastening, 493

Now lost in thought and self-forgetful, now looking down to earth, then raising up his drooping (eye) to heaven, falling at times and then rising again, thus weeping as he went, he pursued his way homewards. 494

VARGA 7. ENTERING THE PLACE (WOOD) OF AUSTERITIES.

The prince having dismissed *K*andaka, as he entered the *Ri*shis' abode, his graceful body brightly

[1] I have supposed that 絳 is for 降. The robe is represented as the cloud surrounding the bright person of Bodhisattva.

[2] He now has put on a dark-colour'd robe.

[3] The painful forest; that is, the forest or wood where painful mortification is practised. 苦行林.

shining, lit up on every side the forest 'place of suffering;' 495

Himself gifted with every excellence (Siddhârtha), according to his gifts, so were they reflected. As the lion, the king of beasts, when he enters among the herd of beasts, 496

Drives from their minds all thoughts of common things[1], as now they watch the true form of their kind[2], so those *Ri*shi masters assembled there, suddenly perceiving the miraculous portent[3], 497

Were struck with awe and fearful gladness[4], as they gazed with earnest eyes and hands conjoined. The men and women too, engaged in various occupations, beholding him, with unchanged attitudes, 498

Gazed as the gods look on king *S*akra, with constant look and eyes unmoved; so the *Ri*shis, with their feet fixed fast, looked at him even thus; 499

Whatever in their hands they held, without releasing it, they stopped and looked; even as the ox when yoked to the wain, his body bound, his mind also restrained; 500

So also the followers of the holy *Ri*shis, each called the other to behold the miracle. The peacocks and the other birds with cries commingled flapped their wings; 501

---

[1] That is, expels the recollection of all inferior shapes or forms.

[2] 'The true form of their kind,' I here take 道 to be equal to the 'way of birth.'

[3] 'The miracle,' 未曾有.

[4] 'Fearful gladness,' 驚喜.

The Brahma*k*ârins holding the rules of deer[1], following the deer wandering through mountain glades, (as the) deer coarse of nature, with flashing eyes [shen shih], regard (or see) the prince with fixed gaze; 502

So following the deer, those Brahma*k*ârins intently gaze likewise, looking at the exceeding glory of the Ikshvâku. As the glory of the rising sun 503

Is able to affect the herds of milch kine, so as to increase the quantity of their sweet-scented milk, so those Brahma*k*ârins, with wondrous joy, thus spoke one to the other: 504

'Surely this is one of the eight Vasu Devas[2];' others, 'this is one of the two A*s*vins[3];' others, 'this is Mâra[4];' others, 'this is one of the[5] Brahmakâyikas;' 505

Others, 'this is Sûryadeva[6] or *K*andradeva, coming down; are they not seeking here a sacrifice which is their due? Come let us haste to offer our religious services!' 506

The prince, on his part, with respectful mien addressed to them polite salutation. Then Bodhisattva, looking with care in every direction on the Brahma*k*ârins occupying the wood, 507

---

[1] Is this a name of a sect of Brahman ascetics? holding-deer-rules.

[2] 八婆藪 the eight Vasus.

[3] 二阿濕波.

[4] Literally, 'the sixth Mâra,' i.e. 'Mâra of the sixth heaven,' or Mâra who rules over the six heavens of the Kâmaloka.

[5] 梵迦夷天.

[6] The sun Devaputra, or the moon Devaputra.

Each engaged in his religious duties, all desirous of the delights of heaven, addressed the senior Brahma*k*ârin, and asked him as to the path of true religion[1]. 508

'Now having but just come here, I do not yet know the rules of your religious life. I ask you therefore for information, and I pray explain to me what I ask.' 509

On this that twice-born (Brahman) in reply explained in succession all the modes of painful discipline, and the fruits expected as their result. 510

(How some ate) nothing brought from inhabited places (villages)[2], (but) that produced from pure water, (others) edible roots and tender twigs, (others) fruits and flowers fit for food, 511

Each according to the rules of his sect, clothing and food in each case different, some living amongst bird-kind, and like them capturing and eating food; 512

Others eating as the deer the grass (and herbs); others living like serpents, inhaling air; others eating nothing pounded in wood or stone; some eating with two teeth, till a wound be formed; 513

Others, again, begging their food and giving it in charity, taking only the remnants for themselves; others, again, who let water continually drip on their heads and those who offer up with fire; 514

---

[1] Or, 'an aged Brahma*k*ârin:' here we have the expression '*Kh*ang suh,' 長宿, for 'aged' (as before).

[2] Literally, 'opposed to village coming out,' or, 'that which comes out of (所出) villages.'

Others who practise water-dwelling like fish[1]; thus there are (he said) Brahma*k*ârins of every sort, who practise austerities, that they may at the end of life obtain a birth in heaven, 515

And by their present sufferings afterwards obtain peaceable fruit. The lord of men[2], the excellent master, hearing all their modes of sorrow-producing penance, 516

Not perceiving any element of truth in them, experienced no joyful emotion in his heart; lost in thought, he regarded the men with pity, and with his heart in agreement his mouth thus spake: 517

'Pitiful indeed are such sufferings! and merely in quest of a human or heavenly reward[3], ever revolving in the cycle of birth or death, how great your sufferings, how small the recompence! 518

'Leaving your friends, giving up honourable position; with a firm purpose to obtain the joys of heaven, although you may escape little sorrows, yet in the end involved in great sorrow; 519

'Promoting the destruction of your outward form, and undergoing every kind of painful penance, and yet seeking to obtain another birth; increasing and prolonging the causes of the five desires, 520

'Not considering that herefrom (result repeated) birth and death, undergoing suffering and, by that, seeking further suffering; thus it is that the world of men, though dreading the approach of death, 521

---

[1] That is, as I understand it, *R*i*shis who live in water like fish. In the former case the 'air-inhaling snake *R*i*shi' would be *R*i*shis who endeavour to live on air like the boa.

[2] 'The lord of two-footed creatures,' i.e. of men.

[3] *G*in-tien po; if it had been tien-*g*in po, it would have simply meant 'a heavenly reward.'

'Yet strive after renewed birth; and being thus born, they must die again. Altho' still dreading (the power of) suffering, yet prolonging their stay in the sea of pain: 522

'Disliking from their heart their present kind of life, yet still striving incessantly after other life; enduring affliction that they may partake of joy; seeking a birth in heaven, to suffer further trouble; 523

'Seeking joys, whilst the heart sinks with feebleness. For this is so with those who oppose right reason; they cannot but be cramped and poor at heart. But by earnestness and diligence, then we conquer. 524

'Walking in the path of true wisdom, letting go both extremes[1], we then reach ultimate perfection; to mortify the body, (if) this is religion,[2] then to enjoy rest, is something not resulting from religion. 525

'To walk religiously and afterwards to receive happiness, this is to make the fruit of religion something different from religion; but bodily exercise is but the cause of death, strength results alone from the mind's intention; 526

---

[1] This line, which (with the following ones) is obscure, may be literally translated, 'a double letting-go, eternal Nirvâ*n*a,' where Nirvâ*n*a is in the original 無爲. The two extremes are worldly life and ascetic life.

[2] The word 法, like dharma, is difficult to translate. It may mean here either 'religion' or 'something formal;' but the idea of the whole verse seems to be this, 'if suffering pain is a part of religion, then to enjoy rest is different from religion, therefore to practise religious austerities with the view of afterwards obtaining rest, is to make the fruit of religion something different from, or opposed to, religion itself.'

'If you remove (from conduct) the purpose of the mind, the bodily act is but as rotten wood; wherefore, regulate the mind, and then the body will spontaneously go right. 527

'(You say that) to eat pure things is a cause of religious merit, but the wild beasts and the children of poverty ever feed on these fruits and medicinal herbs; these then ought to gain much religious merit. 528

'But if you say that the heart being good then bodily suffering is the cause of further merit, (then I ask) why may not those who walk (live) in ease, also possess a virtuous heart? 529

'If joys are opposed to a virtuous heart, a virtuous heart may also be opposed to bodily suffering; if, for instance, all those heretics profess purity because they use water (in various ways), 530

'Then those who thus use water among men, even with a wicked mind (karma), yet ought ever to be pure. But if righteousness is the groundwork of a *R*ishi's purity, then the idea of a sacred spot as his dwelling, 531

'Being the cause of his righteousness (is wrong). What is reverenced, should be known and seen [1]. Reverence indeed is due to righteous conduct, but let it not redound to the place (or, mode of life).' 532

Thus speaking at large on religious questions, they went on till the setting sun. He then beheld their rites in connection with sacrifice to fire, the drilling (for sparks) and the fanning into flame, 533

---

[1] This is, as it seems, the meaning of the line, or it may be rendered, 'What is esteemed of weight ought to be seen in the world.'

Also the sprinkling of the butter libations, also the chanting of the mystic prayers, till the sun went down. The prince considering these acts, 534

Could not perceive the right reason of them, and was now desirous to turn and go. Then all those Brahma*k*ârins came together to him to request him to stay; 535

Regarding with reverence the dignity of Bodhisattva, very desirous, they earnestly besought him: 'You have come from an irreligious place, to this wood where true religion flourishes, 536

'And yet, now, you wish to go away; we beg you, then, on this account, to stay.' All the old Brahma*k*ârins, with their twisted hair and bark clothes, 537

Came following after Bodhisattva, asking him as a god[1] to stay a little while. Bodhisattva seeing these aged ones following him, their bodies worn with macerations, 538

Stood still and rested beneath a tree; and soothing them, urged them to return. Then all the Brahma*k*ârins, young and old, surrounding him, made their request with joined hands: 539

'You who have so unexpectedly arrived here, amid these garden glades so full[2] of attraction, why now are you leaving them and going away, to seek perfection in the wilderness? 540

'As a man loving (long) life, is unwilling to let go his body, so we are even thus; would that you would stop awhile. 541

---

[1] The original is 小留神; probably 神 is for 住.

[2] I am not sure whether I understand the original, or whether there is not a mistake in the text, which is 妙文満.

'This is a spot where Brahmans and *Ri*shis have ever dwelt, royal *Ri*shis and heavenly *Ri*shis, these all have dwelt within these woods. The places on the borders of the snowy mountains, 542

'Where men of high birth[1] undergo their penance, those places are not to be compared to this. All the body of learned masters from this place have reached heaven; 543

'All the learned *Ri*shis who have sought religious merit, have from this place and northwards (found it), those who have attained a knowledge of the true law, and gained divine wisdom come not from southwards; 544

'If you indeed see us remiss and not earnest enough, practising rules not pure, and on that account are not pleased to stay, 545

'Then we are the ones that ought to go; you can still remain and dwell here, all these different Brahma*k*ârins ever desire to find companions in their penances. 546

'And you, because you are conspicuous for your religious earnestness, should not so quickly cast away their society: if you can remain here, they will honour you as god *S*akra, 547

'Yea! as the Devas pay worship to B*ri*haspati[2] (or, Virudhakapati).' Then Bodhisattva answered the Brahma*k*ârins and told them what his desires were: 548

'I am seeking for a true method of escape, I desire solely to destroy all mundane influences; but you, with strong hearts, practise your rules as ascetics, 549

---

[1] Tsang-*kh*ang *g*in, 增長人.
[2] Pi-lai-ho.

'And pay respectful attention to such visitors as may come. My heart indeed is moved with affection towards you, for pleasant conversation is agreeable to all, those who listen are affected thereby; 550

'And so hearing your words, my mind is strengthened in religious feeling; you indeed have all paid me much respect, in agreement with the courtesy of your religious profession; 551

'But now I am constrained to depart, my heart grieves thereat exceedingly, first of all, having left my own kindred, and now about to be separated from you. 552

'The pain of separation from associates, this pain is as great as the other, it is impossible for my mind not to grieve, as it is not to see others' faults [1]. 553

'But you, by suffering pain, desire earnestly to obtain the joys of birth in heaven; whilst I desire to escape from the three worlds, and therefore I give up what my reason (mind) tells me must be rejected [2]. 554

'The law which you practise, you inherit from the deeds of former teachers, but I, desiring to destroy all combination (accumulation), seek a law which admits of no such accident. 555

'And therefore I cannot in this grove delay for a longer while in fruitless discussions.' At this time all the Brahma*k*ârins, hearing the words spoken by Bodhisattva, 556

[1] This and the previous line might perhaps be better rendered thus, 'A joyless life (absence of joy) is opposed to my disposition, moreover (it is my disposition) not to observe the faults of others.'

[2] Literally, the form (body) turning from them even as (而) the mind rejects (乖); or may it be rendered, 'the body giving up, though the mind is still perverse.'

Words full of right reason and truth, very excellent in the distinction of principles, their hearts rejoiced and exulted greatly, and deep feelings of reverence were excited within them. 557

At this time there was one Brahma*k*ârin, who always slept in the dust, with tangled hair and raiment of the bark of trees, his eyes bleared (yellow), preparing himself in an ascetic practice (called) 'high-nose[1].' 558

This one addressed Bodhisattva in the following words: 'Strong in will! bright in wisdom! firmly fixed in resolve to escape (pass beyond) the limits of birth, knowing that in escape from birth there alone is rest, 559

'Not affected by any desire after heavenly blessedness, the mind set upon the eternal destruction of the body (bodily form), you are indeed miraculous in appearance, (as you are) alone in the possession of such a mind. 560

'To sacrifice to the gods, and to practise every kind of austerity, all this is designed to secure a birth in heaven, but here there is no mortification of selfish desire, 561

'There is still a selfish personal aim; but to bend the will to seek final escape, this is indeed the work of a true teacher, this is the aim of an enlightened master; 562

'This place is no right halting-place for you, you ought to proceed to Mount Pi*nd*a (Pâ*nd*ava), there dwells a great Muni, whose name is A-lo-lam (Arâ*d*a Râma). 563

'He only has reached the end (of religious aims), the most excellent eye (of the law). Go therefore

[1] I.e. raising his nose to look up at the sun.

to the place where he dwells, and listen there to
the true exposition of the law. 564

'This will make your heart rejoice, as you learn
to follow the precepts of his system. As for me,
beholding the joy of your resolve, and fearing that
I shall not obtain rest, 565

'I must once more let go (dismiss) those following
me, and seek other disciples; straighten my head
(nose) and gaze with my full eyes; anoint my lips
and cleanse my teeth, 566

'Cover my shoulders and make bright my face,
smooth my tongue and make it pliable. Thus, O
excellently marked, sir! fully drinking (at the fountain of) the water you give (glorious water)[1], 567

'I shall escape from the unfathomable depths. In
the world nought is comparable to this, that which
old men and *Ri*shis have not known, that shall (I)[2]
know and obtain.' 568

Bodhisattva having listened to these words, left
the company of the *Ri*shis, whilst they all, turning
round him to the right, returned to their place. 569

VARGA 8. THE GENERAL GRIEF OF THE PALACE.

*K*andaka leading back the horse, opening the way
for his heart's sorrow, as he went on, lamented and
wept: unable to disburthen his soul. 570

First of all with the royal prince, passing along the
road for one night, but now dismissed and ordered

[1] This line and the context, again, is obscure. Perhaps 醆水 is a mistake for 甘水, which latter expression may mean the 'sweet dew' (am*ri*ta) of Bodhisattva's doctrine.

[2] Or, that (you know) and will obtain.

to return. As the darkness of night closed on him, 571

Irresolute he wavered in mind. On the eighth day approaching the city, the noble horse pressed onwards, exhibiting all his qualities of speed; 572

But yet hesitating as he looked around and beheld not the form of the royal prince; his four members bent down with toil, his head and neck deprived of their glossy look, 573

Whinnying as he went on with grief, he refused night and day his grass and water, because he had lost his lord, the deliverer of men. Returning thus to Kapilavastu, 574

The whole country appeared withered and bare, as when one comes back to a deserted village; or as when the sun hidden behind Sumeru causes darkness to spread over the world. 575

The fountains of water sparkled no more, the flowers and fruits were withered and dead, the men and women in the streets seemed lost in grief and dismay. 576

Thus *K*andaka with the white horse went on sadly and with slow advance, silent to those enquiring, wearily progressing as when accompanying a funeral; 577

So they went on, whilst all the spectators seeing *K*andaka, but not observing the royal *S*âkya prince, raised piteous cries of lamentation and wept; as when the charioteer returned without Râma. 578

Then one by the side of the road, with his body bent, called out to *K*andaka: 'The prince, beloved of the world, the defender of his people, 579

'The one you have taken away by stealth, where

dwells he now?' *K*andaka, then, with sorrowful heart, replied to the people and said: 580

'I with loving purpose followed after him whom I loved; 'tis not I who have deserted the prince, but by him have I been sent away; (by him) who now has given up his ordinary adornments, 581

'And with shaven head and religious garb, has entered the sorrow-giving grove.' Then the men hearing that he had become an ascetic, were oppressed with thoughts of wondrous boding (unusual thoughts); 582

They sighed with heaviness and wept, and as their tears coursed down their cheeks, they spake thus one to the other: 'What then shall we do (by way of expedient)?' 583

Then they all exclaimed at once, 'Let us haste after him in pursuit; for as when a man's bodily functions fail, his frame dies and his spirit flees, 584

'So is the prince our life, and he our life gone, how shall we survive? This city, perfected with slopes and woods; those woods, that cover the slopes of the city, 585

'All deprived of grace, ye lie as Bharata when killed!' Then the men and women within the town, vainly supposing the prince had come back, 586

In haste rushed out to the heads of the way, and seeing the horse returning alone, not knowing whether he (the prince) was safe or lost, began to weep and to raise every piteous sound; 587

(And said, 'Behold!) *K*andaka advancing slowly with the horse, comes back with sighs and tears; surely he grieves because the prince is lost.' And thus sorrow is added to sorrow! 588

Then like a captive warrior is drawn before the

king his master, so did he enter the gates with tears, his eyes filled so that he said nought. 589

Then looking up to heaven he loudly groaned; and the white horse too whined piteously; then all the varied birds and beasts in the palace court, and all the horses within the stables, 590

Hearing the sad whinnying of the royal steed, replied in answer to him, thinking 'now the prince has come back.' But seeing him not, they ceased their cries! 591

And now the women of the after-palace, (hearing the cries of the horses, birds, and beasts,) their hair dishevelled, their faces wan and yellow, their forms sickly to look at, their mouths and lips parched, 592

Their garments torn and unwashed, the soil and heat not cleansed from their bodies, their ornaments all thrown aside, disconsolate and sad, cheerless in face, 593

Raised their bodies, without any grace, even as the feeble (little) morning star (or stars of morning); their garments torn and knotted, soiled like the appearance of a robber, 594

Seeing *K*andaka and the royal horse shedding tears instead of the hoped-for return, they all, assembled thus, uttered their cry, even as those who weep for one beloved just dead; 595

Confused and wildly they rushed about, as a herd of oxen that have lost their way. Mahâpra*g*âpati Gôtamî, hearing that the prince had not returned, 596

Fell fainting on the ground, her limbs entirely deprived of strength, even as some mad tornado wind crushes the golden-colour'd plantain tree; 597

And again, hearing that her son had become a recluse, deeply sighing and with increased sadness she thought, 'Alas! those glossy locks turning to the right, each hair produced from each orifice, 598

'Dark and pure, gracefully shining, sweeping the earth when loose[1], or when so determined, bound together in a heavenly crown, and now shorn and lying in the grass! 599

'Those rounded shoulders and that lion step! Those eyes broad as the ox-king's, that body shining bright as yellow gold; that square breast and Brahma voice; 600

'That you! possessing all these excellent qualities, should have entered on the sorrow-giving forest; what fortune now remains for the world, losing thus the holy king of earth? 601

'That those delicate and pliant feet, pure as the lily and of the same colour, should now be torn by stones and thorns; O how can such feet tread on such ground! 602

'Born and nourished in the guarded palace, clad with garments of the finest texture, washed in richly-scented water, anointed with the choicest perfumes, 603

'And now exposed to chilling blasts and dews of night, O! where during the heat or the chilly morn can rest be found! Thou flower of all thy race! Confessed by all the most renowned! 604

'Thy virtuous qualities everywhere talked of and exalted, ever reverenced, without self-seeking! why hast thou unexpectedly brought thyself upon some morn to beg thy food for life! 605

'Thou who wert wont to repose upon a soft and

---

[1] This description of the prince's hair seems to contradict the head arrangement of the figures of Buddha, unless the curls denote the shaven head of the recluse.

kingly couch, and indulge in every pleasure during thy waking hours, how canst thou now endure the mountain and the forest wilds, on the bare grass to make thyself a resting-place!' 606

Thus thinking of her son—her heart was full of sorrow, disconsolate she lay upon the earth. The waiting women raised her up, and dried the tears from off her face, 607

Whilst all the other courtly ladies, overpowered with grief, their limbs relaxed, their minds bound fast with woe, unmoved they sat like pictured-folk. 608

And now Yasodharâ, deeply chiding, spoke thus to *K*andaka: 'Where now dwells he, who ever dwells within my mind? 609

'You two went forth, the horse a third, but now two only have returned! My heart is utterly o'er-borne with grief, filled with anxious thoughts, it cannot rest. 610

'And you deceitful man! Untrustworthy and false associate! evil contriver! plainly revealed a traitor, a smile lurks underneath thy tears! 611

'Escorting him in going; returning now with wails! Not one at heart—but in league against him—openly constituted a friend and well-wisher, concealing underneath a treacherous purpose; 612

'So thou hast caused the sacred prince to go forth once and not return again! No questioning the joy you feel! Having done ill you now enjoy the fruit; 613

'Better far to dwell with an enemy of wisdom, than work with one who, while a fool, professes friendship. Openly professing sweetness and light, inwardly a scheming and destructive enemy. 614

'And now this royal and kingly house, in one short morn is crushed and ruined! All these fair and queen-like women, with grief o'erwhelmed, their beauty marred, 615

'Their breathing choked with tears and sobs, their faces soiled with crossing tracks of grief! Even the queen (Mâyâ) when in life, resting herself on him, as the great snowy mountains 616

'Repose upon the widening earth, through grief in thought of what would happen, died. How sad the lot of these—within these open lattices—these weeping ones, these deeply wailing! 617

'Born in another state than hers in heaven[1], how can their grief be borne!' Then speaking to the horse she said, 'Thou unjust! what dullness this—to carry off a man, 618

'As in the darkness some wicked thief bears off a precious gem. When riding thee in time of battle, swords, and javelins and arrows, 619

'None of these alarmed or frighted thee! But now what fitfulness of temper this[2], to carry off by violence, to rob my soul of one, the choicest jewel of his tribe. 620

'O! thou art but a vicious reptile, to do such wickedness as this! to-day thy woeful lamentation sounds everywhere within these palace walls, 621

'But when you stole away my cherished one, why wert thou dumb and silent then! if then thy voice

---

[1] This line is obscure; it may be paraphrased thus, 'If she in bearing her son brought about her own death, but yet is now born in heaven, how shall these bear their grief, or shall this grief (of losing him) be borne by these!'

[2] Or, 'how unendurable then your present conduct!'

had sounded loud, and roused the palace inmates from their sleep, 622

'If then they had awoke and slumbered not, there would not have ensued the present sorrow.' *K*andaka, hearing these sorrowful words, drawing in his breath and composing himself, 623

Wiping away his tears, with hands clasped together, answered: 'Listen to me, I pray, in self-justification—be not suspicious of, nor blame the royal[1] horse, nor be thou angry with me either. 624

'For in truth no fault has been committed (by us). It is the gods who have effected this. For I, indeed, extremely reverenced the king's command, it was the gods who drove him to the solitudes, 625

'Urgently leading on the horse with him: thus they went together fleet as with wings, his breathing hushed! suppressed was every sound[2], his feet scarce touched the earth! 626

'The city gates wide opening of themselves! all space self-lighted! this was the work indeed of the gods; and what was I, or what my strength, compared with theirs?' 627

Ya*s*odharâ hearing these words, her heart was lost in deep consideration[3]! the deeds accomplished by the gods could not be laid to others' charge[4], as faults; 628

And so she ceased her angry chiding, and allowed her great, consuming grief to smoulder. Thus prostrate on the ground she muttered out her sad com-

---

[1] The white horse.

[2] They caused no sound (to be heard).

[3] See above, p. 69, n. 3.

[4] Or, to their charge, i. e. to the charge of *K*andaka or the horse.

plaints, 'That the two ringed-birds[1] (doves) should be divided! 629

'Now,' she cried, 'my stay and my support is lost, between those once agreed in life (religious life)[2], separation has sprung up! those who were at one (as to religion) are now divided, (let go their common action)! where shall I seek another mode of (religious) life? 630

'In olden days the former conquerors (*G*inas?) greatly rejoiced to see their kingly retinue; these with their wives in company, in search of highest wisdom, roamed through groves and plains. 631

'And now, that he should have deserted me! and what is the religious state he seeks! the Brahman ritual respecting sacrifice, requires the wife to take part in the offering[3], 632

'And because they both share in the service they shall both receive a common reward hereafter! but you (O prince!) art niggard in your religious rites, driving me away, and wandering forth alone! 633

'Is it that you saw me jealous, and so turned against me! that you now seek some one free from

---

[1] Or, 'that two birds;' it may be doves; or perhaps the symbol 輪 is an error for 頭, meaning the 'double-headed bird.' This double-headed bird is often alluded to in Buddhist books, as in the Fo-pen-hing-tsi-king (Romantic History of Buddha, p. 380). The origin of the story may be perhaps found in the myth of Yama and Yamî.

[2] It may be 'religious life,' but it can as well refer to the common aim of life; as, for example, in the case of the double-headed bird, both heads having one object, viz. the care of the body.

[3] Literally, 'the sacrificial code of the Brahman requires husband and wife to act together.'

jealousy! or did you see some other cause to hate me, that you now seek to find a heaven-born nymph[1]! 634

'But why should one excelling in every personal grace seek to practise self-denying austerities! is it that you despise a common lot with me, that variance rises in your breast against your wife! 635

'Why does not Rahula fondly repose upon[2] your knee. Alas! alas! unlucky master! full of grace without, but hard (diamond) at heart! 636

'The glory and the pride of all your tribe[3], yet hating those who reverence you! O! can it be, you have turned your back for good (upon) your little child, scarce able yet to smile[4]! 637

'My heart is gone! and all my strength! my lord has fled, to wander in the mountains! he cannot surely thus forget me! he is then but a man of wood or stone.' 638

Thus having spoken, her mind was dulled and darkened, she muttered on, or spoke in wild mad words, or fancied that she saw strange sights, and sobbing past the power of self-restraint, 639

Her breath grew less, and sinking thus, she fell asleep upon the dusty ground! The palace ladies seeing this, were wrung with heartfelt sorrow, 640

Just as the full-blown lily, struck by the wind and hail, is broken down and withered. And now the

---

[1] 'A Devî of the Pure abode.' The idea seems to be that, finding Yasodharâ less pure than a Devî, he had gone to seek the company of one of these.

[2] Or, below your knee, i. e. sitting or fondling around the knee.

[3] Or, the full-brightness of your illustrious family.

[4] 'Your child not yet a boy.'

king, his father, having lost the prince, was filled, both night and day, with grief; 641

And fasting, sought the gods (for help). He prayed that they would soon restore him, and having prayed and finished sacrifice, he went from out the sacred[1] gates; 642

Then hearing all the cries and sounds of mourning, his mind distressed became confused, as when heaven's thundering and lightning put to bewildering flight a herd of elephants. 643

Then seeing *K*andaka with the royal steed, after long questioning, finding his son a hermit, fainting he fell upon the earth, as when the flag of Indra falls and breaks. 644

Then all the ministers of state, upraising him, exhort him, as was right[2], to calm himself. After a while, his mind somewhat recovered, speaking to the royal steed, he said: 645

'How often have I ridden thee to battle, and every time have thought upon (commended) your excellence! but now I hate and loathe thee, more than ever I have loved or praised thee! 646

'My son, renowned for noble qualities, thou hast carried off and taken from me; and left him 'mid the mountain forests; and now you have come back alone[3]; 647

'Take me, then, quickly hence and go! And going, never more come back with me! For since you have not brought him back, my life is worth no more preserving; 648

'No longer care I about governing! My son about

---

[1] The heaven-sacrificing-gate.

[2] In agreement with religion.

[3] Or, 'now you return from the desert (hung) alone.'

me was my only joy; as the Brahman *G*ayanta[1] met death for his son's sake, 649

'So I, deprived of my religious son, will of myself deprive myself of life. So Manu, lord of all that lives, ever lamented for his son; 650

'How much more I, a mortal man (ever-man), deprived of mine, must lose all rest! In old time the king A*g*a, loving his son[2], wandering thro' the mountains, 651

'Lost in thought (or deeply affected), ended life, and forthwith was born in heaven. And now I cannot die! Thro' the long night fixed in this sad state, 652

'With this great palace round me, thinking of my son, solitary and athirst as any hungry spirit (Preta); as one who, thirsty, holding water in his hand, but when he tries to drink lets all escape, 653

'And so remains athirst till death ensues, and after death becomes a wandering ghost[3];—so I, in the extremity of thirst, through loss, possessed once of a son[4], but now without a son, 654

'Still live, and cannot end my days! But come! tell me at once where is my son! let me not die athirst (for want of knowing this) and fall among the Pretas. 655

'In former days, at least, my will was strong and firm, difficult to move as the great earth; but now I've lost my son, my mind is dazed, as in old time the king "ten chariots[5]."' 656

---

[1] The Sanskrit text gives Sa*ñg*aya as the Brahman's name.

[2] Or, the son he loved.

[3] Or, is born in the way (i. e. the class) of famishing ghosts.

[4] Obtaining a son, as (a thirsty man obtains) water.

[5] That is, Da*s*aratha.

And now the royal teacher (Purohita), an illustrious sage[1], with the chief minister, famed for wisdom, with earnest and considerate minds, both exhorted with remonstrances, the king. 657

'Pray you (they said) arouse yourself to thought, and let not grief cramp and hold your mind! in olden days there were mighty kings, who left their country, as flowers are scattered[2]; 658

'Your son now practises the way of wisdom; why then nurse (increase) your grief and misery; you should recall the prophecy of Asita, and reasonably count on what was probable! 659

'(Think of) the heavenly joys which you, a universal king, have inherited[3]! But now, so troubled and constrained in mind, how will it not be said, "The Lord of earth can change his golden-jewel-heart!" 660

'Now, therefore, send us forth, and bid us seek the place he occupies, then by some stratagem and strong remonstrances, and showing him our earnestness of purpose, 661

'We will break down his resolution, and thus assuage your kingly sorrow.' The king, with joy, replied and said: 'Would that you both would go in haste, 662

'As swiftly as the Saketa[4] bird flies through the void for her young's sake; thinking of nought but the royal prince, and sad at heart—I shall await your search!' 663

The two men having received their orders, the

[1] 'To-wan-sse,' a celebrated master.

[2] 'As falling flowers,' or 'scattered blossoms,' alluding, as it seems, to the separation of the flower from the tree.

[3] Or it may be rendered, 'A heaven-blessed, universal (wheel) king!'

[4] Sho-ku-to bird.

king retired among his kinsfolk, his heart somewhat more tranquillised, and breathing freely through his throat. 664

VARGA 9. THE MISSION TO SEEK THE PRINCE.

The king now suppressing (regulating) his grief, urged on his great teacher and chief minister, as one urges on with whip a ready horse, to hasten onwards as the rapid stream; 665

Whilst they fatigued, yet with unflagging effort, come to the place of the sorrow-giving grove; then laying on one side the five outward marks[1] of dignity and regulating well their outward gestures, 666

They entered the Brahmans' quiet hermitage, and paid reverence to the *Ri*shis. They, on their part, begged them to be seated, and repeated the law for their peace and comfort. 667

Then forthwith they addressed the *Ri*shis and said: 'We have on our minds a subject on which we would ask (for advice). There is one who is called *S*uddhodana râ*g*a, a descendant of the famous Ikshvâku family, 668

'We are his teacher and his minister, who instruct him in the sacred books as required. The king indeed is like Indra (for dignity); his son, like *K*e-yan-to (*G*ayanta), 669

'In order to escape old age, disease, and death, has become a hermit, and depends on this; on his account have we come hither, with a view to let your worships know of this.' 670

Replying, they said: 'With respect to this youth,

[1] The five marks of dignity were the distinguishing robes of their office.

has he long arms and the signs of a great man? Surely he is the one who, enquiring into our practice, discoursed so freely on the matter of life and death. 671

'He has gone to the abode of Arâ*d*a, to seek for a complete mode of escape.' Having received this certain information, respectfully considering the urgent commands of the anxious king, 672

They dared not hesitate in their undertaking, but straightway took the road and hastened on. Then seeing the wood in which the royal prince dwelt, and him, deprived of all outward marks of dignity, 673

His body still glorious with lustrous shining, as when the sun comes forth from the black cloud[1]; then the religious teacher of the country and the great minister holding to the true law, 674

Put off from them their courtly dress, and descending from the chariot gradually advanced, like the royal Po-ma-ti (? Bharata) and the *R*ishi Vasish*th*a, 675

Went through the woods and forests, and seeing the royal prince Râma, each according to his own prescribed manner, paid him reverence, as he advanced to salute him; 676

Or as *S*ukra, in company with Aṅgiras, with earnest heart paid reverence, and sacrificed to Indra râ*g*a. 677

Then the royal prince in return paid reverence to the royal teacher and the great minister, as the divine Indra placed at their ease *S*ukra and Aṅgiras; 678

[1] The character which I have translated 'black' is 烏, which also means 'a crow.'

Then, at his command, the two men seated themselves before the prince, as Pou-na (Punarvasû) and Pushya, the twin stars attend beside the moon; 679

Then the Purohita and the great minister respectfully explained to the royal prince, even as Pi-li-po-ti (B*ri*haspati) spoke to that *G*ayanta: 680

'Your royal father, thinking of the prince, is pierced in heart, as with an iron point; his mind distracted, raves in solitude; he sleeps upon the dusty ground; 681

'By night and day he adds to his sorrowful reflections; his tears flow down like the incessant rain; and now to seek you out, he has sent us hither. Would that you would listen with attentive mind; 682

'We know that you delight to act religiously; it is certain, then, without a doubt, this is not the time for you to be a hermit (to enter the forest wilds); a feeling of deep pity consumes our heart! 683

'You, if you be indeed moved by religion, ought to feel some pity for our case; let your kindly feelings flow abroad, to comfort us who are worn at heart; 684

'Let not the tide of sorrow and of sadness completely overwhelm the outlets of our heart; as the torrents (which roll down) the grassy mountains; or the calamities of tempest, fiery heat, and lightning; 685

'For so the grieving heart has these four sorrows, turmoil and drought, passion and overthrow. But come! return to your native place, the time will arrive when you can go forth again as a recluse. 686

'But now to disregard your family duties, to turn against father and mother, how can this be called love and affection? that love which overshadows and embraces all. 687

'Religion requires not the wild solitudes; you can practise a hermit's duties in your home; studiously thoughtful, diligent in expedients, this is to lead a hermit's life in truth. 688

'A shaven head, and garments soiled with dirt,—to wander by yourself through desert wilds,—this is but to encourage constant fears, and cannot be rightly called "an awakened hermit's (life)." 689

'Would rather we might take you by the hand, and sprinkle[1] water on your head, and crown you with a heavenly diadem, and place you underneath a flowery canopy, 690

'That all eyes might gaze with eagerness upon you; after this, in truth, we would leave our home with joy. The former kings Teou-lau-ma (Druma?), A-neou-*k*e-o-sa (Anu*g*asa or Anu*d*âsa), 691

'Po-*k*e-lo-po-yau (Va*g*rabâhu), Pi-po-lo-'an-ti (Vaibhrâ*g*a), Pi-ti-o-*k*e-na (Vatâ*g*ana?), Na-lo-sha-po-lo (Narasavara?), 692

'All these several kings refused not the royal crown, the jewels, and the ornaments of person; their hands and feet were adorned with gems, 693

'Around them were women to delight and please, these things they cast not from them, for the sake of escape; you then may also come back home, and undertake both necessary duties[2]; 694

'Your mind prepare itself in higher law, whilst for the sake of earth you wield the sceptre; let there be no more weeping, but comply with what we say, and let us publish it; 695

---

[1] I have here substituted 雨 for 兩.

[2] That is, the duties of religion and also of the state.

'And having published it with your authority, then you may return and receive respectful welcome. Your father and your mother, for your sake, in grief shed tears like the great ocean; 696

'Having no stay and no dependence now—no source from which the *S*âkya stem may grow—you ought, like the captain of the ship, to bring it safely across to a place of safety. 697

'The royal prince Pi-san-ma, as also Lo-me-po-ti, they respectfully attended to the command of their father, you also should do the same! 698

'Your loving mother who cherished you so kindly, with no regard for self, through years of care, as the cow deprived of her calf, weeps and laments, forgetting to eat or sleep; 699

'You surely ought to return to her at once, to protect her life from evil; as a solitary bird, away from its fellows, or as the lonely elephant, wandering through the jungle, 700

'Losing the care of their young, ever think of protecting and defending them, so you the only child, young and defenceless, not knowing what you do, bring trouble and solicitude; 701

'Cause, then, this sorrow to dissipate itself; as one who rescues the moon[1] from being devoured, so do you reassure the men and women of the land, and remove from them the consuming grief, 702

'(And suppress) the sighs that rise like breath to heaven, which cause the darkness that obscures their sight; seeking you, as water, to quench the fire, the fire quenched, their eyes shall open.' 703

---

[1] Referring to an eclipse of the moon.

Bodhisattva, hearing of his father the king, experienced the greatest distress of mind, and sitting still, gave himself to reflection; and then, in due course, replied respectfully: 704

'I know indeed that my royal father is possessed of a loving and deeply[1] considerate mind, but my fear of birth, old age, disease, and death has led me to disobey, and disregard his extreme kindness. 705

'Whoever neglects right consideration about his present life, and because he hopes to escape in the end, therefore disregards all precautions (in the present), on this man comes the inevitable doom of death. 706

'It is the knowledge of this, therefore, that weighs with me, and after long delay has constrained me to a hermit's life; hearing of my father, the king, and his grief, my heart is affected with increased love; 707

'But yet, all is like the fancy of a dream, quickly reverting to nothingness. Know then, without fear of contradiction, that the nature of existing things is not uniform; 708

'The cause of sorrow is not necessarily[2] the relationship of child with parent, but that which produces the pain of separation, results from the influence of delusion[3]; 709

'As men going along a road suddenly meet midway with others, and then a moment more are separated, each one going his own way[4], 710

---

[1] Or, as we should say, 'of deep consideration.'

[2] Or, does not necessarily exist either in child or parent.

[3] Delusion is here equivalent to 'moha.'

[4] This line may be more literally translated 'each one acting for himself according to his own purpose.' The words run thus, 'opposite purpose, private, of himself.'

'So by the force of concomitance, relationships are framed, and then, according to each one's destiny [1], there is separation; he who thoroughly investigates this false connection of relationship ought not to cherish in himself grief; 711

'In this world there is rupture of family love, in another life (world) it is sought for again; brought together for a moment, again rudely divided [2], everywhere the fetters of kindred are formed [3]! 712

'Ever being bound, and ever being loosened! who can sufficiently lament such constant separations; born into the world [4], and then gradually changing, constantly separated by death and then born again. 713

'All things which exist in time must perish [5], the forests and mountains all things thus exist [6]; in time are born all sensuous things (things possessing the five desires), so is it both with worldly substance [7] and with time. 714

'Because, then, death pervades all time, get rid of death [8], and time will disappear. You desire to

---

[1] The word for 'destiny' is li; it means the 'reason' or 'rule of action.'

[2] Or, separated in opposite directions.

[3] In every place (place-place) there is no (place) without relationships.

[4] From the moment of conception (placed in the womb) gradually changing.

[5] All things (in) time have death.

[6] The text is very curt, 'mountains, forests, what (is there) without time.'

[7] 'Seeking wealth (in?) time, even thus;' or, 'Seeking wealth and time, are even thus.'

[8] 'Exclude the laws of death (sse fă), there will be no time.'

make me king, and it is difficult to resist the offices of love; 715

'But as a disease (is difficult to bear) without medicine, so neither can I bear (this weight of dignity); in every condition, high or low, we find folly and ignorance, (and men) carelessly following the dictates of lustful passion; 716

'At last, we come[1] to live in constant fear; thinking anxiously of the outward form, the spirit droops; following the ways of men[2], the mind resists the right[3]; but, the conduct of the wise is not so. 717

'The sumptuously ornamented[4] and splendid palace (I look upon) as filled with fire; the hundred dainty dishes (tastes) of the divine kitchen, as mingled with destructive poisons; 718

'The lily growing on the tranquil lake, in its midst harbours countless noisome insects; and so the towering abode of the rich is the house of calamity; the wise will not dwell therein. 719

'In former times illustrious kings, seeing the many crimes of their home and country, affecting as with poison the dwellers therein, in sorrowful disgust sought comfort in seclusion[5]; 720

'We know, therefore, that the troubles of a royal estate are not to be compared with the repose of a religious life; far better dwell in the wild mountains[6], and eat the herbs like the beasts of the field; 721

---

[1] 'In the end the body (that is, the person) ever fearful.'

[2] Following the multitude.

[3] The heart opposes religion (fă).

[4] The seven-jewelled, beautiful palace hall.

[5] Became hermits.

[6] In the mountains. I take 'lin' in the expression 'shan lin' in this and other passages to be the sign of the plural. It corresponds

'Therefore I dare not dwell in the wide[1] palace, for the black snake has its dwelling there. I reject the kingly estate and the five desires [desires of the senses], to escape such sorrows I wander thro' the mountain wilds. 722

'This, then, would be the consequence of compliance, that I, who, delighting in religion, am gradually getting wisdom[2], should now quit these quiet woods, and returning home, partake of sensual pleasures, 723

'And thus by night and day increase[3] my store of misery. Surely this is not what should be done! that the great leader of an illustrious tribe, having left his home from love of religion, 724

'And for ever turned his back upon tribal honour[4], desiring to confirm his purpose as a leader[5],—that he,—discarding outward form, clad in religious garb, loving religious meditation, wandering thro' the wilds,— 725

'Should now reject his hermit vestment, tread down his sense of proper shame (and give up his aim). This, though I gained heaven's kingly state, cannot be done! how much less to gain an earthly, though distinguished[6], home! 726

---

with 'vana' so used in other languages (the Sinhalese, according to Childers).

[1] The wide or deep palace seems to refer to the well-guarded and secure condition of a royal abode.

[2] Am gradually increasing enlightenment.

[3] Here the increase of sorrow is contrasted with the increase of wisdom, in the previous verse.

[4] Or, on his honourable, or renowned, tribe.

[5] Here the word leader (*k*ang fu) refers to a religious leader, in contrast with a leader of a tribe, or family.

[6] There seems to be a fine and delicate sarcasm in these words.

'For having spued forth lust, passion, and ignorance, shall I return to feed upon it? as a man might go back to his vomit! such misery, how could I bear? 727

'Like a man whose house has caught fire, by some expedient finds a way to escape, will such a man forthwith go back and enter it again? such conduct would disgrace a man[1]! 728

'So I, beholding the evils, birth, old age, and death, to escape the misery, have become a hermit; shall I then go back and enter in, and like a fool dwell in their company? 729

'He who enjoys a royal estate and yet seeks rescue[2], cannot dwell thus, this is no place for him; escape (rescue) is born from quietness and rest; to be a king is to add distress and poison; 730

'To seek for rest and yet aspire to royal condition is but a contradiction, royalty and rescue, motion and rest, like fire and water, having two principles[3], cannot be united. 731

'So one resolved to seek escape cannot abide possessed of kingly dignity! and if you say a man may be a king[4], and at the same time prepare deliverance for himself, 732

'There is no certainty in this[5]! to seek certain

[1] How would such a man be not accounted insignificant (tim, a dot or spot).

[2] I have translated 'kiai tuh,' rescue; it means rescue from sorrow, or deliverance in the sense of salvation.

[3] Two, or different, principles (li).

[4] A man may occupy a kingly estate.

[5] This is still opposed to certainty; or, this cannot be established.

escape is not to risk it thus[1]; it is through this uncertain frame of mind that once a man gone forth is led to go back home again; 733

'But I, my mind is not uncertain[2]; severing the baited hook[3] of relationship, with straightforward purpose[4], I have left my home. Then tell me, why should I return again?' 734

The great minister, inwardly reflecting, (thought), 'The mind of the royal prince, my master[5], is full of wisdom, and agreeable to virtue[6], what he says is reasonable and fitly framed[7].' 735

Then he addressed the prince and said: 'According to what your highness states, he who seeks religion must seek it rightly; but this is not the fitting time (for you); 736

'Your royal father, old and of declining years, thinking of you his son, adds grief to grief; you say indeed, "I find my joy in rescue. To go back would be apostacy[8]." 737

'But yet your joy denotes unwisdom[9], and argues want of deep reflection; you do not see, because you seek the fruit, how vain to give up present duty[10]. 738

---

[1] Certain escape, or certainty in escape, is not thus.

[2] But now I have attained to certainty.

[3] That is, taking the bait off the hook of relationship; the love of kindred is the bait.

[4] Using a right (or straight) expedient (upâya).

[5] The purpose of the prince, the master (*k*ang fu).

[6] Deep in knowledge, virtuously accordant.

[7] Or, has reasonable sequence (cause and effect).

[8] Fi-fă, opposed to religion; or, a revulsion from religion.

[9] Although you rejoice, it comes forth from no-wisdom.

[10] This is a free rendering; the original is, 'in fă kwan,' which means 'present religious consideration.'

'There are some who say, There is "hereafter[1];" others there are who say, "Nothing hereafter." So whilst this question hangs in suspense, why should a man give up his present pleasure? 739

'If perchance there is "hereafter," we ought to bear (patiently) what it brings[2]; if you say, "Hereafter is not[3]," then there is not either rescue (salvation)! 740

'If you say, "Hereafter is," you would not say, "Salvation causes it[4]." As earth is hard, or fire is hot, or water moist, or wind is mobile, 741

'"Hereafter" is just so. It has its own distinct nature. So when we speak of pure and impure, each comes from its own distinctive nature. 742

'If you should say, "By some contrivance this can be removed," such an opinon argues folly. Every root within the moral world[5] (world or domain of conduct) has its own nature predetermined; 743

'Loving remembrance and forgetfulness, these have their nature fixed and positive; so likewise

---

[1] A discussion now begins as to the certainty or otherwise of 'a hereafter;' the words in the text which I have translated 'hereafter,' are 'heou shai,' i. e. after world. The phrase seems to correspond with the Pâli 'paro loko,' as in the sentence, 'N' ev' atthi na n' atthi paro loko' (see Childers' Pâli Dict., sub voce na).

[2] We ought to trust it, whatever it is.

[3] These two lines may also be translated thus, 'If you say the after world is nothingness, then nothingness is also rescue (from the present world).'

[4] This seems to mean that if we say there is another world, we cannot mean that escape from the present world is the cause of the future. Literally and word for word, 'Not-say-escape-the cause.'

[5] 'The word 'root' here means 'sense.' The sentence seems to mean 'every sense united with its object.'

age, disease, and death, these sorrows, who can escape by strategy[1]? (contrivance, upâya). 744

'If you say, "Water can put out fire," or "Fire can cause water to boil and pass away," (then this proves only that) distinctive natures may be mutually destructive; but nature in harmony produces living things; 745

'So man when first conceived within the womb, his hands, his feet, and all his separate members, his spirit and his understanding, of themselves are perfected; but who is he who does it? 746

'Who is he that points the prickly thorn? This too is nature, self-controlling[2]. And take again the different kinds of beasts, these are what they are, without desire (on their part[3]); 747

'And so, again, the heaven-born beings, whom the self-existent (Isvara) rules[4], and all the world of his creation; these have no self-possessed power of expedients; 748

'For if they had a means of causing birth, there would be also (means) for controlling death, and then what need of self-contrivance, or seeking for deliverance? 749

'There are those who say, "I[5]" (the soul) is the cause of birth, and others who affirm, "I" (the soul) is the cause of death. There are some who say,

---

[1] The word translated 'strategy' is of very frequent occurrence. It means contrivance, use of means to an end.

[2] Tsz' in, 'of itself.'

[3] This line seems to mean that these beasts are made, or come into being, without desire on their part.

[4] I have supposed that the symbol 爲 in the text is for 主, but the first symbol may be retained, and then the passage would mean 'whom the self-existent made.'

[5] The word 'I' here seems to mean 'the self,' or, the soul.

"Birth comes from nothingness, and without any plan of ours we perish[1]." 750

'Thus one is born a fortunate child, removed from poverty, of noble family, or learned in testamentary lore of *Ri*shis, or called to offer mighty sacrifices to the gods, 751

'Born in either state, untouched by poverty, then their famous name becomes to them "escape," their virtues handed down by name to us[2]; yet if these attained their happiness (found deliverance), 752

'Without contrivance of their own, how vain and fruitless is the toil of those who seek "escape." And you, desirous of deliverance, purpose to practise some high expedient, 753

'Whilst your royal father frets and sighs; for a short while you have assayed the road, and leaving home have wandered thro' the wilds, to return then would not now be wrong; 754

'Of old, king Ambarîsha for a long while dwelt in the grievous forest, leaving his retinue and all his kinsfolk, but afterwards returned and took the royal office; 755

'And so Râma, son of the king of the country, leaving his country occupied the mountains, but hearing he was acting contrary to usage[3], returned[4] and governed righteously. 756

---

[1] I have taken the symbol 'iu' here in the sense of 'without,' like the Latin 'careo.'

[2] The sense seems to be that the great name and renown of such persons handed down through successive generations is 'salvation' or 'deliverance;' not the reward of another world, but the immortal character of their good deeds in this.

[3] So I translate the expression 'fung-tsuh-li,' usage-separation.

[4] There is a symbol here which may denote the name of the

'And so the king of Sha-lo-po, called To-lo-ma (Druma)[1], father and son, both wandered forth as hermits, but in the end came back again together; 757

'So Po-'sz-tsau Muni (Vasish*th*a?), with On-tai-tieh (Âtreya?), in the wild mountains practising as Brahma*k*ârins, these too returned to their own country. 758

'Thus all these worthies of a by-gone age, famous for their advance in true religion, came back home and royally governed, as lamps enlightening the world. 759

'Wherefore for you to leave the mountain wilds, religiously to rule, is not a crime.' The royal prince, listening to the great minister, loving words without excess of speaking, 760

Full of sound argument, clear and unconfused, with no desire to wrangle after the way of the schools, with fixed purpose, deliberately speaking, thus answered the great minister: 761

'The question of being and not-being is an idle one, only adding to the uncertainty of an unstable mind, and to talk of such matters I have no strong (fixed) inclination[2]; 762

'Purity of life, wisdom, the practice of asceticism[3], these are matters to which I earnestly apply myself[4], the world is full of empty studies (discoveries) which our teachers in their office skilfully involve; 763

'But they are without any true principle, and I

---

place to which he returned; 'wei' is often used in the composition of proper names, especially those ending in 'vastu.'

[1] Drumâksha, king of the *S*âlvas.

[2] 取=upâdâna.

[3] Or, purely and wisely to practise self-denial (mortification).

[4] Or, these are the certainties I for myself know.

will none of them! The enlightened man distinguishes truth from falsehood; but how can truth[1] (faith) be born from such as those? 764

'For they are like the man born blind, leading the blind man as a guide; as in the night, as in thick darkness [both wander on], what recovery is there for them? 765

'Regarding the question of the pure and impure, the world involved in self-engendered doubt cannot perceive the truth; better to walk along the way of purity, 766

'Or rather follow the pure law of self-denial, hate the practice of impurity, reflect on what was said of old[2], not obstinate in one belief or one tradition, 767

'With sincere (empty) mind, accepting all true words, and ever banishing sinful sorrow (i. e. sin, the cause of grief). Words which exceed sincerity (simplicity of purpose) are vainly (falsely) spoken; the wise man uses not such words. 768

'As to what you say of Râma and the rest, leaving their home, practising a pure life, and then returning to their country, and once more mixing themselves in sensual pleasures, 769

'Such men as these walk vainly; those who are wise place no dependence on them. Now, for your sakes, permit me, briefly, to recount this one true principle (i. e. purpose) (of action): 770

'"The sun, the moon may fall to earth, Sumeru and all the snowy mountains overturn, but I will never change my purpose; rather than enter a forbidden place, 771

---

[1] The word 'sin' 信 may mean faith or truth.

[2] Consider what has been handed down.

'"Let me be cast into the fierce fire; not to accomplish rightly (what I have entered on), and to return once more to my own land, there to enter the fire of the five desires, 772

'"Let it befall me as my own oath records:"—so spake the prince, his arguments as pointed as the brightness of the perfect sun; then rising up he passed some distance off.' 773

The Purohita and the minister, their words and discourse prevailing nothing, conversed together, after which, resolving to depart on their return, 774

With great respect they quietly inform[1] the prince, not daring to intrude their presence on him further; and yet regarding the king's commands, not willing to return with unbecoming haste, 775

They loitered quietly along the way, and whomsoever they encountered, selecting those who seemed like wise men, they interchanged such thoughts as move the learned, 776

Hiding their true position, as men of title; then passing on, they speeded on their way.

---

[1] They breathe it to the prince.

KIOUEN III.

VARGA 10. BIMBASÂRA RÂGA INVITES THE PRINCE.

The royal prince departing from the court-master (i. e. the Purohita) and the great minister, Saddharma[1], keeping along[2] the stream, then crossing the Ganges, he took the road towards the Vulture Peak[3], 777

[1] Saddharma may be the name of the minister, or it may be rendered 'the great minister of the true law,' i. e. of religion.

[2] For the symbol 冐 I have substituted 望 'to go towards.' The whole line may be translated 'following the turbulent (streams) he crossed the Ganges,' in this case 冐 would be for 倡. But the sentence is obscure, as 'lang tsai' may be a proper name.

[3] The distance from the place of the interview with the ministers to the Vulture Peak would be in a straight line about 150 miles. In the Southern books (Nidâna-kathâ; Buddhist Birth Stories, by Mr. Rhys Davids, pp. 85 and 87 n.) it is said that from Kapilavastu to the River Anomâ, near which the interview took place, is thirty *yoganas*; this is greatly in excess of the real distance, which is about thirty-three miles, or five *yoganas*. Then again from the Anomâ River, or the village of Maneya (Mhaniya), where the Bodhisattva halted (see Romantic Legend of Buddha, p. 140, and compare vol. xii, plate viii, Archæological Survey of India), to Râgagriha by way of Vaisâli would not be more than 180 miles, so that the whole distance from Kapilavastu (assuming Bhuila to represent this old town) would be about 215 miles, or about thirty *yoganas*. Hence we assume that the thirty *yoganas* of the Southern account is intended to represent the entire distance from Kapilavastu, and not from the River Anomâ. Mr. Rhys Davids supposes the distance from Kapilavastu to Râgagriha (viâ Vaisalî) to be sixty *yoganas* (loc. cit. Birth Stories). In the Southern account the journey from the Anomâ to Râgagriha is described as having been accomplished in one day.

Hidden among the five mountains[1], standing alone a lovely peak as a roof amid (the others). The trees and shrubs and flowers in bloom, the flowing fountains, and the cooling rills, 778

(All these he gazed upon)—then passing on, he entered the city of the five peaks, calm and peaceful, as one come down from heaven[2]. The country folk, seeing the royal prince, his comeliness and his excessive grace, 779

Though young in years, yet glorious in his person, incomparable as the appearance of a great master, seeing him thus, strange thoughts affected them, as if they gazed upon the banner (curtain) of I*s*vara[3]. 780

They stayed the foot, who passed athwart the path; those hastened on, who were behind; those going before, turned back their heads and gazed with earnest, wistful[4] look. 781

The marks and distinguishing points of his person[5], on these they fixed their eyes without fatigue, and then approached with reverent homage, joining both their hands in salutation: 782

---

[1] The five mountains, viz., which surrounded Râ*g*agriha, see Fah-hian, p. 112 n. The text seems to imply that the Vulture Peak towered above the others, but its base was hidden among the five.

[2] As a Deva, outside (heaven).

[3] The banner of I*s*vara (Indra) is frequently represented in Buddhist sculptures. There is a pleasing figure of it in Mrs. Speir's Ancient India, p. 230; see also Tree and Serpent Worship, plate xxxviii and elsewhere.

[4] Unsatisfied look, that is, constant or fixed gaze.

[5] The marks and distinguishing points are the signs to be found on the person of one destined to be a Buddha. In the text the expression 'on the four limbs' means 'on the body.'

With all there was a sense of wondrous joy, as in their several ways they offered what they had, looking at his noble and illustrious features; bending down their bodies[1] modestly, 783

Correcting every careless or unseemly gesture, thus they showed their reverence to him silently[2]; those who with anxious heart, seeking release, were moved by love, with feelings composed, bowed down the more[3]. 784

Great men and women, in their several engagements[4], at the same time arrested on their way, paid to his person and his presence homage: and following him as they gazed, they went not back. 785

For the white circle between his eyebrows[5] adorning his wide and violet colour'd[6] eyes, his noble body bright as gold, his pure and web-joined fingers, 786

All these, though he were but a hermit, were marks of one who was a holy king; and now the men and women of Râ*g*agriha, the old and young alike, were moved, 787

(And cried), 'This man so noble as a recluse, what common joy is this for us[7]!' At this time Bimbasâra Râ*g*a, placed upon a high tower of observation, 788

Seeing all those men and women, in different ways

---

[1] Their different bodies, or forms.

[2] Silently they added their respectful homage.

[3] These lines seem to refer to the ease of mind given to the care-worn by the presence of Bodhisattva.

[4] Whether engaged on public or private affairs; so at least the text seems to mean, 公私業.

[5] That is, the urna, or circle of hair, supposed to be on the forehead of every great man.

[6] The colour is indefinite blue-like; compare the Greek *κύανος*.

[7] That is, 'what an occasion for uncommon joy is this!'

exhibiting one mark of surprise[1], calling before him some man outside, enquired at once the cause of it; 789

This one bending his knee below the tower, told fully what he had seen and heard, 'That one of the *S*âkya race, renowned of old, a prince most excellent and wonderful, 790

'Divinely wise, beyond the way of this world, a fitting king to rule the eight regions, now without home, is here, and all men are paying homage to him.' 791

The king on hearing this was deeply moved at heart[2], and though his body was restrained, his soul had gone[3]. Calling his ministers speedily before him, and all his nobles and attendants, 792

He bade them follow secretly the (prince's) steps, to observe what charity was given[4]. (So in obedience to the command) they followed and watched him steadfastly, as with even gait and unmoved presence 793

He entered on the town and begged his food, according to the rule of all great hermits, with joyful mien and undisturbed mind, not anxious whether much or little alms were given; 794

Whatever he received, costly or poor, he placed within his bowl, then turned back to the wood, and having eaten it and drank of the flowing stream, he joyous sat upon the immaculate mountain[5]. 795

---

[1] Scared in different ways, assuming one attitude, or unvarying attitude; the line simply means they all showed the same indication of astonishment.

[2] Rejoiced with fear, or with astonishment.

[3] His body held (to the place), his soul (shin) had already hastened, i.e. to the spot where Bodhisattva was.

[4] Or, what religious offering should be made.

[5] The White Mountain, meaning probably the Royal Mountain.

(There he beheld) the green trees fringing with their shade the crags, the scented flowers growing between the intervals, whilst the peacocks and the other birds, joyously flying, mingled their notes; 796

His sacred garments bright and lustrous, (shone) as the sun-lit mulberry leaves; the messengers beholding his fixed composure, one by one (returning), reported what they had seen; 797

The king hearing it, was moved at heart, and forthwith ordered his royal equipment to be brought, his god-like crown and his flower-bespangled robes; then, as the lion-king, he strided forth, 798

And choosing certain aged persons of consideration, learned men, able calmly and wisely to discriminate, he (with them) led the way followed by a hundred thousand people, who like a cloud ascended with the king the royal mountain. 799

And now beholding the dignity of Bodhisattva, every outward gesture (spring of action) under government, sitting with ease upon the mountain crag[1], as the moon shining limpid in the pure heavens, 800

So (was) his matchless beauty and purity of grace; then as the converting presence of religion[2] dwelling within the heart makes it reverential[3], so (beholding him) he reverently approached, 801

Even as divine *S*âkara comes to the presence of

[1] On the lofty abode of the mountain (peak).

[2] This expression is singular, it will bear no other translation than this, 'the converting body (or, presence) of the law, i.e. religion.'

[3] Or, causes reverence (on the part of the beholder).

Mo-hi-su-ma[1], so with every outward form of courtesy and reverence[2] (the king approached) and asked him respectfully of his welfare. 802

Bodhisattva, answering as he was moved[3], in his turn made similar enquiries. Then the king, the questioning over, sat down with dignity upon a clean-faced rock. 803

And so he steadfastly beheld the divine appearance (of the prince), the sweetness and complacency of his features[4] revealing[5] what his station was and high estate, his family renown, received by inheritance, 804

The king who for a time restrained his feelings, now wishful to get rid of doubts, (enquired) (why one) descended from the royal family of the sun-brightness having attended to religious sacrifices thro' ten thousand generations, 805

Whereof the virtue had descended as his full inheritance, increasing and accumulating until now[6], (why he) so excellent in wisdom, so young in years, had now become a recluse, 806

Rejecting the position of a *K*akravartin's[7] son, begging his food, despising family fame, his beau-

---

[1] Probably the symbol ma is here used for va, in which case the name would be restored to Mâhe*s*vara.

[2] It is difficult to render such passages as this literally, but it might be translated thus, 'With collected air and every mark of decorum.'

[3] That is, according to the circumstances of the enquiry.

[4] The sweet expression blended with a joyfulness of countenance.

[5] Or it may be rendered, 'Correctly hearing his name and high degree,' as though one of the king's attendants had whispered the name and family of Bodhisattva in his ear.

[6] Largely possessed (or, collected) in his own person.

[7] Son of a holy king.

teous form, fit for perfumes and anointings, why clothed with coarse Kasâya garments; 807

The hand which ought to grasp the reins of empire, instead thereof, taking its little stint of food; if indeed (the king continued) you were not of royal descent, and would receive as an offering the transfer of this land, 808

Then would I divide with you my empire[1]; saying this, he scarcely hoped to excite his feelings, who had left his home and family, to be a hermit. Then forthwith the king proceeded thus: 809

'Give just weight I pray you to my truthful words, desire for power is kin to nobleness, and so is just pride of fame or family or wealth or personal appearance; 810

'No longer having any wish to subdue the proud, or to bend (others) down and so get thanks from men, it were better, then, to give to the strong and warlike martial arms to wear, for them to follow war and by their power to get supremacy; 811

'But when by one's own power a kingdom falls to hand, who would not then accept the reins of empire? The wise man knows the time to take religion, wealth, and worldly pleasure. 812

'But if he obtains not[2] the three (or, threefold profit), then in the end he abates his earnest efforts, and reverencing religion, he lets go material wealth. Wealth is the one desire[3] of worldly men; 813

---

[1] The absence of covetousness in Bimbasâra has passed into a proverb or a typical instance in Buddhist literature. (Compare Asvaghosha's Sermons, passim.)

[2] If he desires not to possess the three, that is, wealth, pleasure, religion.

[3] Wealth affects (makes) all men of the world.

'To be rich and lose all desire for religion, this is to gain but outside wealth. But to be poor and even thus despise religion, what pleasure can indulgence give in such a case! 814

'But when possessed of all the three, and when enjoyed with reason and propriety, then religion, wealth, and pleasure make what is rightly called a great master; 815

'Permit not, then, your perfectly-endowed body to lay aside (sacrifice) its glory, without reward (merit); Mandha(ri) the *K*akravartin, as a monarch, ruled the four empires of the world, 816

'And shared with *S*akra his royal throne, but was unequal to the task of ruling heaven. But you, with your redoubtable strength, may well grasp both heavenly and human power; 817

'I do not rely upon my kingly power[1], in my desire to keep you here by force, but seeing you change your comeliness of person, and wearing the hermit's garb, 818

'Whilst it makes me reverence you for your virtue, moves me with pity and regret for you as a man; you now go begging your food, and I offer you (desire to offer) the whole land as yours; 819

'Whilst you are young and lusty enjoy yourself[2]. During middle life acquire wealth, and when old and all your abilities ripened, then is the time for following the rules of religion; 820

'When young to encourage religious fervour, is to destroy the sources of desire; but when old and

[1] That is, I do not command you as a king, but desire you to share my kingly power.

[2] Receive the pleasure of the five enjoyments (of sense), i.e. the indulgence of the five senses.

the breath (of desire) is less eager, then is the time to seek religious solitude; 821

'When old we should avoid, as a shame, desire of wealth, but get honour in the world by a religious life; but when young, and the heart light and elastic, then is the time to partake of pleasure, 822

'In boon companionship to indulge in gaiety, and partake to the full of mutual intercourse; but as years creep on, giving up indulgence, to observe the ordinances of religion, 823

'To mortify the five desires, and go on increasing a joyful and religious heart, is not this the law of the eminent kings of old, who as a great company paid worship to heaven, 824

'And borne on the dragon's back, received the joys of celestial abodes? All these divine and victorious monarchs, glorious in person, richly adorned, 825

'Thus having as a company performed their religious offering, in the end received the reward of their conduct in heaven.' Thus Bimbasâra Râga (used) every kind of winning expedient in argument; 826

The royal prince unmoved and fixed remained firm as Mount Sumeru.

VARGA 11. THE REPLY TO BIMBASÂRA RÂGA.

Bimbasâra Râga having, in a decorous manner, and with soothing speech, made his request, the prince on his part respectfully replied, in the following words, deep and heart-stirring: 827

'Illustrious and world renowned! Your words are

not opposed to reason, descendant of a distinguished family—an Aryan[1]—amongst men[2] a true friend indeed, 828

'Righteous and sincere to the bottom of your heart, it is proper for religion's sake to speak thus[3]. In all the world, in its different sections, there is no chartered place[4] for solid virtue (right principles), 829

'For if virtue flags and folly rules, what reverence can there be, or honour paid, to a high name or boast of prowess, inherited from former generations! 830

'And so there may be in the midst of great distress, large goodness, these are not mutually opposed. This then is so with the world in the connection of true worth and friendship. 831

'A true friend who makes good (free) use of wealth—is rightly called a fast and firm treasure, but he who guards and stints the profit he has made, his wealth will soon be spent and lost; 832

'The wealth of a country is no constant treasure, but that which is given in charity is rich in returns, therefore charity is a true friend, altho' it scatters, yet it brings no repentance; 833

'You indeed are known as liberal and kind, I make no reply in opposition to you, but simply as we meet, so with agreeable purpose we talk. 834

---

[1] The symbols are 'ho-lai;' the translation may be simply 'descendant of a noble (ariya) and renowned family.'

[2] Or, for men's sake.

[3] This line literally translated is, 'Religion requires (me) thus to speak,' or, if the expression '*g*u shi' refers to what has been said (as it generally does), then the line will run thus, 'Religion justifies you in speaking as you have.'

[4] We cannot place (i. e. fix the place) where religion (or, virtue and right principle) must dwell.

'I fear birth, old age, disease, and death, and so I seek to find a sure mode of deliverance; I have put away thought of relatives and family affection, how is it possible then for me to return to the world (five desires) 835

'And not to fear to revive the poisonous snake, (and after)[1] the hail to be burned in the fierce fire; indeed I fear the objects of these several desires, this whirling in the stream (of life) troubles my heart, 836

'These five desires, the inconstant thieves[2]—stealing from men their choicest treasures, making them unreal, false, and fickle—are like the man called up as an apparition[3]; 837

'For a time the beholders are affected (by it), but it has no lasting hold upon the mind; so these five desires are the great obstacles, for ever disarranging the way of peace; 838

'If the joys of heaven are not worth having, how much less the desires common to men, begetting the thirst of wild love, and then lost in the enjoyment, 839

'As the fierce wind fans the fire, till the fuel be spent and the fire expires; of all unrighteous things in the world, there is nothing worse than the domain of the five desires; 840

'For all men maddened by the power of lust, giving themselves to pleasure, are dead to reason. The wise man fears these desires, he fears to fall into the way of unrighteousness; 841

---

[1] Like frozen hail and fierce burning fire.

[2] Robbers of impermanency.

[3] That is, are as unreal as an apparition.

'For like a king who rules all within the four seas, yet still seeks beyond for something more, (so is lust); like the unbounded ocean, it knows not when and where to stop. 842

'Mandha, the *K*akravartin, when the heavens rained yellow gold, and he ruled all within the seas, yet sighed after the domain of the thirty-three heavens; 843

'Dividing with *S*akra his seat, and so thro' the power of this lust he died; Nung-Sha (Nyâsa?), whilst practising austerities, got power to rule the thirty-three heavenly abodes, 844

'But from lust he became proud and supercilious, the *Ri*shi whilst stepping into his chariot, through carelessness in his gait, fell down into the midst of the serpent pit. 845

'Yen-lo (Yama?) the universal monarch (*K*akravartin) wandering abroad thro' the Trayastri*ms*as heaven, took a heavenly woman (Apsara) for a queen, and unjustly extorted[1] the gold of a *Ri*shi; 846

'The *Ri*shi, in anger, added a charm, by which the country was ruined, and his life ended. Po-lo, and *S*akra king of Devas[2], *S*akra king of Devas, and Nung-sha (Nyâsa), 847

'Nung-sha returning (or, restoring) to *S*akra; what certainty (constancy) is there, even for the lord of heaven? Neither is any country safe, though kept by the mighty strength of those dwelling in it. 848

---

[1] The literal translation of this line would be, 'Taxing the gold of Lim the *Ri*shi;' or, 'of the harvest ingathered by the *Ri*shi.'

[2] These lines refer to the transfer of heavenly power from *S*akra to others, but the myth is not known to me; and there is confusion in the text, which is probably corrupt.

'But when one's clothing consists of grass, the berries one's food, the rivulets one's drink, with long hair flowing to the ground, silent as a Muni, seeking nothing, 849

'In this way practising austerities, in the end lust shall be destroyed. Know then, that the province (indulgence) of the five desires is avowedly an enemy of the religious man. 850

'Even the one-thousand-armed invincible king, strong in his might, finds it hard to conquer this. The *Ri*shi Râma perished because of lust, 851

'How much more ought I, the son of a Kshatriya, to restrain lustful desire; but indulge in lust a little, and like the child it grows apace, 852

'The wise man hates it therefore; who would take poison for food? every sorrow is increased and cherished by the offices of lust. 853

'If there is no lustful desire, the risings of sorrow are not produced, the wise man seeing the bitterness of sorrow, stamps out and destroys the risings of desire; 854

'That which the world calls virtue, is but another form of this baneful law[1]; worldly men enjoying the pleasure of covetous desire then every form of careless conduct results; 855

'These careless ways producing hurt, at death, the subject of them reaps perdition (falls into one of the evil ways). But by the diligent use of means, and careful continuance therein, 856

'The consequences of negligence are avoided, we should therefore dread the non-use of means; recol-

[1] The sense of this passage seems to be that what is called by men a virtuous life, is but a form of regulated vice.

lecting that all things are illusory, the wise man covets them not; 857

'He who desires such things, desires sorrow, and then goes on again ensnared in love, with no certainty of ultimate freedom; he advances still and ever adds grief to grief, 858

'Like one holding a lighted torch burns his hand, and therefore the wise man enters on no such things. The foolish man and the one who doubts, still encouraging the covetous and burning heart, 859

'In the end receives accumulated sorrow, not to be remedied by any prospect of rest; covetousness and anger are as the serpent's poison; the wise man casts away 860

'The approach of sorrow as a rotten bone; he tastes it not nor touches it, lest it should corrupt his teeth, that which the wise man will not take, 861

'The king will go through fire and water to obtain, the wicked sons[1] labour for wealth as for a piece of putrid flesh, o'er which the hungry flocks of birds contend. 862

'So should we regard riches; the wise man is ill pleased at having wealth stored up, the mind wild with anxious thoughts, 863

'Guarding himself by night and day, as a man who fears some powerful enemy, like as a man's feelings revolt with disgust at the (sights seen) beneath the slaughter post of the East Market, 864

'So the high post which marks the presence of lust, and anger, and ignorance, the wise man always avoids; as those who enter the mountains or the seas have much to contend with and little rest, 865

'As the fruit which grows on a high tree, and is

[1] The foolish world.

grasped at by the covetous at the risk of life, so is the region (matter) of covetous desire, tho' they see the difficulty of getting it, 866

'Yet how painfully do men scheme after wealth, difficult to acquire, easy to dissipate, as that which is got in a dream, how can the wise man hoard up (such trash)! 867

'Like covering over with a false surface a hole full of fire, slipping thro' which the body is burnt, so is the fire of covetous desire. The wise man meddles not with it. 868

'Like that Kaurava [Kau-lo-po], or Pih-se-ni Nanda, or Ni-*k'h*e-lai Danta, as some *k*andala's (butcher's) appearance[1], 869

'Such also is the appearance of lustful desire; the wise man will have nothing to do with it, he would rather throw his body into the water or fire, or cast himself down over a steep precipice. 870

'Seeking to obtain heavenly pleasures, what is this but to remove the place of sorrow, without profit. Sün-tau, Po-sun-tau (Sundara and Vasundara), brothers of Asura, 871

'Lived together in great affection, but on account of lustful desire slew one another, and their name perished; all this then comes from lust; 872

'It is this which makes a man vile, and lashes and goads him with piercing sorrow; lust debases a man, robs him of all hope, whilst through the long night his body and soul are worn out; 873

'Like the stag[2] that covets the power of speech

[1] This line may be translated, 'as the appearance of the shambles.'

[2] I do not know to what this refers; the symbol 'shing' may not only mean 'the power of speech,' but also 'musical power' or 'music;' or it may mean 'celebrity.'

and dies, or the winged bird that covets[1] sensual pleasure (the net), or the fish that covets the baited hook, such are the calamities that lust brings; 874

'Considering what are the requirements of life, none of these possess permanency; we eat to appease the pain of hunger, to do away with thirst we drink, 875

'We clothe ourselves to keep out the cold and wind, we lie down to rest to get sleep, to procure locomotion we seek a carriage, when we would halt we seek a seat, 876

'We wash to cleanse ourselves from dirt, all these things are done to avoid inconvenience; we may gather therefore that these five desires have no permanent character; 877

'For as a man suffering from fever seeks and asks for some cooling medicine, so covetousness seeks for something to satisfy its longings; foolish men regard these things as permanent, 878

'And as the necessary requirements of life, but, in sooth, there is no permanent cessation of sorrow; for by coveting to appease these desires we really increase them, there is no character of permanency therefore about them. 879

'To be filled and clothed are no lasting pleasures, time passes, and the sorrow recurs; summer is cool during the moon-tide shining; winter comes and cold increases; 880

'And so through all the eightfold laws of the world they possess no marks of permanence, sorrow and joy cannot agree together, as a person slave-governed loses his renown. 881

---

[1] Or, 'that follows after form-covetousness.'

'But religion causes all things to be of service, as a king reigning in his sovereignty; so religion controls sorrow, as one fits on a burthen according to power of endurance. 882

'Whatever our condition in the world, still sorrows accumulate around us. Even in the condition of a king, how does pain multiply, though bound to others by love, yet this is a cause of grief; 883

'Without friends and living alone, what joy can there be in this? Though a man rules over the four kingdoms, yet only one part can be enjoyed; 884

'To be concerned in ten thousand matters, what profit is there in this, for we only accumulate anxieties. Put an end to sorrow, then, by appeasing desire, refrain from busy work, this is rest. 885

'A king enjoys his sensual pleasures; deprived of kingship there is the joy of rest; in both cases there are pleasures (but of different kinds); why then be a king! 886

'Make then no plan or crafty expedient, to lead me back to the five desires; what my heart prays for, is some quiet place and freedom (a free road); 887

'But you desire to entangle me in relationships and duties, and destroy the completion of what I seek; I am in no fear of a hated house (family hatred), nor do I seek the joys of heaven; 888

'My heart hankers after no vulgar profit, so I have put away my royal diadem; and contrary to your way of thinking, I prefer, henceforth, no more to rule. 889

'A hare rescued from the serpent's mouth, would it go back again to be devoured? holding a torch and burning himself, would not a man let it go? 890

'A man blind and recovering his sight, would he again seek to be in darkness? the rich, does he sigh for poverty? the wise, does he long to be ignorant? 891

'Has the world such men as these? then will I again enjoy my country. (But) I desire to get rid of birth, old age, and death, with body restrained, to beg my food; 892

'With appetites moderated, to keep in my retreat; and then to avoid the evil modes of a future life, this is to find peace in two worlds: now then I pray you pity me not. 893

'Pity, rather, those who rule as kings! their souls ever vacant and athirst, in the present world no repose, hereafter receiving pain as their meed. 894

'You, who possess a distinguished family name, and the reverence due to a great master, would generously share your dignity with me, your worldly pleasures and amusements; 895

'I, too, in return, for your sake, beseech you to share my reward with me; he who indulges in (practises) the threefold kinds of pleasure, this man the world calls "Lord," 896

'But this is not according to reason either, because these things cannot be retained, but where there is no birth, or life, or death, he who exercises himself in this way, is Lord indeed! 897

'You say that while young a man should be gay, and when old then religious (a recluse), but I regard the feebleness of age as bringing with it loss of power (to be religious), 898

'Unlike the firmness and power of youth, the will determined and the heart established; but death as a robber with a drawn sword follows us all, desiring to catch his prey; 899

'How then should we wait for old age, ere we bring our mind to a religious life? Inconstancy is the great hunter, age his bow, disease his arrows, 900

'In the fields of life and death he hunts for living things as for the deer; when he can get his opportunity, he takes our life; who then would wait for age? 901

'And what the teachers say and do, with reference to matters connected with life and death, exhorting the young, mature, or middle-aged, all to contrive by any means, 902

'To prepare vast meetings for sacrifices, this they do indeed of their own ignorance; better far to reverence the true law (religion), and put an end to sacrifice to appease the gods! 903

'Destroying life to gain religious merit, what love can such a man possess? even if the reward of such sacrifices were lasting, even for this, slaughter would be unseemly; 904

'How much more, when the reward is transient! Shall we (in search of this) slay that which lives, in worship? this is like those who practise wisdom, and the way of religious abstraction, but neglect the rules of moral conduct. 905

'It ill behoves us then to follow with the world, and attend these sacrificial assemblies, and seek some present good in killing that which lives; the wise avoid destroying life! 906

'Much less do they engage in general sacrifices, for the purpose of gaining future reward! the fruit (reward) promised in the three worlds is none of mine to choose for happiness! 907

'All these are governed by transient, fickle laws, like the wind, or the drop that is blown from the grass; such things therefore I put away from me, and I seek for true escape. 908

'I hear there is one O-lo-lam (Ârâ*d*a Kâlâma) who eloquently (well) discourses on the way of escape, I must go to the place where he dwells, that great *Ri*shi and hermit. 909

'But in truth, sorrow must be banished; I regret indeed leaving you; may your country have repose and quiet! safely defended (by you) as (by) the divine *S*akra-râ*g*a! 910

'May wisdom be shed abroad as light upon your empire, like the brightness of the meridian sun! may you be exceedingly victorious as lord of the great earth, with a perfect heart ruling over its destiny! 911

'May you direct and defend its sons! ruling your empire in righteousness! Water and snow and fire are opposed to one another, but the fire by its influence causes vapour, 912

'The vapour causes the floating clouds, the floating clouds drop down rain; there are birds in space, who drink the rain, with rainless bodies[1] (?) 913

'Slaughter and peaceful homes are enemies! those who would have peace hate slaughter, and if those who slaughter are so hateful, then put an end, O king, to those who practise it! 914

'And bid these find release, as those who drink

[1] This line literally translated is, 'Who drink rain, not rain-body;' there may be a misprint, but I cannot see how to correct the text. The sense of the text and context appears to be this, that as there are those who drink the rain-clouds and yet are parched with thirst, so there are those who constantly practise religious duties and yet are still unblest. Compare Epistle by Jude, ver. 12, 'Clouds without water.'

and yet are parched with thirst.' Then the king clasping together his hands, with greatest reverence and joyful heart, 915

(Said), 'That which you now seek, may you obtain quickly the fruit thereof; having obtained the perfect fruit, return I pray and graciously receive me!' 916

Bodhisattva, his heart inwardly acquiescing, purposing to accomplish his prayer, departing, pursued his road, going to the place where Ârâ*d*a Kâlâma dwelt, 917

Whilst the king with all his retinue, their hands clasped, themselves followed a little space, then with thoughtful and mindful heart, returned once more to Râ*g*ag*ri*ha! 918

Varga 12. Visit to Ârâda Udrarâma[1].

The child of the glorious sun of the Ikshvâku race, going to that quiet peaceful grove, reverently stood before the Muni, the great *Ri*shi Ârâ*d*a Râma; 919

The dark-clad (?) followers of the Kalam (Saṅghârâma) seeing afar off Bodhisattva approaching, with loud voice raised a joyful chant, and with suppressed breath muttered 'Welcome,' 920

As with clasped hands they reverenced him. Approaching one another, they made mutual enquiries; and this being done, with the usual apologies, according to their precedence (in age)[2] they sat down; 921

The Brahma*k*ârins observing the prince, (beheld) his personal beauty and carefully considered his

[1] The compound in the original probably represents Ârâ*d*a Kâlâma and Udra(ka) Râmaputra.

[2] Tsi'ang tsu may mean 'after invitation.'

appearance; respectfully[1] they satisfied themselves of his high qualities, like those who, thirsty, drink the 'pure dew.' 922

(Then) with raised hands they addressed the prince, 'Have you[2] (or, may we know whether you have) been long an ascetic, divided from your family and broken from the bonds of love, like the elephant who has cast off restraint? 923

'Full of wisdom (your appearance), completely enlightened, (you seem) well able to escape the poisonous fruit (of this world)[3]. In old time the monarch Ming Shing[4] (brightly victorious) gave up his kingly estate to his son, 924

'As a man who has carried a flowery wreath, when withered casts it away: but such is not your case, full of youthful vigour, and yet not enamoured with the condition of a holy king; 925

'We see that your will is strong and fixed, capable of becoming a vessel of the true law, able to embark in the boat of wisdom, and to cross over the sea of life and death: 926

'The common class[5], enticed to come to learn, their talents first are tested, then they are taught; but as I understand your case, your mind is already fixed and your will firm: 927

---

[1] 'High qualities,' powers of his mind; probably the same as the taigasa of the Gainas (see Colebrooke, Essays, p. 282). This line may be literally translated, 'bathing themselves in a respectful admiration of his high qualities.'

[2] The symbol 'ki' may possibly mean 'friend,' in which case the line would be, 'O friend! have you long been a homeless one?'

[3] Or the poisonous fruit of that which is low or base.

[4] I have taken 'Ming Shing' as a proper name, but it may be also translated 'illustrious conquering (kings).'

[5] 'Fan fu,' the common class of philosophers, or students. The vulgar herd.

'And now you have undertaken the purpose of learning, (I am persuaded) you will not in the end shrink from it.' The prince hearing this exhortation, with gladness made reply: 928

'You have with equal intention, illustrious[1]! cautioned me with impartial mind; with humble heart I accept the advice, and pray that it may be so with me, (as you anticipate); 929

'That I may in my night-journey obtain a torch, to guide me safely thro' treacherous places; a handy boat to cross over the sea;—may it be so even now with me! 930

'But as I am somewhat in doubt and anxious to learn, I will venture to make known my doubts, and ask, with respect to old age, disease, and death, how are these things to be escaped?' 931

At this time O-lo-lam (Ârâ*d*a Kâlâma) hearing the question asked by the prince, briefly from the various Sûtras and *S*âstras, quoted passages in explanation of a way of deliverance. 932

'But thou (he said) illustrious youth! so highly gifted, and eminent among the wise! hear what I have to say, as I discourse upon the mode of ending birth and death; 933

'Nature, and change, birth, old age, and death, these five (attributes) belong to all[2]; "nature" is (in itself)[3] pure and without fault; the involution of this with the five elements[4], 934

---

[1] Or, 'illustriously admonished me without preference or dislike;' or 'against preference or dislike.'

[2] The discourse following is very obscure, being founded on the philosophical speculations of Kapila and others.

[3] Or, Nature is that which is pure and unsullied (tabula rasa).

[4] The five 'great' (Mahat).

'Causes an awakening and power of perception, which, according to its exercise[1], is the cause of "change;" form, sound, order, taste, touch, these are called the five objects of sense (dhâtu); 935

'As the hand and foot are called the "two ways" (methods of moving?) so these are called "the roots" of action (the five skandhas); the eye, the ear, the nose, the tongue, the body, these are named the "roots" (instruments) of understanding. 936

'The root of "mind" (manas)[2] is twofold, being both material, and also intelligent; "nature" by its involutions is "the cause," the knower of the cause is "I" (the soul); 937

'Kapila the *R*ishi and his numerous followers, on this deep principle of "soul[3]," practising wisdom (Buddhi), found deliverance. 938

'Kapila and now Vâ*k*aspati[4], by the power of "Buddhi" perceiving the character of birth, old age, and death, declare that on this is founded true philosophy[5]; 939

'Whilst all opposed to this, they say, is false. "Ignorance" and "passion," causing constant "transmigration," 940

---

[1] That is, as the power of perception is exercised, 'change' is experienced.

[2] Refer to Colebrooke, on the Sâṅkhya philosophy.

[3] Much of this discourse might be illustrated from the Chinese version of 'the seventy golden *S*astra' (Sâṅkhya Kârikâ) of Kapila; but the subject would require distinct treatment.

[4] This verse is obscure, and the translation doubtful. Literally rendered it runs as follows: 'That Kapila (or, that which Kapila said) now (is affirmed respecting) Pra*g*âpati [po-*k*e-po-ti; this may be restored to Vâkpati, or to Pra*g*âpati; the latter however (as I am told) is the reading found in the Sanskrit original] (by the power of) Buddhi, knowing birth,' &c.

[5] This, they say, is called 'to see.'

'Abiding in the midst of these (they say) is the lot of "all that lives." Doubting the truth of "soul" is called "excessive doubt," and without distinguishing aright, there can be no method of escape. 941

'Deep speculation as to the limits of perception is but to involve the "soul;" thus unbelief leads to confusion, and ends in differences of thought and conduct. 942

'Again, the various speculations on "soul" (such as) "I say," "I know and perceive," "I come" and "I go" or "I remain fixed," these are called the intricacies (windings) of "soul[1]." 943

'And then the fancies raised in different natures, some saying "this is so," others denying it, and this condition of uncertainty is called the state of "darkness[2]." 944

'Then there are those who say that outward things (resembling forms) are one with "soul," who say that the "objective" is the same as "mind," who confuse "intelligence" with "instruments," who say that "number" is the "soul." 945

'Thus not distinguishing aright, these are called "excessive quibbles," "marks of folly," "nature changes," and so on. 946

'To worship and recite religious books, to slaughter living things in sacrifice, to render pure by fire and water, and thus awake the thought of final rescue, 947

'All these ways of thinking are called "without right expedient," the result of ignorance and doubt, by means of word or thought or deed; 948

---

[1] The 'soul' is the 'I' (aha*m*kâra) of the Sâṅkhya system, concerning which see Colebrooke (Essays), p. 153.

[2] Tamas.

'Involving outward relationships, this is called "depending on means;" making the material world the ground of "soul," this is called "depending on the senses." 949

'By these eight sorts of speculation are we involved in birth and death. The foolish masters of the world make their classifications in these five ways, (viz.) 950

'Darkness, folly, and great folly, angry passion, with timid fear. Indolent coldness is called "darkness;" birth and death are called "folly;" 951

'Lustful desire is "great folly;" because of great men subjected to error[1], cherishing angry feelings, "passion" results; trepidation of the heart is called "fear." 952

'Thus these foolish men dilate upon the five desires; but the root of the great sorrow of birth and death, the life destined to be spent in the five ways, 953

'The cause of the whirl of life, I clearly perceive, is to be placed in the existence of "I;" because of the influence of this cause, result the consequences of repeated birth and death; 954

'This cause is without any nature of its own, and its fruits have no nature; rightly considering what has been said, there are four matters which have to do with escape, 955

'Kindling wisdom—opposed to dark ignorance,—making manifest—opposed to concealment and obscurity,—if these four matters be understood, then we may escape birth, old age, and death. 956

[1] Literally 'great men producing error,' or it may be 'because of the birth-error (delusion) of great men.'

'Birth, old age, and death being over, then we attain a final place; the Brahmans[1] all depending on this principle, 957

'Practising themselves in a pure life, have also largely dilated on it, for the good of the world.' The prince hearing these words again enquired of Ârâ*d*a: 958

'Tell me what are the expedients you name, and what is the final place to which they lead, and what is the character of that pure (Brahman) life; and again what are the stated periods 959

'During which such life must be practised, and during which such life is lawful; all these are principles to be enquired into; and on them I pray you discourse for my sake.' 960

Then that Ârâ*d*a, according to the Sûtras and *S*âstras, spoke, 'Yourself using wisdom is the expedient; but I will further dilate on this a little; 961

'First by removing from the crowd and leading a hermit's life, depending entirely on alms for food, extensively practising rules of decorum, religiously adhering to right rules of conduct, 962

'Desiring little and knowing when to abstain, receiving whatever is given (in food), whether pleasant or otherwise, delighting to practise a quiet (ascetic) life, diligently studying all the Sûtras and *S*âstras, 963

'Observing the character of covetous longing and fear, without remnant of desire to live in purity, to govern well the organs of life, the mind quieted and silently at rest, 964

'Removing desire, and hating vice, all the sorrows

[1] The Brahmans in the world.

of life (the world of desire) put away, then there is happiness; and we obtain the enjoyment of the first[1] dhyâna. 965

'Having obtained this first dhyâna, then with the illumination thus obtained, by inward meditation is born reliance on thought alone, and the entanglements of folly are put away; 966

'The mind depending on this, then after death, born in the Brahma heavens, the enlightened are able to know themselves; by the use of means is produced further inward illumination; 967

'Diligently persevering, seeking higher advance, accomplishing the second dhyâna, tasting of that great joy, we are born in the Kwong-yin[2] heaven (Âbhâsvara); 968

'Then by the use of means putting away this delight, practising the third dhyâna, resting in such delight and wishing no further excellence, there is a birth in the *S*ubhak*ri*tsna (hin-tsing) heaven; 969

'Leaving the thought of such delight, straightway we reach the fourth dhyâna, all joys and sorrows done away, the thought of escape produced, 970

'We dwell in this fourth dhyâna, and are born in the V*ri*hat-phala heaven; because of its long enduring years, it is thus called V*ri*hat-phala (extensive-fruit); 971

'Whilst in that state of abstraction rising (higher), perceiving there is a place beyond any bodily condition, adding still and persevering further in practising wisdom, rejecting this fourth dhyâna, 972

[1] The dhyânas are the conditions of ecstasy, enjoyed by the inhabitants of the Brahmaloka heavens.

[2] We have here an account of the different heavens of the Brahmalokas, concerning which consult Burnouf, 'Introduction to Indian Buddhism.'

'Firmly resolved to persevere in the search, still contriving to put away every desire after form, gradually from every pore of the body there is perceived a feeling of empty release, 973

'And in the end this extends to every solid part, so that the whole is perfected in an apprehension of emptiness. In brief, perceiving no limits to this emptiness, there is opened to the view boundless knowledge. 974

'Endowed with inward rest and peace, the idea of "I" departs, and the object of "I:" clearly discriminating the non-existence of matter (bhava), this is the condition of immaterial life. 975

'As the Mu*ñ*ga (grass) when freed from its horny case, or as the wild bird which escapes from its prison trap, so, getting away from all material limitations, we thus find perfect release. 976

'Thus ascending above the Brahmans (Brahmalokas?), deprived of every vestige of bodily existence, we still endure[1]. Endued with wisdom[2]! let it be known this is real and true deliverance. 977

'You ask what are the expedients for obtaining this escape; even as I have before detailed, those who have deep faith will learn. 978

'The *Ri*shis *G*aigîshavya, *G*anaka, V*ri*ddha Parâ*s*ara[3], and other searchers after truth, 979

'All by the way I have explained, have reached true deliverance.' The prince hearing these words, deeply pondering on the outline of these principles, 980

And reaching back to the influences produced by

---

[1] Literally, 'endurance not exhausted.'

[2] That is, 'O thou! endued with wisdom,' or, generally, 'those endued with wisdom.'

[3] These proper names were supplied from the Sanskrit text.

our former lives, again asked with further words: 'I have heard your very excellent system of wisdom, the principles very subtle and deep-reaching, 981

'From which I learn that because of not "letting go" (by knowledge as a cause), we do not reach the end of the religious life; but by understanding nature in its involutions, then, you say, we obtain deliverance; 982

'I perceive this law of birth has also concealed in it another law as a germ; you say that the "I" (i. e. "the soul," of Kapila) being rendered pure[1], forthwith there is true deliverance; 983

'But if we encounter a union of cause and effect, then there is a return to the trammels of birth; just as the germ in the seed, when earth, fire, water, and wind 984

'Seem to have destroyed in it the principle of life, meeting with favourable concomitant circumstances will yet revive, without any evident cause, but because of desire; so those who have gained this supposed release, (likewise) 985

'Keeping the idea of "I" and "living things," have in fact gained no final deliverance; in every condition, letting go the "three classes[2]" and again reaching the three[3] "excellent qualities," 986

'Because of the eternal existence of soul, by the subtle influences of that, (influences resulting from the past,) the heart lets go the idea of expedients, 987

'And obtains an almost endless duration of years. This, you say, is true release; you say "letting go the ground on which the idea of soul rests," that this frees us from "limited[4] existence," 988

---

[1] See Colebrooke, l. c. p. 150.
[2] Three sorts of pain.
[3] Perception, inference, affirmation.
[4] Bhava.

'And that the mass of people have not yet removed the idea of soul, (and are therefore still in bondage). But what is this letting go "gu*n*as[1]" (cords fettering the soul); if one is fettered by these "gu*n*as," how can there be release? 989

'For gu*n*î (the object) and "gu*n*a" (the quality) in idea are different, but in substance one; if you say that you can remove the properties of a thing (and leave the thing) by arguing it to the end, this is not so. 990

'If you remove heat from fire, then there is no such thing as fire, or if you remove surface (front) from body, what body can remain? 991

'Thus "gu*n*a" is as it were surface, remove this and there can be no "gu*n*î." So that this deliverance, spoken of before, must leave a body yet in bonds. 992

'Again, you say that by "clear knowledge" you get rid of body; there is then such a thing as knowledge or the contrary; if you affirm the existence of clear knowledge, then there should be some one who possesses it (i.e. possesses this knowledge); 993

'If there be a possessor, how can there be deliverance (from this personal "I")? If you say there is no "knower," then who is it that is spoken of as "knowing?" 994

'If there is knowledge and no person, then the subject of knowledge may be a stone or a log; moreover, to have clear knowledge of these minute causes of contamination and reject them thoroughly, 995

'These being so rejected, there must be an end, then, of the "doer." What Ârâ*d*a has declared cannot satisfy my heart. 996

[1] Colebrooke, p. 157.

'This clear knowledge is not "universal wisdom," I must go on and seek a better explanation.' Going on then to the place of Udra[1] *Ri*shi, he also expatiated on this question of 'I.' 997

(But) although he refined the matter to the utmost, laying down a term of 'thought' and 'no thought' taking the position of removing 'thought' and 'no thought,' yet even so he came not out of the mire; 998

For supposing creatures attained that state, still (he said) there is a possibility of returning to the coil, whilst Bodhisattva sought a method of getting out of it. So once more leaving Udra *Ri*shi, 999

He went on in search of a better system, and came at last to Mount Kia-*k*e[2] [the forest of mortification], where was a town called Pain-suffering forest (Uravilva?). Here the five Bhikshus had gone before. 1000

When then he beheld these five, virtuously keeping in check their senses (passion-members), holding to the rules of moral conduct, practising mortification, dwelling in that grove of mortification[3]; 1001

Occupying a spot beside the Naira*ñg*ana river, perfectly composed and filled with contentment, Bodhisattva forthwith by them (selecting) one spot, quietly gave himself to thought. 1002

The five Bhikshus knowing him with earnest heart to be seeking escape, offered him their services with devotion, as if reverencing Î*s*vara Deva. 1003

---

[1] Yuh-to. [2] Gayâ, or Gayâ*s*îrsha.

[3] Or is the word fu-hing = the name of a plant, such as the uruvu (betel)?

Having finished their attentions and dutiful services, then going on he took his seat not far off, as one about to enter on a course of religious practice, composing all his members as he desired. 1004

Bodhisattva diligently applied himself to 'means,' as one about to cross over old age, disease, and death. With full purpose of heart (he set himself) to endure mortification, to restrain every bodily passion, and give up thought about sustenance, 1005

With purity of heart to observe the fast-rules, which no worldly man (active man) can bear; silent and still, lost in thoughtful meditation; and so for six years he continued, 1006

Each day eating one hemp grain, his bodily form shrunken and attenuated, seeking how to cross (the sea) of birth and death, exercising himself still deeper and advancing further; 1007

Making his way perfect by the disentanglements of true wisdom, not eating, and yet not (looking to that as) a cause (of emancipation), his four members although exceedingly weak, his heart of wisdom increasing yet more and more in light; 1008

His spirit free, his body light and refined, his name spreading far and wide, as 'highly gifted,' even as the moon when first produced, or as the Kumuda flower spreading out its sweetness; 1009

Everywhere thro' the country his excellent fame extended; the daughters of the lord of the place both coming to see him, his mortified body like a withered branch, just completing the period of six years, 1010

Fearing the sorrow of birth and death, seeking earnestly the method (cause) of true wisdom, he came to the conviction that these were not the means to extinguish desire and produce ecstatic contemplation; 1011

Nor yet (the means by which) in former time, seated underneath the *G*ambu tree[1], he arrived at that miraculous condition, that surely was the proper way, (he thought), 1012

The way opposed to this of 'withered body.' I should therefore rather seek strength of body, by drink and food refresh my members, and with contentment cause my mind to rest. 1013

My mind at rest, I shall enjoy silent composure; composure is the trap for getting ecstasy (dhyâna); whilst in ecstasy perceiving the true law (right law, i. e. truth), then the force of truth (the law) obtained, disentanglement will follow. 1014

And thus composed, enjoying perfect quiet, old age and death are put away; and then defilement is escaped by this first means; thus then by equal steps the excellent law results from life restored by food and drink. 1015

Having carefully considered this principle, bathing in the Nairañ*g*ana river, he desired afterwards to leave the water (pool), but owing to extreme exhaustion was unable to rise; 1016

Then a heavenly spirit holding out (pressing down) a branch, taking this in his hand he (raised himself and) came forth. At this time on the opposite side of the grove there was a certain chief herdsman, 1017

Whose eldest daughter was called Nandâ. One of the *S*uddhavâsa Devas addressing her said, 'Bodhi-

[1] See above, p. 48, ver. 335.

sattva dwells in the grove, go you then, and present to him a religious offering.' 1018

Nandâ Balada (or Balaga or Baladhya) with joy came to the spot, above her hands (i. e. on her wrists) white chalcedony bracelets, her clothing of a grey (bluish) colour (dye); 1019

The grey and the white together contrasted in the light, as the colours of the rounded river bubble; with simple heart and quicken'd step she came, and, bowing down at Bodhisattva's feet, 1020

She reverently offered him perfumed rice milk, begging him of his condescension to accept it[1]. Bodhisattva taking it, partook of it (at once), whilst she received, even then, the fruits of her religious act. 1021

Having eaten it, all his members refreshed, he became capable of receiving Bodhi; his body and limbs glistening with (renewed strength), and his energies swelling higher still[2], 1022

As the hundred streams swell the sea, or the first quarter'd moon daily increases in brightness. The five Bhikshus having witnessed this, perturbed, were filled with suspicious reflection; 1023

They supposed (said) that his religious zeal (heart) was flagging, and that he was leaving and looking for a better abode, as though he had obtained deliverance, the five elements entirely removed[3]. 1024

---

[1] See Tree and Serpent Worship, plate l.

[2] This is a free translation; the text is probably defective, 開 being a mistake for 開 or for 尊.

[3] 'The five elements,' in the original 'the five great;' the sense seems to be that the Bodhisattva was acting as though he had attained his aim, and overcome the powers of sense. At the same

Bodhisattva wandered on alone, directing his course to that 'fortunate[1]' tree, beneath whose shade he might accomplish his search after complete enlightenment[2]. 1025

(Over) the ground wide and level, producing soft and pliant grass, easily he advanced with lion step, pace by pace, (whilst) the earth shook withal; 1026

And as it shook, Kâla nâga aroused, was filled with joy, as his eyes were opened to the light. Forthwith he exclaimed: 'When formerly I saw the Buddhas of old, there was the sign of an earthquake as now; 1027

'The virtues of a Muni are so great in majesty, that the great earth cannot endure[3] them; as step by step his foot treads upon the ground, so is there heard the sound of the rumbling earth-shaking; 1028

'A brilliant light now illumes the world, as the shining of the rising sun; five hundred bluish tinted birds (I see), wheeling round to the right, flying through space; 1029

'A gentle, soft, and cooling breeze blows around in an agreeable way; all these auspicious (miraculous) signs are the same as those of former Buddhas; 1030

'Wherefore I know that this Bodhisattva will certainly arrive at perfect wisdom. And now, behold! from yonder man, a grass cutter, he obtains some pure and pliant grass, 1031

'Which spreading out beneath the tree, with upright body, there he takes his seat; his feet placed

time it is possible that 'the five great' may allude to the five Bhikshus. But in any case it is better to hold to the literal sense.

[1] The 'fortunate tree,' the tree 'of good omen,' the Bodhi tree.

[2] Samyak-Sambodhi.

[3] Cannot excel or surpass them.

under him, not carelessly arranged (moving to and fro), but like the firmly fixed and compact body of a Nâga; 1032

'Nor shall he rise again from off his seat till he has completed his undertaking.' And so he (the Nâga) uttered these words by way of confirmation. The heavenly Nâgas, filled with joy, 1033

(Caused a) cool refreshing breeze to rise; the trees and grass were yet unmoved by it, and all the beasts, quiet and silent, (looked on in wonderment.) 1034

These are the signs that Bodhisattva will certainly attain enlightenment. 1035

VARGA 13. DEFEATS MÂRA.

The great *Ri*shi, of the royal tribe of *Ri*shis, beneath the Bodhi tree firmly established, resolved by oath to perfect the way of complete deliverance. 1036

The spirits, Nâgas, and the heavenly multitude [1], all were filled with joy; but Mâra Devarâ*g*a, enemy of religion, alone was grieved, and rejoiced not; 1037

Lord of the five desires [2], skilled in all the arts of warfare, the foe of those who seek deliverance, therefore his name is rightly given Pi*s*una [3]. 1038

Now this Mâra râ*g*a had three daughters, mincingly beautiful and of a pleasant countenance, in every way fit by artful ways to enflame a man with love, highest in this respect among the Devîs. 1039

The first was named Yuh-yen (lust-pollution), the second Neng-yueh-*g*in (able to delight a man),

[1] 天衆.

[2] I. e. king of sensuality.

[3] The wicked one.

the third Ngai-loh[1] (love-joy). These three, at this time, advanced together, 1040

And addressed their father Pisuna and said: 'May we not know the trouble that afflicts you?' The father calming his feelings, addressed his daughters thus: 1041

'The world has now a great Muni, he has taken a strong oath as a helmet, he holds a mighty bow in his hand, wisdom is the diamond shaft he uses, 1042

'His object is to get the mastery in the world, to ruin and destroy my territory (domain); I am myself unequal to him, for all men will believe in him, 1043

'And all find refuge in the way of his salvation; then will my land be desert and unoccupied. But as when a man transgresses the laws of morality, his body (or, he himself) is then empty (i. e. unprotected), 1044

'So now, the eye of wisdom, not yet opened (in this man), whilst my empire still has peace (quiet), I will go and overturn his purpose, and break down and divide the ridge-pole (of his house)[2].' 1045

Seizing then his bow and his five arrows, with all his retinue of male and female attendants, he went to that grove of 'fortunate rest' with the vow that the world (all flesh) should not find peace[3]. 1046

Then seeing the Muni, quiet and still (silent), preparing to cross the sea of the three worlds, in his left hand grasping his bow, with his right hand pointing his arrow, 1047

---

[1] See Childers, sub Mâro, for the name of the daughters. In Sanskrit, Rati, Prîti, and T*r*ish*n*â.

[2] 'I will return to the house . . . . , he findeth it swept and garnished, but empty.'

[3] Should not find 'rest.' There is a play on the word.

He addressed Bodhisattva and said: 'Kshatriya! rise up quickly! for you may well fear! your death is at hand; you may practise your own religious system[1], 1048

'But let go this effort after the law of deliverance (for others); wage warfare in the field of charity[2] as a cause of merit, appease the tumultuous world, and so in the end reach your reward in heaven; 1049

'This is a way renowned and well established, in which former saints (victors) have walked, *Ri*shis and kings and men of eminence; but this system of penury and alms-begging is unworthy of you. 1050

'Now then if you rise not, you had best consider with yourself, that if you give not up your vow, and tempt me to let fly an arrrow, 1051

'How that Aila, grandchild of Soma[3], by one of these arrows just touched, as by a fanning of the wind, lost his reason and became a madman; 1052

'And how the *Ri*shi Vimala, practising austerities, hearing the sound of one of these darts, his heart possessed by great fear, bewildered and darkened he lost his true nature; 1053

'How much less can you—a late-born one—hope to escape this dart of mine. Quickly arise then! if hardly you may get away! 1054

'This arrow full of rankling poison, fearfully insidious where it strikes a foe! See now! with all my force, I point it! and are you resting in the face of such calamity? 1055

'How is it that you fear not this dread arrow? say! why do you not tremble?' Mâra uttered such fear-inspiring threats, bent on overawing Bodhisattva. 1056

[1] Or, a system of religion for yourself. [2] Religious almsgiving.
[3] Ai*d*a, the grandson of Soma (i. e. Purûravas, the lover of Urvasî?).

But Bodhisattva's heart remained unmoved; no doubt, no fear was present. Then Mâra instantly discharged his arrow, whilst the three women came in front; 1057

Bodhisattva regarded not the arrow, nor considered ought the women three. Mâra râ*g*a now was troubled much with doubt, and muttered thus 'twixt heart and mouth: 1058

'Long since the maiden of the snowy mountains, shooting at Mahe*s*vara, constrained him to change his mind; and yet Bodhisattva is unmoved, 1059

'And heeds not even this dart of mine, nor the three heavenly women! nought prevails to move his heart or raise one spark of love within him. 1060

'Now must I assemble my army-host, and press him sore by force;' having thought thus awhile, Mâra's army suddenly assembled round; 1061

Each (severally) assumed his own peculiar form; some were holding spears, others grasping swords, others snatching up trees, others wielding diamond maces; (thus were they) armed with every sort of weapon; 1062

Some had heads like hogs, others like fishes, others like asses, others like horses; some with forms like snakes or like the ox or savage tiger; lion-headed, dragon-headed, (and like) every other kind of beast; 1063

Some had many heads on one body-trunk, with faces having but a single eye, and then again with many eyes; some with great-bellied mighty bodies, 1064

And others thin and skinny, bellyless; others long-legged, mighty-knee'd; others big-shanked and fat-calved; some with long and claw-like nails; 1065

Some were headless, breastless, faceless; some with two feet and many bodies; some with big faces looking every way; some pale and ashy-coloured, 1066

Others colour'd like the bright star rising, others steaming fiery vapour, some with ears like elephants, with humps like mountains, some with naked forms covered with hair, 1067

Some with leather skins for clothing, their faces party-coloured, crimson and white; some with tiger skins as robes, some with snake skins over them, 1068

Some with tinkling bells around their waists, others with twisted screw-like hair, others with hair dishevelled covering the body, some breath-suckers, 1069

Others body-snatchers, some dancing and shrieking awhile, some jumping onwards with their feet together, some striking one another as they went, 1070

Others waving (wheeling round) in the air, others flying and leaping between the trees, others howling, or hooting, or screaming, or whining, with their evil noises shaking the great earth; 1071

Thus this wicked goblin troop encircled on its four sides the Bodhi tree; some bent on tearing his body to pieces, others on devouring it whole; 1072

From the four sides flames belched forth, and fiery steam ascended up to heaven; tempestuous winds arose on every side[1]; the mountain forests shook and quaked; 1073

---

[1] Kik for pien?

Wind, fire, and steam, with dust combined, (produced) a pitchy darkness, rendering all invisible. And now the Devas well affected to the law, and all the Nâgas and the spirits (kwei-shin), 1074

All incensed at this host of Mâra, with anger fired, wept tears of blood; the great company of *S*uddhavâsa gods, beholding Mâra tempting[1] Bodhisattva, 1075

Free from low-feeling, with hearts undisturbed by passion, moved by pity towards him and commiseration, came in a body to behold the Bodhisattva, so calmly seated and so undisturbed, 1076

Surrounded with an uncounted host of devils, shaking the heaven and earth with sounds ill-omened. Bodhisattva silent and quiet in the midst remained, his countenance as bright as heretofore, unchanged; 1077

Like the great lion-king placed amongst all the beasts howling and growling round him (so he sat), a sight unseen before, so strange and wonderful! 1078

The host of Mâra hastening, as arranged, each one exerting his utmost force, taking each other's place in turns, threatening every moment to destroy him, 1079

Fiercely staring, grinning with their teeth, flying tumultuously, bounding here and there; but Bodhisattva, silently beholding them, (watched them) as one would watch the games of children; 1080

And now the demon host waxed fiercer and more angry, and added force to force, in further conflict; grasping at stones they could not lift, or lifting them, they could not let them go; 1081

---

[1] Confusing.

Their flying spears, lances, and javelins, stuck fast in space, refusing to descend; the angry thunder-drops and mighty hail, with these, were changed into five-colour'd lotus flowers, 1082

Whilst the foul poison of the dragon snakes was turned to spicy-breathing air. Thus all these countless sorts of creatures, wishing to destroy the Bodhisattva, 1083

Unable to remove him from the spot, were with their own weapons wounded. Now Mâra had an aunt-attendant whose name was Ma-kia-ka-li (Mâha Kâlî?), 1084

Who held a skull-dish in her hands, and stood in front of Bodhisattva, and with every kind of winsome gesture, tempted to lust the Bodhisattva. 1085

So all these followers of Mâra, possessed of every demon-body form, united in discordant uproar, hoping to terrify Bodhisattva; 1086

But not a hair of his was moved, and Mâra's host was filled with sorrow. Then in the air the crowd of angels (spirits), their forms invisible, raised their voices, saying: 1087

'Behold the great Muni; his mind unmoved by any feeling of resentment, whilst all that wicked Mâra race, besotted, are vainly bent on his destruction; 1088

'Let go your foul and murderous thoughts against that silent Muni, calmly seated! You cannot with a breath move the Sumeru mountain; 1089

'Fire may freeze, water may burn, the roughened earth may grow soft and pliant, but ye cannot hurt the Bodhisattva! Thro' ages past disciplined by suffering, 1090

'Bodhisattva rightly trained in thought, ever

advancing in the use of "means," pure and illustrious for wisdom, loving and merciful to all, 1091

'These four conspicuous (excellent) virtues cannot with him be rent asunder, so as to make it hard or doubtful whether he gain the highest wisdom. 1092

'For as the thousand rays of yonder sun must drown the darkness of the world, or as the boring wood must kindle fire, or as the earth deep-dug gives water, 1093

'So he who perseveres in the "right means," by seeking thus, will find. The world without instruction, poisoned by lust and hate and ignorance, 1094

'Because he pitied "flesh," so circumstanced, he sought on their account the joy of wisdom. Why then would you molest and hinder one who seeks to banish sorrow from the world? 1095

'The ignorance that everywhere prevails is due to false pernicious books (sûtras), and therefore Bodhisattva, walking uprightly, would lead and draw men after him. 1096

'To obscure and blind the great world-leader, this undertaking is impossible[1], for 'tis as though in the Great Desert a man would purposely mislead the merchant-guide; 1097

'So "all flesh" having fallen into darkness, ignorant of where they are going, for their sakes he would light the lamp of wisdom; say then! why would you extinguish it? 1098

'All flesh engulphed and overwhelmed in the great sea of birth and death, this one prepares the boat of wisdom; say then! why destroy and sink it? 1099

'Patience is the sprouting of religion, firmness

---

[1] In the sense of 'not commendable.'

its root, good conduct is the flower, the enlightened heart the boughs and branches, 1100

'Wisdom supreme the entire tree, the "transcendent law[1]" the fruit, its shade protects all living things; say then! why would you cut it down? 1101

'Lust, hate, and ignorance, (these are) the rack and bolt, the yoke placed on the shoulder of the world; through ages long he has practised austerities to rescue men from these their fetters, 1102

'He now shall certainly attain his end, sitting on this right-established throne; (seated) as all the previous Buddhas, firm and compact like a diamond; 1103

'Though all the earth were moved and shaken, yet would this place be fixed and stable; him, thus fixed and well assured, think not that you can overturn. 1104

'Bring down and moderate your mind's desire, banish these high and envious thoughts, prepare yourselves for right reflection, be patient in your services.' 1105

Mâra hearing these sounds in space, and seeing Bodhisattva still unmoved, filled with fear and banishing his high and supercilious thoughts, again took up his way to heaven above; 1106

Whilst all his host (were scattered), o'erwhelmed with grief and disappointment, fallen from their high estate, 'reft of their warrior pride, their warlike weapons and accoutrements thrown heedlessly and cast away 'mid woods and deserts. 1107

Like as when some cruel chieftain slain, the hateful

[1] Anuttara-dharma.

band is all dispersed and scattered, so the host of Mâra disconcerted, fled away. The mind of Bodhisattva (now reposed) peaceful and quiet. 1108

The morning sun-beams brighten with the dawn, the dust-like mist dispersing, disappears; the moon and stars pale their faint light, the barriers of the night are all removed, 1109

Whilst from above a fall of heavenly flowers pay their sweet tribute to the Bodhisattva. 1110.

VARGA 14. O-WEI-SAN-POU-TI (ABHISAMBODHI)[1].

Bodhisattva having subdued Mâra, his firmly fixed mind at rest, thoroughly exhausting the first principle of truth[2], he entered into deep and subtle contemplation, 1111

Self-contained. Every kind of Sâmadhi in order passed before his eyes. During the first watch he entered on 'right perception[3],' and in recollection all former births passed before his eyes; 1112

Born in such a place, of such a name, and downwards to his present birth, so through hundreds, thousands, myriads, all his births and deaths he knew; 1113

Countless in number were they, of every kind and sort; then knowing, too, his family relationships, great pity rose within his heart. 1114

This sense of deep compassion passed, he once again considered 'all that lives,' and how they moved within the six[4] portions of life's revolution, no final term to birth and death; 1115

---

[1] The condition that looks wisdom face to face.

[2] 'Eternally exhausting the highest truth' (paramartha).

[3] The word for 'perception' is vedanâ (sheu).

[4] The six modes of birth (transmigration).

Hollow all, and false and transient (unfixed) as the plantain tree, or as a dream, or phantasy. Then in the middle watch of night, he reached to knowledge (eyes) of the pure Devas[1], 1116

And beheld before him every creature, as one sees images upon a mirror; all creatures born and born again to die, noble and mean, the poor and rich, 1117

Reaping the fruit of right or evil doing, and sharing happiness or misery in consequence. First he considered and distinguished evil-doers (works), that such must ever reap an evil birth; 1118

Then he considered those who practise righteous deeds, that these must gain a place with men or gods; but those again born in the nether hells, (he saw) participating in every kind of misery; 1119

Swallowing (drinking) molten brass (metal), the iron skewers piercing their bodies, confined within the boiling caldron, driven and made to enter the fiery oven (dwelling), 1120

Food for hungry, long-toothed dogs, or preyed upon by brain-devouring birds; dismayed by fire, then (they wander through) thick woods, with leaves like razors gashing their limbs, 1121

While knives divide their (writhing) bodies, or hatchets lop their members, bit by bit; drinking the bitterest poisons, their fate yet holds them back from death. 1122

Thus those who found their joy in evil deeds, he saw receiving now their direst sorrow; a momentary taste of pleasure here, a dreary length of suffering there; 1123

A laugh or joke because of others' pain, a crying

[1] Deva sight.

out and weeping now at punishment received. Surely if living creatures saw the consequence of all their evils deeds, self-visited, 1124

With hatred would they turn and leave them, fearing the ruin following—the blood and death. He saw, moreover, all the fruits of birth as beasts, each deed entailing its own return, 1125

(And) when death ensues born in some other form (beast shape), different in kind according to the deeds. Some doomed to die for the sake of skin or flesh [1], some for their horns or hair or bones or wings, 1126

Others torn or killed in mutual conflict, friend or relative before, contending thus; (some) burthened with loads or dragging heavy weights, (others) pierced and urged on by pricking goads, 1127

Blood flowing down their tortured forms, parched and hungry—no relief afforded; then, turning round, (he saw) one with the other struggling, possessed of no independent strength; 1128

Flying through air or sunk in deep water, yet no place as a refuge left from death. He saw, moreover, those, misers and covetous, born now as hungry ghosts, 1129

Vast bodies like the towering mountain, with mouths as small as any needle-tube, hungry and thirsty, nought but fire and poison'd flame to enwrap their burning forms within. 1130

Covetous, they would not give to those who sought, or duped the man who gave in charity, now born among the famished ghosts, they seek for food, but cannot find withal. 1131

The refuse of the unclean man they fain would

[1] That is, some born as beasts, whose hides are of value, and for which they are killed.

eat, but this is changed and lost (before it can be eaten); oh! if a man believes that covetousness is thus repaid, as in their case, 1132

Would he not give his very flesh in charity even as *S*ivi râ*g*a did! Then, once more (he saw), those reborn as men, with bodies like some foul sewer, 1133

Ever moving 'midst the direst sufferings, born from the womb to fear and trembling, with body tender, touching anything its feelings painful, as if cut with knives; 1134

Whilst born in this condition, no moment free from chance of death, labour, and sorrow, yet seeking birth again, and being born again, enduring pain. 1135

Then (he saw those who) by a higher merit were enjoying heaven; a thirst for love ever consuming them, their merit ended with the end of life, the five signs[1] warning them of death (their beauty fades), 1136

Just as the blossom that decays, withering away, is robbed of all its shining tints; not all their associates, living still, though grieving, can avail to save the rest; 1137

The palaces and joyous precincts empty now, the Devîs all alone and desolate, sitting or asleep upon the dusty earth, weep bitterly in recollection of their loves; 1138

Those who are born, sad in decay; those who are dead, belovéd, cause of grief; thus ever struggling on, preparing future pain, covetous they seek the joys of heaven, 1139

---

[1] The five signs are the indications of a Deva's life in heaven coming to an end.

Obtaining which, these sorrows come apace; despicable joys! oh, who would covet them! using such mighty efforts (means) to obtain, and yet unable thence to banish pain. 1140

Alas, alas! these Devas, too, alike deceived—no difference is there! thro' lapse of ages bearing suffering, striving to crush desire and lust, 1141

Now certainly expecting long reprieve, and yet once more destined to fall! in hell enduring every kind of pain, as beasts tearing and killing one the other, 1142

As Pretas parched with direst thirst, as men worn out, seeking enjoyment; although, they say, when born in heaven, 'then we shall escape these greater ills,' 1143

Deceived, alas! no single place exempt, in every birth incessant pain! Alas! the sea of birth and death revolving thus—an ever-whirling wheel— 1144

All flesh immersed within its waves cast here and there without reliance! thus with his pure Deva eyes he thoughtfully considered the five domains of life. 1145

He saw that all was empty and vain alike! with no dependence! like the plantain or the bubble. Then, on the third eventful watch, he entered on the deep, true[1] apprehension[2]; 1146

He meditated on the entire world of creatures, whirling in life's tangle, born[3] to sorrow; the crowds who live, grow old, and die, innumerable for multitude, 1147

---

[1] 受 for 念.

[2] That is, the deep apprehension of truth.

[3] Sorrow self-natured.

Covetous, lustful, ignorant, darkly-fettered, with no way known for final rescue. Rightly considering, inwardly he reflected from what source birth and death proceed; 1148

He was assured that age and death must come from birth as from a source. For since a man has born with him a body, that body must inherit pain (disease). 1149

Then looking further whence comes birth, he saw it came from life-deeds done elsewhere; then with his Deva-eyes scanning these deeds, he saw they were not framed by Isvara; 1150

They were not self-caused, they were not personal existences, nor were they either uncaused; then, as one who breaks the first bamboo joint finds all the rest easy to separate, 1151

Having discerned the cause of birth and death, he gradually came to see the truth; deeds come from upâdâna (cleaving), like as fire which catches hold of grass; 1152

Upâdâna (tsu) comes from *trishnâ* ('ngai), just as a little fire enflames the mountains; *trishnâ* comes from vedanâ (shau), (the perception of pain and pleasure, the desire for rest); 1153

As the starving or the thirsty man seeks food and drink, so 'sensation' (perception) brings 'desire' for life; then contact (sparsa) is the cause of all sensation, producing the three kinds of pain or pleasure, 1154

Even as by art of man the rubbing wood produces fire for any use or purpose; sparsa (contact) is born from the six entrances (âyatanas)[1],

[1] The six organs of sense.

(a man is blind because he cannot see the light)[1]; 1155

The six entrances are caused by name and thing, just as the germ grows to the stem and leaf; name and thing are born from knowledge (vigñâna), as the seed which germinates and brings forth leaves. 1156

Knowledge, in turn, proceeds from name and thing, the two are intervolved leaving no remnant; by some concurrent cause knowledge engenders name and thing, whilst by some other cause concurrent, name and thing engender knowledge; 1157

Just as a man and ship advance together, the water and the land mutually involved[2]; thus knowledge brings forth name and thing; name and thing produce the roots (âyatanas); 1158

The roots engender contact; contact again brings forth sensation; sensation brings forth longing desire; longing desire produces upâdâna; 1159

Upâdâna is the cause of deeds; and these again engender birth; birth again produces age and death; so does this one incessant round 1160

Cause the existence of all living things. Rightly illumined, thoroughly perceiving this, firmly established, thus was he enlightened; destroy birth, old age and death will cease; 1161

Destroy bhava then will birth cease; destroy 'cleaving' (upâdâna) then will bhava end; destroy *tri*sh*n*â (desire) then will cleaving end; destroy sensation then will *tri*sh*n*â end; 1162

---

[1] This clause is obscure, it may mean, 'blind to darkness therefore he sees.'

[2] It is difficult to catch the meaning here; literally translated the passage runs thus: 'Water and dry land cause mutual involution.'

Destroy contact then will end sensation; destroy the six entrances, then will contact cease; the six entrances all destroyed, from this, moreover, names and things will cease; 1163

Knowledge destroyed, names and things[1] will cease; sa*m*skâra (names and things) destroyed, then knowledge perishes; ignorance destroyed, then the sa*m*skâra[2] will die; the great *Ri*shi was thus perfected in wisdom (sambodhi). 1164

Thus perfected, Buddha then devised for the world's benefit the eightfold path, right sight, and so on, the only true path for the world to tread. 1165

Thus did he complete the end (destruction) of 'self,' as fire goes out for want of grass; thus he had done what he would have men do; he first had found the way of perfect knowledge; 1166

He finished thus the first great lesson (paramârtha); entering the great *Ri*shi's house[3], the darkness disappeared; light coming on, perfectly silent, all at rest, 1167

He reached at last the exhaustless source of truth (dharma); lustrous with all wisdom the great *Ri*shi sat, perfect in gifts, whilst one convulsive throe shook the wide earth. 1168

And now the world was calm again and bright, when Devas, Nâgas, spirits, all assembled, amidst the void raise heavenly music, and make their offerings as the law[4] directs; 1169

A gentle cooling breeze sprang up around, and

[1] Here evidently equivalent to sa*m*skâra.

[2] Sa*m*skâra, i. e. the five skandhas, or constituents of individual life.

[3] I. e. attained Nirvâ*n*a.

[4] 'As the law directs;' that is, 'religious offerings' (dharma dâna).

from the sky a fragrant rain distilled; exquisite flowers, not seasonable[1], bloomed; sweet fruits before their time were ripened; 1170

Great Mandâras[2], and every sort of heavenly precious flower, from space in rich confusion fell, as tribute[3] to the illustrious monk. 1171

Creatures of every different kind were moved one towards the other lovingly; fear and terror altogether put away, none entertained a hateful thought; 1172

And all things living in the world with faultless men[4] consorted freely; the Devas giving up their heavenly joys, sought rather to alleviate the sinner's sufferings; 1173

Pain and distress grew less and less, the moon of wisdom waxed apace; whilst all the *Ri*shis of the Ikshvâku clan who had received a heavenly birth, 1174

Beholding Buddha thus benefitting men, were filled with joy and satisfaction; and whilst throughout the heavenly mansions religious offerings fell as raining flowers, 1175

The Devas and the Nâga spirits[5], with one voice, praised the Buddha's virtues; men seeing the religious offerings, hearing, too, the joyous hymn of praise, 1176

Were all rejoiced in turn; they leapt for unre-

---

[1] 'Not seasonable;' that is, out of season; or, before their season.

[2] The Mahâ Mandâra, or Mandârava; one of the five trees of the paradise of Indra (Wilson); the Erythrina fulgens. See Burnouf, Lotus, p. 306.

[3] As a religious offering to the Muni-lord.

[4] Wou lau *g*in, leakless men. It means that all things living consorted freely with the good.

[5] The Devas, Nâgas, and heavenly spirits (kwei shin).

strained joy; Mâra, the Devarâ*g*a, only, felt in his heart great anguish. 1177

Buddha for those seven days, in contemplation lost, his heart at peace, beheld and pondered on the Bodhi tree, with gaze unmoved and never wearying: 1178

'Now resting here, in this condition, I have obtained,' he said, 'my ever-shifting[1] heart's desire, and now at rest I stand, escaped from self[2].' The eyes of Buddha[3] then considered 'all that lives,' 1179

And forthwith rose there in him deep compassion; much he desired to bring about their welfare (purity), but how to gain for them that most excellent deliverance, 1180

From covetous desire, hatred, ignorance, and false teaching (this was the question); how to suppress this sinful heart by right direction; not by anxious use of outward means, but by resting quietly in thoughtful silence. 1181

Now looking back and thinking of his mighty vow, there rose once more within his mind a wish to preach the law; and looking carefully throughout the world, he saw how pain and sorrow ripened and increased everywhere. 1182

Then Brahma-deva knowing his thoughts, and considering[4] it right to request him to advance religion for the wider spread of the Brahma-glory, in the deliverance of all flesh from sorrow, 1183

---

[1] My heart which has experienced constant and differing birth-changes.

[2] Wou-ngo, in a condition without personal (ngo) limitations. The sense seems to be, that, by casting away the limitations of the finite, he had apprehended the idea of the infinite.

[3] The eye of Buddha; the last of the pa*ñk*a*k*akkhus, for which see Childers, Pâli Dict. sub voce.

[4] The sense may be, 'thinking that he ought to be requested to preach.'

Coming, beheld upon the person of the reverend monk all the distinguishing marks of a great preacher, visible in an excellent degree; fixed and unmoved (he sat) in the possession of truth and wisdom, 1184

Free from all evil impediments, with a heart cleansed from all insincerity or falsehood. Then with reverent and a joyful heart, (great Brahma stood and) with hands joined, thus made known his request: 1185

'What happiness in all the world so great as when a loving master meets the unwise[1]; the world with all its occupants, filled with impurity and dire confusion[2], 1186

'With heavy grief oppressed, or, in some cases, lighter sorrows, (waits deliverance); the lord of men, having escaped by crossing the wide and mournful sea of birth and death, 1187

'We now entreat to rescue others—those struggling creatures all engulphed therein; as the just worldly man, when he gets profit, gives some rebate withal[3], 1188

'So the lord of men enjoying such religious gain, should[4] also give somewhat to living things. The world indeed is bent on large personal gain, and hard it is to share one's own with others; 1189

'O! let your loving heart be moved with pity towards the world burthened[5] with vexing cares.'

---

[1] In the sense of 'the uninstructed.'

[2] With sense-pollution and distracted heart, oppressed with heavy grief, or, may be, with lighter and less grievous sorrow.

[3] These lines are obscure; the sense, however, is plainly that given in the text.

[4] In the way of request, 'would that the lord of men,' &c.

[5] Oppressed amidst oppressions (calamities).

Thus having spoken by way of exhortation, with reverent mien he turned back to the Brahma heaven. 1190

Buddha regarding the invitation of Brahma-deva rejoiced at heart, and his design was strengthened; greatly was his heart of pity nourished, and purposed was his mind to preach. 1191

Thinking he ought to beg some food, each of the four kings offered him a Pâtra; Tathâgata[1], in fealty to religion, received the four and joined them all in one. 1192

And now some merchant men were passing by, to whom 'a virtuous friend[2],' a heavenly spirit, said: 'The great *R*ishi, the venerable monk, is dwelling in this mountain grove, 1193

'(Affording) in the world a noble field for merit[3]; go then and offer him a sacrifice!' Hearing the summons, joyfully they went, and offered the first meal religiously. 1194

Having partaken of it, then he deeply pondered, who first should hear the law[4]; he thought at once of Ârâ*d*a Kâlâma and Udraka Râmaputra, 1195

[1] Here the Buddha is called Tathâgata. It is a point to be observed that this title is only used after the Bodhisattva's enlightenment.

[2] There is a great deal said in Buddhist books about this expression 'virtuous,' or, 'good friend.' In general it means Bodhi or wisdom. It is used also in Zend literature to denote the sun (mithra); see Haug (Parsis), p. 209.

[3] That is, giving the world a noble opportunity of obtaining religious merit. The expression 'field for merit' is a common one, as we say, 'field for work,' 'field for usefulness,' and so on.

[4] Who ought to be first instructed in religion; or, who should hear the first religious instruction (sermon). The first sermon is that which is sometimes called 'the foundation of the kingdom of righteousness.' It is given further on.

As being fit to accept the righteous law; but now they both were dead. Then next he thought of the five men, that they were fit to hear the first sermon. 1196

Bent then on this design to preach Nirvâ*n*a[1], as the sun's glory bursts thro' the darkness, so went he on towards Benares, the place where dwelt the ancient *Ri*shis; 1197

With eyes as gentle as the ox king's, his pace as firm and even as the lion's, because he would convert the world he went on towards the Kâ*s*i[2] city; 1198

Step by step, like the king of beasts, did he advance watchfully through the grove of wisdom (Uruvilva wood). 1199

Varga 15. Turning the Law-wheel[3].

Tathâgata piously composed and silent, radiant with glory, shedding light around, with unmatched dignity advanced alone, as if surrounded by a crowd of followers. 1200

Beside the way he encountered a young Brahman[4], whose name was Upaka[5]; struck[6] with the

[1] To preach the law of perfect quietude (quiet extinction; that is, quietness or rest, resulting from the extinction of sorrow).

[2] That is, Benares.

[3] Concerning this expression, which means 'establishing the dominion of truth,' see Childers, Pâli Dict., sub voce pavatteti.

[4] A Brahma*k*ârin, a religious student, one who was practising a life of purity.

[5] Called 'Upagana' by Burnouf (Introd. p. 389), and in the Lalita Vistara an Agîvaka (hermit), (Foucaux, 378). For some useful remarks on this person's character, see Études Buddhiques (Leon Féer), pp. 15, 16, 17.

[6] So I construe '*k*ih *k*i;' it means 'taken by,' or 'attracted by'

deportment of the Bhikshu, he stood with reverent mien on the road side; 1201

Joyously he gazed at such an unprecedented sight, and then, with closed hands, he spake[1] as follows: 'The crowds who live around are stained with sin, without a pleasing feature, void of grace, 1202

'And the great world's heart is everywhere disturbed; but you alone, your senses all composed, with visage shining as the moon when full, seem to have quaffed the water of the immortals' stream; 1203

'The marks of beauty yours, as the great man's (Mahâpurusha); the strength of wisdom, as an all-sufficient (independent) king's (samrâ*g*); what you have done must have been wisely done, what then your noble tribe and who your master?' 1204

Answering he said, 'I have no master; no honourable tribe; no point of excellence[2]; self-taught in this profoundest doctrine, I have arrived at superhuman wisdom[3]. 1205

'That which behoves the world to learn, but through the world no learner found, I now myself

---

the demeanour of the mendicant (Bhikshu). This incident is introduced as the first instance of Buddha's mendicant life and its influence on others.

[1] Or, 'he questioned thus.'

[2] 'Nothing that has been conquered.'

[3] I have attained to that which man has not attained. That is, I have arrived at superhuman wisdom. It appears to me that this point in Buddha's history is a key to the whole system of his religion. He professes to have grasped absolute truth (the word 'absolute' corresponds with 'unfettered'); and by letting go the finite, with its limitations and defilements, to have passed into the free, boundless, unattached infinite.

and by myself[1] have learned throughout; 'tis rightly called Sambodhi (*k*ing kioh); 1206

'That hateful family of griefs the sword of wisdom has destroyed; this then is what the world has named, and rightly named, the "chiefest victory." 1207

'Through all Benares soon will sound the drum of life, no stay is possible—I have no name[2]—nor do I seek profit or pleasure, 1208

'But simply to declare the truth; to save men (living things) from pain, and to fulfil my ancient oath, to rescue all not yet delivered. 1209

'The fruit of this my oath is ripened now, and I will follow out my ancient vow. Wealth, riches, self all given up, unnamed, I still am named "Righteous Master[3]." 1210

'And bringing profit to the world (empire), I also have the name "Great Teacher[4];" facing sorrows, not swallowed up by them, am I not rightly called Courageous Warrior? 1211

'If not a healer of diseases, what means the name of Good Physician? seeing the wanderer, not showing him the way, why then should I be called "Good Master-guide?" 1212

'Like as the lamp shines in the dark, without a

[1] This assertion is a fundamental one (see Mr. Rhys Davids' Dhamma-*k*akka-ppavattana-sutta, Sacred Books of the East, vol. xi, throughout); so that Buddha disclaims any revelation in the sense of the result of a higher wisdom than his own. The cloud, in fact, of sin moved away, the indwelling of light, by itself, revealed itself.

[2] 'I am a voice.'

[3] (Called by the) not-called name, 'Master of righteousness.'

[4] Here follow a list of names applied to Tathâgata in virtue of his office. He gives up his name Gautama, and claims to be known only by his religious titles.

purpose of its own, self-radiant, so burns the lamp of the Tathâgata, without the shadow of a personal feeling. 1213

'Bore wood in wood, there must be fire; the wind blows of its own free self in space; dig deep and you will come to water; this is the rule of self-causation. 1214

'All the Munis who perfect wisdom, must do so at Gayâ; and in the Kâ*s*i country they must first turn the Wheel of Righteousness.' 1215

The young Brahman Upâka, astonished, breathed the praise of such strange doctrine[1], and called to mind like thoughts he had before experienced[2]; lost in thought at the wonderful occurrence, 1216

At every turning of the road he stopped to think; embarrassed in every step he took. Tathâgata proceeding slowly onwards, came to the city of Kâ*s*i, 1217

The land so excellently adorned as the palace of *S*akradevendra; the Ganges and Bara*n*â[3], two twin rivers flowed amidst; 1218

The woods and flowers and fruits so verdant, the peaceful cattle wandering together, the calm retreats

[1] Sighed 'oh!' and praised in under tone the strange behaviour of Tathâgata.

[2] Or perhaps the following translation is better: 'following in mind the circumstances which led to the strange encounter.'

[3] The account in the text makes the city of Benares to be between the Ganges and the Bara*n*â or Vara*n*â; General Cunningham (Archæolog. Report, vol. i, p. 104) says, 'The city of Benares is situated on the left bank of the Ganges, between the Barnâ Nadi on the north-east and the Asi Nâla on the south-west. The Barnâ is a considerable rivulet which rises to the north of Allahabad, and has a course of about 100 miles. The Asi is a mere brook of no length.'

free from vulgar noise, such was the place where the old *Ri*shis dwelt. 1219

Tathâgata glorious and radiant, redoubled the brightness of the place; the son of the Kau*nd*inya-tribe (Kau*nd*inya-kulaputra), and next Da*s*abala-kâ*s*yapa, 1220

And the third Vâshpa, the fourth A*s*va*g*it, the fifth called Bhadra, practising austerities as hermits, 1221

Seeing from far Tathâgata approaching, sitting together all engaged in conversation, (said), 'This Gautama, defiled by worldly indulgence, leaving the practice of austerities, 1222

'Now comes again to find us here, let us be careful not to rise in salutation, nor let us greet him when he comes, nor offer him the customary refreshments; 1223

'Because he has broken his first vow, he has no claim to hospitality;' [for men on seeing an approaching guest by rights prepare things for his present and his after wants, 1224

They arrange a proper resting-couch, and take on themselves care for his comfort.][1] Having spoken thus and so agreed, each kept his seat, resolved and fixed. 1225

And now Tathâgata slowly approached, when, lo! these men unconsciously, against their vow, rose and invited him to take a seat; offering to take his robe and Pâtra, 1226

They begged to wash and rub his feet, and asked him what he required more; thus in everything attentive, they honour'd him and offered all to him as teacher. 1227

They did not not cease however to address him

[1] This [ ] seems to be parenthetical.

still as Gautama, after his family[1]. Then spake the Lord to them and said: 'Call me not after my private name, 1228

'For it is a rude and careless way of speaking to one who has obtained Arhatship[2]; but whether men respect or disrespect me, my mind is undisturbed and wholly quiet; 1229

'But you[3]—your way is not so courteous, let go, I pray, and cast away your fault. Buddha can save the world; they call him, therefore, Buddha; 1230

'Towards all living things, with equal heart he looks as children, to call him then by his familiar name is to despise a father; this is sin[4].' 1231

Thus Buddha, by exercise of mighty love, in deep compassion spoke to them; but they, from ignorance and pride, despised the only wise[5] and true one's words. 1232

They said that first he practised self-denial, but having reached thereby no profit, now giving rein to body, word, and thought[6], how by these means (they asked) has he become a Buddha? 1233

Thus equally entangled by doubts, they would not credit that he had attained the way. Thoroughly versed in highest truth, full of all-embracing wisdom, 1234

---

[1] The address 'Bho Gotama' or 'Gotama,' according to Childers (Pâli Dict. p. 150), was an appellation of disrespect used by unconverted Brahmins in addressing Buddha. The title Gautama Buddha is rarely met with in Northern translations.

[2] The Arhat is the highest grade among the Buddhist saints. See Burnouf, Introd. p. 295.

[3] Here the appeal is to them as religious persons.

[4] Or, is the sin of dishonouring a father.

[5] The true words of the Only Enlightened; that is, of the Buddha.

[6] 樂 for 意.

Tathâgata on their account briefly declared to them the one true way; the foolish masters practising austerities, and those who love to gratify their senses, 1235

He pointed out to them these two distinctive classes[1], and how both greatly erred. 'Neither of these (he said) has found the way of highest wisdom, nor are their ways of life productive of true rescue. 1236

'The emaciated devotee by suffering produces in himself confused and sickly thoughts, not conducive even to worldly knowledge, how much less to triumph over sense! 1237

'For he who tries to light a lamp with water, will not succeed in scattering the darkness, (and so the man who tries) with worn-out body to trim the lamp of wisdom shall not succeed, nor yet destroy his ignorance or folly. 1238

'Who seeks with rotten wood to evoke the fire will waste his labour and get nothing for it; but boring hard wood into hard, the man of skill forthwith gets fire for his use; 1239

'In seeking wisdom then it is not by these austerities a man may reach the law of life. But (likewise) to indulge in pleasure is opposed to right, this is the fool's barrier against wisdom's light; 1240

'The sensualist cannot comprehend the Sûtras or the *S*âstras, how much less the way of overcoming all desire! As some man grievously afflicted eats food not fit to eat, 1241

'And so in ignorance aggravates his sickness, so

[1] The two extremes.

how can he get rid of lust who pampers lust? Scatter the fire amid the desert grass, dried by the sun, fanned by the wind, 1242

'The raging flames who shall extinguish? Such is the fire of covetousness and lust (or, hankering lust), I, then, reject both these extremes, my heart keeps in the middle way. 1243

'All sorrow at an end and finished, I rest at peace, all error put away; my true sight[1] greater than the glory of the sun, my equal and unvarying wisdom[2], vehicle of insight, 1244

'Right words[3] as it were a dwelling-place, wandering through the pleasant groves of right conduct[4], making a right life[5] my recreation, walking along the right road of proper means[6], 1245

'My city of refuge in right recollection[7], and my sleeping couch right meditation[8]; these are the eight even and level roads[9] by which to avoid the sorrows of birth and death; 1246

'Those who come forth by these means from the slough, doing thus, have attained the end; such shall fall neither on this side or the other, amidst the sorrow-crowd of the two periods[10]. 1247

'The tangled sorrow-web of the three worlds by this road alone can be destroyed; this is my own way, unheard of before; by the pure eyes of the true law, 1248

---

[1] Samyag d*ri*sh*t*i.
[2] Samyak sa*m*kalpa.
[3] Samyag vâ*k*.
[4] Samyak karma.
[5] Samyag â*g*îva.
[6] Samyag vyâyâma.
[7] Samyak sm*ri*ti.
[8] Samyak samâdhi.
[9] The right roads (orthodox ways).
[10] Or rather, of the 'two ages;' this age and the next.

'Impartially seeing the way of escape, I, only I, now first make known this way; thus I destroy the hateful company of T*ri*sh*n*â's[1] host, the sorrows of birth and death, old age, disease, 1249

'And all the unfruitful aims of men, and other springs of suffering. There are those who warring against desire are still influenced by desire; who whilst possessed of body, act as tho' they had none; 1250

'Who put away from themselves all sources of true merit, briefly will I recount their sorrowful lot. Like smothering a raging fire, though carefully put out, yet a spark left, 1251

'So in their abstraction, still the germ of "I[2]," the source[3] of great sorrow still surviving, perpetuates the suffering caused by lust (t*ri*sh*n*â), and the evil consequences of every kind of deed survive; 1252

'These are the sources of further pain, but let these go and sorrow dies, even as the seed of corn taken from the earth and deprived of water dies; 1253

'The concurrent causes not uniting, then the bud and leaf cannot be born; the intricate bonds of every kind of existence, from the Deva down to the evil ways of birth, 1254

'Ever revolve and never cease; all this is produced from covetous desire; falling from a high estate to lower ones, all is the fault of previous deeds; 1255

'But destroy the seed of covetousness and the rest, then there will be no intricate binding, but all

---

[1] For some account of T*ri*sh*n*â, Pâli Ta*n*ha, see Rhys Davids (op. cit.), p. 149 note.

[2] The germ of self; that is, of individual existence.

[3] Having the nature of great sorrow.

effect of deeds destroyed, the various degrees of sorrow then will end for good; 1256

'Having this, then, we must inherit that; destroying this, then that is ended too; no birth, old age, disease, or death; no earth, or water, fire, or wind; 1257

'No beginning, end, or middle; and no deceptive systems of philosophy; this is the standpoint of wise men and sages; the certain and exhausted termination, (complete Nirvâ*n*a). 1258

'Such do the eight right ways declare; this one expedient has no remains; that which the world sees not, engrossed by error (I declare), 1259

'I know the way to sever all these sorrow-sources; the way to end them is by right reason, meditating on these four highest truths, following and perfecting this highest wisdom. 1260

'This is what means the "knowing" sorrow; this is to cut off the cause of all remains of being; these destroyed, then all striving, too, has ended, the eight right ways have been assayed. 1261

'(Thus, too), the four great truths have been acquired, the eyes of the pure law completed. In these four truths, the equal (i.e. true or right) eyes not yet born, 1262

'There is not mention made of gaining true deliverance, it is not said what must be done is done, nor that all (is finished), nor that the perfect truth has been acquired. 1263

'But now because the truth is known, then by myself is known "deliverance gained," by myself is known that "all is done," by myself is known "the highest wisdom."' 1264

And having spoken thus respecting truth, the

member of the Kau*nd*inya family, and eighty thousand of the Deva host, were thoroughly imbued with saving knowledge; 1265

They put away defilement from themselves, they got the eyes of the pure law; Devas and earthly masters thus were sure, that what was to be done was done. 1266

And now with lion-voice he joyfully enquired, and asked Kau*nd*inya, 'Knowest thou yet?' Kau*nd*inya forthwith answered Buddha, 'I know the mighty master's law;' 1267

And for this reason, knowing it, his name was Â*gñ*âta Kau*nd*inya (â*gñ*âta, known). Amongst all the disciples of Buddha, he was the very first in understanding. 1268

Then as he understood the sounds of the true law, hearing (the words of) the disciple—all the earth spirits together raised a shout triumphant, 'Well done! deeply seeing (the principles of) the law, 1269

'Tathâgata, on this auspicious day, has set revolving that which never yet revolved, and far and wide, for gods and men, has opened the gates of immortality[1]. 1270

'(Of this wheel) the spokes are the rules of pure conduct; equal contemplation, their uniformity of length; firm wisdom is the tire; modesty and thoughtfulness, the rubbers (sockets in the nave in which the axle is fixed); 1271

'Right reflection is the nave; the wheel itself the law of perfect truth; the right truth now

[1] The way or gate of sweet dew.

has gone forth in the world, not to retire before another teacher.' 1272

Thus the earth spirits shouted, the spirits of the air took up the strain, the Devas all joined in the hymn of praise, up to the highest Brahma heaven. 1273

The Devas of the triple world, now hearing what the great *Ri*shi taught, in intercourse together spoke, 'The widely-honoured Buddha moves the world! 1274

'Wide-spread, for the sake of all that lives, he turns the wheel of the law of complete purity!' The stormy winds, the clouds, the mists, all disappeared; down from space the heavenly flowers descended; 1275

The Devas revelled in their joys celestial, filled with unutterable gladness. 1276

KIOUEN IV.

VARGA 16. BIMBISÂRA RÂGA BECOMES A DISCIPLE.

And now those five men, Asva*g*it, Vâshpa, and the others, having heard that he (Kau*nd*inya) 'knew' the law, with humble mien and self-subdued, 1277

Their hands joined, offered their homage, and looked with reverence in the teacher's face. Tathâgata, by wise expedient, caused them one by one to embrace the law. 1278

And so from first to last the five Bhikshus obtained reason and subdued their senses, like the five stars which shine in heaven, waiting upon the brightening moon. 1279

At this time in the town of Ku-i[1] (Ku*s*inârâ) there was a noble's son (called) Yasas; lost in night-sleep suddenly he woke, and when he saw his attendants all, 1280

Men and women, with ill-clad bodies, sleeping, his heart was filled with loathing; reflecting on the root of sorrow, (he thought) how madly foolish men were immersed in it; 1281

Clothing himself, and putting on his jewels, he left his home and wandered forth; then on the way he stood and cried aloud, 'Alas! alas! what endless chain of sorrows.' 1282

---

[1] The scene of this history of Yasas is generally laid in Benares; see Romantic Legend, p. 261; Sacred Books of the East, vol. xiii, p. 102.

Tathâgata, by night, was walking forth, and hearing sounds like these, 'Alas! what sorrow,' forthwith replied, 'You are welcome! here, on the other hand, there is a place of rest, 1283

'The most excellent, refreshing, Nirvâna, quiet and unmoved, free from sorrow.' Yasas hearing Buddha's exhortation, there rose much joy within his heart, 1284

And in the place of the disgust he felt, the cooling streams of holy wisdom found their way, as when one enters first a cold pellucid lake. Advancing then, he came where Buddha was; 1285

His person decked with common ornaments, his mind already freed from all defects; by power of the good root obtained in other births, he quickly reached the fruit of an Arhat; 1286

The secret light of pure wisdom's virtue (li) enabled him to understand, on listening to the law; just as a pure silken fabric[1] with ease is dyed a different colour; 1287

Thus having attained to self-illumination, and done that which was to be done, (he was converted); then looking at his person richly ornamented, his heart was filled with shame. 1288

Tathâgata knowing his inward thoughts, in gâthas spoke the following words: 'Tho' ornamented with jewels, the heart may yet have conquered sense; 1289

'Looking with equal mind on all that lives, (in such a case) the outward form does not affect religion; the body, too, may wear the ascetic's garb, the heart, meanwhile, be immersed in worldly thoughts; 1290

[1] Sacred Books of the East, vol. xiii, p. 105.

'Dwelling in lonely woods, yet covetous of worldly show, such men are after all mere worldlings; the body may have a worldly guise, the heart mount high to things celestial; 1291

'The layman and the hermit are the same, when only both have banished thought of "self," but if the heart be twined with carnal bonds, what use the marks of bodily attention? 1292

'He who wears martial decorations, does so because by valour he has triumphed o'er an enemy,—so he who wears the hermit's colour'd robe, does so for having vanquished sorrow as his foe.' 1293

Then he bade him come, and be a member of his church (a Bhikshu); and at the bidding lo! his garments changed! and he stood wholly attired in hermit's dress, complete; in heart and outward look, a *S*rama*n*a. 1294

Now (Yasas) had in former days some light companions, in number fifty and four; when these beheld their friend a hermit, they too, one by one, attained true wisdom [entered the true law]; 1295

By virtue of deeds done in former births, these deeds now bore their perfect fruit. Just as when burning ashes are sprinkled by water, the water being dried, the flame bursts forth. 1296

So now, with those above, the *S*râvakas (disciples) were altogether sixty, all Arhats; entirely obedient and instructed in the law of perfect discipleship[1]. So perfected he taught them further: 1297

'Now ye have passed the stream and reached "the other shore," across the sea of birth and death;

[1] The law of Arhats.

what should be done, ye now have done! and ye may now receive the charity of others. 1298

'Go then through every country, convert those not yet converted; throughout the world that lies burnt up with sorrow, teach everywhere; (instruct) those lacking right instruction; 1299

'Go, therefore! each one travelling by himself[1]; filled with compassion, go! rescue and receive. I too will go alone, back to yonder Kia-*k*e[2] mountain; 1300

'Where there are great *Ri*shis, royal *Ri*shis, Brahman *Ri*shis too, these all dwell there, influencing men according to their schools; 1301

'The *Ri*shi Kâ*s*yapa, enduring pain, reverenced by all the country, making converts too of many, him will I visit and convert.' 1302

Then the sixty Bhikshus respectfully receiving orders to preach, each according to his fore-determined purpose, following his inclination, went thro' every land; 1303

The honour'd of the world went on alone, till he arrived at the Kia-*k*e mountain, then entering a retired religious dell, he came to where the *Ri*shi Kâ*s*yapa was. 1304

Now this one had a 'fire grot' where he offered sacrifice, where an evil Nâga dwelt[3], who wandered here and there in search of rest, through mountains and wild places of the earth. 1305

---

[1] In after time the disciples were not allowed to travel alone, but two and two.

[2] Gayâ*s*îrsha, or Gayâsîsa in the Pâli (Sacred Books of the East, vol. xiii, p. 134).

[3] The episode here translated is found amongst the Sanchi sculptures. See Tree and Serpent Worship, plate xxiv.

The honoured of the world, (wishing) to instruct this hermit and convert him, asked him, on coming, for a place to lodge that night. Kâ*s*yapa, replying, spake to Buddha thus: 'I have no resting-place to offer for the night, 1306

'Only this fire grot where I sacrifice, this is a cool and fit place for the purpose, but an evil dragon dwells there, who is accustomed, as he can, to poison men.' 1307

Buddha replied, 'Permit me only, and for the night I'll take my dwelling there.' Kâ*s*yapa made many difficulties, but the world-honoured one still asked the favour. 1308

Then Kâ*s*yapa addressed Buddha, 'My mind desires no controversy, only I have my fears and apprehensions, but follow you your own good pleasure.' 1309

Buddha forthwith stepped within the fiery grot, and took his seat with dignity and deep reflection; and now the evil Nâga seeing Buddha, belched forth in rage his fiery poison, 1310

And filled the place with burning vapour. But this could not affect the form of Buddha. Throughout the abode the fire consumed itself, the honoured of the world still sat composed: 1311

Even as Brahma, in the midst of the kalpa-fire that burns and reaches to the Brahma heavens, still sits unmoved, without a thought of fear or apprehension, 1312

(So Buddha sat); the evil Nâga seeing him, his face glowing with peace, and still unchanged, ceased his poisonous blast, his heart appeased; he bent his head and worshipped. 1313

Kâ*s*yapa in the night seeing the fire-glow, sighed;

'Ah! alas! what misery! this most distinguished man is also burnt up by the fiery Nâga,' 1314

Then Kâsyapa and his followers at morning light came one and all to look. Now Buddha having subdued the evil Nâga, had straightway placed him in his pâtra, 1315

(Beholding which) and seeing the power of Buddha, Kâsyapa conceived within him deep and secret thoughts: 'This Gotama,' he thought, 'is deeply versed (in religion), but still he said, "I am a master of religion."' 1316

Then Buddha, as occasion offered, displayed all kinds of spiritual changes[1], influencing his (Kâsyapa's) heart-thoughts, changing and subduing them; 1317

Making his mind pliant and yielding, until at length prepared to be a vessel of the true law, he confessed that his poor wisdom could not compare with the complete wisdom of the world-honoured one. 1318

And so, convinced at last, humbly submitting, he accepted right instruction. (Thus) U-pi-lo (Uravilva) Kâsyapa, and five hundred of his followers 1319

Following their master, virtuously submissive, in turn received the teaching of the law. Kâsyapa and all his followers were thus entirely converted. 1320

The *Ri*shi then, taking his goods and all his sacrificial vessels, threw them together in the river, which floated down upon the surface of the current. 1321

Nadi and Gada, brothers, who dwelt adown the stream, seeing these articles of clothing (and the rest) floating along the stream disorderly, 1322

---

[1] The different wonders wrought by Buddha are detailed in Spence Hardy's Manual, and in the Romantic Legend of Buddha.

Said, 'Some great change has happened,' and deeply pained, were restlessly (concerned). The two, each with five hundred followers, going up the stream to seek their brother, 1323

Seeing him now dressed as a hermit, and all his followers with him, having got knowledge of the miraculous law—strange thoughts engaged their minds— 1324

'Our brother having submitted thus, we too should also follow him (they said).' Thus the three brothers, with all their band of followers, 1325

Were brought to hear the lord's discourse on the comparison of a fire sacrifice[1]: (and in the discourse he taught), 'How the dark smoke of ignorance arises[2], whilst confused thoughts, like wood drilled into wood, create the fire, 1326

'Lust, anger, delusion, these are as fire produced, and these enflame and burn all living things. Thus the fire of grief and sorrow, once enkindled, ceases not to burn, 1327

'Ever giving rise to birth and death; but whilst this fire of sorrow ceases not, yet are there two kinds of fire, one that burns but has no fuel left; 1328

'So when the heart of man has once conceived distaste for sin, this distaste removing covetous desire, covetous desire extinguished, there is rescue; 1329

'If once this rescue has been found, then with it is born sight and knowledge, by which distinguishing

---

[1] So I translate i sse fo pi; it may mean, however, 'in respect of the matter of the fire comparison.'

[2] This is the sermon on 'The Burning;' see Sacred Books of the East, vol. xiii, p. 135.

the streams of birth and death, and practising pure conduct, 1330

'All is done that should be done, and hereafter shall be no more life (bhava).' Thus the thousand Bhikshus hearing the world-honoured preach, 1331

All defects[1] for ever done away, their minds found perfect and complete deliverance. Then Buddha for the Kâ*s*yapas' sakes, and for the benefit of the thousand Bhikshus, having preached, 1332

And done all that should be done, himself with purity and wisdom and all the concourse of high qualities excellently adorned, he gave them, as in charity, rules for cleansing sense. 1333

The great *Ri*shi, listening to reason, lost all regard for bodily austerities, and, as a man without a guide, was emptied of himself, and learned discipleship. 1334

And now the honoured one and all his followers go forward to the royal city[2] (Râ*g*ag*ri*ha), remembering, as he did, the Magadha king, and what he heretofore had promised. 1335.

The honoured one when he arrived, remained within the 'staff grove[3];' Bimbisâra Râ*g*a hearing thereof, with all his company of courtiers, 1336

Lords and ladies all surrounding him, came to where the master was. Then at a distance seeing Buddha seated, with humbled heart and subdued presence, 1337

Putting off his common ornaments, descending from his chariot, forward he stepped; even as

[1] The Â*s*ravas.

[2] So also in the Pâli.

[3] The '*K*ang lin,' called in Sanskrit Yash*t*ivana.

*S*akra, king of gods, going to where Brahmadeva-râ*g*a dwells. 1338

Bowing down at Buddha's feet, he asked him, with respect, about his health of body; Buddha in his turn, having made enquiries, begged him to be seated on one side. 1339

Then the king's mind reflected silently: 'This *S*âkya must have great controlling power, to subject to his will these Kâ*s*yapas who now are round him as disciples.' 1340

Buddha, knowing all thoughts, spoke thus to Kâ*s*yapa, questioning him: 'What profit have you found in giving up your fire-adoring law?' 1341

Kâ*s*yapa hearing Buddha's words, rising with dignity before the great assembly, bowed lowly down, and then with clasped hands and a loud voice addressing Buddha, said: 1342

'The profit I received, adoring the fire spirit, was this,—continuance in the wheel of life, birth and death with all their sorrows growing,—this service I have therefore cast away; 1343

'Diligently I persevered in fire-worship, seeking to put an end to the five desires, in return I found desires endlessly increasing, therefore have I cast off this service. 1344

'Sacrificing thus to fire with many Mantras, I did but miss (i.e. I did not find) escape from birth; receiving birth, with it came all its sorrows, therefore I cast it off and sought for rest. 1345

'I was versed, indeed, in self-affliction, my mode of worship largely adopted, and counted of all most excellent, and yet I was opposed to highest wisdom. 1346

'Therefore have I discarded it, and gone in quest

of the supreme Nirvâ*n*a. Removing from me birth, old age, disease, and death, I sought a place of undying rest and calm. 1347

'And as I gained the knowledge of this truth, then I cast off the law of worshipping the fire (or, by fire).' The honoured-of-the-world, hearing Kâ*s*yapa declaring his experience of truth, 1348

Wishing to move the world throughout to conceive a heart of purity and faith, addressing Kâ*s*yapa further, said, 'Welcome! great master, welcome! 1349

'Rightly have you distinguished law from law, and well obtained the highest wisdom; now before this great assembly, pray you! exhibit your excellent endowments; 1350

'As any rich and wealthy noble opens for view his costly treasures, causing the poor and sorrow-laden multitude to increase their forgetfulness awhile; 1351

'(So do you now) and honour well your lord's instruction.' Forthwith in presence of the assembly, gathering up his body and entering Samâdhi, calmly he ascended into space, 1352

And there displayed himself, walking, standing, sitting, sleeping, emitting fiery vapour from his body, on his right and left side water and fire, not burning and not moistening him; 1353

Then clouds and rain proceeded from him, thunder with lightning shook the heaven and earth; thus he drew the world to look in adoration, with eyes undazzled as they gazed; 1354

With different mouths, but all in language one, they magnified and praised this wondrous spectacle, then afterwards drawn by spiritual force, they came and worshipped at the master's feet, 1355

(Exclaiming), 'Buddha is our great teacher! we are the honoured one's disciples.' Thus having magnified his work and finished all he purposed doing, 1356

Drawing the world as universal witness, the assembly was convinced that he, the world-honoured, was truly the 'Omniscient!' 1357

Buddha, perceiving that the whole assembly was ready as a vessel to receive the law, spoke thus to Bimbisâra Râ*g*a: 'Listen now and understand; 1358

'The mind, the thoughts, and all the senses are subject to the law of life and death. This fault[1] of birth and death, once understood, then there is clear and plain perception; 1359

'Obtaining this clear perception, then there is born knowledge of self, knowing oneself and with this knowledge laws of birth and death, then there is no grasping and no sense-perception. 1360

'Knowing oneself, and understanding how the senses act, then there is no room for "I," or ground for framing it; then all the accumulated mass of sorrow, sorrows born from life and death, 1361

'Being recognised as attributes of body, and as this body is not "I," nor offers ground for "I," then comes the great superlative (discovery), the source of peace unending; 1362

'This thought (view) of "self" gives rise to all these sorrows, binding as with cords[2] the world, but having found there is no "I" that can be bound, then all these bonds are severed. 1363

'There are no bonds indeed—they disappear—

[1] This fault; that is, this flaw.

[2] As with fetters.

and seeing this there is deliverance. The world holds to this thought of "I," and so, from this, comes false apprehension. 1364

'Of those who maintain the truth of it, some say the "I" endures, some say it perishes; taking the two extremes of birth and death, their error is most grievous! 1365

'For if they say the "I" (soul) is perishable, the fruit they strive for, too, will perish; and at some time there will be no hereafter, this is indeed a meritless deliverance. 1366

'But if they say the "I" is not to perish, then in the midst of all this life and death there is but one identity (as space), which is not born and does not die. 1367

'If this is what they call the "I," then are all things living, one—for all have this unchanging self—not perfected by any deeds, but self-perfect; 1368

'If so, if such a self it is that acts, let there be no self-mortifying conduct, the self is lord and master; what need to do that which is done? 1369

'For if this "I" is lasting and imperishable, then reason would teach it never can be changed. But now we see the marks of joy and sorrow, what room for constancy then is here? 1370

'Knowing that birth brings this deliverance then I put away all thought of sin's defilement; the whole world, everything, endures! what then becomes of this idea of rescue. 1371

'We cannot even talk of putting self away, truth is the same as falsehood, it is not "I" that do a thing, and who, forsooth, is he that talks of "I?" 1372

'But if it is not "I" that do the thing, then there is no "I" that does it, and in the absence of these both, there is no "I" at all, in very truth. 1373

'No doer and no knower, no lord, yet notwithstanding this, there ever lasts this birth and death, like morn and night ever recurring. But now attend to me and listen; 1374

'The senses six and their six objects united cause the six kinds of knowledge, these three (i. e. senses, objects, and resulting knowledge) united bring forth contact, then the intervolved effects of recollection (follow). 1375

'Then like the burning glass and tinder thro' the sun's power cause fire to appear, so thro' the knowledge born of sense and object, the lord (of knowledge) (self) (like the fire) is born. 1376

'The shoot springs from the seed, the seed is not the shoot, not one and yet not different, such is the birth of all that lives.' 1377

The honoured of the world preaching the truth, the equal and impartial paramârtha, thus addressed the king with all his followers. Then king Bimbisâra filled with joy, 1378

Removing from himself defilement, gained religious sight, a hundred thousand spirits also, hearing the words of the immortal law, shook off and lost the stain of sin. 1379

VARGA 17. THE GREAT DISCIPLE BECOMES A HERMIT.

At this time Bimbisâra Râga, bowing his head, requested the honoured of the world to change his place of abode for the bamboo grove[1]; graciously accepting it, Buddha remained silent. 1380

Then the king, having perceived the truth, offered his adoration and returned to his palace. The world-honoured, with the great congregation, proceeded on foot, to rest for awhile in the bamboo garden[2]. 1381

(There he dwelt) to convert all that breathed[3], to kindle once for all[4] the lamp of wisdom, to establish Brahma and the Devas, and to confirm the lives[5] of saints and sages. 1382

At this time Asvagit and Vâshpa[6], with heart composed and every member (sense) subdued, the time having come for begging food, entered into the town of Râgagriha: 1383

Unrivalled in the world were they for grace of person, and in dignity of carriage excelling all. The lords and ladies of the city seeing them, were filled with joy; 1384

Those who were walking stood still, those before waited, those behind hastened on. Now the *Ri*shi Kapila amongst all his numerous disciples 1385

---

[1] This garden, called the Karanda Venuvana, was a favourite residence of Buddha. For an account of it, see Spence Hardy, Manual of Buddhism, p. 194. It was situated between the old city of Râgagriha and the new city, about three hundred yards to the north of the former (see Fă-hien, chap. xxx, Beal's translation, p. 117 and note 2).

[2] I have translated Ku'an 'to rest awhile,' it might be supposed to refer to the rest of the rainy season. But it is doubtful whether this ordinance was instituted so early.

[3] All living things.

[4] To establish and settle the brightness of the lamp of wisdom.

[5] To establish the settlement of sages and saints.

[6] He is sometimes called Dasabala Kâsyapa (Eitel, Handbook, p. 158 b).

Had one of wide-spread fame, whose name was *S*âriputra; he, beholding the wonderful grace of the Bhikshus, their composed mien and subdued senses, 1386

Their dignified walk and carriage, raising his hands, enquiring, said: 'Young in years, but pure and graceful in appearance, such as I before have never seen, 1387

'What law most excellent (have you obeyed)? and who your master that has taught you? and what the doctrine you have learned? Tell me, I pray you, and relieve my doubts.' 1388

Then of the Bhikshus, one[1], rejoicing at his question, with pleasing air and gracious words, replied: 'The omniscient, born of the Ikshvâku family, 1389

'The very first 'midst gods and men, this one is my great master. I am indeed but young, the sun of wisdom has but just arisen, 1390

'How can I then explain the master's doctrine? Its meaning is deep and very hard to understand, but now, according to my poor capability (wisdom), I will recount in brief the master's doctrine: 1391

'"Whatever things exist all spring from cause, the principles (cause) of birth and death (may be) destroyed, the way is by the means he has declared[2]."' 1392

---

[1] In the Pâli account of this incident A*s*vag*i*t alone is represented as begging his food; but here A*s*vag*i*t and Vâshpa are joined according to the later rule (as it would seem) which forbad one mendicant to proceed alone through a town. (Compare Sacred Books of the East, vol. xiii, p. 144.)

[2] For the Southern version of this famous stanza, see Sacred Books of the East, vol. xiii, p. 146; also Manual of Buddhism,

Then the twice-born Upata (Upatishya), embracing heartily what he had heard, put from him all sense-pollution, and obtained the pure eyes of the law. 1393

The former explanations he had trusted, respecting cause and what was not the cause, that there was nothing that was made, but was made by Îsvara, 1394

All this, now that he had heard the rule of true causation, understanding (penetrating) the wisdom of the no-self, adding thereto the knowledge of the minute (dust) troubles[1], which can never be overcome in their completeness (completely destroyed), 1395

But by the teaching of Tathâgata, all this he now for ever put away; leaving no room for thought of self, the thought of self will disappear[2]. 1396

'Who, when the brightness of the sun gives light, would call for the dimness of the lamp? for, like the severing of the lotus, the stem once cut, the pods (?) will also die; 1397

'So Buddha's teaching cutting off the stem of sorrow, no seeds are left to grow or lead to further increase.' Then bowing at the Bhikshu's feet, with grateful mien, he wended homewards. 1398

The Bhikshus after having begged their food, likewise went back to the bamboo grove. *S*âri-

p. 196. For a similar account from the Chinese, see Wong Puh, § 77.

[1] The 'dust troubles' are the troubles caused by objects of sense, as numerous as motes in a sunbeam.

[2] 'Look upon the world as void, O Mogharâ*g*an, being always thoughtful; having destroyed the view of oneself (as really existing), so one may overcome death; the king of death will not see him who thus regards the world,' Sutta Nipâta, Fausböll, p. 208.

putra on his arrival home, (rested) with joyful face and full of peace. 1399

His friend the honoured Mugalin (Maudgalyâyana), equally renowned for learning, seeing *S*âriputra in the distance[1], his pleasing air and lightsome step, 1400

Spoke thus: 'As I now see thee, there is an unusual look I notice, your former nature seems quite changed, the signs of happiness I now observe, 1401

'All indicate the possession of eternal truth, these marks are not uncaused.' Answering he said: 'The words of the Tathâgata are such as never yet were spoken;' 1402

And then, requested, he declared (what he had heard). Hearing the words and understanding them, he too put off the world's defilement, and gained the eyes of true religion, 1403

The reward of a long-planted virtuous cause; and, as one sees by a lamp that comes to hand, so he obtained an unmoved faith in Buddha; and now they both set out for Buddha's presence, 1404

With a large crowd of followers, two hundred men and fifty. Buddha seeing the two worthies[2] coming, spoke thus to his disciples: 1405

'These two men who come shall be my two most eminent followers, one unsurpassed for wisdom, the other for powers miraculous;' 1406

And then with Brahma's voice[3], profound and

[1] 'Then the paribbâ*g*aka Sâriputta went to the place where the paribbâ*g*aka Moggallâna was,' Sacred Books of the East, vol. xiii, p. 147.

[2] The two 'bhadras,' i. e. 'sages,' or 'virtuous ones.'

[3] Or, with 'Brahma-voice' (Brahmaghosha), for which, see Childers sub voce.

sweet, he forthwith bade them 'Welcome!' Here is the pure and peaceful law (he said); here the end of all discipleship! 1407

Their hands grasping the triple-staff[1], their twisted hair holding the water-vessel[2], hearing the words of Buddha's welcome, they forthwith changed into complete *S*rama*n*as[3]; 1408

The leaders two and all their followers, assuming the complete appearance of Bhikshus, with prostrate forms fell down at Buddha's feet, then rising, sat beside him[4]: 1409

And with obedient heart listening to the word, they all became Rahats. At this time there was a twice-(born) sage[5], Kâ*s*yapa Shi-ming-teng (Eggidatta) (Agnidatta), 1410

Celebrated and perfect in person, rich in possessions, and his wife most virtuous. But all this he

[1] This triple (three-wonderful) staff is, I suppose, a mark of a Brahman student.

[2] Twisted hair holding the pitcher; this may also refer to some custom among the Brahmans. Or the line may be rendered, 'their hair twisted and holding their pitchers.'

[3] This sudden transformation from the garb and appearance of laymen into shorn and vested Bhikshus, is one often recounted in Buddhist stories.

[4] Or, sat on one side (ekamantam).

[5] This expression, which might also be rendered 'two religious leaders' ('rh sse), may also, by supplying the word 'sing,' be translated a 'twice-born sage,' i.e. a Brahman; and this appears more apposite with what follows, and therefore I have adopted it. The Brahman alluded to would then be called Kâ*s*yapa Agnidatta. The story of Eggidatta is given by Bigandet (Legend, p. 180, first edition), but there is nothing said about his name Kâ*s*yapa. Eitel (Handbook, sub voce Mahâkâ*s*yapa) gives an explanation of the name Kâ*s*yapa, 'he who swallowed light;' but the literal translation of the words in our text is, 'Kâ*s*yapa giving in charity a bright lamp.'

had left and become a hermit, seeking the way of salvation. 1411

And now in the way by the To-tseu[1] tower he suddenly encountered *S*âkya Muni, remarkable for his dignified and illustrious appearance, as the embroidered flag of a Deva (temple); 1412

Respectfully and reverently approaching, with head bowed down, he worshipped his feet, whilst he said: 'Truly, honoured one, you are my teacher, and I am your follower, 1413

'Much and long time have I been harassed with doubts, oh! would that you would light the lamp[2] (of knowledge).' Buddha knowing that this twice-(born) sage was heartily desirous of finding the best mode of escape[3], 1414

With soft and pliant voice, he bade him come and welcome. Hearing his bidding and his heart complying, losing all listlessness of body or spirit, 1415

His soul embraced the terms of this most excellent salvation[4]. Quiet and calm, putting away defilement, the great merciful, as he alone knew how, briefly explained the mode of this deliverance, 1416

Exhibiting the secrets of his law, ending with

---

[1] This 'many children' tower is perhaps the one at Vai*s*âlî alluded to by Fâ-hien, chap. xxv.

[2] Here the phrase 'teng ming,' light of the lamp, seems to be a play on the name 'ming teng,' bright lamp. The method and way in which a disciple (saddhivihârika) chooses a master (upa*gg*hâya) is explained, Sacred Books of the East, vol. xiii, p. 154.

[3] Literally, '(had) a heart rejoicing in the most complete method of salvation (moksha).'

[4] Or, 'the mode of salvation explained by the most excellent (Buddha).'

the four indestructible acquirements[1]. The great sage, everywhere celebrated, was called Mahâ Kâsyapa, 1417

His original faith was that 'body and soul are different,' but he had also held that they are the same, that there was both 'I' and a place[2] for I; but now he for ever cast away his former faith, 1418

And considered only (the truth) that 'sorrow' is ever accumulating; so (he argued) by removing sorrow there will be 'no remains' (i. e. no subject for suffering); obedience to the precepts and the practice of discipline, though not themselves the cause, yet he considered these the necessary mode by which to find deliverance. 1419

With equal and impartial mind, he considered the nature of sorrow, for evermore freed from a cleaving heart. Whether we think 'this is,' or 'this is not' (he thought), both tend to produce a listless (idle) mode of life; 1420

But when with equal mind we see the truth, then certainty is produced and no more doubt. If we rely for support on wealth or form, then wild confusion and concupiscence result, 1421

Inconstant and impure. But lust and covetous desire removed, the heart of love and equal thoughts produced, there can be then no enemies or friends (variance), 1422

But the heart is pitiful and kindly disposed to all, and thus is destroyed the power of anger and of hate. Trusting to outward things and their relationships, then crowding thoughts of every kind are gendered; 1423

---

[1] *K*atu*h*-samyak-pradhâna?

[2] 所 'the place of.'

Reflecting well, and crushing out confusing thought, then lust for pleasure is destroyed. Though born in the Arûpa world (he saw) that there would be a remnant of life still left; 1424

Unacquainted with the four right truths, he had felt an eager longing for this deliverance, for the quiet resulting from the absence of all thought. And now putting away for ever covetous desire for such a formless state of being, 1425

His restless heart was agitated still, as the stream is excited by the rude wind. Then entering on deep reflection in quiet he subdued his troubled mind, 1426

And realised the truth of there being no 'self,' and that therefore birth and death are no realities; but beyond this point he rose not, his thought of 'self' destroyed, all else was lost. 1427

But now the lamp of wisdom lit, the gloom of every doubt dispersed, he saw an end to that which seemed without an end; ignorance finally dispelled, 1428

He considered the ten points of excellence; the ten seeds of sorrow destroyed, he came once more to life, and what he ought to do, he did. And now regarding with reverence the face of his lord, 1429

He put away the three[1] and gained the three[2]; so were there three disciples[3] in addition to the

---

[1] The three poisons, lust, hatred, ignorance.

[2] The three treasures (triratna), Buddha, the law, the community.

[3] The three disciples, as it seems, were *S*âriputra, Maudgalyâyana, and Agnidatta (Kâ*s*yapa).

three[1]; and as the three stars range around the Trayastrimsas heaven, 1430

Waiting upon the three and five[2], so the three wait on Buddha. 1431

Varga 18. Conversion of[3] the 'Supporter of the Orphans and Destitute[4]' (Anâthapindada).

At this time there was a great householder[5] whose name was 'Friend of the Orphan and Destitute;' he was very rich and of unbounded means, and widely charitable in helping the poor and needy. 1432

Now this man coming far away from the north, even from the country of Kosala[6], stopped at the house of a friend whose name was Sheu-lo[7] (in Râgagriha). 1433

Hearing that Buddha was in the world and dwell-

[1] In addition to the three brothers (the Kâsyapas).

[2] The allusion here is obscure; there may be a misprint in the text.

[3] Literally, 'he converts,' &c.

[4] This is the Chinese explanation of the name of Anâthapindada (or Anâthapindika), 'the protector or supporter of the destitute.' He is otherwise called Sudatta (see Jul. II, 294).

[5] The Chinese is simply 'ta kang ké,' but this is evidently the equivalent of 'Mahâ-setthi,' a term applied emphatically to Anâthapindada (see Rhys Davids, Sacred Books of the East, vol. xiii, p. 102, note 2). Where I have translated it 'nobleman,' the word 'treasurer' might be substituted; the term 'elder' cannot be allowed. Yasa the son of a setthi is called by Rh. D. a 'noble youth' (op. cit., p. 102, § 7).

[6] That is, Uttara Kosala (Northern Kosala), the capital of which was Srâvastî.

[7] Rhys Davids gives the name of one of the rich merchant's daughters, Kûla-Subhaddâ (Birth Stories, p. 131); perhaps his friend at Râgagriha was called Sûla or Kûla (see also Manual of Buddhism, p. 219).

ing in the bamboo grove near at hand, understanding moreover his renown and illustrious qualities, he set out that very night[1] for the grove. 1434

Tathâgata, well aware of his character, and that he was prepared to bring forth purity and faith[2], according to the case, called him by his true[3] (name), and for his sake addressed him in words of religion: 1435

'Having rejoiced in the true law[4], and being humbly[5] desirous for a pure and believing heart, thou hast overcome desire for sleep, and art here to pay me reverence; 1436

'Now then will I for your sake discharge fully the duties of a first meeting[6]. In your former births the root of virtue planted firm in pure and rare expectancy[7], 1437

'Hearing now the name of Buddha, you rejoiced because you are a vessel fit for righteousness, humble

---

[1] The statements that he came 'by night,' and that Buddha called him by his name—or, as the Chinese might be translated, called him 'true' (? guileless)—appear as though borrowed from the Gospel narrative. Nicodemus was rich, and Nathaniel (Bartholomew) preached in India (Euseb. Lib. v. cap. 10). He is said to have carried the Gospel of St. Matthew there, where it was discovered by Pantaenus.

[2] That is, that he was ripe for conversion.

[3] The name by which he was called, according to Spence Hardy (Manual of Buddhism, p. 217), was Sudatta.

[4] That is, 'because' you have rejoiced. The 'true law' is the same as 'religious truth.'

[5] Literally, 'pure and truthful of heart, with meekness thirsting (after knowledge).'

[6] The meaning is, as we have now met for the first time, I will explain my doctrine (preach) in a formal (polite) way.

[7] That is, your merit in former births has caused you to reap a reward in your present condition.

in mind, but large in gracious deeds, abundant in your charity to the poor and helpless— 1438

'The name you possess wide spread and famous, (this is) the just reward (fruit) of former merit. The deeds you now perform are done of charity, done with the fullest purpose and of single heart. 1439

'Now, therefore, take from me[1] the charity of perfect rest (Nirvâ*n*a), and for this end accept my rules of purity. My rules[2] are full of grace, able to rescue from destruction (evil ways of birth), 1440

'And cause a man to ascend to heaven and share in all its pleasures. But yet to seek for these (pleasures) is a great evil, for lustful longing in its increase brings much sorrow. 1441

'Practise then the art of "giving up[3]" all search, for "giving up" desire is the joy of perfect rest (Nirvâ*n*a)[4]. Know[5] then! that age, dis-

---

[1] The construction here is difficult. There seems to be a play on the word 'shi,' religious charity; the sense is, that as Anâthapi*nd*ada was remarkable for his liberality now, he should be liberally rewarded by gaining a knowledge of salvation (Nirvâ*n*a).

[2] Instead of 'my rules,' it would be better to understand the word in an indefinite sense as 'rules of morality' (sîla).

[3] 'Giving up,' that is, putting away all desire and giving up 'self,' even in relation to future reward; compare the hymn of S. Francis Xavier,

> 'O Deus, ego amo Te
> Nec amo Te ut salves me,' etc.

And again,

> 'Non ut in coelo salves me
> Nec praemii ullius spe.'

[4] This definition of Nirvâ*n*a, as a condition of perfect rest resulting from 'giving up' desire, is in agreement with the remarks of Mr. Rhys Davids and others, who describe Nirvâ*n*a as resulting from the absence of a 'grasping' disposition.

[5] It would seem, from the context, that the word '*k*i' (know), in this line, is a mistake for 'sing,' birth.

ease, and death, these are the great sorrows of the world. 1442

'Rightly considering the world, we put away birth and old age, disease and death; (but now) because we see that men at large inherit sorrow caused by age, disease, and death, 1443

'(We gather that) when born in heaven, the case is also thus; for there is no continuance there for any, and where there is no continuance there is sorrow, and having sorrow there is no "true self." 1444

'And if the state of "no continuance" and of sorrow is opposed to "self," what room is there for such idea or ground for "self[1]?" Know then! that "sorrow" is this very sorrow (viz. of knowledge), and its repetition is "accumulation[2];" 1445

'Destroy[3] this sorrow and there is joy, the way[4] is in the calm and quiet place. The restless busy nature of the world, this I declare is at the root of pain. 1446

'Stop then the end by choking up the source[5].

[1] The argument is, that there can be no personal self, in other words, no 'soul,' where there is no continuance, or power of independent existence. This is one of the principles of Buddhism, viz. that what has had a beginning must come to an end; the 'soul,' therefore, as it began with the birth of the individual, must die (and as the Buddhists said) with the individual. If we put this into modern phraseology, it will be something like this, 'the very nature of phenomena demonstrates that they must have had a beginning, and that they must have an end' (Huxley, Lay Sermons, p. 17).

[2] The sorrow of 'accumulation' is the second of the 'four truths' (according to Northern accounts).

[3] 'Destruction' is the third great truth.

[4] The 'way' is the fourth truth.

[5] The sentiment here enunciated is repeated, under various forms, in Dhammapada; the first paragraph in the Sûtra of Forty-two Sections, also, exhibits the same truth.

Desire not either life (bhava) or its opposite; the raging fire of birth, old age, and death burns up the world on every side. 1447

'Seeing the constant toil (unrest) of birth and death we ought to strive to attain a passive state (no-thought), the final goal of Sammata[1], the place of immortality[2] and rest. 1448

'All is empty! neither "self," nor place for "self," but all the world is like a phantasy; this is the way to regard ourselves, as but a heap of composite qualities (sa*m*skâra).' 1449

The nobleman hearing the spoken law forthwith attained the first[3] degree of holiness, he emptied, as it were, the sea of birth and death, one drop[4] alone remaining. 1450

By practising, apart from men, the banishment of all desire he soon attained the one impersonal

---

[1] Sammata or Sammati seems to be the same as Samatha in Pâli (concerning which, see Childers, Pâli Dict. sub voce). The Chinese expression 'yih sin' (one heart) is generally equivalent to 'sammata,' ecstatic union. It cannot here be rendered by samâdhi.

[2] The place of 'sweet dew' (am*ri*ta).

[3] That is, of a Srotâpanna. Spence Hardy, in his Manual of Buddhism, p. 218, also says that Anâthapi*nd*ada entered the first path after hearing the sermon; but in his account the sermon consisted of two stanzas only, 'He who is free from evil desire attains the highest estate and is always in prosperity. He who cuts off demerit, who subdues the mind and attains a state of perfect equanimity, secures Nirvâ*n*a; this is his prosperity.' In this account the idea of 'prosperity' is the same as the 'charity of Nirvâ*n*a' in our version.

[4] This appears to allude to the circumstance that at the dedication of the Vihâra Anâthapi*nd*ada arrived at the third degree of holiness, after which there was but one birth (drop) more to experience before reaching Nirvâ*n*a (Manual of Buddhism, p. 220).

condition, not[1] as common folk do now-a-day who speculate upon the mode of true deliverance; 1451

For he who does not banish sorrow-causing sa*m*skâras does but involve himself in every kind of question; and though he reaches to the highest form of being, yet grasps not the one and only truth; 1452

Erroneous thoughts as to the joy of heaven are still entwined by the fast cords of lust[2]. The nobleman attending to the spoken law the cloud of darkness opened before the shining splendour; 1453

Thus he attained true sight, erroneous views for ever dissipated; even as the furious winds of autumn sway to and fro and scatter all the heaped-up clouds. 1454

He argued[3] not that Î*s*vara was cause, nor did he advocate some cause heretical, nor yet again did he affirm there was no cause for the beginning of the world. 1455

'If the world was made by Î*s*vara deva[4], there should be neither young nor old, first nor after, nor the five ways of birth (transmigration); and when once born there should be no destruction. 1456

'Nor should there be such thing as sorrow or calamity, nor doing wrong nor doing right; for all,

---

[1] These lines appear to be by way of reflection.

[2] 'Lust' in the sense of 'appetite.'

[3] Here follows a long dissertation on the subject of the 'maker' of the world. The theories refuted are (1) that Î*s*vara is maker, (2) that self-nature is the cause, (3) that time is the maker, (4) that self (in the sense of 'universal self') is the cause, (5) that there is no cause.

[4] Here I begin with inverted commas, as if the discourse were either spoken by Buddha or interpolated by A*s*vaghosha.

both pure and impure deeds, these must come from Îsvara deva. 1457

'Again, if Îsvara deva made the world there should be never question (doubt) about the fact, even as a son born of his father ever confesses him and pays him reverence. 1458

'Men when pressed by sore calamity ought not (if Îsvara be creator) to rebel against him, but rather reverence him completely, as the self-existent. Nor ought they to adore more gods than one (other spirits). 1459

'Again, if Îsvara be the maker he should not be called the self-existent[1], because in that he is the maker now he always should have been the maker (ever making). 1460

'But if ever making, then ever self-remembering[2], and therefore not the self-existent one. And if he made without a mind (purpose) then is he like the sucking child; 1461

'But if he made having an (ever prompting) purpose, then is he not, with such a purpose, self-existent. Sorrow and joy spring up in all that lives, these at least are not the works of Îsvara; 1462

'For if he causes grief[3] and joy, he must himself

---

[1] In the sense of 'existing in himself' or independently. How entirely Northern Buddhism changed its character shortly after Asvaghosha's time, is evident from the fact that Avalokitesvara, 'the god who looks down' (in the sense of protector), became an object of almost universal worship, and was afterwards regarded as the creating god.

[2] That is, ever 'purposing' to make, and so not complete in himself.

[3] 'This question, "unde malum et quare,"' was the question that of old met the thoughtful at every turn. And it has always

have love (preference) and hate; but if he loves unduly, or has hatred, he cannot properly be named the self-existent. 1463

'Again, if Î*s*vara be the maker, all living things should silently submit, patient beneath the maker's power, and then what use to practise virtue? 1464

''Twere equal, then, the doing right or wrong, there should be no reward of works; the works themselves being his making, then all things are the same with him, the maker. 1465

'But if all things are one with him, then our deeds, and we who do them, are also self-existent. But if Î*s*vara be uncreated, then all things (being one with him) are uncreated. 1466

'But if you say there is another cause beside him as creator, then Î*s*vara is not the "end of all" (Î*s*vara, who ought to be inexhaustible, is not so), and therefore all that lives may after all be uncreated (without a maker). 1467

'Thus, you see, the thought of Î*s*vara is overthrown in this discussion (*s*âstra); and all such contradictory assertions should be exposed; if not, the blame is ours [1]. 1468

'Again, if it be said self-nature [2] is the maker, this

---

done so. Many of the arguments used in the text may be found in works treating on the subject of 'evil' and its origin.

[1] So the passage must be translated; but if so, it would appear, as before stated, that this discourse on the 'maker' is introduced here parenthetically by A*s*vaghosha, not as spoken by Buddha. No doubt the theories and their confutations were such as prevailed in his day.

[2] By self-nature, or, original nature, is evidently meant 'svabhâva.' The theory of such a cause had evidently gained ground at this time in the North, although it seems unknown amongst

is as faulty as the first assertion; nor has either of the Hetuvidyâ[1] *s*âstras asserted such a thing as this, till now. 1469

'That which depends on nothing cannot as a cause make that which is; but all things round us come from a cause, as the plant comes from the seed; 1470

'We cannot therefore say that all things are produced by self-nature. Again, all things which exist (are made) spring not from one (nature) as a cause; 1471

'And yet you say self-nature is but one, it cannot then be cause of all. If you say that that self-nature pervades and fills all places, 1472

'If it pervades and fills all things, then certainly it cannot make them too; for there would be nothing, then, to make, and therefore this cannot be the cause. 1473

'If, again, it fills all places and yet makes all things that exist, then it should throughout "all time" have made for ever that which is. 1474

'But if you say it made things thus, then there is nothing to be made "in time[2];" know then for certain self-nature cannot be the cause of all. 1475

'Again, they say that that self-nature excludes all

Southern Buddhists. Nâgasena wrote a *S*âstra ('of one *s*loka') to disprove it.

[1] The usual Chinese expression for 'hetuvidyâ' is 'in ming;' here the phrase is 'ming in;' but I suppose this to be either an error, or equivalent with the other. The Hetuvidyâ *s*âstra is a treatise on the 'explanation of causes.'

[2] The argument seems to be that self-nature must have made all things from the first as they are; there is no room therefore for further creation, but things are still made, therefore self-nature cannot be the cause.

gu*n*as[1] (modifications), therefore all things made by it ought likewise to be free from gu*n*as. 1476

'But we see, in fact, that all things in the world are fettered throughout by gu*n*as, therefore, again, we say that self-nature cannot be the cause of all. 1477

'If, again, you say that that self-nature is different from such qualities (gu*n*as), (we answer), since self-nature must have ever caused, it cannot differ in its nature (from itself); 1478

'But if the world (all living things) be different from these qualities (gu*n*as), then self-nature cannot be the cause. Again, if self-nature be unchangeable, so things should also be without decay; 1479

'If we regard self-nature as the cause, then cause and consequence of reason should be one; but because we see decay in all things, we know that they at least are caused. 1480

'Again, if self-nature be the cause, why should we seek to find "escape?" for we ourselves possess this nature; patient then should we endure both birth and death. 1481

'For let us take the case that one may find "escape," self-nature still will re-construct the evil of birth. If self-nature in itself be blind, yet 'tis the maker of the world that sees. 1482

'On this account again it cannot be the maker, because, in this case, cause and effect would differ in their character, but in all the world around us, cause and effect go hand in hand. 1483

'Again, if self-nature have no purpose[2] (aim), it

[1] That is, that it is nirgu*n*a, devoid of qualities.

[2] 'No purpose'—no heart; if we take the two powers of soul

cannot cause that which has such purpose. We know on seeing smoke there must be fire, and cause and result are ever classed together thus. 1484

'We are forbidden, then, to say an unthinking cause can make a thing that has intelligence. The gold of which the cup is made is gold throughout from first to last. 1485

'Self-nature then that makes these things from first to last must permeate all it makes. Once more, if "time" is maker of the world, 'twere needless then to seek "escape," 1486

'For "time" is constant and unchangeable, let us in patience bear the "intervals" of time. The world in its successions has no limits, the "intervals" of time are boundless also. 1487

'Those then who practise a religious life need not rely on "methods" or "expedients." The To-lo-piu Kiu-na[1] (Tripuna gu*n*a *s*âstra?), the one strange *S*âstra in the world, 1488

'Although it has so many theories (utterings), yet still, be it known, it is opposed to any single cause. But if, again, you say that "self[2]" is maker, then surely self should make things pleasingly, 1489

'But now things are not pleasing for oneself, how then is it said that self is maker? But if he did not wish to make things so, then he who wishes for things pleasing, is opposed to self, the maker. 1490

(according to the scholastic method) to be a 'vis cognitiva' and a 'vis effectiva,' the expression in the text appears to correspond with the latter.

[1] I do not know any other way of restoring these symbols than the one I have used. But what is the Tripuna gu*n*a *s*âstra?

[2] 'Self' in the sense of a 'universal cause' co-extensive with the things made.

'Sorrow and joy are not self-existing, how can these be made by "self?" But if we allow that self was maker, there should not be, at least, an evil karman[1]; 1491

'But yet our deeds produce results both good and evil, know then that "self" cannot be maker. But perhaps you say "self" is the maker according to occasion[2] (time), and then the occasion ought to be for good alone; 1492

'But as good and evil both result from "cause," it cannot be that "self" has made it so. But if you adopt the argument—there is no maker—then it is useless practising expedients[3]; 1493

'All things are fixed and certain of themselves, what good to try to make them otherwise? Deeds of every kind, done in the world, do, notwithstanding, bring forth every kind of fruit; 1494

'Therefore we argue all things that exist are not without some cause or other. There is both "mind" and "want of mind," all things come from fixed causation; 1495

'The world and all therein is not the result of "nothing" as a cause.' The nobleman[4] (householder), his heart receiving light, perceived throughout the most excellent system of truth, 1496

Simple, and of wisdom born; thus firmly settled

---

[1] There should not be works producing birth in one of the evil ways.

[2] I do not understand the point here; literally the passage is 'saying self according to time makes'—the Chinese 'ts'ui shi' means 'whenever convenient,' or 'at a good time;' so that the passage may mean 'but if you say that self creates only when so prompted by itself.'

[3] That is, using means for salvation or escape from sorrow.

[4] Here the narrative seems to take up the thread dropped at v. 1451.

in the true doctrine he lowly bent in worship at the feet of Buddha and with closed hands made his request: 1497

'I dwell indeed at *S*râvastî (Sâvatthi)[1], a land rich in produce, and enjoying peace; Prasena*g*it (Pasenit)[2] is the great king thereof, the offspring of the "lion" family; 1498

'His high renown and fame spread everywhere, reverenced by all both far and near. Now am I wishful there to found a Vihâra, I pray you of your tenderness accept it from me. 1499

'I know the heart of Buddha has no preferences, nor does he seek a resting-place from labour, but on behalf of all that lives refuse not my request.' 1500

Buddha, knowing the householder's heart, that his great charity was now the moving cause, untainted and unselfish charity, nobly considerate of the heart of all that lives 1501

(He said), 'Now you have seen the true doctrine, your guileless heart loves to exercise its charity, for wealth and money are inconstant treasures, 'twere better quickly to bestow such things on others. 1502

'For when a treasury has been burnt, whatever precious things may have escaped the fire, the wise

[1] She-po-ti; evidently a Pâli or Prâkrit form of the Sanskrit *S*râvastî. The Chinese explanation of this name is (as found in the next line) a 'country of abundance.' It has been identified by General Cunningham with Sâhet Mâhet.

[2] Po-sze-nih, i.e. Prasena*g*it (victorious army). With respect to this king, we know from Hiouen Thsang (Jul. II, 317) that he did not belong to the *S*âkya race, but he became a convert to Buddhism. His son Virû*dh*aka massacred a number of the *S*âkyas, 'and the ground was covered with their dead bodies as with pieces of straw' (Jul. II, 317). The king is here described as belonging to the Si*m*ha race; probably he was a Scyth, of the same family as the Va*gg*is, one tribe of whom was called the 'lion' tribe.

man, knowing their inconstancy, gives freely, doing acts of kindness with his saved possessions. 1503

'But the niggard guards them carefully, fearing to lose them, worn by anxiety, but never fearing (worst of all!) "inconstancy[1]," and that accumulated sorrow, when he loses all! 1504

'There is a proper time and a proper mode in charity, just as the vigorous warrior goes to battle, so is the man "able to give," he also is an able warrior; a champion strong and wise in action. 1505

'The charitable man is loved by all, well-known and far-renowned! his friendship prized by the gentle and the good, in death his heart at rest and full of joy! 1506

'He suffers no repentance, no tormenting fear, nor is he born a wretched ghost or demon! this is the opening flower of his reward, the fruit that follows—hard to conjecture[2]! 1507

'In all the six conditions born there is no sweet companion like pure charity; if born a Deva or a man, then charity brings worship and renown on every hand; 1508

'If born among the lower creatures (beasts), the result of charity will follow in contentment got; wisdom leads the way to fixed composure without dependence and without number[3]. 1509

'And if we even reach the immortal path, still by continuous acts of charity we fulfil ourselves in

---

[1] 'Inconstancy,' or 'death.'

[2] This is a singular expression, implying that the character of a good man's final condition is difficult to describe: 'it has not entered the heart.'

[3] These two lines appear to be irrelevant; nor do I understand the last phrase 'without number,' in its connection with the context.

consequence of kindly charity done elsewhere. Training ourselves in the eightfold [1] path of recollection, 1510

'In every thought the heart is filled with joy, firm fixed in holy contemplation (samâdhi), by meditation still we add to wisdom, able to see aright (the cause of) birth and death; 1511

'Having beheld aright the cause of these, then follows in due order perfect deliverance. The charitable man discarding earthly wealth, nobly excludes the power of covetous desire; 1512

'Loving and compassionate now, he gives with reverence and banishes all hatred, envy, anger. So plainly may we see the fruit of charity, putting away all covetous and unbelieving ways, 1513

'The bands of sorrow all destroyed, this is the fruit of kindly charity. Know then! the charitable man has found the cause of final rescue; 1514

'Even as the man who plants the sapling, thereby secures the shade, the flowers, the fruit (of the tree full grown); the result of charity is even so, its reward is joy and the great Nirvâ*n*a. 1515

'The charity which unstores [2] wealth leads to returns of well-stored fruit. Giving away our food we get more strength, giving away our clothes we get more beauty, 1516

'Founding religious rest-places [3] (pure abodes) we

[1] The eight recollections (nim); doubtless these are the eight 'samâpattis' (attainments or endowments), concerning which we may consult Childers' Pâli Dict., sub 'samâpatti.'

[2] That is, which does not store up wealth, but unstores it to give away. There seems to be here a tacit allusion to Sudatta's wealth, which he unstored and gave in charity by purchasing the garden of *G*eta.

[3] That is, Vihâras.

reap the perfect fruit of the best charity. There is a way of giving, seeking pleasure by it; there is a way of giving, coveting to get more; 1517

'Some also give away to get a name for charity, others to get the happiness of heaven, others to avoid the pain of being poor (hereafter), but yours, O friend! is a charity without such thoughts, 1518

'The highest and the best degree of charity without self-interest or thought of getting more. What your heart inclines you now to do, let it be quickly done and well completed! 1519

'The uncertain and the lustful heart goes wandering here and there, but the pure eyes (of virtue) opening, the heart comes back and rests[1]!' The nobleman accepting Buddha's teaching, his kindly heart receiving yet more light, 1520

He invited Upatishya[2], his excellent friend, to accompany him on his return to Kosala; and then going round to select a pleasant site, 1521

He saw the garden of the heir-apparent, *G*eta, the groves and limpid streams most pure. Proceeding where the prince was dwelling, he asked for leave to buy the ground; 1522

The prince, because he valued it so much, at first was not inclined to sell, but said at last: 'If you can cover it with gold then, but not else, you may possess it[3].' 1523

---

[1] These two lines are probably proverbial, something of this kind, 'the uncertain, amorous mind is profligate (wandering), the enlightened man comes to himself.'

[2] Upatissa is the same as *S*âriputra. Hiouen Thsang (Jul. II, 296) says that Buddha sent *S*âriputra with Sudatta, to advise and counsel him.

[3] The famous contract between Sudatta and *G*eta, the heir-apparent, is well known, and may be read in all the translations of the

The nobleman, his heart rejoicing, forthwith began to spread his gold. Then *G*eta said: 'I will not give, why then spread you your gold?' 1524

The nobleman replied, 'Not give; why then said you, "Fill it with yellow gold?"' And thus they differed and contended both, till they resorted to the magistrate. 1525

Meanwhile the people whispered much about his unwonted[1] (charity), and *G*eta too, knowing the man's sincerity, asked more about the matter: what his reasons were. On his reply, 'I wish to found a Vihâra, 1526

'And offer it to the Tathâgata and all his Bhikshu followers,' the prince, hearing the name of Buddha, received at once illumination, 1527

And only took one half the gold, desiring to share in the foundation: 'Yours is the land (he said), but mine the trees; these will I give to Buddha as my share in the offering.' 1528

Then the noble took the land, *G*eta the trees, and settled both in trust on *S*âriputra. Then they began to build the hall, labouring night and day to finish it; 1529

Lofty it rose and choicely decorated, as one of the four kings' palaces, in just proportions, following the

---

lives of Buddha. There is a representation of the proceeding in plate lvii (Bharhut Stûpa). I may observe here that the figure immediately in front (by the side of *G*eta, the prince, who is apparently giving away the trees, whilst Sudatta below him is giving the land), whistling with thumb and forefinger, and waving the robe, is typical of a number of others in these sculptures similarly engaged (see e.g. plate xiii [outer face]).

[1] Or, the unwonted circumstance; or, the 'unusual' character of Sudatta.

directions which Buddha had declared the right ones; 1530

Never yet so great a miracle as this! the priests shone in the streets of *S*râvastî! Tathâgata, seeing the divine shelter, with all his holy ones resorted to the place to rest[1]; 1531

No followers there to bow in prostrate service, his followers rich in wisdom only. The nobleman reaping his reward, at the end of life ascended up to heaven, 1532

Leaving to sons and grandsons a good foundation, through successive generations, to plough the field of merit. 1533

Varga 19. Interview between Father and Son.

Buddha in the Magadha country (employing himself in) converting all kinds of unbelievers[2] (heretics), entirely changed them by the one and self-same[3] law he preached, even as the sun drowns with its brightness all the stars. 1534

Then leaving the city of the five mountains[4] with the company of his thousand disciples, and with a

---

[1] The expression 'to rest' may also mean 'to observe the rainy season rest,' if the ordinance of Wass had been enacted at this time.

[2] 'I tau,' different persuasions. It was during Buddha's stay near Râ*g*agr*i*ha that different rules for the direction of the 'Order' were framed. See Romantic Legend, p. 340 seq. There is no reference in our text to the stately march of Buddha to Kapilavastu, or of the different messages sent to him, as related by Bigandet, p. 160, and in Hardy's Manual of Buddhism, pp. 198, 199, also Romantic Legend, p. 349.

[3] Yih-mi-fă, 'one-taste law.'

[4] That is, Râ*g*agr*i*ha; the city surrounded by five mountains.

great multitude who went before and came after him, he advanced towards the Ni-kin[1] mountain, 1535

Near Kapilavastu; and there he conceived in himself a generous purpose to prepare an offering according to his religious doctrine[2] to present to his father, the king. 1536

And now in anticipation of his coming the royal teacher (purohita) and the chief minister had sent forth certain officers and their attendants to observe on the right hand and the left (what was taking place); and they soon espied him (Buddha) as he advanced or halted on the way. 1537

Knowing that Buddha was now returning to his country they hastened back[3] and quickly announced the tidings, 'The prince who wandered forth afar to obtain enlightenment, having fulfilled his aim, is now coming back.' 1538

The king hearing the news was greatly rejoiced, and forthwith went out with his gaudy equipage to meet (his son); and the whole body of gentry (sse) belonging to the country, went forth with him in his company. 1539

Gradually advancing he beheld Buddha from afar, his marks of beauty sparkling with splendour two-

---

[1] This may be the Nyagrodha garden alluded to by Spence Hardy, Manual of Buddhism, p. 200, and also in the Romantic Legend, p. 350. The symbols ni-kin, however, seem to have some other equivalent, such as Nigantha.

[2] This of course means 'a religious offering,' or 'service of religion,' i. e. agreeable to religion.

[3] There is no reference here to their conversion as in the Southern accounts. The account in the Manual of Buddhism, p. 200, of the king's preparation to meet his son, bears the appearance of a late date, and in exaggeration surpasses all we find in the Northern books.

fold greater than of yore; placed in the middle of the great congregation he seemed to be even as Brahma râga. 1540

Descending from his chariot and advancing with dignity, (the king) was anxious lest there should be any religious[1] difficulty (in the way of instant recognition); and now beholding his beauty he inwardly rejoiced, but his mouth found no words to utter. 1541

He reflected, too, how that he was still dwelling among the unconverted throng, whilst his son had advanced and become a saint (*Ri*shi); and although he was his son, yet as he now occupied the position of a religious lord[2], he knew not by what name to address him. 1542

Furthermore he thought with himself how he had long ago desired earnestly (this interview), which now had happened unawares[3] (without arrangement). Meantime his son in silence took a seat, perfectly composed and with unchanged countenance. 1543

Thus for some time sitting opposite each other, with no expression of feeling (the king reflected thus)[4], 'How desolate and sad does he now make my heart, as that of a man, who, fainting, longs for water, upon the road espies a fountain pure and cold; 1544

'With haste he speeds towards it and longs to

---

[1] That is, whether religion required a greeting first from him, the father.

[2] An Arhat or distinguished saint.

[3] Without any summons.

[4] I supply this (as in many other cases); in the text we are without direction when and where to bring in these explanatory phrases.

drink, when suddenly the spring dries up and disappears. Thus, now I see my son, his well-known features as of old; 1545

'But how estranged his heart! and how his manner high and lifted up! There are no grateful outflowings of soul, his feelings seem unwilling to express themselves; cold and vacant (there he sits); and like a thirsty man before a dried-up fountain (so am I).' 1546

Still distant thus (they sat), with crowding thoughts rushing through the mind, their eyes full met, but no responding joy; each looking at the other, seemed as one who thinking of a distant friend, gazes by accident upon his pictured form[1]. 1547

'That you' (the king reflected) 'who of right might rule the world, even as that Mândhât*ri* râ*g*a, should now go begging here and there your food! what joy or charm has such a life as this? 1548

'Composed and firm as Sumeru[2], with marks of beauty bright as the sunlight, with dignity of step like the ox king, fearless as any lion, 1549

'And yet receiving not the tribute of the world, but begging food sufficient for your body's nourishment!' Buddha, knowing his father's mind, still kept to his own filial purpose. 1550

And then to open out his[3] mind, and moved with

---

[1] This translation is doubtful; there is some question as to the correct reading.

[2] Buddha is often called 'the golden mountain,' and in this particular, as in many others, there is in Buddhism a marked resemblance with traditions known among primitive races; Bel, for example, is called 'the great mountain.'

[3] That is, as I understand it, to move his father's mind. It may be understood, however, in the sense of carrying out his own purpose.

pity for the multitude of people, by his miraculous power he rose in mid-air, and with his hands (appeared) to grasp the sun and moon[1]. 1551

Then he walked to and fro in space, and underwent all kinds of transformation, dividing his body into many parts, then joining all in one again. 1552

Treading firm on water as on dry land, entering the earth as in the water, passing through walls of stone without impediment, from the right side and the left water and fire produced[2]! 1553

The king, his father, filled with joy, now dismissed all thought of son and father[3]; then upon a lotus throne, seated in space, he (Buddha) for his father's sake declared the law. 1554

'I know that the king's heart (is full of) love and recollection, and that for his son's sake he adds grief to grief; but now let the bands of love that bind him, thinking of his son, be instantly unloosed and utterly destroyed. 1555

'Ceasing from thoughts of love, let your calmed mind receive from me, your son, religious nourishment; such as no son has offered yet to father, such do I present to you the king, my father. 1556

'And what no father yet has from a son received, now from your son you may accept, a gift miraculous for any mortal king to enjoy, and seldom had by any heavenly king! 1557

'The way superlative of life immortal[4] (sweet

[1] Here we have an account of the grotesque miracles that distinguish this part of the narrative in all Northern Buddhist books; see Romantic Legend, p. 352.

[2] This is probably the twin-miracle (yamaka-pâ*t*ihâriya*m*) referred to by Mr. Rhys Davids, Birth Stories, p. 105 n.

[3] That is, of the relative duties of father and son.

[4] This phrase, 'the way of sweet dew,' I can only restore to 'the

dew) I offer now the Mahârâga; from accumulated deeds comes birth, and as the result of deeds comes recompense; 1558

'Knowing then that deeds bring fruit, how diligent should you be to rid yourself of worldly deeds! how careful that in the world your deeds should be only good and gentle! 1559

'Fondly affected by relationship or firmly bound by mutual ties of love, at end of life the soul (spirit) goes forth alone,—then, only our good deeds befriend us.— 1560

'Whirled in the five ways of the wheel of life, three kinds of deeds produce three kinds of birth [1], and these are caused by lustful hankering, each kind different in its character. 1561

'Deprive these of their power by the practice now of (proper) deeds of body and of word; by such right preparation day and night strive to get rid of all confusion of the mind and practise silent (contemplation); 1562

'Only this brings profit in the end, besides this there is no reality; for be sure! the three worlds are but as the froth and bubble of the sea. 1563

'Would you have pleasure, or would you practise that which brings it near? then prepare yourself by

way of immortality;' of course it means 'immortality' (amritam) according to Buddhist ideas, that is, Nirvâna. Childers tells us that 'Buddhaghosa says that Nirvâna is called amata, because not being born it does not decay or die' (Pâli Dict., sub amatam). This definition of Nirvâna is the usual one found in Chinese books, that state which admits 'neither of birth nor death.'

[1] Referring to the three inferior kinds of birth, as a beast, a preta, or in hell.

deeds that bring the fourth birth[1]: but (still) the
five ways in the wheel of birth and death are like
the uncertain wanderings of the stars; 1564
'For heavenly beings too must suffer change:
how shall we find with men (a hope of) constancy;
Nirvâ*n*a! that is the chief rest; composure! that
the best of all enjoyments! 1565
'The five indulgences (pleasures) enjoyed by
mortal kings are fraught with danger and distress,
like dwelling with a poisonous snake; what pleasure,
for a moment, can there be in such a case? 1566
'The wise man sees the world as compassed
round with burning flames; he fears always, nor
can he rest till he has banished, once for all, birth,
age, and death. 1567
'Infinitely quiet is the place where the wise man
finds his abode; no need of arms (instruments) or
weapons there! no elephants or horses, chariots or
soldiers there! 1568
'Subdued the power of covetous desire and angry
thoughts and ignorance, there's nothing left in the
wide world to conquer! Knowing what sorrow is,
he cuts away the cause of sorrow; 1569
'This destroyed, by practising right means, rightly
enlightened in the four true principles[2], he casts off
fear and escapes the evil ways of birth.' The king
when first he saw his wondrous spiritual power (of
miracle) rejoiced in heart; 1570
But now his feelings deeply affected by the joy
of (hearing) truth, he became a perfect vessel for
receiving true religion, and with clasped hands he

[1] The 'fourth birth' would be as 'a man;' but it may refer here to birth as 'a Deva.'

[2] That is, in the 'four truths.'

breathed forth his praise: 'Wonderful indeed! the fruit of your resolve (oath)[1] completed thus! 1571

'Wonderful indeed! the overwhelming sorrow passed away! Wonderful indeed, this gain to me! At first my sorrowing heart was heavy, but now my sorrow has brought forth only profit! 1572

'Wonderful indeed! for now, to-day, I reap the full fruit of a begotten son. It was right he should reject the choice pleasures of a monarch (conqueror); it was right he should so earnestly and with diligence practise penance; 1573

'It was right he should cast off his family and kin; it was right he should cut off every feeling of love and affection. The old *Ri*shi kings boasting of their penance gained no merit; 1574

'But you, living in a peaceful, quiet place, have done all and completed all; yourself at rest now you give rest to others, moved by your mighty sympathy (compassion) for all that lives! 1575

'If you had kept your first estate with men, and as a *K*akravartin monarch ruled the world, possessing then no self-depending power of miracle, how could my soul have then received deliverance? 1576

'Then there would have been no excellent law declared, causing me such joy to-day; no! had you been a universal sovereign, the bonds of birth and death would still have been unsevered; 1577

'But now you have escaped from birth and death; the great pain of transmigration overcome, you are able, for the sake of every creature, widely to preach the law of life immortal (sweet dew), 1578

---

[1] That is, the oath to become enlightened and a deliverer.

'And to exhibit thus your power miraculous, and (show) the deep and wide power of wisdom; the grief of birth and death eternally destroyed, you now have risen far above both gods and men. 1579

'You might have kept the holy state of a *K*akravartin monarch; but no such good as this would have resulted.' Thus his words of praise concluded, filled with increased reverence and religious love, 1580

He who occupied the honoured place of a royal father, bowed down respectfully and did obeisance. Then all the people of the kingdom, beholding Buddha's miraculous power, 1581

And having heard the deep and excellent law, seeing, moreover, the king's grave reverence, with clasped hands bowed down and worshipped. Possessed with deep portentous thoughts, 1582

Satiated with sorrows attached to lay-life, they all conceived a wish to leave their homes[1]. The princes, too, of the *S*âkya tribe, their minds enlightened to perceive the perfect fruit of righteousness, 1583

Entirely satiated with the glittering joys of the world, forsaking home, rejoiced to join his company (become hermits). Ânanda, Nanda, Kin-pi (Kimbila)[2], Anuruddha, 1584

Nandupananda, with *K*u*nd*adana[3], all these principal nobles and others of the *S*âkya family, 1585

---

[1] That is, to become mendicants, or religious followers of Buddha.

[2] The conversion of Nanda &c. is referred to in Spence Hardy's Manual of Buddhism, p. 227. I have restored Kin-pi to Kimbila from this authority, p. 228. Perhaps also in the Romantic Legend, p. 386, it ought to have been so restored.

[3] *K*un-*k*a-to-na. I do not remember having met with this name before. It may be meant for *Kh*andaka, see Schiefner, 'Lebensbeschreibung *S*âkyamuni's,' p. 266.

From the teaching of Buddha became disciples and accepted the law. The sons of the great minister of state, Udâyin being the chief, 1586

With all the royal princes following in order became recluses. Moreover, the son of Atalî, whose name was Upâli, 1587

Seeing all these princes and the sons of the chief minister becoming hermits, his mind opening for conversion, he, too, received the law of renunciation. 1588

The royal father seeing his son possessing the great qualities of *Ri*ddhi, himself entered on the calm flowings (of thought), the gate of the true law of eternal life. 1589

Leaving his kingly estate and country, lost in meditation, he drank sweet dew. Practising (his religious duties) in solitude, silent and contemplative he dwelt in his palace, a royal *Ri*shi. 1590

Tathâgata following a peaceable[1] life, recognised fully by his tribe, repeating the joyful news of religion, gladdened the hearts of all his kinsmen hearing him. 1591

And now, it being the right time for begging food, he entered the Kapila country (Kapilavastu); in the city all the lords and ladies, in admiration, raised this chant of praise: 1592

'Siddhârtha! fully enlightened! has come back again!' The news flying quickly in and out of doors, the great and small came forth to see him; 1593

Every door and every window crowded, climbing on shoulders[2], bending down the eyes, they gazed

[1] Or, living in peaceful prosecution of his work.

[2] Or it may be 'shoulder to shoulder.'

upon the marks of beauty on his person, shining and glorious! 1594

Wearing his Kashâya garment outside, the glory of his person from within shone forth, like the sun's perfect wheel; within, without, he seemed one mass of splendour[1]. 1595

Those who beheld were filled with sympathising[2] joy; their hands conjoined, they wept (for gladness)[3]; and so they watched him as he paced with dignity the road, his form collected, all his organs well-controlled! 1596

His lovely body exhibiting the perfection[4] of religious beauty, his dignified compassion adding to their regretful joy! his shaven head, his personal beauty sacrificed! his body clad in dark and sombre vestment, 1597

His manner natural and plain, his unadorned appearance; his circumspection as he looked upon the earth in walking! 'He who ought to have had held over him the feather-shade' (they said), 'whose hands should grasp "the reigns of the flying[5] dragon," 1598

'See how he walks in daylight on the dusty road! holding his alms-dish, going to beg! Gifted enough to tread down every enemy, lovely enough to gladden woman's heart, 1599

---

[1] The glory of his person within and without, together, like a mass of light.

[2] Compassion and joy.

[3] That is, they wept for pity and for joy.

[4] Manifesting religious uprightness or rectitude.

[5] This appears to be a Chinese phrase, adapted perhaps from some expression in the Sanskrit original signifying 'supreme power.'

'With glittering vesture and with godlike crown reverenced he might have been by servile crowds! But now, his manly beauty hidden, with heart restrained, and outward form subdued, 1600

'Rejecting the much-coveted and glorious apparel, his shining body clad with garments grey, what aim, what object, now! Hating the five delights that move the world, 1601

'Forsaking virtuous wife and tender child, loving the solitude, he wanders friendless; hard, indeed, for virtuous wife through the long night[1], cherishing her grief; 1602

'And now to hear he is a hermit! She enquires not now (so lost to life) of the royal *S*uddhodana if he has seen his son or not! 1603

'But as she views his beauteous person, (to think) his altered form is now a hermit's! hating his home, still full of love; his father, too, what rest for him (they say)! 1604

'And then his loving child Râhula, weeping with constant sorrowful desire! And now to see no change, or heart-relenting; and this the end of such enlightenment! 1605

'All these attractive marks, the proofs of a religious calling, whereas, when born, all said, these are marks of a "great man," who ought to receive tribute from the four seas! 1606

'And now to see what he has come to! all these predictive words vain and illusive.' Thus they talked together, the gossiping multitude, with confused accents. 1607

Tathâgata, his heart unaffected, felt no joy and

[1] I. e. her life of widowhood.

no regret. But he was moved by equal love to all the world, his one desire that men should escape the grief of lust; 1608

To cause the root of virtue to increase, and for the sake of coming ages, to leave the marks of self-denial[1] behind him, to dissipate the clouds and mists of sensual desire, 1609

He entered, thus intentioned, on the town to beg. He accepted food both good or bad, whatever came, from rich or poor, without distinction; having filled his alms-dish, he then returned back to the solitude. 1610

VARGA 20. RECEIVING THE *G*ETAVANA VIHÂRA.

The lord of the world, having converted[2] the people of Kapilavastu according to (their several) circumstances[3], his work being done, he went with the great body of his followers, 1611

And directed his way to the country of Ko*s*ala, where dwelt king Prasena*g*it (Po-se-nih). The *G*etavana was now fully adorned, and its halls and courts carefully prepared; 1612

The fountains and streams flowed through the garden which glittered with flowers and fruit; rare birds sat by the pools (water side), and on the land

---

[1] Little desire.

[2] The expression in the original is 'having opened for conversion.'

[3] It is not necessarily 'according to their circumstances,' but it may also be rendered 'according to circumstances,' or 'as the occasion required.'

they sang in sweet concord, according to their kind; 1613

Beautiful in every way as the palace of Mount Kilas (Kailâsa)[1], (such was the *G*etavana.) Then the noble friend of the orphans, surrounded by his attendants, who met him on the way, 1614

Scattering flowers and burning incense, invited the lord to enter the *G*etavana. In his hand he carried a golden dragon-pitcher[2], and bending low upon his knees he poured the flowing water 1615

As a sign of the gift of the *G*etavana Vihâra for the use of the priesthood throughout the world[3]. The lord then received it, with the prayer[4] that 'overruling all evil influences it might give the kingdom permanent rest, 1616

'And that the happiness of Anâthapi*nd*ada might flow out in countless streams.' Then the king Prasena*g*it, hearing that the lord had come, 1617

With his royal equipage went to the *G*etavana to worship at the lord's feet[5]. (Having arrived) and

---

[1] Mount Kailâsa, the fabulous residence of Kuvera; the paradise of *S*iva.

[2] In the Barahut sculpture there is a figure carrying a pitcher in the act of pouring out the water; but the figure is not kneeling.

[3] 'The four quarters,' that is, 'the world.'

[4] 'The prayer,' the 'devout incantation;' it has often been questioned whether 'prayer' is possible with Buddhists; the expression in the Chinese is the same as that used for prayer in other books; but it may of course denote sincere or earnest desire, coming from the heart.

[5] There are various representations of Prasena*g*it going to the *G*etavana in the Barahut sculptures. In plate xiii (Cunningham's Barahut) the Vihâra is represented, the wheel denoting the sermon which Buddha preached; the waving of garments and whistling with fingers denoting the joy of the hearers.

taken a seat on one side, with clasped hands he spake to Buddha thus: 1618

'O that my unworthy and obscure kingdom should thus suddenly have met such fortune! For how can misfortunes or frequent calamities possibly affect it, (in the presence of) so great a man? 1619

'And now that I have seen your sacred features, I may perhaps partake of the converting streams of your teaching. A town although it is composed of many sections[1], yet both ignoble and holy persons may enter the surpassing[2] stream; 1620

'And so the wind which fans the perfumed grove causes the scents to unite and form one pleasant breeze; and as the birds which collect on Mount Sumeru (are many), and the various shades that blend in shining gold, 1621

'So an assembly may consist of persons of different capacities, individually insignificant, but a glorious body. The desert master by nourishing the *Ri*shi, procured a birth as the san-tsuh (three leg or foot) star[3]; 1622

'Worldly profit is fleeting and perishable, religious (holy) profit is eternal and inexhaustible; a man though a king is full of trouble, a common man, who is holy, has everlasting rest.' 1623

---

[1] I cannot be sure of this translation; yet I can suggest no other. The line is 部雖處凡品.

[2] 'The victorious stream;' this may refer to the Rapti, on the banks of which *S*râvastî was situated. The object of the allusion is that as both rich and poor, noble and ignoble may enter the stream of the river, so all may seek the benefit of the stream of religious doctrine.

[3] I am unable to explain the reference here; nor do I know what the 'three-footed star' can be.

Buddha knowing the state of the king's heart,—that he rejoiced in religion as *S*akrarâ*g*a[1],—considered the two obstacles that weighted him, viz. too great love of money, and of external pleasures[2]; 1624

Then seizing the opportunity, and knowing the tendencies of his heart, he began, for the king's sake, to preach: 'Even those who, by evil karman[3], have been born in low degree, when they see a person of virtuous character, feel reverence for him; 1625

'How much rather ought an independent[4] king, who by his previous conditions of life has acquired much merit, when he encounters Buddha, to conceive even more reverence. Nor is it difficult to understand, 1626

'That a country should enjoy more rest and peace, by the presence of Buddha, than if he were not to dwell therein[5]. And now, as I briefly declare my law, let the Mahârâ*g*a listen and weigh my words, 1627

'And hold fast that which I deliver! See now the end of my perfected merit[6], my life is done,

---

[1] General Cunningham (Barahut Stûpa, plate xiii) has remarked that the Preaching Hall visited by Prasena*g*it resembles in detail the Palace of *S*akrarâ*g*a; the reference in the text seems to allude to this.

[2] Reference is often made in Buddhist books to the self-indulgence of king Prasena*g*it. Compare section xxix of the Chinese Dhammapada.

[3] That is, in consequence of evil deeds.

[4] This expression 'tsze tsai,' which I render 'independent,' means 'self-sufficient,' or 'self-existing;' the reference is probably to a lord paramount (samrâ*g*).

[5] This exordium appears intended to take down the pride of the king.

[6] Buddha points to himself as having gained the end of all his

there is for me no further body or spirit, but freedom from all ties of kith or kin! 1628

'The good or evil deeds we do from first to last (beginning to end) follow us as shadows; most exalted then the deeds (karman) of the king of the law[1]. The prince[2] (son) who cherishes his people, 1629

'In the present life gains renown, and hereafter ascends to heaven; but by disobedience and neglect of duty, present distress is felt and future misery! 1630

'As in old times Lui-'ma (lean horse)[3] râ*g*a, by obeying the precepts, was born in heaven, whilst Kin-pu (gold step) râ*g*a, doing wickedly, at the end of life was born in misery. 1631

'Now then, for the sake of the great king, I will briefly relate the good and evil law (the law of good and evil). The great requirement[4] is a loving heart! to regard the people as we do an only son, 1632

'Not to oppress, not to destroy; to keep in due check every member of the body, to forsake unrighteous doctrine and walk in the straight path; not to exalt oneself by treading down others (or inferiors), 1633

'But to comfort and befriend those in suffer-

---

previous meritorious conduct, in the attainment of his present condition.

[1] Dharmarâ*g*a, an epithet of every Buddha (Eitel).

[2] The symbol here stands for 'son;' it may mean 'prince' in the sense of 'son of the king of the law' (fă wang tseu), which is a common one in Buddhist books, and is often rendered by 'Kumâra bhûta.'

[3] Lui-'ma may be a phonetic equivalent of the name of the king, or a translation of the name, viz. K*r*i*s*â*s*va. So also in the next line Hira*n*yaka*s*ipu may be meant.

[4] The 'great deficiency,' or 'the great need.'

ing; not to exercise oneself in false theories[1] (treatises), nor to ponder much on kingly dignity (strength), nor to listen to the smooth words of false teachers; 1634

'Not to vex oneself by austerities, not to exceed (or transgress) the right rules of kingly conduct, but to meditate on Buddha and weigh his righteous law, and to put down and adjust all that is contrary to religion; 1635

'To exhibit true superiority by virtuous conduct and the highest exercise of reason, to meditate deeply on the vanity of earthly things, to realise the fickleness of life by constant recollection; 1636

'To exalt the mind to the highest point of reflection, to seek sincere faith (truth) with firm purpose; to retain an inward sense of happiness resulting from oneself[2], (and to look forward to) increased happiness hereafter; 1637

'To lay up a good name for distant ages, this will secure the favour of Tathâgata[3], as men now loving sweet fruit will hereafter be praised by their descendants[4]. 1638

'There is a way of darkness out of light[5], there is a way of light out of darkness; there is darkness which follows after the gloom (signs of gloom),

[1] In false theories and 'vidyâs' (ming).

[2] Self-dependent happiness.

[3] Whether the phrase '*gu*-lai' ought to be here translated Tathâgata, or whether it refers simply to 'future generations,' is a question.

[4] This again is an uncertain translation, although the meaning is plain, that those who here love 'sweet fruit,' will not set their children's teeth on edge hereafter.

[5] In this and the following lines the reference is apparently to the possibility of growing worse or better by our deeds.

there is a light which causes the brightening of light. 1639

'The wise man leaving first principles[1], should go on to get more light[2]; evil words will be repeated far and wide by the multitude, but there are few to follow good direction; 1640

'It is impossible however to avoid result of works[3], the doer cannot escape; if there had been no first works, there had been in the end no result of doing, 1641

'—No reward for good, no hereafter joy—; but because works are done, there is no escape. Let us then practise good works; 1642

'(Let us) inspect our thoughts that we do no evil, because as we sow so we reap[4]. As when enclosed in a four-stone [stone or rock-encircled] mountain, there is no escape or place of refuge for any one, 1643

'So within this mountain-wall of old age, birth, disease, and death, there is no escape for the world[5]. Only by considering and practising the true law can we escape from this sorrow-piled mountain. 1644

'There is, indeed, no constancy in the world, the end of the pleasures of sense is as the lightning flash, whilst old age and death are as the piercing bolts; what profit, then, in doing (practising) iniquity[6]! 1645

---

[1] San p'hin, the 'three sections.'

[2] 'Ought to learn from first to last, illumination.' Does it refer to books or vidyâs (ming) of instruction?

[3] There is not such a thing as 'not making fruit,' or the fruit of 'not making;' but the former is the more likely. 'Fruit,' of course, refers to the result of works.

[4] 'Because as we ourselves do, we ourselves receive.'

[5] For all living creatures.

[6] 'Why then ought we to do iniquity!' (fi fă.)

'All the ancient conquering kings, who were as gods[1] on earth, thought by their strength to overcome decay[2]; but after a brief life they too disappeared[3]. 1646

'The Kalpa-fire will melt Mount Sumeru, the water of the ocean will be dried up, how much less can our human frame, which is as a bubble, expect to endure for long upon the earth! 1647

'The fierce wind scatters the thick mists, the sun's rays encircle (hide) Mount Sumeru, the fierce fire licks up the place of moisture, so things are ever born once more to be destroyed! 1648

'The body is a thing (vessel) of unreality, kept through the suffering of the long night[4], pampered by wealth, living idly and in carelessness, 1649

'Death suddenly comes and it is carried away as rotten wood in the stream! The wise man expecting these changes with diligence strives against sloth; 1650

'The dread of birth and death acts as a spur to keep him from lagging on the road; he frees himself from engagements, he is not occupied with self-pleasing, he is not entangled by any of the cares of life, 1651

'He holds to no business, seeks no friendships, engages in no learned career, nor yet wholly separates himself from it; for his learning is the wisdom

[1] Who were as Îsvaradeva.

[2] Literally, 'to conquer emptiness;' it may mean to 'surpass the sky'—to climb to heaven.

[3] They were ground to dust and disappeared.

[4] The suffering of the 'long night' (the period of constant transmigration) keeps and guards it.

of not-perceiving[1] wisdom, but yet perceiving that which tells him of his own impermanence; 1652

'Having a body, yet keeping aloof from defilement, he learns to regard defilement as the greatest evil. (He knows) that tho' born in the Arûpa world, there is yet no escape from the changes of time; 1653

'His learning, then, is to acquire the changeless body; for where no change is, there is peace. Thus the possession of this changeful body is the foundation of all sorrow. 1654

'Therefore, again, all who are wise make this their aim—to seek a bodiless condition; all the various orders of sentient creatures, from the indulgence of lust, derive pain; 1655

'Therefore all those in this condition ought to conceive a heart, loathing lust; putting away and loathing this condition, then they shall receive no more pain; 1656

'Though born in a state with or without an external form, the certainty of future change is the root of sorrow; for so long as there is no perfect cessation of personal being, there can be, certainly, no absence of personal desire; 1657

'Beholding, in this way, the character of the three worlds, their inconstancy and unreality, the presence of ever-consuming pain, how can the wise man seek enjoyment therein? 1658

'When a tree is burning with fierce flames how

[1] 'The wisdom of not perceiving;' the symbol 'sheu' corresponds with 'vedanâ,' perception, or sensation. The meaning therefore is that true wisdom depends not on the power of sense; but yet he perceives by his senses that he (his body) is impermanent.

can the birds congregate therein? The wise man, who is regarded as an enlightened sage, without this knowledge is ignorant; 1659

'Having this knowledge, then true wisdom dawns; without it, there is no enlightenment. To get this wisdom is the one aim, to neglect it is the mistake of life. 1660.

'All the teaching of the schools should be centred here; without it is no true reason. To recount this excellent system is not for those who dwell in family connection; 1661

'Nor is it, on that account, not to be said[1], for religion concerns a man individually [is a private affair]. Burned up with sorrow, by entering the cool stream, all may obtain relief and ease; 1662

'The light of a lamp in a dark room lights up equally objects of all colours, so is it with those who devote themselves to religion,—there is no distinction between the professed disciple and the unlearned (common). 1663

'Sometimes the mountain-dweller (i.e. the religious hermit) falls into ruin, sometimes the humble householder mounts up to be a *Ri*shi; the want of faith (doubt) is the engulfing sea, the presence of disorderly belief is the rolling flood, 1664

'The tide of lust carries away the world; involved in its eddies there is no escape; wisdom is the handy boat, reflection is the hold-fast. 1665

'The drum-call of religion (expedients), the barrier (dam) of thought, these alone can rescue from

---

[1] This and the preceding line are obscure. The sense of the whole passage seems to point to the adaptation of religion for the life of all persons, laïc or cleric.

the sea of ignorance.' At this time the king sincerely attentive to the words of the All-wise[1], 1666

Conceived a distaste for the world's glitter and was dissatisfied with the pleasures of royalty, even as one avoids a drunken elephant, or returns to right reason after a debauch. 1667

Then all the heretical teachers, seeing that the king was well affected to Buddha, besought the king (mahârâ*g*a), with one voice, to call on Buddha to exhibit[2] his miraculous gifts. 1668

Then the king addressed the lord of the world: 'I pray you, grant their request!' Then Buddha silently acquiesced[3]. And now all the different professors of religion, 1669

The doctors who boasted of their spiritual power, came together in a body to where Buddha was; then he manifested before them his power of miracle; ascending up into the air, he remained seated, 1670

Diffusing his glory as the light of the sun he shed abroad the brightness of his presence. The heretical teachers were all abashed, the people all were filled with faith. 1671

Then for the sake of preaching to his mother, he forthwith ascended to the heaven of the thirty-three gods; and for three months dwelt in heavenly mansions[4]. There he converted the occupants (Devas) of that abode, 1672

---

[1] The words of him who knew all things.

[2] To substantiate his claim by exhibiting miraculous power.

[3] By his silence showed his acquiescence.

[4] There is an account of Buddha's ascent to this heaven in the Manual of Buddhism, pp. 298 seq. Also in Fă-hien, cap. xvii. There are pictures (sculptures) of the scene of his descent in Tree and Serpent Worship, plate xvii, and in the account of the Stûpa of Barahut.

And having concluded his pious mission to his mother, the time of his sojourn in heaven finished, he forthwith returned, the angels accompanying him on wing[1]; he travelled down a seven-gemmed ladder, 1673

And again arrived at *G*ambudvîpa. Stepping down he alighted on the spot where all the Buddhas return[2], countless hosts of angels accompanied him, conveying with them their palace abodes (as a gift); 1674

The people of *G*ambudvîpa with closed hands looking up with reverence, beheld him. 1675

Varga 21. Escaping the Drunken Elephant and Devadatta.

Having instructed his mother in heaven with all the angel host, and once more returned to men, he went about converting those capable of it. 1676

*G*utika, *G*îva(ka)[3], Sula, and *K*ûr*n*a, the noble's son Aṅga and the son of the fearless king (Abhaya) 1677

Nyagrodha[4] and the rest; *S*rîkutaka (or, *S*rî-

[1] It would be curious, if this translation were absolutely certain, to find that A*s*vaghosha had heard of angels with 'wings.' In the sculptures the Devas are represented as ordinary mortals. The Chinese may, however, simply mean 'accompanying him, as if on wing,' i.e. following him through the air.

[2] That is, at Sankisa (Sâṅkâ*s*ya), [see the Archæological Survey of India, 1862–1863.]

[3] This I suppose is the physician *G*îvaka. The names of many of the persons in the context may be found in Spence Hardy, M. B., passim.

[4] For Nyagrodha, see M. B., p. 39.

guptaka), Upâli the Nirgrantha[1], (all these) were thoroughly converted. 1678

So also the king of Gandhâra, whose name was Fo-kia-lo (Pudgala?); he, having heard the profound and excellent law, left his country and became a recluse. 1679

So also the demons Himapati and Vâtagiri, on the mountain Vibhâra, were subdued and converted; 1680

The Brahma*k*ârin Prayan(tika), on the mountain Va*g*ana (Po-sha-na), by the subtle meaning of half a gâtha, he convinced and caused to rejoice in faith; 1681

The village of Dânamati (Khânumat)[2] had one Kûtadanta, the head of the twice-born (Brahmans); at this time he was sacrificing countless victims; 1682

Tathâgata by means (upâya, expedients) converted him, and caused him to enter the true path. On Mount Bhatika[3] (?) a heavenly being of eminent distinction, 1683

Whose name was Pa*ñk*a*s*ikha[4], receiving the law, attained Dhyâna[5]; in the village of Vainu-

---

[1] For Upâli the Nirgrantha, see M. B., p. 267.

[2] The village Dânamati must be the same as that called Khânumat by Spence Hardy, M. B., p. 271.

[3] For this event, see Spence Hardy's M. B., p. 288. He calls the mountain or rock by the name of Wédi.

[4] For Pa*ñk*a*s*ikha and his conversion, see M. B., p. 289; also Fă-hien, cap. xxviii. [I may here correct my translation of the passage in my 'Buddhist Pilgrims' (p. 110), instead of 'each one possessing a five-stringed lute,' it should be 'attended by the divine musician Pa*ñk*a*s*ikha.'] For Pa*ñk*a*s*ikha, see Childers' Pali Dict., sub voce Pañcasikho; also Eitel's Handbook.

[5] Or attained rest, or a fixed mind.

sh*t*a, he converted the mother of the celebrated Nanda[1]; 1684

In the town of A*ññ*kavari (Agrâ*t*avî), he subdued the powerful (mahâbâla) spirit; Bhanabhadra (patala), *S*ronadanta; 1685

The malevolent and powerful Nâgas, the king of the country and his harem, received together the true law, as he opened to them the gate of immortality (sweet dew). 1686

In the celebrated Vi*gg*i village (or in the village Pavi*gg*i) Kina and Sila, earnestly seeking to be born in heaven, he converted and made to enter the right path; 1687

The Aṅgulimâla[2], in that village of Sumu, through the exhibition of his divine power, he converted and subdued; 1688

There was that noble's son, Puri*g*îvana, rich in wealth and stores as Punavatî (punyavatî?), 1689

Directly he was brought to Buddha (Tathâgata) accepting the doctrine, he became vastly liberal. So in that village of Padatti he converted the celebrated Patali (or, Potali), 1690

And also Patala, brothers, and both demons. In Bhidhavali (Pi-ti-ho-fu-li) there were two Brahmans, 1691

One called Great-age (Mahâyus?), the other Brahma-age (Brahmâyus?). These by the power of a discourse he subdued, and caused them to attain knowledge of the true law; 1692

---

[1] The mother of Nanda was Pra*g*âpatî; for her conversion, see M. B., p. 307. She was the foster-mother of Buddha.

[2] For the history of the conversion of the Aṅgulimâla, see M. B., p. 249.

When he came to Vai*s*âlî, he converted all the Raksha demons, and the lion (Si*m*ha) of the Li*k*-*kh*avis, and all the Li*kkh*avis, 1693

Sa*k*a[1] the Nirgrantha, all these he caused to attain the true law. Hama kinkhava had a demon Potala, 1694

And another Potalaka (in) Potalagâma [these he converted]. Again he came to Mount Ala, to convert the demon Alava, 1695

And a second called Kumâra, and a third Asidaka; then going back to Mount Ga*g*a (Gayâsîrsha) he converted the demon Ka*ñg*ana, 1696

And Kamo (kin-mau) the Yaksha, with the sister and son. Then coming to Benares, he converted the celebrated Katyâyana[2]; 1697

Then afterwards going, by his miraculous power, to Sruvala (Sou-lu-po-lo), he converted the merchants Davakin and Nikin (?), 1698

And received their sandal-wood hall, exhaling its fragrant odours till now. Going then to Mahîvatî, he converted the *R*ishi Kapila, 1699

And the Muni remained with him; his foot stepping on the stone, the thousand-spoked twin-wheels appeared, which never could be erased. 1700

Then he came to the place Po-lo-na (Prâ*n*a), where he converted the demon Po-lo-na; coming to the country of Mathurâ, he converted the demon Godama (Khadama ?); 1701

In the Thurakusati (? neighbourhood of Mathurâ)

---

[1] For Sa*k*a the Nirgrantha, see M. B., p. 255; also Dhammapada from the Chinese, p. 126.

[2] That is, Mahâkâtyâyana. There was another Kâtyâyana, mentioned by Hiouen Thsang, who lived 300 years after the Nirvâ*n*a.

he also converted Pi*nd*apâla (or, vara); coming to the village of Vaira*ñg*a, he converted the Brahman; 1702

In the village of Kalamasa (or Kramasa), he converted Savasasin, and also that celebrated A*g*irivasa. 1703

Once more returning to the *S*râvastî country, he converted the Gautamas *G*âtisruna and Dakâtili; 1704

Returning to the Ko*s*ala country, he converted the leaders of the heretics Vakrapali (or, Vikravari) and all the Brahma*k*ârins. 1705

Coming to Satavaka, in the forest retreat, he converted the heretical *Ri*shis, and constrained them to enter the path of the Buddha *Ri*shi. 1706

Coming to the country of Ayodhyâ, he converted the Demon Nâgas; coming to the country of Kimbila, he converted the two Nâgarâ*g*as; 1707

One called Kimbila, the other called Kâlaka. Again coming to the Va*gg*i country, he converted the Yaksha demon, 1708

Whose name was Pisha[1], the father and mother of Nâgara, and the great noble also, he caused to believe gladly in the true law. 1709

Coming to the Kau*s*âmbî country, he converted Goshira[2], and the two Upasikâs, Va*g*uttarâ 1710

And her companion Uvarî; and besides these, many others, one after the other. Coming to the

[1] Pi-sha, i.e. Vai*s*rava*n*a, the Regent of the North: converted by Buddha.

[2] For Goshira, see Jul. II, 285; Fă-hien cap. xxxiv.

country of Gandhâra he converted the Nâga Apalâla[1]; 1711

Thus in due order all these air-going, water-loving natures he completely converted and saved, as the sun when he shines upon some dark and sombre cave. 1712

At this time Devadatta[2], seeing the remarkable excellences of Buddha, conceived in his heart a jealous hatred; losing all power of thoughtful abstraction, 1713

He ever plotted wicked schemes, to put a stop to the spread of the true law; ascending the G*ri*dhrakû*t*a (Ghi*gg*akû*t*a) mount he rolled down a stone to hit Buddha[3]; 1714

The stone divided into two parts, each part passing on either side of him. Again, on the royal highway he loosed a drunken, vicious elephant[4]; 1715

With his raised trunk trumpeting as thunder (he ran), his maddened breath raising a cloud around him, his wild pace like the rushing wind to be avoided more than the fierce tempest; 1716

His trunk and tusks and tail and feet, when touched only, brought instant death. (Thus he ran) through the streets and ways of Râ*g*agriha, madly wounding and killing men; 1717

Their corpses lay across the road, their brains

[1] For the conversion of Apalâla, see Jul. II, 135.

[2] Devadatta, the envious; he was the son of Suprabuddha, the father-in-law of Buddha, M. B., p. 61.

[3] This event is related by Fă-hien, cap. xxix, p. 115 (Buddhist Pilgrims). Fă-hien says, 'The stone is still there,' but he does not say that it was divided. See also M. B., p. 383, where the account somewhat differs.

[4] This story of the drunken elephant is related in nearly all the 'lives of Buddha.' The sculptures at Amarâvatî and Barahut also include this episode. See also Fă-hien, p. 113.

and blood scattered afar. Then all the men and women filled with fear, remained indoors; 1718

Throughout the city there was universal terror, only piteous shrieks and cries were heard; beyond the city men were running fast, hiding themselves in holes and dens. 1719

Tathâgata, with five hundred followers, at this time came towards the city; from tops of gates and every window, men, fearing for Buddha, begged him not to advance; 1720

Tathâgata, his heart composed and quiet, with perfect self-possession, thinking only on the sorrow caused by hate, his loving heart desiring to appease it, 1721

Followed by guardian angel-nâgas, slowly approached the maddened elephant. The Bhikshus all deserted him[1], Ânanda only remained by his side; 1722

Joined by every tie of duty, his steadfast nature did not shake or quail. The drunken elephant, savage and spiteful, beholding Buddha, came to himself at once, 1723

And bending, worshipped at his feet[2] just as a mighty mountain falls to earth. With lotus hand the master pats his head, even as the moon lights up a flying cloud. 1724

And now, as he lay crouched before the master's feet, on his account he speaks some sacred words: 'The elephant cannot hurt the mighty dragon[3], hard it is to fight with such a one; 1725

---

[1] It is said, in the later accounts, that 'they rose into the air.'

[2] See Tree and Serpent Worship, plate lviii; also Burgess' Western Caves, plate xvii.

[3] Buddha was also called the great Nâga or dragon.

'The elephant desiring so to do will in the end obtain no happy state of birth; deceived by lust, anger, and delusion, which are hard to conquer, but which Buddha has conquered. 1726

'Now, then, this very day, give up this lust, this anger and delusion! You! swallowed up in sorrow's mud! if not now given up, they will increase yet more and grow.' 1727

The elephant, hearing Buddha's words, escaped from drunkenness, rejoiced in heart; his mind and body both found rest, as one athirst (finds joy) who drinks of heavenly dew. 1628

The elephant being thus converted, the people around were filled with joy; they all raised a cry of wonder at the miracle, and brought their offerings of every kind. 1729

The scarcely-good arrived at middle-virtue, the middling-good passed to a higher grade, the unbelieving now became believers, those who believed were strengthened in their faith. 1730

A*g*âta*s*atru, mighty king, seeing how Buddha conquered the drunken elephant, was moved at heart by thoughts profound; then, filled with joy, he found a twofold growth of piety. 1731

Tathâgata, by exercise of virtue, exhibited all kinds of spiritual powers; thus he subdued and harmonised the minds of all, and caused them in due order to attain religious truth; 1732

And through the kingdom virtuous seeds were sown, as at the first when men began to live (i. e. were first created). But Devadatta, mad with rage, because he was ensnared by his own wickedness, 1733

At first by power miraculous able to fly, now fallen, dwells in lowest hell[1]. 1734

Varga 22. The Lady Âmra[2] (Âmrapâlî) sees Buddha.

The lord of the world having finished his wide work of conversion conceived in himself a desire (heart) for Nirvâ*n*a. Accordingly proceeding from the city of Râ*g*ag*ri*ha, he went on towards the town of Pa-lin-fo (Pâ*t*aliputra)[3]. 1735

Having arrived there, he dwelt in the famous Pâ*t*ali *k*etiya[4]. Now this (town of Pâ*t*aliputra) is

[1] For a full account of the deeds and punishment of Devadatta, see M. B., pp. 328, 329. We are told that Suprabuddha, the father of Devadatta, also went to hell, M. B., p. 339 seq.

[2] This lady is called Ambapâlî, the courtezan, in the southern records.

[3] Pâ*t*aliputra, so called, as it seems, from a flower, pâ*t*ali (Bignonia suaveolens). It was otherwise called Kusumapura, 'the city of flowers.' The Palimbothra of the Greeks, Arrian, Hist. Ind. p. 324 (ed. Gronovii); supposed to be the modern Patna. The story found in the text, viz. that the place was an unfortified village or frontier station of Magadha when Buddha was seventy-nine years old, compared with the statement that in the time of Megasthenes it was one of the largest and most prosperous towns of India (Arrian, as above), seems to show that some considerable time had elapsed between the Nirvâ*n*a and the period of the Greek conquest. It is singular however (as I stated in Buddhist Pilgrims, p. lxiv) that Fă-hien in his account of this town (cap. xxvii) makes no allusion to the Buddhist council said to have been held there under Dharmâ*s*oka. (For further notice of Pâ*t*aliputra, compare Sacred Books of the East, vol. xi, pp. 16, 17; also Bigandet, p. 257, and Spence Hardy, passim.)

[4] There is no mention of the Pâ*t*ali *k*etiya (unless the rest-house is the same as the *K*etiya hall) in the Mahâ-parinibbâna-Sutta, but in Bigandet, p. 257, it is stated that the people prepared the 'dzeat,' or hall, for his use. This 'dzeat' had been erected by

the frontier town of Magadha, defending the outskirts of the country. 1736

Ruling the country was a Brahman[1] of wide renown and great learning in the scriptures (sûtras); and (there was also) an overseer of the country, to take the omens of the land with respect to rest or calamity. 1737

At this time the king of Magadha sent to that officer of inspection (overseer) a messenger to warn and command him to raise fortifications in the neighbourhood (round) of the town for its security and protection. 1738

And now the lord of the world, as they were raising the fortifications, predicted that in consequence of the Devas and spirits who protected and kept (the land), the place should continue strong and free from calamity (destruction). 1739

---

king Agâtasatru for receiving the Likkhavi princes of Vaisâlî, who had come to a conference at this place to settle their affairs with the king. This hall is probably represented at Agantâ, Cave xvi (see Burgess' Report, vol. i, plate xiii, fig. 2; also Mrs. Speirs' Ancient India, p. 197); at least it would seem so from the exact account left us of the position Buddha took on this occasion, 'he entered the hall and took his seat against the central pillar of the hall' (Rhys Davids and Bigandet in loc.) Does this hall, built by king Agâtasatru, and called in our text a '*K*etiya hall,' bear any resemblance to a Basilica?

[1] Rhys Davids (Sacred Books of the East, vol. xi, p. 18) tells us that 'the chief magistrates of Magadha Sunîdha and Vassakâra were building a fortress at Pâtaligâma to repel the Vaggians;' I have therefore in my translation supposed the '*k*u kwŏ' and the 'yang kwan' to be the two officers referred to. It would seem that these titles 'ruling the country' and 'overseer' were recognised at the time. The text, however, would bear another translation, making the Brahman ruler the same as the omen-taking overseer.

On this the heart of the overseer greatly rejoiced[1], and he made religious offerings to Buddha, the law, and the church. Buddha now leaving the city gate went on towards the river Ganges. 1740

The overseer from his deep reverence for Buddha named the gate (through which the lord had passed) the 'Gautama gate[2].' Meanwhile the people all by the side of the river Ganges went forth to pay reverence to the lord of the world. 1741

They prepared for him every kind of religious offering, and each one with his gaudy boat (decorated boat)[3] invited him to cross over. The lord of the world, considering the number of the boats, feared lest by an appearance of partiality in accepting one, he might hurt the minds of all the rest. 1742

Therefore in a moment by his spiritual power he transported himself and the great congregation (across the river), leaving this shore he passed at once to that, 1743

Signifying thereby the passage in the boat of wisdom[4] (from this world to Nirvâ*n*a), a boat large enough to transport all that lives (to save the world), even as without a boat he crossed without hindrance the river (Ganges). 1744

---

[1] The account here given is less exact than that of the Mahâparinibbâna-Sutta, and it would seem as if it were borrowed from a popular form of that work.

[2] This is in agreement with the Southern account (see Rhys Davids, Sacred Books of the East, vol. xi, p. 21).

[3] There is no mention here made of the river being 'brimful and overflowing' as in the Southern books, nor of the search for rafts of wood or basket-work.

[4] Compare the account given by Rhys Davids (Sacred Books of the East, vol. xi, p. 21) and the verse or song there preserved.

Then all the people on the bank of the river, with one voice, raised a rapturous shout[1], and all declared this ford should be called the Gautama ford. 1745

As the city gate is called the Gautama gate, so this Gautama ford is so known through ages; and shall be so called through generations to come[2]. 1746

Then Tathâgata, going forward still, came to that celebrated Kuli[3] village, where he preached and converted many; again he went on to the Nâdi[4] village, 1747

Where many deaths had occurred among the people. The friends of the dead then came (to the lord) and asked, 'Where have our friends and relatives deceased, now gone to be born, after this life ended[5]?' 1748

Buddha, knowing well the sequence of deeds, answered each according to his several case. Then going forward to Vaisâlî[6], he located himself in the Âmra grove[7]. 1749

The celebrated Lady Âmrâ, well affected to Buddha, went to that garden followed by her waiting

[1] Or rather 'shouted out, "miraculous!"'

[2] Is there any name corresponding to the 'Gautama' ford known near Patna?

[3] No doubt the same as Koṭigâma (op. cit., p. 23) called Kantikama by Bigandet, p. 259.

[4] 'Come, Ânanda, let us go to the villages of Nâdika,' Rhys Davids, p. 24.

[5] The names of the dead are given in the Pâli; the account here is evidently an abstract only.

[6] 'Come, Ânanda, let us go on to Vesâli,' Rh. D., p. 28.

[7] 'And there at Vesâli the Blessed One stayed at Ambapâlî's grove,' Rh. D., p. 28.

women, whilst the children from the schools[1] paid her respect. 1750

Thus with circumspection and self-restraint, her person lightly and plainly clothed, putting away all her ornamented robes and all adornments of scent and flowers, 1751

As a prudent and virtuous woman goes forth to perform her religious duties, so she went on, beautiful to look upon, like any Devî in appearance. 1752

Buddha seeing the lady in the distance approaching, spake thus to all the Bhikshus[2]: 'This woman is indeed exceedingly beautiful, able to fascinate the minds (feelings) of the religious; 1753

'Now then, keep your recollection straight! let wisdom keep your mind in subjection! Better fall into the fierce tiger's mouth, or under the sharp knife of the executioner, 1754

'Than to dwell with a woman and excite in yourselves lustful thoughts. A woman is anxious to exhibit her form and shape[3], whether walking, standing, sitting, or sleeping. 1755

'Even when represented as a picture, she desires most of all to set off the blandishments of her beauty, and thus to rob men of their steadfast heart! How then ought you to guard yourselves? 1756

'By regarding her tears and her smiles as enemies, her stooping form, her hanging arms, and all her disentangled hair as toils designed to entrap man's heart. 1757

---

[1] So I translate ts'iang tsin; it may mean grown-up scholars, however, or 'students.'

[2] This sermon against 'woman's wiles' is not found in the Pâli.

[3] Tsz' t'ai, her bewitching movements or airs.

'Then how much more (should you suspect) her studied, amorous beauty! when she displays her dainty outline, her richly ornamented form, and chatters gaily with the foolish man! 1758

'Ah, then! what perturbation and what evil thoughts, not seeing underneath the horrid, tainted shape, the sorrows of impermanence, the impurity, the unreality! 1759

'Considering these as the reality, all lustful thoughts die out; rightly considering these, within their several limits, not even an Apsaras would give you joy. 1760

'But yet the power of lust is great with men, and is to be feared withal; take then the bow of earnest perseverance, and the sharp arrow points of wisdom, 1761

'Cover your head with the helmet of right-thought, and fight with fixed resolve against the five desires. Better far with red-hot iron pins bore out both your eyes, 1762

'Than encourage in yourselves lustful thoughts, or look upon a woman's form with such desires. Lust beclouding a man's heart, confused with woman's beauty, 1763

'The mind is dazed, and at the end of life that man must fall into an "evil way." Fear then the sorrow of that "evil way!" and harbour not the deceits of women. 1764

'The senses not confined within due limits, and the objects of sense not limited as they ought to be, lustful and covetous thoughts grow up between the two, because the senses and their objects are unequally yoked. 1765

'Just as when two ploughing oxen are yoked

together to one halter and cross-bar, but not together pulling as they go, so is it when the senses and their objects are unequally matched. 1766

'Therefore, I say, restrain the heart, give it no unbridled license.' Thus Buddha, for the Bhikshus' sake, explained the law in various ways. 1767

And now that Âmrâ lady gradually approached the presence of the lord; seeing Buddha seated beneath a tree, lost in thought and wholly absorbed by it, 1768

She recollected that he had a great compassionate heart, and therefore she believed he would in pity receive her garden grove. With steadfast heart and joyful mien and rightly governed feelings, 1769

Her outward form restrained, her heart composed, bowing her head at Buddha's feet, she took her place as the lord bade her, whilst he in sequence right declared the law: 1770

'Your heart (O lady!) seems composed and quieted, your form without external ornaments; young in years and rich, you seem well-talented as you are beautiful. 1771

'That one, so gifted, should by faith be able to receive the law of righteousness is, indeed, a rare thing in the world! The wisdom of a master[1], derived from former births, enables him to accept the law with joy, this is not rare; 1772

'But that a woman, weak of will, scant in wisdom, deeply immersed in love, should yet be able to delight in piety, this, indeed, is very rare. 1773

'A man born in the world, by proper thought comes to delight in goodness, he recognises the

[1] That is, of a man.

impermanence of wealth and beauty, and looks upon religion as his best ornament. 1774

'He feels that this alone can remedy the ills of life and change the fate of young and old; the evil destiny that cramps another's life cannot affect him, living righteously; 1775

'Always removing that which excites desire, he is strong in the absence of desire; seeking to find, not what vain thoughts suggest, but that to which religion points him. 1776

'Relying on external help, he has sorrow; self-reliant, there is strength and joy. But in the case of woman, from another comes the labour, and the nurture of another's child. 1777

'Thus then should every one consider well, and loath and put away the form of woman.' Âmrâ the lady, hearing the law, rejoiced. 1778

Her wisdom strengthened, and still more enlightened, she was enabled to cast off desire, and of herself dissatisfied with woman's form, was freed from all polluting thoughts. 1779

Though still constrained to woman's form, filled with religious joy, she bowed at Buddha's feet and spoke: 'Oh! may the lord, in deep compassion, receive from me, though ignorant, 1780

'This offering, and so fulfil my earnest vow.' Then Buddha knowing her sincerity, and for the good of all that lives, 1781

Silently accepted her request, and caused in her full joy, in consequence; whilst all her friends attentive, grew in knowledge, and, after adoration, went back home. 1782

KIOUEN V.

VARGA 23. BY SPIRITUAL POWER FIXING HIS (TERM OF) YEARS[1].

At this time the great men among the Li*kkh*avis[2], hearing that the lord of the world had entered their country and was located in the Âmra garden, 1783

(Went thither) riding in their gaudy chariots with silken canopies and clothed in gorgeous robes, both blue and red and yellow and white, each one with his own cognizance. 1784

Accompanied by their body guard surrounding them, they went; others prepared the road in front; and with their heavenly crowns and flower-bespangled robes (they rode), richly dight with every kind of costly ornament. 1785

Their noble forms resplendent increased the glory of that garden grove; now taking off the five dis-

[1] This title may also be rendered, 'By spiritual power stopping his years of life.' It probably refers to the incident related by Mr. Rhys Davids (Sacred Books of the East, vol. xi, p. 35), 'Let me now, by a strong effort of the will, bend this sickness down and keep my hold on life till the allotted time be come.' There is no mention, however, in the text of Buddha's sickness, which caused the determination here referred to. The sickness is mentioned in the Chinese copy of the Parinirvâ*n*a Sûtra, which in the main agrees with the Pâli.

[2] The Li*kkh*avis were residents of Vai*s*âlî. I have shown elsewhere (Journal of the R. A. S., Jan. 1882) that they were probably of Scythic origin. The account given in the text of their gorgeous chariots, cognizances, &c. is quite in keeping with the customs of the Northern nations. The account given in the Mahâ-parinibbâna-Sutta is in agreement with the text (Sacred Books of the East, vol. xi, p. 31).

tinctive ornaments[1], alighting from their chariots, they advanced afoot. 1786

Slowly thus with bated breath, their bodies reverent (they advanced). Then they bowed down and worshipped Buddha's foot[2], and, a great multitude, they gathered round the lord, shining as the sun's disc, full of radiance. 1787

(There was) the lion Li*kkh*avi[3], among the Li*kkh*avis the senior, his noble form (bold) as the lion's, standing there with lion eyes, 1788

But without the lion's pride, taught by the *S*âkya lion[4] (who thus began): 'Great and illustrious personages, famed as a tribe for grace and comeliness! 1789

'Put aside, I pray, the world's high thoughts, and now accept the abounding lustre[5] of religious teaching. Wealth and beauty, scented flowers and ornaments like these, are not to be compared for grace with moral rectitude! 1790

---

[1] These five distinctive ornaments were, probably, crowns, earrings, necklets, armlets, and sandals.

[2] The worship of the foot of Buddha is exemplified in many of the plates of the Sanchi and Amarâvatî sculptures, where we see worshippers adoring the impression of his foot on the stool before the throne (plates lviii, lxxi, &c.)

[3] This and following lines are somewhat obscure, as it is not plain whether the reference is to one, or all the Li*kkh*avis. I have preferred to refer it to one of them, the chief or leader; for so we read in Spence Hardy's Manual, p. 282: 'A number of the Lichawi princes then went to the king (i. e. the chief of their tribe), whose name was Maha-li.' It would seem as if 'li' were a component part of the name Li*kkh*avi, and meant 'a lion,'—the chief would then be 'the great lion.' Compare the root 'ur' in the Assyrian urmakh, 'great lion;' and the Hebrew layish, 'a great or strong lion.'

[4] The *S*âkya lion was Buddha, the lion of the *S*âkyas (*S*âkyasi*m*ha).

[5] The 'abounding lustre,' that is, the additional glory or lustre of religion. The sermon appears to be addressed principally against pride of person, and anger.

'Your land productive and in peaceful quiet—this is your great renown; but true gracefulness of body and a happy people depend upon the heart well-governed. 1791

'Add but to this a reverent (joyful) feeling for religion, then (a people's) fame is at its height! a fertile land and all the dwellers in it, as a united body, virtuous[1]! 1792

'To-day then learn this virtue[2], cherish with carefulness the people, lead them as a body in the right way of rectitude[3], even as the ox-king leads the way across the river-ford. 1793

'If a man with earnest recollection ponder on things of this world and the next, he will consider how by right behaviour[4] (right morals) he prepares, as the result of merit, rest in either world. 1794

'For all in this world will exceedingly revere him, his fame will spread abroad through every part, the virtuous will rejoice to call him friend, and the outflowings of his goodness will know no bounds for ever. 1795

'The precious gems found in the desert wilds are all from earth engendered; moral conduct, likewise, as the earth, is the great source of all that is good[5]. 1796

---

[1] Much of this discourse seems to refer to the fertility of the land occupied by these Li*kkh*avis in the valley of the Ganges, and to their good rules of government. The character of their government is alluded to in pp. 3, 4, Sacred Books of the East, vol. xi.

[2] The symbol 'tih,' which I have translated by 'virtue,' means 'quality' (gu*n*a) or 'lustre' (te*g*as).

[3] The literal rendering of this line is 'lead the body of them all in the clear and right (path).'

[4] Right behaviour, right morality, here refer to the Buddhist rules of right conduct (*s*îla).

[5] All that is illustrious (shen).

'By this, without the use of wings, we fly through space, we cross the river needing not a handy boat; but without this a man will find it hard indeed to cross (the stream of) sorrow (or, stay the rush of sorrow). 1797

'As when a tree with lovely flowers and fruit, pierced by some sharp instrument, is hard to climb, so is it with the much-renowned for strength and beauty, who break through the laws of moral rectitude! 1798

'Sitting upright in the royal palace (the palace of the conqueror) the heart of the king was grave and majestic[1]; with a view to gain the merit of a pure and moral life, he became a convert of a great *Ri*shi. 1799

'With garments dyed and clad with hair, shaved, save one spiral knot[2] (he led a hermit's life), but, as he did not rule himself with strict morality, he was immersed in suffering and sorrow. 1800

'Each morn and eve he used the three ablutions, sacrificed to fire and practised strict austerity, let his body be in filth as the brute beast, passed through fire and water, dwelt amidst the craggy rocks, 1801

'Inhaled the wind, drank from the Ganges' stream, controlled himself with bitter fasts—but all! far short of moral rectitude[3]. 1802

---

[1] This line is difficult; I was prepared to regard 端坐 as a proper name. Dr. Legge, however, has kindly suggested the translation in the text. But who is the king referred to?

[2] The spiral knot of hair may be seen in many of the sculptures (e. g. plate lxx, Tree and Serpent Worship).

[3] This is a free rendering; I have supposed that the description throughout refers to the 'king' alluded to above; this line may mean, '(he did all this) having put aside right morals.'

'For though a man inure himself to live as any brute, he is not on that account a vessel of the righteous law[1]; whilst he who breaks the laws of right behaviour invites detraction, and is one no virtuous man can love; 1803

'His heart is ever filled (ever cherishes) with boding fear, his evil name pursues him as a shadow. Having neither profit nor advantage in this world, how can he in the next world reap content (rest)? 1804

'Therefore the wise man ought to practise pure behaviour (morals); passing through the wilderness of birth and death, pure conduct is to him a virtuous guide. 1805

'From pure behaviour comes self-power, which frees a man from (many) dangers; pure conduct, like a ladder, enables us to climb to heaven. 1806

'Those who found themselves on right behaviour, cut off the source of pain and grief; but they who by transgression destroy this mind, may mourn the loss of every virtuous principle. 1807

'(To gain this end)[2] first banish every ground of

---

[1] A vessel of righteousness.

[2] I have supplied this, although the sentence would make complete sense without it. In the context 'every ground of self' ('ngo sho) seems to refer to the aim after selfish ends. The sermon from this point refers to 'pride of self,' and its evil consequences; in the latter portion he joins hatred or anger with pride; the whole reminds us of Milton's description:

> 'Round he throws his baleful eyes
> That witnessed huge affliction and dismay
> Mixed with obdurate pride and steadfast hate.'
>
> Paradise Lost, I, 57, 58.

Whilst the war of Devas and Asuras is just Milton's idea when he says, "self;" this thought of "self" shades every lofty (good) aim, even as the ashes that conceal the fire, treading on which the foot is burned. 1808

'Pride and indifference shroud this heart, too, as the sun is obscured by the piled-up clouds; supercilious thoughts root out all modesty of mind, and sorrow saps the strongest will. 1809

'(As) age and disease waste youthful beauty, (so) pride of self destroys all virtue; the Devas and Asuras, thus from jealousy and envy, raised mutual strife. 1810

'The loss of virtue and of merit which we mourn proceeds from "pride of self," throughout; and as I am a conqueror (*G*ina) amid conquerors[1], so he who (they who) conquers self, is one with me. 1811

'He who little cares to conquer self, is but a foolish master; beauty (or, earthly things), family renown (and such things), all are utterly inconstant, and what is changeable can give no rest of interval[2]. 1812

'Storming fury rose
And clamour, such as heard in heaven till now
Was never.' Ibid. VI, 207–209.

[1] Here there is allusion to Buddha's name 'Deva among Devas.' The construction of these sentences is obscure on account of the varied use of the word 'I' ('ngo); this symbol is used sometimes, as in the line under present consideration, as a pronoun, but in the next line it means the evil principle of 'self.' I have found it difficult to avoid comparing this use of the word 'I,' meaning the 'evil self,' with the phrase the 'carnal mind.' The question, in fact, is an open one, whether the Buddhist teaching respecting the non-existence of 'I,' i.e. a personal self or soul, may not justly be explained as consisting in the denial of the reality of the 'carnal self.'

[2] I should like to translate it no 'interval of rest,' but it seems to

'If in the end the law of entire destruction (is exacted) what use is there in indolence and pride? Covetous desire (lust) is the greatest (source of) sorrow, appearing as a friend in secret 'tis our enemy. 1813

'As a fierce fire excited from within (a house), so is the fire of covetous desire: the burning flame of covetous desire is fiercer far than fire which burns the world (world-fire). 1814

'For fire may be put out by water in excess, but what can overpower the fire of lust? The fire which fiercely burns the desert grass (dies out), and then the grass will grow again; 1815

'But when the fire of lust burns up the heart, then how hard for true religion there to dwell! for lust seeks worldly pleasures, these pleasures add to an impure karman[1]; 1816

'By this evil karman a man falls into perdition (evil way), and so there is no greater enemy to man than lust. Lusting, man gives way to amorous indulgence (lit. "lust, then it brings forth love"), by this he is led to practise (indulge in) every kind of lustful longing; 1817

'Indulging thus, he gathers frequent sorrow (all sorrow, or accumulated sorrow, referring to the second of the "four truths"). No greater evil (excessive evil) is there than lust. Lust is a dire disease, and the foolish master stops (i.e. neglects) the medicine of wisdom. 1818

'(The study of) heretical books not leading to

mean the only rest given is momentary, no rest from interval, i. e. constant change.

[1] The impure karman is, of course, the power of evil (in the character) to bring about suffering by an evil birth.

right thought, causes the lustful heart to increase and grow, for these books are not correct (pure) on the points of impermanency, the non-existence of self, and any object (ground) for "self[1]." 1819

'But a true and right apprehension through the power of wisdom, is effectual to destroy that false desire (heretical longing), and therefore our object (aim or purpose) should be to practise this true apprehension. 1820

'Right apprehension (views) once produced then there is deliverance from covetous desire, for a false estimate of excellency produces a covetous desire to excel, whilst a false view of demerit produces anger (and regret); 1821

'But the idea of excelling and also of inferiority (in the sense of demerit) both destroyed, the desire to excel and also anger (on account of inferiority) are destroyed. Anger! how it changes the comely face, how it destroys the loveliness of beauty! 1822

'Anger dulls (clouds) the brightness of the eye (or, the bright eye), chokes all desire to hear the principles of truth, cuts and divides the principle of family affection, impoverishes and weakens every worldly aim[2]. 1823

---

[1] The meaning is, that heretical books, i. e. books of the Brahmans and so on, teach no sound doctrine as to the unreality of the world, the non-existence of a 'personal self,' and the impropriety of any personal selfish aim, and therefore not teaching these, men who follow them are taken up with the idea that there is reality in worldly pleasures, that there is a personal self capable of enjoying them, and that the aim after such enjoyment is a right aim. All this Buddha and his doctrine exclude.

[2] I am not sure whether this is a right translation, it appears rather to contradict Buddha's teaching about the unreality of the world; literally the line is this, 'it makes the world what is light and poor.'

'Therefore let anger be subdued, yield not (a moment) to the angry impulse (heart); he who can hold his wild and angry heart is well entitled "illustrious charioteer." 1824

'For men call such a one "illustrious team-breaker[1]" (who can) with bands restrain the unbroken steed; so anger not subdued, its fire unquenched, the sorrow of repentance burns like fire. 1825

'A man who allows wild passion to arise within, himself first burns his heart, then after burning adds the wind[2] thereto which ignites the fire again, or not (as the case may be)[3]. 1826

'The pain of birth, old age, disease, and death press heavily upon the world, but adding "passion" to the score, what is this but to increase our foes when pressed by foes? 1827

'But rather, seeing how the world is pressed by throngs of grief, we ought to encourage in us love[4] (a loving heart), and as the world (all flesh) produces grief on grief, so should we add as antidotes unnumbered remedies.' 1828

Tathâgata, illustrious in expedients, according to

---

[1] This expression and that in the verse preceding is allied to the Pâli purisadammasârathi, 'trainer or breaker-in of the human steer,' the unconverted man being (as Childers says, Dict. sub voce puriso) like to a refractory bullock. In the Northern books the comparison generally refers to a 'breaker-in of horses,' derived doubtless from the associations of the Northern people (converts to Buddhism), who excelled in chariot racing.

[2] The wind of repentance, the frequent 'sighs' and moans of penitence.

[3] It seems to mean that the wind may sometimes revive the fire, but sometimes not.

[4] This remedy of 'love' is a singular feature in the Buddhist doctrine.

the disease, thus briefly spoke; even as a good physician in the world, according to the disease, prescribes his medicine. 1829

And now the Li*kkh*avis, hearing the sermon preached by Buddha, arose forthwith and bowed at Buddha's feet, and joyfully they placed them on their heads[1]. 1830

Then they asked both Buddha and the congregation on the morrow to accept their poor religious offerings. But Buddha told them that already Âmrâ (the lady) had invited him. 1831

On this the Li*kkh*avis, harbouring thoughts of pride and disappointment[2], (said): 'Why should that one take away our profit?' But, knowing Buddha's heart to be impartial and fair, they once again regained their cheerfulness. 1832

Tathâgata, moreover, nobly (virtuously or illustriously) seizing the occasion (or, following the right plan), appeasing them, produced within a joyful heart; and so subdued, their grandeur of appearance came again, as when a snake subdued by charms glistens with shining skin. 1833

And now, the night being passed, the signs of dawn appearing, Buddha and the great assembly go to the abode of Âmrâ, and having received her entertainment, 1834

They went on to the village of Pi-nau[3] (Beluva),

---

[1] Placing the foot on the head is a symbol of submission—the custom of putting relic-caskets on the head is illustrated in Tree and Serpent Worship, plate xxxviii.

[2] 'We are outdone by this mango girl,' Sacred Books of the East, vol. xi, p. 31.

[3] 'Now when the Blessed One had remained as long as he wished at Ambapâlî's grove, he addressed Ânanda, and said, "Come,

and there he rested during the rainy season; the three months' rest being ended, again he returned to Vais*â*lî, 1835

And dwelt beside the Monkey[1] Tank; sitting there in a shady grove, he shed a flood of glory from his person; aroused thereby, Mâra Pis*u*na 1836

Came to the place where Buddha was, and with closed palms[2] exhorted him thus: 'Formerly, beside the Nairañgana river, when you had accomplished your true and steadfast aim, 1837

'(You said), "When I have done all I have to do, then will I pass at once to Nirvâ*n*a;" and now you have done all you have to do, you should, as then you said, pass to Nirvâ*n*a.' 1838

Then Buddha spake to Pis*u*na[3]: 'The time of my complete deliverance is at hand, but let three months elapse, and I shall reach Nirvâ*n*a.' 1839

Then Mâra, knowing that Tathâgata had fixed the time for his emancipation, his earnest wish being thus fulfilled, joyous returned to his abode in heaven[4]. 1840

Ânanda, let us go on to Beluva,"' Sacred Books of the East, vol. xi, p. 34.

[1] The Marka*t*ahrada.

[2] Here the description of Mâra, 'with closed palms,' leaves no doubt that the figure in Tree and Serpent Worship (plate xxvi, fig. 1, 1st ed.) represents Mâra in this scene, 'requesting Buddha to depart.' It is satisfactory to know that the Buddhist idea of the appearance of 'the Wicked One' (Pis*u*na) was not in agreement with our modern conception of the form of Satan. He is here represented as a Deva, 'lord of the world of desires' (kâmaloka).

[3] Compare this account of Mâra's appeal with Rhys Davids (Pâli Suttas, p. 53).

[4] His abode in heaven. He is represented in Tree and Serpent Worship (plate xxx, fig. 1) as standing on the platform above the

Tathâgata, seated beneath a tree, straightway was lost in ecstasy, and willingly rejected his allotted years, and by his spiritual power fixed the remnant of his life. 1841

On this, Tathâgata thus giving up his years, the great earth shook and quaked through all the limits of the universe; great flames of fire were seen around, 1842

The tops of Sumeru were shaken (fell), from heaven there rained showers of flying stones, a whirling tempest rose on every side, the trees were rooted up and fell, 1843

Heavenly music rose with plaintive notes, whilst angels for a time were joyless. Buddha rising from out his ecstasy, announced to all the world: 1844

'Now have I given up my term of years; I live henceforth by power of Samâdhi[1] (faith); my body like a broken chariot stands, no further cause of "coming" or of "going;" 1845

'Completely freed from the three worlds, I go enfranchised, as a chicken from its egg.' 1846

Varga 24. The Differences of the Likkhavis.

The venerable Ânanda, seeing the earth shaking on every side, his heart was fearful and his hair erect; he asked the cause thereof of Buddha. 1847

Trayastrimsas heaven (where the Devas are worshipping the tiara),—this is his right place as lord of the world of desires.

[1] Rhys Davids says samâdhi corresponds to the Christian faith, Buddhist Suttas, p. 145.

Buddha replied: 'Ânanda! I have fixed three months to end my life, the rest of life I utterly give up; this is the reason why the earth is greatly shaken.' 1848

Ânanda, hearing the instruction of Buddha, was moved with pity and the tears flowed down his face, even as when an elephant of mighty strength shakes (with a blow) the sandal-wood tree. 1849

Thus was (Ânanda) shaken and his mind perturbed, whilst down (his cheeks) the tears, like drops of perfume, flowed; so much he loved the lord his master, so full of kindness (was he), and, as yet, not freed from earthly thoughts (desire)[1]. 1850

Thinking then on these four things[2] alone, he gave his grief full liberty, nor could he master it, (but said), 'Now I hear the lord declare that he has fixed for good his time to die (Nirvâ*n*a), 1851

'My body fails, my strength is gone, my mind is dazed, my soul is all discordant, and all the words of truth forgotten; a wild deserted waste seems heaven and earth. 1852

'Have pity! save me, master (lord of the world)! perish not so soon[3]! Perished with bitter cold[4], I chanced upon a fire—forthwith it disappeared. 1853

---

[1] 'Freedom from desire' (vîtarâga) was the distinction of an Arhat; Ânanda had not yet arrived at this condition.

[2] 'These four things,' or, the things of the world; 'the four' denoting the 'four quarters,' that is, 'the world.'

[3] This and the previous line may otherwise be translated, 'Have pity! save the world, O lord! from this so unexpected an end (of your life).'

[4] These and the succeeding comparisons represent the condition of Ânanda in prospect of Buddha's death.

'Wandering amid the wilds of grief and pain, deceived, confused, I lost my way—suddenly a wise and prudent guide encountered me, but hardly saved from my bewilderment, he once more vanished. 1854

'Like some poor man treading through endless mud, weary and parched with thirst, longs for the water, suddenly he lights upon a cool refreshing lake, he hastens to it—lo! it dries before him. 1855

'The deep blue, bright, refulgent eye[1], piercing through all the worlds, with wisdom brightens the dark gloom, the darkness (but) for a moment is dispelled[2]. 1856

'As when the blade shoots through the yielding earth, the clouds collect and we await the welcome shower, then a fierce wind drives the big clouds away, and so with disappointed hope we watch the dried-up field! 1857

'Deep darkness reigned for want of wisdom, the world of sentient creatures groped for light, Tathâgata lit up the lamp of wisdom, then suddenly extinguished it—ere he had brought it out[3].' 1858

Buddha, hearing Ânanda speaking thus, grieved at his words, and pitying his distress, with soothing accents and with gentle presence spake with purpose to declare the one true[4] law: 1859

---

[1] That is, the eye of Buddha, about which so much is said in the books.

[2] Such appears to be the meaning of the passage, implying that the disappearance of darkness is but for a moment.

[3] Or, alas! why bring it out!

[4] The expression here, as in other cases, is a strong affirmative, 'the true law of truth,' 'the only true law;' the word 'law' means religious system.

'If men but knew their own[1] nature, they would not dwell (indulge) in sorrow; everything that lives, whate'er it be[2], all this is subject to destruction's law; 1860

'I have already told you plainly, the law (nature) of things "joined[3]" is to "separate;" the principle of kindness and of love[4] is not abiding, 'tis better then to reject this pitiful and doting heart. 1861

'All things around us bear the stamp of instant change; born, they perish; no self-sufficiency[5]; those who would wish to keep them long, find in the end no room for doing so. 1862

'If things around us could be kept for aye, and were not liable to change or separation, then this would be salvation[6]! where then can this be sought? 1863

'You, and all that lives, can seek in me this great deliverance! That which you may all attain

[1] '(The character of) self-nature,' or as in the text.

[2] 'All things that have a personal or individual existence.' It would be well to compare the spirit of this sermon with the old belief of the Veda, respecting the birth of the 'one nature' from which the visible world took shape (History of Ancient Sanskrit Literature by Max Müller, p. 561). It seems that the effort of Buddha was to transcend the time of the birth of this nature, and thus arrive at the condition of the original first cause, which 'breathed breathless;' in other words, this is the condition of Nirvâ*n*a.

[3] As in the concluding verse of the Va*g*ra*kkh*edikâ Sûtra, 'târakâ timira*m*,' &c. Analecta Oxoniensia, Aryan Series, vol. I, part i, p. 46.

[4] 'Love' in the sense of parental love; or the love which produced the world.

[5] In the Rig-veda (according to Dr. Muir) the gods though spoken of as immortal are not regarded as unbeginning or self-existent; see Journal of the Royal Asiatic Society, 1864, p. 62.

[6] That is, there would be no need to seek salvation, for it would be already possessed.

I have already told you, (and tell you) to the end. 1864

'Why then should I preserve this body? The body of the excellent law[1] shall long endure! I am resolved; I look for rest! This is the one thing needful[2]. 1865

'So do I now instruct all creatures, and as a guide, not seen before, I lead them; prepare yourselves to cast off consciousness[3], fix yourselves well in your own island[4]. 1866

'Those who are thus fixed (mid-stream), with single aim and earnestness striving in the use of means, preparing quietly a quiet place, not moved by others' way of thinking, 1867

'Know well, such men are safe on the law's island. Fixed in contemplation, lighted by the lamp of wisdom, they have thus finally destroyed ignorance and gloom. Consider well the world's four bounds, 1868

'And dare to seek for true religion only; forget "yourself," and every "ground of self," the bones, the nerves, the skin, the flesh, the mucus, the blood that flows through every little vein; 1869

---

[1] The 'body of the law' represents the teaching of the word of Buddha, which teaching is supposed to be accompanied with or attended by a living power, ever dwelling with the congregation of the faithful.

[2] 'That which is wanting only resides in this.'

[3] The Chinese 'siang' is equivalent to Sanskrit *sañgñâ*, the third skandha (constituents of personal being). It is the receptive (subjective) power, in distinction to the perceptive power (vedanâ). Buddha denied the necessity of personal consciousness (i. e. of self-consciousness, or consciousness of self) as an element of life, i. e. life in the abstract.

[4] This idea of 'an island' (dvîpa), fixed amid the running stream of life, is found in Dhammapada, verse 25.

'Behold these things as constantly impure, what joy then can there be in such a body? every sensation born from cause, like the bubble floating on the water. 1870

'The sorrow coming from (the consciousness of) birth and death and inconstancy, removes all thought of joy—the mind acquainted with the law of production[1], stability, and destruction, (recognises) how again and once again things follow or (succeed one another) with no endurance. 1871

'But thinking well about Nirvâ*n*a[2], the thought of endurance is for ever dismissed, (we see how) the sa*m*skâras[3] from causes have arisen, and how these aggregates will again dissolve, all of them impermanent. 1872

'The foolish man conceives the idea of "self," the wise man sees there is no ground on which to build the idea of "self," thus through the world he rightly looks and well concludes, 1873

'All, therefore, is but evil (one perverse way)—the aggregate amassed by sorrow must perish (in the end)! if once confirmed in this conviction, that man perceives the truth. 1874

---

[1] The law of production, stability, and destruction; this refers to the Buddhist theory of the successive stages in the development of the world. The world is produced from chaos, established for a period, and then destroyed; and this law is a perpetual one, extending through all space (the infinite systems of worlds) and through all time.

[2] Nirvâ*n*a, quietness and extinction.

[3] The sa*m*skâras, the elements of being, i. e. individual being (for a full account of this term, see Childers' Pâli Dict. sub voce). With regard to the use of the Chinese 'hing' for sa*m*skâra, see Eitel, Handbook, sub sa*m*skâra; also consult Colebrooke, Hindu Philosophy, p. 254, and Burnouf (Introduction, pp. 504, 505, note 2).

'This body, too, of Buddha now existing (soon will) perish, the law is one and constant, and without exception.' Buddha having delivered this excellent sermon, appeased the heart of Ânanda. 1875

Then all the Li*kkh*avis, hearing the report[1], with fear and apprehension assembled in a body; devoid of their usual ornaments, they hastened to the place where Buddha was. 1876

Having saluted him according to custom, they stood on one side, wishing to ask him a question, but not being able to find words. Buddha, knowing well their heart, by way of remedy, in the right use of means[2], spake thus: 1877

'Now I perfectly understand that you have in your minds unusual thoughts, not referring to worldly matters, but wholly connected with subjects of religion; 1878

'And now you wish to hear from me, what may be known respecting the report about my resolve to terminate my life, and my purpose to put an end to the repetition of birth. 1879

'Impermanence is the nature of all that exists[3], constant change and restlessness its conditions; unfixed, unprofitable, without the marks of long endurance. 1880

'In ancient days the *Ri*shi kings, Vasish*th*a *Ri*shi,

---

[1] 'Hearing it,' in the original, i.e. hearing the report of Buddha's approaching death.

[2] 'The right use of means' is the rendering of the Chinese 'fang pien,' the Sanskrit upâya; this term may mean 'by artifice,' or, 'by way of expedient;' but generally it refers to the use of means to an end, where the 'means' are evanescent and illusory; the end attained, lasting and real.

[3] Here we have the well-known Pâli formula 'sabbe sa*m*khârâ ani*kk*â.'

Mândhâtri, the Kakravartin monarchs, and the rest, these and all others like them, 1881

'The former conquerors (Ginas), who lived with strength like Îsvara, these all have long ago perished, not one remains till now; 1882

'The sun and moon, Sakra himself, and the great multitude of his attendants, will all, without exception, perish[1]; there is not one that can for long endure; 1883

'All the Buddhas of the past ages, numerous as the sands of the Ganges, by their wisdom enlightening the world, have all gone out as a lamp[2]; 1884

'All the Buddhas yet to come will also perish in the same way; why then should I alone be different? I too will pass into Nirvâna; 1885

'But as they prepared others for salvation, so now should you press forward in the path; Vaisâlî may be glad indeed, if you should find the way of rest! 1886

'The world, in truth, is void of help, the "three worlds" not enough for joy—stay then the course of sorrow, by engendering a heart without desire. 1887

'Give up for good the long and straggling (way of life), press onward on the northern track[3], step by

[1] That the gods were considered to be mortal appears, as Wilson says (Rig-veda, vol. i, p. 7 n), from the title (nara) given to them. Compare also Coxe, Mythol. II, p. 13, and Muir, Journal of the Royal Asiatic Society, 1864, p. 62.

[2] This idea of a lamp going out is a fundamental one as a definition of Nirvâna (paggotassa nibbânam). Its meaning has been discussed by Professor Max Müller in his Introduction to Buddhaghosha's Parables (by Captain Rogers).

[3] That is, the northern track of the sun.

step advance along the upward road, as the sun skirts along (approaches) the western[1] mountains.' 1888

At this time the Li*kkh*avis, with saddened hearts, went back along the way; lifting their hands to heaven and sighing bitterly: 'Alas! what sorrow this! 1889

'His body like the pure gold mountain[2], the marks upon his person so majestic, ere long and like a towering crag he falls; not to live, then why not, "not to love[3]?" 1890

'The powers of birth and death, weakened awhile, the lord Tathâgata, himself the fount (mother) of wisdom (appeared), and now to give it up and disappear! without a saviour now, what check to sorrow. 1891

'The world long time endured in darkness, and men were led by a false light along the way—when lo! the sun of wisdom rose; and now, again, it fades and dies—no warning given. 1892

'Behold the whirling waves of ignorance engulfing all the world! (Why is) the bridge or raft of wisdom in a moment cut away? 1893

'The loving and the great physician king (came) with remedies of wisdom, beyond all price, to heal the hurts and pains of men—why suddenly goes he away? 1894

'The excellent and heavenly flag of love adorned with wisdom's blazonry, embroidered with the dia-

[1] The idea appears to be, that as the sun advances in his course, he approaches the western mountains as his true setting place, i. e. he approaches the equinoctial point.

[2] This comparison of Buddha's body to the golden mountain (sumeru) is a very frequent one, and is probably allied in its origin with the idea of Bel, 'the great mountain' (sadu rabu).

[3] The sense is, 'if he dies, where is the proof of his love?'

mond heart, the world not satisfied with gazing on it, 1895

'The glorious flag of heavenly worship[1]! Why in a moment is it snapped? Why such misfortune for the world, when from the tide of constant revolutions 1896

'A way of escape was opened—but now shut again! and there is no escape from weary sorrow!' Tathâgata, possessed of fond and loving heart, now steels himself and goes away; 1897

He holds his heart[2] so patient and so loving, and, like the Wai-ka-ni (Vakkani ?) flower, with thoughts cast down (irresolute) and tardy, he goes depressed along the road; 1898

Or like a man fresh from a loved one's grave, the funeral past and the last farewell taken, comes back (with anxious look). 1899

VARGA 25. PARINIRVÂ*N*A.

When Buddha went towards the place of his Nirvâ*n*a, the city of Vai*s*âlî was (as if) deserted, as when upon a dark and cloudy night the moon and stars withdraw their shining. 1900

The land that heretofore had peace, was now afflicted and distressed; as when a loving father dies, the orphan daughter yields to constant grief. 1901

Her personal grace unheeded, her clever skill but lightly thought of, with stammering lips she finds expression for her thoughts; how poor her brilliant wit and wisdom now! 1902

---

[1] Religious sacrifices.

[2] That is, he restrains himself.

Her spiritual powers (spirits [1]) ill regulated (without attractiveness [2]), her loving heart [3] faint (poor) and fickle (false), exalted high [4] but without strength, and all her native grace neglected (without rule) [5]; 1903

Such was the case at Vaisâlî; all outward show [6] now fallen (sorry-looking), like autumn verdure in the fields bereft of water, withered up and dry; 1904

Or like the smoke of a half-smouldering [7] fire, or like those who having food before them yet forget to eat, so these forgot their common household [8] duties, and nought prepared they for the day's emergencies. 1905

Thinking thus on Buddha, lost in deep reflection, silent they sat nor spoke a word. And now the lion-Li*kkh*avis [9], manfully enduring their great sorrow, 1906

---

[1] Shin-tung generally means 'spiritual (miraculous) powers,' but here it refers to the 'spirits' or 'good spirits,' i. e. the bearing or cheerful tone of mind.

[2] Without dignity.

[3] That is, her heart capable of love now poor and estranged, i. e. incapable of earnest attachment.

[4] The symbol 'shing' denotes not only 'power' generally, and hence used for the Sanskrit '*g*ina,' but also 'a head-dress worn by females.' It thus corresponds with the Greek ἐξουσία (1 Cor. xi. 10). The phrase in the text may therefore mean 'her horn (head-dress) exalted, but bereft of power,' where there is a play on the second word 'lih' (power).

[5] 'Dignified and yet no ruler.'

[6] Outward glory.

[7] Like the smoking (ashes) of a fire put out.

[8] Kung sz' may mean 'public and private,' or as in the text.

[9] The difficulty here, as before, is to know whether one Li*kkh*avi is referred to, or the whole clan. We may observe that there is an Accadian root 'lig' or 'lik,' meaning 'lion.' Sayce, Assyrian Grammar.

With flowing tears and doleful sighs, signifying thereby their love of kindred, destroyed for ever all their books of heresy, to show their firm adherence to the true law[1]. 1907

Having put down all heresy (or heretics), they left it once for all[2] (never to return); severed from the world and the world's doctrines, convinced that non-continuance (impermanence) was the great disease (evil). 1908

(Moreover thus they thought): 'The lord of men now enters the great quiet place (Nirvâ*n*a), (and we are left) without support and with no saviour; the highest lord of "means" (means of saving men) is now about to extinguish all his glory in the final[3] place (of death). 1909

'Now we indeed have lost our steadfast will, as fire deprived of fuel; greatly to be pitied is the world, now that the lord gives up his world-protecting (office), 1910

'Even as a man bereft of spiritual power (right reason) throughout the world is greatly pitied. Oppressed by heat we seek the cooling lake, nipped by the cold we use the fire; 1911

'But in a moment all is lost[4], the world is left without resource[5]; the excellent law (superlative

---

[1] *Kh*ing-fă = saddharma.

[2] The passage may possibly mean that they sent away all heretics from their city; but the whole verse is obscure.

[3] The 'final' or 'highest' place.

[4] This is a doubtful translation; the original is sih kwoh in, 'all openly or widely (gone).'

[5] Without a place of refuge, or a lodging-place. The line literally translated is, 'All things that live, what refuge have they?'

law), indeed, is left, to frame the world anew, as a metal-caster frames anew his work[1]. 1912

'The world has lost its master-guide, and, men bereaved of him, the way is lost; old age, disease, and death, self-sufficient[2], now that the road is missed, pervade the world without a way. 1913

'What is there now throughout the world equal to overcome the springs of these great sorrows? The great cloud's rain alone can make the raging and excessive fire, that burns the world, go out. 1914

'So only he can make the raging fire of covetous desire go out; and now he, the skilful maker of comparisons[3], has firmly fixed his mind to leave the world! 1915

'And why, again, is the sword of wisdom, ever ready to be used for an uninvited friend (i. e. on behalf of the friendless), only like the draught of wine given to him about to undergo the torture and to die[4]? 1916

'Deluded by false knowledge the mass of living things are only born to die again; as the sharp knife divides the wood, so constant change divides the world. 1917

'The gloom of ignorance like the deep water, lust like the rolling billow, sorrow like the float-

---

[1] This is the idea, as it seems, of the original, implying that the law of Buddha alone was left to take the place of the teacher.

[2] Tsz'-tsai, independent, without control.

[3] 'Powerful in making comparisons,' one of Buddha's characteristic names. The construction of these lines is unlike Chinese, and is evidently adapted from the Sanskrit original.

[4] The sense seems to be that the sword of Buddha's wisdom, instead of rescuing the friendless, has only been used, as the executioner's draught, to lull the pain of death.

ing bubbles, false views (heresy) like the Makara[1] fish, 1918

'(Amidst all these) the ship of wisdom only can carry us across the mighty sea. The mass of ills (diseases) are like the flowers of the (sorrow) tree, old age and all its griefs, the tangled boughs; 1919

'Death the tree's tap-root, deeds done in life the buds, the diamond sword of wisdom only strong enough to cut down the mundane tree! 1920

'Ignorance (is like) the burning fire-glass, covetous desire the scorching rays, the objects of the five desires the (dry) grass, wisdom alone the water to put out the fire. 1921

'The perfect law, surpassing every law, having destroyed the gloom of ignorance, we see the straight road leading to quietness and rest, the end of every grief and sorrow. 1922

'And now the loving (one), converting men, impartial in his thoughts to friend or foe, the all-knowing, perfectly instructed, even he is going to leave the world! 1923

'He with his soft and finely modulated voice, his compact body and broad shoulders, he, the great *R*ishi[2], ends his life! Who then can claim exemption? 1924

'Enlightened, now he quickly passes hence! let

---

[1] A mythical sea monster (see for a probable representation of it, Bharhut Stûpa, plate xxxiv, fig. 2).

[2] The great *R*ishi (Mahesi), even he has come to die, who then can claim exemption? It would seem, from this episode, that the Li*kkh*avis were now convinced of the law of impermanence, and this was the lesson they most needed to learn, being of a proud and haughty disposition.

us therefore seek with earnestness the truth, even as a man meets with the stream beside the road, then drinks and passes on. 1925

'Inconstancy, this is the dreaded enemy—the universal destroyer—sparing neither rich nor poor; rightly perceiving this and keeping it in mind, this man, though sleeping, yet is the only ever-wakeful.' 1926

Thus the Li*kkh*avi lions, ever mindful of the Buddha's wisdom, disquieted with (the pain of) birth and death, sighed forth their fond remembrance of the man-lion[1]. 1927

Retaining in their minds no love of worldly things, aiming to rise above the power of every lustful quality[2], subduing in their hearts the thought of light or trivial matters, training their thoughts (hearts) (to seek) the quiet, peaceful place; 1928

Diligently practising (the rules) of unselfish, charitable conduct; putting away all listlessness, they found their joy in quietness and seclusion, meditating only on religious truth. 1929

And now the all-wise (omniscient), turning his body round with a lion-turn[3], once more gazed upon Vai*s*âlî, and uttered this farewell verse: 1930

---

[1] That is, of Buddha, the lion of the *S*âkya tribe (*S*âkyasi*m*ha). There is here, of course, reference to the Li*kkh*avi lion, as contrasted with the *S*âkya lion. It will be well to bear in mind that the beautiful pillar described by Stephenson, Cunningham, and others, found near the site of Vai*s*âlî, was surmounted by a 'lion.'

[2] Tih, corresponding to gu*n*a.

[3] In the text it is yuen shin, 'his round or perfect body;' in Fă-hien the symbol is hwui, 'turning' (cap. xxv). The passage in Fă-hien may be translated 'turning his body with a right-turn-look.' Here the passage is 'turning (yuen for hwui) his body with a lion-turn;' in the Pâli (Sacred Books of the East, vol. xi, p. 64) it is 'he

'Now this, the last time this, I leave (wander forth from) Vai*s*âlî—the land where heroes[1] live and flourish! Now am I going to die.' 1931

Then gradually advancing, stage by stage[2] he came to Bhoga-nagara (Po-ki'a-shing), and there he rested in the *S*âla[3] grove, where he instructed all his followers (Bhikshus) in the precepts: 1932

'Now having gone on high (ascended into heaven)[4] I shall enter on Nirvâ*n*a: ye must rely upon the law (religious truth)—this is your highest, strongest, vantage ground[5]. 1933

'What is not found (what enters not) in Sûtra, or what disagrees with rules of Vinaya, opposing the one true system (of my doctrine), this must not be held by you[6]. 1934

'What opposes Dharma, what opposes Vinaya, or

---

gazed at Vesâli with an elephant look' (nâgapalokita*m*), on which word Mr. Rhys Davids has an interesting note. The lion appears to be the favourite with Northern Buddhists, the elephant (nâga) with the Southern.

[1] Lih sse, generally translated 'Mallas;' in Fa-hien 'Kin kang lih sse' has been translated by Va*g*rapâ*n*i (cap. xxiv), but this is not correct; it is singular that 'lih sse'—in old Chinese 'lik sse'—should be applied as another term for Li*kkh*avis. As stated above, lik is an Accadian root for 'lion'—is the Chinese symbol 'lik,' strong, allied to this?

[2] The stages according to the Pâli (Sacred Books of the East, vol. xi, p. 66) were from Vesâli to Bha*nd*a-gâma, from Bha*nd*a-gâma to Hatthi-gâma, from Hatthi-gâma to Amba-gâma, from Amba-gâma to *G*ambu-gâma, and thence to Bhoga-nagara.

[3] At the Ânanda *K*etiya (in the Pâli, as above).

[4] This is a singular phrase, 'having ascended into heaven I shall enter Nirvâ*n*a'—it may refer to the process hereafter named through which the mind of Buddha passed (entering the dhyânas &c.) ere he died; but anyhow, it is a curious phrase.

[5] This then is the noble, conquering place.

[6] It will be well to compare this sermon with that in the Pâli (op. cit. pp. 67, 68).

what is contrary to my words, this is the result (speech) of ignorance, ye must not hold such doctrine, but with haste reject it. 1935

'Receiving that which has been said aright (in the light)[1], this is not subversive of true doctrine, this is what I have said[2], as the Dharma and Vinaya say. 1936

'Accepting that which I, the law, and the Vinaya declare, this is (the truth) to be believed. But words which neither I, the law, nor the Vinaya declare, these are not to be believed. 1937

'Not gathering (explaining) the true and hidden meaning, but closely holding to the letter[3], this is the way of foolish teachers, but contrary to my doctrine (religion) and a false way of teaching. 1938

'Not separating the true from false, accepting in the dark without discrimination, is like a shop where gold and its alloys are sold together, justly condemned by all the world. 1939

'The foolish masters, practising (the ways of) superficial wisdom, grasp not the meaning of the truth; but to receive the law (religious doctrine) as it explains itself, this is to accept the highest mode of exposition (this is to accept the true law). 1940

---

[1] This dictum has been often quoted as illustrating the breadth of Buddha's teaching, 'keep and receive the right (vidyâ) spoken (words),' or 'whatever is according to right reason' (see Wassiljew, Buddhismus, pp. 18, 68).

[2] The distinction between Dharma Vinaya and 'what I have said,' seems to point to the numerous discourses which are called 'Fo shwo' (in Chinese, i. e. spoken by Buddha. Compare with this phrase the Pâli 'Tathâgatena vutto,' see Leon Féer, Études, p. 192; Childers, Pâli Dict. sub vutti).

[3] This 'holding to the letter' is also alluded to in the Pâli (see Childers, sub voce vyañganam).

'Ye ought therefore thus to investigate true principles, to consider well the true law and the Vinaya, even as the goldsmith does who melts and strikes and then selects the true (metal). 1941

'Not to know the Sûtras and the *S*âstras, this is to be devoid of wisdom; not saying properly that which is proper, is like doing that which is not fit to see. 1942

'Let all be done (accepted) in right and proper order, according as the meaning of the sentence guides, for he who grasps a sword unskilfully, does but inflict a wound upon his hand. 1943

'Not skilfully to handle words and sentences, the meaning then is hard to know; as in the night time travelling and seeking for a house, if all be dark within, how difficult to find. 1944

'Losing the meaning, then the law (dharma) is disregarded, disregarding the law the mind becomes confused; therefore every wise and prudent master neglects not to discover the true and faithful meaning.' 1945

Having spoken these words respecting the precepts of religion, he advanced to the town of Pâvâ [1], where all the Mallas (lih sse) prepared for him religious offerings of every kind. 1946

At this time a certain householder's son [2], whose

[1] Sacred Books of the East, vol. xi, p. 70. It would seem from the people of Pâvâ being called Mallas that they were allied with the Li*kkh*avis.

[2] There is nothing said in the text about *K*unda being a worker in metals, or about the character of his offering, or its consequences on Buddha's health. The expression 'householder's son' may be also translated a 'householder,' the symbol 'tseu' (son) being often used, as Wassiljew (Buddhismus, p. 168) has observed, as an honorific expletive.

name was *K*unda, invited Buddha to his house, and there he gave him, as an offering, his very last repast. 1947

Having partaken of it and declared the law (preached), he onward went to the town of Kusi (Ku*s*inagara), crossing the river Tsae-kieuh (Tsaku) and the Hira*n*yavatî (Hi-lan)[1]. 1948

Then in that *S*âla grove, a place of quiet and seclusion (hermit-rest), he took his seat: entering the golden river (Hira*n*yavatî) he bathed his body, in appearance like a golden mountain. 1949

Then he spake his bidding thus to Ânanda: 'Between those twin *S*âla trees, sweeping and watering, make a clean space, and then arrange my sitting-mat (couch), 1950

'At midnight coming, I shall die' (enter Nirvâ*n*a). Ânanda hearing the bidding of his master (Buddha), his breath was choked with heart-sadness; 1951

But going and weeping he obeyed the instruction, and spreading out the mat he came forthwith back to his master and acquainted him. Tathâgata having lain down with his head towards the north and on his right side, slept thus. 1952

Resting upon his hand as on a pillow with his feet crossed[2], even as a lion-king; all grief is passed, his last-born body from this one sleep shall never rise. 1953

His followers (disciples) round him, in a circle

---

[1] Ku*s*inagara is the present Kasia. I do not find any reference in General Cunningham's account of this city (Archæological Survey of India, I, 76 seq.) to the river Tsaku, but the Hira*n*yavatî is still known as the Hirana.

[2] 'With one leg resting on the other,' Sacred Books of the East, vol. xi, p. 86.

gathered, sigh dolefully: 'The eye of the (great) world is now put out!' The wind is hushed, the forest streams are silent, no voice is heard of bird or beast. 1954

The trees sweat out large flowing drops, flowers and leaves out of season singly fall, whilst men and Devas, not yet free from desire, are filled with overwhelming fear. 1955

(Thus were they) like men wandering through the arid desert, the road full dangerous, who fail to reach the longed-for hamlet; full of fear they go on still, dreading they may not find it, their heart borne down with fear they faint and droop. 1956

And now Tathâgata, aroused from sleep, addressed Ânanda thus: 'Go! tell the Mallas, the time of my decease (Nirvâ*n*a) is come; 1957

'They, if they see me not, will ever grieve and suffer deep regret.' Ânanda listening to the bidding of his master (Buddha), weeping went along the road. 1958

And then he told those Mallas all—'The lord is near to death.' The Mallas hearing it, were filled with great, excessive grief (fear). 1959

The men and women hurrying forth, bewailing as they went, came to the spot where Buddha was; with garments torn and hair dishevelled, covered with dust and sweat they came. 1960

With piteous cries they reached the grove, as when a Deva's day of merit (heavenly merit or enjoyment) comes to an end[1], so did they bow

[1] The time when a Deva's sojourn in heaven is approaching its end is indicated by certain signs (fading of the head-garland, restlessness on his couch, &c.), on observing which there is general grief among the Devîs and others, his companions.

weeping and adoring at the feet of Buddha, grieving (to behold) his failing strength. 1961

Tathâgata, composed and quiet, spake: 'Grieve not! the time is one for joy; no call for sorrow or for anguish here; 1962

'That which for ages I have aimed at, now am I just about to obtain; delivered now from the narrow bounds of sense, I go to the place of never-ending rest and peace (purity). 1963

'I leave these things, earth, water, fire, and air, to rest secure where neither birth nor death can come. Eternally delivered there from grief, oh! tell me! why should I be sorrowful? 1964

'Of yore on *S*îrsha's[1] mount, I longed to rid me of this body, but to fulfil my destiny I have remained till now with men (in the world); 1965

'I have kept (till now) this sickly, crumbling body, as dwelling with a poisonous snake; but NOW I am come to the great resting-place, all springs of sorrow now for ever stopped. 1966

'No more shall I receive a body, all future sorrow now for ever done away; it is not meet for you, on my account, for evermore, to encourage any anxious fear.' 1967

The Mallas hearing Buddha's words, that he was now about to die (enter the great, peaceful, quiet state), their minds confused, their eyes bedimmed, as if they saw before them nought but blackness, 1968

With hands conjoined, spake thus to Buddha: 'Buddha is leaving now the pain of birth and death, and entering on the eternal joy of rest (peaceful extinction); doubtless we ought to rejoice thereat. 1969

---

[1] Near Gayâ.

'Even as when a house is burnt a man rejoices if his friends are saved from out the flames; the gods! perhaps they rejoice—then how much more should men! 1970

'But—when Tathâgata has gone and living things no more may see him, eternally cut off from safety and deliverance—in thought of this we grieve and sorrow. 1971

'Like as a band of merchants crossing with careful steps a desert, with only a single guide, suddenly he dies! 1972

'Those merchants now without a protector, how can they but lament! The present age, coming to know their true case[1], has found the omniscient, and looked to him, 1973

'But yet has not obtained the final conquest;—how will the world deride! Even as it would laugh at one who, walking o'er a mountain full of treasure, yet ignorant thereof, hugs still the pain of poverty.' 1974

So spake the Mallas, and with tearful words excuse themselves to Buddha, even as an only child pleads piteously before a loving father. 1975

Buddha then, with speech most excellent, exhibited and declared the highest principle (of truth), and thus addressed the Mallas: 'In truth, 'tis as you say; 1976

'Seeking the way, you must exert yourselves and strive with diligence—it is not enough to have seen me! Walk, as I have commanded you; get rid of all the tangled net of sorrow; 1977

---

[1] Men now living having learned their case, or condition, from the teaching of Buddha.

'Walk in the way with steadfast aim; 'tis not from seeing me this comes,—even as a sick man depending on the healing power of medicine, 1978

'Gets rid of all his ailments easily without beholding the physician. He who does not do what I command sees me in vain, this brings no profit; 1979

'Whilst he who lives far off from where I am, and yet walks righteously, is ever near me! A man may dwell beside me, and yet, being disobedient, be far away from me. 1980

'Keep your heart carefully—give not place to listlessness! earnestly practise every good work. Man born in this world is pressed by all the sorrows of the long career (night) [of suffering], 1981

'Ceaselessly troubled—without a moment's rest, as any lamp blown by the wind!' The Mallas all, hearing Buddha's loving instruction, 1982

Inwardly composed, restrained their tears, and, firmly self-possessed, returned. 1983

Varga 26. Mahâparinirvâna.

At this time there was a Brahma*k*ârin whose name was Su-po-to-lo[1] (Subhadra); he was well known for his virtuous qualities (bhadra), leading a pure life according to the rules of morality, and protecting all living things. 1984

When young[2] he had adopted heretical views and become a recluse among unbelievers—this one, wishing to see the lord, spake to Ânanda thus: 1985

'I hear that the system of Tathâgata is of a

[1] Called Subhadda in the Southern accounts.

[2] This may also be translated 'of small endowments.'

singular character and very profound (difficult to fathom), and that he (has reached) the highest wisdom (anuttarâ(sam)bodhi) in the world, the first of all horse-tamers[1]. 1986

'(I hear moreover) that he is now about to die (reach Nirvâna), it will be difficult[2] indeed to meet with him again, and difficult to see those who have seen him with difficulty, even as it is to catch in a mirror the reflection of the moon. 1987

'I now desire respectfully to see him the greatest and most virtuous guide (of men), because I seek to escape this mass of sorrow (accumulated sorrow) and reach the other shore of birth and death. 1988

'The sun of Buddha now about to quench its rays, O! let me for a moment gaze upon him.' The feelings of Ânanda now were much affected, thinking that this request was made with a view to controversy, 1989

Or that he (i.e. Subhadra) felt an inward joy because the lord was on the eve of death. He was not willing therefore to permit the interview with Buddha (the Buddha-sight). Buddha, knowing the man's (that one's) earnest desire and that he was a vessel fit for true religion (right doctrine), 1990

Therefore addressed Ânanda thus: 'Permit that heretic to advance; I was born to save mankind[3], make no hindrance therefore or excuse!' 1991

---

[1] Compare 'Purisa-damma-sârathi,' as before. We observe, again, how the reference here is to taming of 'horses,' in the Southern accounts to the taming of the 'steer,' showing the associations of the people using the figure.

[2] 'Sometimes and full seldom do Tathâgatas appear in the world,' Sacred Books of the East, vol. xi, p. 104.

[3] Here again the construction is inverted and un-Chinese, but

Subhadra, hearing this, was overjoyed at heart, and his religious feelings (his feelings of joy in religion) were much enlarged, as with increased reverence he advanced to Buddha's presence. 1992

Then, as the occasion required[1], he spoke becoming words and with politeness made his salutation[2], his features pleasing and with hands conjoined (he said): 'Now I desire to ask somewhat from thee; 1993

'The world has many teachers of religion[3] (those who know the law) as I am myself; but I hear that Buddha has attained a way which is the end of all, complete emancipation. 1994

'O that you would, on my account, briefly explain (your method), moisten my empty, thirsty soul (heart)! not with a view to controversy or from a desire to gain the mastery (but with sincerity I ask you so to do).' 1995

Then Buddha, for the Brahma*k*ârin's sake, in brief recounted the eight 'right ways' (noble paths)—on hearing which, his empty soul (meek heart) accepted it, as one deceived accepts direction in the right road. 1996

---

the sense appears plain, ngo wei to *g*in sing, 'I, to save men am born.' The idea of Buddha as a saviour of men seems to be a development of his character as 'teacher' or 'sage.' It expanded afterwards in Northern Buddhism into the idea of a universal saviour, and was afterwards merged in the character of Avalokite*s*vara, a being 'engaged by an eternal oath (covenant) to save all living things.' The presence of Western modes of thought cannot be doubted here.

[1] According to the occasion; or, as it was customary on such an occasion.

[2] Compare the Pâli sarâ*n*iya*m* vitisâretvâ; 'wen sun,' however, in the Chinese, appears to correspond with the Pâli abhivâdeti.

[3] These teachers are named in the Pâli.

Perceiving now, he knew that what he had before perceived was not the final way (of salvation), but now he felt he had attained what he had not before attained, and so he gave up and forsook his books of heresy. 1997

Moreover, now he rejected (turned his back) on the gloomy hindrances of doubt (moha), reflecting how by his former practices, mixed up with anger, hate, and ignorance, he had long cherished no real (good) joy[1]. 1998

For if (he argued) the ways of lust and hate and ignorance are able to produce a virtuous karman (good works), then 'hearing much' and 'persevering wisdom' (or, wisdom and perseverance (vîrya)) these, too, are born from lust, (which cannot be.) 1999

But if a man is able to cut down hate and ignorance, then also he puts off all consequences of works (karman), and these being finally destroyed, this is complete emancipation. 2000

Those thus freed from works are likewise freed from subtle questionings (investigation of subtle principles), (such as) what the world says 'that all things, everywhere, possess a self-nature[2].' 2001

But if this be the case and therefore lust, hate, and ignorance possess a self-implanted nature, then this nature must inhere in them; what then means the word 'deliverance?' 2002

For even if we rightly cause[3] the overthrow

---

[1] I think 樂 is for 業, in which case the line would be, 'he had long cherished works (karman) not good' (善).

[2] This theory of a 'self-nature' (svabhâva) appears to have prevailed widely about the time of A*s*vaghosha, the Svabhâvika sect of Buddhists perhaps had their origin about this time.

[3] That is, 'by the use of right means.'

(destruction) of hate and ignorance, yet if lust (love) remains, then there is a return of birth; even as water, cold in its nature, may by fire be heated, 2003

But when the fire goes out then it becomes cold again, because this is its constant nature; so (we may) ever know that the nature which lust has is permanent [or, 'endurance, we may know, is the nature of lust'], and neither hearing, wisdom, or perseverance can alter it. 2004

Neither capable of increase or diminution, how can there be deliverance? I held aforetime (thus he thought) that (those things capable of) birth and death resulted thus, from their own innate nature; 2005

But now I see that such a belief excludes deliverance; for what is (born) by nature must endure so, what end can such things have? 2006

Just as a burning lamp cannot but give its light; the way (doctrine) of Buddha is the only true one, that lust, as the root-cause, brings forth the things that live (the world); 2007

Destroy this lust (love) then there is Nirvâ*n*a (quiet extinction); the cause destroyed then the fruit is not produced. I formerly maintained that 'I' (self) was a distinct entity (body), not seeing that it has no maker. 2008

But now I hear the right doctrine preached by Buddha, there is no 'self' (personal self) in all the world, for all things are produced by cause, and therefore there is no creator (Î*s*vara). 2009

If then sorrow is produced by cause (or, if then cause producing things, there is sorrow), the cause may likewise be destroyed; for if the world is cause-produced, then is the view correct, that by destruction of the cause, there is an end. 2010

The cause destroyed, the world brought to an end, there is no room for such a thought as permanence, and therefore all my former views (he said) are 'done away,' and so he deeply 'saw' the true doctrine taught by Buddha. 2011

Because of seeds well sown in former times, he was enabled thus to understand the law on hearing it; thus he reached the good and perfect state of quietness, the peaceful, never-ending place (of rest). 2012

His heart expanding to receive the truth, he gazed with earnest look on Buddha as he slept, nor could he bear to see Tathâgata depart and die (leave the world and attain Nirvâ*n*a); 2013

'Ere yet,' he said, 'Buddha shall reach the term (of life) I will myself first leave the world (become extinct);' and then with hands close joined, retiring from the holy form (face or features), he took his seat apart, and sat composed and firm [1]. 2014

Then giving up his life (years), he reached Nirvâ*n*a, as when the rain puts out a little fire. Then Buddha spake to all his followers (Bhikshus): 'This my very last disciple 2015

'Has now attained Nirvâ*n*a, cherish him (his remains) properly.' Then Buddha the first night (watch) passed, the moon bright shining and all the stars clear in their lustre, 2016

The quiet grove without a sound, moved by his great compassionate heart, declared to his disciples

[1] Compare this account with the Pâli (Sacred Books of the East, vol. xi, p. 110, and note).

this his bequeathed precepts[1] (his testamentary
rules). 'After my Nirvâ*n*a, 2017

'Ye ought to reverence and obey the Pratimoksha,
(receive it) as your master, a shining lamp in the
dark night, 2018

'Or as a great jewel (treasured by) a poor man.
The injunctions I have ever given, these you ought
to obey and follow carefully, and treat in no way
different from myself. 2019

'Keep pure your body, words, and conduct, put
from you all concerns of daily life (business), lands,
houses, cattle, storing wealth or hoarding grain. 2020

'All these should be avoided as we avoid a fiery
pit; (so also) sowing the land, cutting down shrubs,
healing of wounds or the practice of medicine, 2021

'Star-gazing and astrology, forecasting lucky or
unfortunate events by signs (palm signs), prognos-
ticating good or evil, all these are things for-
bidden. 2022

'Keeping the body temperate, eat at proper times;
receive no mission as a go-between; compound no
philteries; abhor dissimulation; 2023

'Follow right doctrine, and be kind to all that
lives; receive in moderation what is given; receive
but hoard not up; these are, in brief, my spoken
precepts. 2024

'These form the groundwork of my rules, these
also are the ground of full emancipation[2]. Enabled

[1] These 'bequeathed precepts' form a separate tract in the Chinese Buddhist Canon; it is generally bound up with the 'Sûtra of 42 Sections.' I have translated it in my first Report on the Chinese Buddhist Books in the Library of the India Office. [This Sûtra in Chinese is called 'an epitome of the Vinaya.' Is it the 'substance of the Vinaya' referred to in the Bairât Edict of A*s*oka?]

[2] Full emancipation seems here to be a synonym of 'Prati-

thus to live (relying on this law, able to live) this is rightly to receive all (other things). 2025

'This is true wisdom which embraces all, this is the way (cause) to attain the end; this code of rules, therefore, ye should hold and keep, and never let it slip or be destroyed. 2026

'For when pure rules of conduct are observed (not broken), then there is true religion; without these, virtue languishes; found yourselves therefore well on these my precepts (moral rules); 2027

'Grounded thus in rules of purity, the springs of feeling (animal feeling) will be well controlled, even as the well-instructed cowherd guides well his cattle (permits them neither to loiter nor hurry on). 2028

'Ill-governed feelings (senses), like the horse, run wild through all the six domains of sense, bringing upon us in the present world unhappiness, and in the next, birth in an evil way. 2029

'So, like the horse ill-broken, these land us in the ditch; therefore the wise and prudent man will not allow his senses licence. 2030

'For these senses (organs of sense) are, indeed, our greatest foes, causes of misery; for men enamoured thus by sensuous things cause all their miseries to recur. 2031

'Destructive as a poisonous snake, or like a savage tiger, or like a raging fire, the greatest evil in the world, he who is wise, is freed from fear of these. 2032

'But what he fears is only this—a light and trivial heart, which drags a man to future misery (evil way

moksha.' The rules of the Pratimoksha (250 rules) were probably later in their origin than the rules here given.

of birth)—just for a little sip of pleasure not looking at the yawning gulf (before us); 2033

'Like the wild elephant freed from the iron curb (ankusa), or like the ape that has regained the forest trees, such is the light and trivial heart;—the wise man should restrain and hold it therefore. 2034

'Letting the heart go loose without restraint, that man shall not attain Nirvâna; therefore we ought to hold the heart in check, and go apart from men and seek a quiet resting-place (hermit's abode). 2035

'Know when to eat and the right measure; and so with reference to the rules of clothing and of medicine; take care you do not by the food you take, encourage in yourselves a covetous or an angry mind. 2036

'Eat your food to satisfy your hunger and (drink to satisfy) your thirst, as we repair an old or broken chariot, or like the butterfly that sips the flower destroying not its fragrance or its texture. 2037

'The Bhikshu, in begging food, should beware of injuring the faithful mind of another[1]; if a man opens his heart in charity, think not about his capabilities (i. e. to overtax him), 2038

'For 'tis not well to calculate too closely the strength of the ox, lest by loading him (beyond his strength) you cause him injury. At morning, noon, and night, successively, store up good works. 2039

'During the first and after watch at night be not overpowered by sleep, but in the middle watch, with heart composed, take sleep (and rest)—be thoughtful towards the dawn of day. 2040

[1] This seems to refer to the offence given by a Bhikshu in asking food, either seeking much or of different quality to that offered.

'Sleep not the whole night through, making the body and the life relaxed and feeble; think! when the fire shall burn the body always, what length of sleep will then be possible? 2041

'For when the hateful brood of sorrow rising through space, with all its attendant horrors, meeting the mind o'erwhelmed by sleep and death, shall seize its prey, who then shall waken it? 2042

'The poisonous snake dwelling within a house can be enticed away by proper charms, so the black toad that dwells within his heart, the early waker disenchants and banishes. 2043

'He who sleeps on heedlessly (without plan), this man has no modesty; but modesty is like a beauteous robe, or like the curb that guides the elephant. 2044

'Modest behaviour keeps the heart composed, without it every virtuous root will die. Who has this modesty, the world applauds (calls him excellent); without it, he is but as any beast. 2045

'If a man with a sharp sword should cut the (another's) body bit by bit (limb by limb), let not an angry thought, or of resentment, rise, and let the mouth speak no ill word. 2046

'Your evil thoughts and evil words but hurt yourself and not another; nothing so full of victory as patience, though your body suffer the pain of mutilation. 2047

'For recollect that he who has this patience cannot be overcome, his strength being so firm; therefore give not way to anger or evil words towards men in power[1]. 2048

[1] So I translate the symbol 'kia.'

'Anger and hate destroy the true law; and they destroy dignity and beauty of body; as when one dies we lose our name for beauty, so the fire of anger itself burns up the heart. 2049

'Anger is foe to all religious merit, he who loves virtue let him not be passionate; the layman who is angry when oppressed by many sorrows is not wondered at, 2050

'But he who has "left his home[1]" indulging anger, this is indeed opposed to principle, as if in frozen water there were found the heat of fire. 2051

'If indolence (an indolent mind) arises in your heart, then with your own hand smooth down your head[2], shave off your hair, and clad in sombre (dyed or stained) garments, in your hand holding the begging-pot, go ask for food; 2052

'On every side the living perish, what room for indolence? the worldly man, relying on his substance or his family, indulging in indolence, is wrong; 2053

'How much more the religious man, whose purpose is to seek the way of rescue, who encourages within an indolent mind; this surely is impossible! 2054

'Crookedness and truth (straightness) are in their nature opposite and cannot dwell together more than frost and fire; for one who has become religious, and practises the way of straight behaviour, a false and crooked way of speech is not becoming. 2055

'False and flattering speech is like the magician's

[1] That is, the hermit, or professed disciple.

[2] Does this refer to smoothing the hair previous to shaving it off? But the sense in any case is obscure, for how could a person admit himself to the 'order?'

art; but he who ponders on religion cannot speak falsely (wildly). To "covet much," brings sorrow; desiring little, there is rest and peace. 2056

'To procure rest (peace of mind), there must be small desire—much more in case of those who seek deliverance (salvation). The niggard dreads the much-seeking man lest he should filch away his property (wealth and jewels), 2057

'But he who loves to give has also fear, lest he should not possess enough to give; therefore we ought to encourage small desire, that we may have to give to him who wants, without such fear. 2058

'From this desiring-little-mind we find the way of true deliverance; desiring true deliverance (seeking salvation) we ought to practise knowing-enough (contentment). 2059

'A contented mind is always joyful, but joy like this is but religion[1]; the rich and poor alike, having contentment, enjoy perpetual rest. 2060

'The ill-contented man though he be born to heavenly joys, because he is not contented would ever have a mind burned up by the fire of sorrow. 2061

'The rich, without contentment, endures the pain of poverty; though poor, if yet he be contented, then he is rich indeed! 2062

'That ill-contented man, the bounds of the five desires extending further still, (becomes) insatiable in his requirements, (and so) through the long night (of life) gathers increasing sorrow. 2063

'Without cessation thus he cherishes his careful (anxious) plans, whilst he who lives contented, freed

[1] So the line plainly means fun hi tsih shi fă, 'joy, like this, is but religion.'

from anxious thoughts about relationships (family concerns), his heart is ever peaceful and at rest. 2064

'And so because he rests and is at peace within, the gods and men revere and do him service. Therefore we ought to put away all cares about relationship (the encumbrance of close or distant relationships). 2065

'For like a solitary desert tree in which the birds and monkeys gather, so is it when we are cumbered much with family associations; through the long night we gather many sorrows. 2066

'Many dependents (relationships) are like the many bands (that bind us), or like the old elephant that struggles in the mud. By diligent perseverance a man may get much profit; 2067

'Therefore night and day men ought with ceaseless effort to exert themselves; the tiny streams that trickle down the mountain slopes (valleys) by always flowing eat away the rock. 2068

'If we use not earnest diligence in drilling wood in wood for fire, we shall not obtain the spark, so ought we to be diligent and persevere, as the skilful master drills the wood for fire. 2069

'A "virtuous friend[1]" though he be gentle is not to be compared with right reflection (thought)—right thought kept well in the mind, no evil thing can ever enter there. 2070

'Wherefore those who practise (a religious life) should always think about "the body" (their true condition—themselves); if thought upon oneself be

[1] This 'virtuous friend' is here, probably, to be taken in its literal sense. The 'right reflection' is samyak smriti. And so the others that follow are the eight portions of the holy path.

absent, then all virtue (virtuous intentions or purposes) dies. 2071

'For as the champion warrior relies for victory upon his armour's strength, so "right thought" is like a strong cuirass able to withstand the six sense-robbers (the robber-objects of the six senses). 2072

'Right faith[1] (samâdhi) enwraps[2] the enlightened heart, (so that a man) perceives the world throughout (is liable to) birth and death; therefore the religious man should practise "samâdhi." 2073

'Having found peace (quietness and peace) in samâdhi, we put an end to all the mass of sorrows, wisdom then can enlighten us, and so we put away the rules by which we acquire (knowledge by the senses). 2074

'By inward thought and right consideration following with gladness the directions of the "true law," this is the way in which both lay (men of the world) and men who have left their homes (religious men) should walk. 2075

'Across the sea of birth and death, "wisdom" is the handy bark; "wisdom" is the shining lamp that lightens up the dark and gloomy (world). 2076

'"Wisdom" is the grateful medicine for all the defiling ills [of life] (âsravas); "wisdom" is the axe wherewith to level all the tangled (prickly) forest trees of sorrow. 2077

'"Wisdom" is the bridge that spans the rushing stream of ignorance and lust—therefore, in every

---

[1] Mr. Rhys Davids (Sacred Books of the East, vol. xi, p. 145) is of opinion that samâdhi in Buddhism corresponds to 'faith' in Christianity. There is much to bear out this opinion.

[2] The ἔνδυμα (in a gnostic sense) of the awakened heart; the atmosphere in which the enlightened heart lives.

way, by thought and right attention (listening), a man should diligently inure himself to engender "wisdom." 2078

'Having acquired the threefold[1] wisdom, then, though blind, the eye of wisdom sees throughout; but without wisdom the mind is poor and insincere (false); such things cannot suit (agree with) the man who has left his home. 2079

'Wherefore let the enlightened man lay well to heart that false and fruitless (vain) things become him not, and let him strive with single mind for that pure (refined and excellent) joy which can be found alone in perfect rest and quietude (the place of rest and peace, i. e. Nirvâ*n*a). 2080

'Above all things be not careless, for carelessness is the chief foe of virtue; if a man avoid this fault he may be born where *S*akra-râ*g*a dwells. 2081

'He who gives way to carelessness of mind must have his lot where the Asuras dwell. Thus have I done my task, my fitting task, (in setting forth the way of) quietude, the proof (work) of love[2]. 2082

'On your parts be diligent[3] (earnest)! with virtuous purpose practise well these rules (works), in quiet solitude of desert hermitage nourish and cherish a still and peaceful heart. 2083

---

[1] Is this the wisdom of Buddha, dharma and saṅgha? or does it refer to the trividyâs, the knowledge of impermanence, sorrow, and unreality? See Childers, Pâli Dict. sub vijja; also Mr. Rhys Davids' Tevi*gg*a Sutta, Introduction, Sacred Books of the East, vol. xi.

[2] I have finished my task of love in setting forth to you the way of rest.

[3] 'Behold now, brethren, I exhort you, saying, "Decay is inherent in all component things! Work out your salvation with diligence!"' Sacred Books of the East, vol. xi, p. 114.

'Exert yourselves to the utmost, give no place to remissness, for as in worldly matters when the considerate physician prescribes fit medicine for the disease he has detected, 2084

'Should the sick man neglect to use it, this cannot be the physician's fault, so I have told you (now) the truth, and set before you this the one and level road (the road of plain duty). 2085

'Hearing my words and not with care obeying them, this is not the fault of him who speaks; if there be anything not clearly understood in the principles of the "four truths," 2086

'You now may ask me, freely; let not your inward thoughts be longer hid.' The lord in mercy thus instructing them, the whole assembly remained silent. 2087

Then Anuruddha, observing that the great congregation continued silent and expressed no doubt, with closed hands thus spake to Buddha: 2088

'The moon may be warm, the sun's rays be cool, the air be still[1], the earth's nature mobile; these four things, though yet unheard of in the world, (may happen); 2089

'But this assembly never can have doubt about the principles of sorrow, accumulation, destruction, and the way (the four truths)—the incontrovertible truths, as declared by the lord. 2090

'But because the lord is going to die, we all have sorrow (are deeply affected); and we cannot raise our thoughts to the high theme of the lord's preaching. 2091

'Perhaps some fresh disciple, whose feelings are

[1] In the sense of 'fixed' or 'solid.'

yet not entirely freed (from other influences) [might doubt]; but we, who now have heard this tender, sorrowful discourse, have altogether freed ourselves from doubt. 2092

'Passed the sea of birth and death, without desire, with nought to seek, we only know how much we love, and, grieving, ask, why Buddha dies so quickly?' 2093

Buddha regarding Anuruddha, perceiving how his words were full of bitterness (sorrow-laden), again with loving heart, appeasing him, replied: 2094

'In the beginning[1] things were fixed, in the end again they separate; different combinations cause other substances, for there is no uniform and constant principle (in nature). 2095

'But when all mutual purposes be answered (what is for oneself and for another, be done), what then shall chaos and creation do! the gods and men alike that should be saved, shall all have been completely saved! 2096

'Ye then! my followers, who know so well the perfect law, remember! the end must come (complete destruction of the universe must come); give not way again to sorrow! 2097

'Use diligently the appointed means; aim to reach the home where separation cannot come; I have lit the lamp of wisdom, its rays alone can drive away the gloom that shrouds the world. 2098

'The world is not for ever fixed! Ye should

[1] This is a very singular passage; it refers to the Buddhist theory that the world (universe) is continually renewed and destroyed, but here we have the novel addition that in 'the end' all this will cease, and there will be no chaos ('void,' hung) and no renovation (re-creation).

rejoice therefore! as when a friend, afflicted grievously, his sickness healed, escapes from pain. 2099

'For I have put away this painful vessel (my painful body), I have stemmed the flowing sea (sea current) of birth and death, free for ever now, from pain (the mass of sorrow)! for this you should exult with joy! 2100

'Now guard yourselves aright, let there be no remissness! that which exists will all return to nothingness! and now I die. 2101

'From this time forth my words are done, this is my very last instruction.' Then entering the Samâdhi of the first Dhyâna, he went successively through all the nine in a direct order; 2102

Then inversely he returned throughout and entered on the first, and then from the first he raised himself and entered on the fourth. 2103

Leaving the state of Samâdhi, his soul without a resting-place (a house to lodge in), forthwith he reached Nirvâ*n*a. And then, as Buddha died, the great earth quaked throughout. 2104

In space, on every hand, was fire like rain (it rained fire) [or, possibly, 'there was rain and fire'], no fuel, self-consuming[1]. And so from out the earth great flames arose on every side (the eight points of the earth), 2105

Thus up to the heavenly mansions flames burst forth; the crash of thunder shook the heavens and earth, rolling along the mountains and the valleys, 2106

Even as when the Devas and Asuras fight with sound of drums and mutual conflict. A wind tempestuous from the four bounds of earth arose—

[1] That is, the fire was self-originated, and was supported without fuel.

whilst from the crags and hills, dust and ashes fell like rain. 2107

The sun and moon withdrew their shining; the peaceful streams on every side were torrent-swollen; the sturdy forests shook like aspen leaves, whilst flowers and leaves untimely fell around, like scattered rain. 2108

The flying dragons, carried on pitchy clouds, wept down their tears[1] (five-headed tears); the four kings and their associates, moved by pity[2], forgot their works of charity. 2109

The pure Devas came to earth from heaven, halting mid-air they looked upon the changeful scene (or, the death scene), not sorrowing, not rejoicing. 2110

But yet they sighed to think of the world, heedless of its sacred teacher, hastening to destruction. The eightfold heavenly spirits[3], on every side filled space, 2111

Cast down at heart and grieving, they scattered flowers as offerings. Only Mâra-râ*g*a rejoiced, and struck up sounds of music in his exultation. 2112

Whilst *G*ambudvîpa[4], shorn of its glory, (seemed to grieve) as when the mountain tops fall down to earth, or like the great elephant robbed of its tusks, or like the ox-king spoiled of his horns; 2113

Or heaven without the sun and moon, or as the lily beaten by the hail; thus was the world bereaved when Buddha died! 2114

---

[1] This passage is obscure, it may mean the dragons wept tears from their five heads, but it is doubtful.

[2] Here again is an error in the text, the symbol 舍 being clearly a misprint.

[3] That is, Nâgas, Kinnaras, and the rest.

[4] That is, 'the world,' as Buddhists count it.

VARGA 27. PRAISING NIRVÂNA.

At this time there was a Devaputra, riding on (or in) his thousand[1] white-swan palace[2] in the midst of space, who beheld the Parinirvâna of Buddha. 2115

This one, for the universal benefit of the Deva assembly, sounded forth at large these verses (gâthas) on impermanence: 'Impermanency is the nature of all (things), quickly born, they quickly die. 2116

'With birth there comes the rush[3] of sorrows, only in Nirvâna[4] is there joy. The accumulated fuel heaped up by the power of karman[5] (deeds), this the fire of wisdom alone can consume. 2117

'Though the fame (of our deeds[6]) reach up to heaven as smoke, yet in time the rains which descend will extinguish all, as the fire that rages at the kalpa's end is put out by the judgment[7] (calamity) of water.' 2118

---

[1] The symbol for 'thousand' is probably an error for the preposition 'u' upon.

[2] The hamsa is the vehicle of Brahmâ. The white hamsa is probably the same.

[3] The accumulation, or crowd of sorrows.

[4] Ts'ie mih, quiet extinction, or the destruction ending in quietness.

[5] The collection of the pile of fuel of the deeds (or beams) of conduct (samskâras).

[6] Or, simply, 'though our fame;' or it may refer to the renown of Buddha.

[7] Referring to the Buddhist account of the destruction and renovation of the universe; the last 'calamity' or 'judgment' was the destruction by water.

Again there was a Brahma-*Ri*shi-deva, like a most exalted *Ri*shi (a highest-principle *Ri*shi[1]), dwelling in heaven, possessed of superior happiness, with no taint in his bliss (heavenly inheritance), 2119

Who thus sighed forth his praises of Tathâgata's Nirvâ*n*a, with his mind fixed in abstraction as he spoke: 'Looking through all the conditions of life (of the three worlds), from first to last nought is free from destruction. 2120

'But the incomparable seer dwelling in the world, thoroughly acquainted with the highest truth[2], whose wisdom grasps that which is beyond the (world's) ken[3], he it is who can save the worldly-dwellers[4]. 2121

'He it is who can provide lasting escape (preservation) from the destructive power of impermanence. But, alas! through the wide world, all that lives is sunk in unbelief (heretical teaching).' 2122

At this time Anuruddha, 'not stopped' (ruddha)[5] by the world, 'not stopped' from being delivered

---

[1] This may refer to one of the highest *Ri*shis, or Pra*g*âpati *Ri*shis, belonging to the Vedic literature.

[2] Here is the same phrase, 'ti yih i,' the first, or highest, truth, or principle of truth (paramârtha).

[3] Whose wisdom sees that which (*k*é) is above, or superior, (to man.)

[4] The difficulty is to find a word in English corresponding to the Buddhist phrase 'all in the world;' it is not only 'mankind' (Sacred Books of the East, vol. xi, p. 133) that are invited to trust in Buddha, but all things that have life. The Chinese phrase is '*k*ung sing,' all that lives.

[5] Not 'liu to,' where 'liu to' is equivalent to 'ruddha' in the proper name Anuruddha. I take the word, therefore, in the sense of 'stopped'—it is used, of course, as a figure of speech; so also in the next phrase. Anuruddha is here taken as A-niruddha.

(delivered and not stopped), the stream of birth and death for ever 'stopped[1]' (niruddha), 2123

Sighed forth the praises of Tathâgata's Nirvâ*n*a : 'All living things completely blind and dark[2]! the mass of deeds (sa*m*skâra) all perishing (inconstant), even as the fleeting cloud-pile[3]! 2124

'Quickly arising and as quickly perishing! the wise man holds not to such a refuge, for the diamond mace of inconstancy can (even) overturn the mountain of the *R*ishi hermit[4] (muni). 2125

'How despicable and how weak the world! doomed to destruction, without strength! Impermanence, like the fierce lion, can even spoil the Nâga-elephant-great-*R*ishi[5]. 2126

'Only the diamond curtain of Tathâgata can overwhelm[6] inconstancy! How much more should those not yet delivered from desire (passion), fear and dread its power. 2127

'From the six seeds there grows one sprout[7], one kind of water from the rain, the origin of the

---

[1] Ni-liu-to, equal to 'niruddha.'

[2] 宜 for 冥.

[3] The Chinese 'feou' means a 'floating' pile or mass, whether of clouds or fanciful worlds. Hence its use in the later Buddhist development to mean a 'series of worlds' (as in the successive stages of the pagoda).

[4] Or, the *R*ishi-hermit-mountain, referring probably to Buddha.

[5] Referring again to Buddha.

[6] The literal translation would be, 'only makes impermanence, destruction.' There may be an error in the text, but this sense is sufficiently plain. The meaning of the word 'curtain,' or, perhaps, 'standard,' is not quite so evident in this connection, it is evidently used in opposition to the 'diamond mace,' in the preceding clause.

[7] This and the following lines are obscure; the reference must be gathered from Sanskrit rather than Chinese. The line before us, rendered literally, is 'six seeds, one bud.'

four points[1] is far removed, five kinds of fruit from the two "koo[2];" 2128

'The three periods (past, present, future) are but one in substance; the Muni-great-elephant plucks up the great tree of sorrow, and yet he (even he) cannot avoid the power of impermanence. 2129

'For like the crested[3] (*s*ikhin) bird delights (within) the pool (water) to seize the poisonous snake, but when from sudden drought he is left in the dry pool, he dies; 2130

'Or as the prancing steed advances fearlessly to battle, but when the fight has passed goes back subdued and quiet; or as the raging fire burns with the fuel, but when the fuel is done, expires; 2131

'So is it with Tathâgata, his task accomplished he returns[4] to (find his refuge in) Nirvâ*n*a: just as the shining of the radiant moon sheds everywhere its light and drives away the gloom, 2132.

'All creatures grateful for its light, (then suddenly) it disappears concealed by Sumeru; such is the case with Tathâgata, the brightness of his wisdom lit up the gloomy darkness, 2133

'And for the good of all that lives drove it away, when suddenly it disappears behind the mountain of Nirvâ*n*a. The splendour of his fame throughout the world diffused, 2134

---

[1] The four 'yin' may be the four points of the compass. But the text is without note or comment.

[2] The Chinese symbol 'koo' means a 'libation cup.'

[3] The symbols 'shi-hi' correspond with Sanskrit *s*ikhin; I have therefore taken it in the sense of 'crested.' There may be a bird, however, called *S*ikhin.

[4] The expression 'he returns to Nirvâ*n*a' is unusual; I have therefore used the alternative meaning which the symbol 'kwei' sometimes has, 'finding refuge in.'

'Had banished all obscurity, but like the stream that ever flows, it rests not with us; the illustrious charioteer with his seven prancing steeds[1] flies through the host (and disappears); 2135

'The bright-rayed[2] Sûrya-deva, entering the Yen-tsz'[3] cave, was, with the moon, surrounded with fivefold barriers; "all things that live," deprived of light, 2136

'Present their offerings to heaven; but from their sacrifice nought but the blacken'd smoke ascends[4]; thus is it with Tathâgata, his glory hidden, the world has lost its light. 2137

'Rare was the expectancy of grateful love[5] that filled the heart of all that lives; that love, reached its full limit, then was left to perish! 2138

'The cords of sorrow all removed, we found the true and only way; but now he leaves the tangled mesh of life, and enters on the quiet place! 2139

'His spirit (or, by spiritual power) mounting through space, he leaves the sorrow-bearing vessel of his body! the gloom of doubt and the great

---

[1] This passage is a difficult one; if the construction is closely followed, the rendering would be this, 'The illustrious charioteer (with) his seven swift steeds, the army host quickly (or, the wings of the army host) following him about.' Possibly it must be connected with the lines which follow, and refers to the saptâ*s*vavâhana of Sûrya.

[2] Kwong-kwong, well-rayed.

[3] The Yen-tsz' cave is the fabulous hiding-place of the sun. The fable is a common one, particularly in Japanese mythology. I do not know whether it is found in Sanskrit literature.

[4] The reference in this and the preceding lines is to the disappearance of the sun and moon, and the darkness of the world, compared to the Nirvâ*n*a of Tathâgata.

[5] This is a free translation; I have taken 'tsiueh' as an intensitive particle.

(heaped-up) darkness all dispelled, by the bright rays of wisdom! 2140

'The earthy soil of sorrow's dust his wisdom's water purifies! no more, no more, returns he here! for ever gone to the place of rest! 2141

'(The power of) birth and death destroyed, the world (all things) instructed in the highest doctrine! he bids the world rejoice in (knowledge of) his law, and gives to all the benefit of wisdom! 2142

'Giving complete rest to the world, the virtuous streams[1] flow forth! his fame known (spread) throughout the world, shines still with increased splendour! 2143

'How great his pity and his love to those who opposed his claims, neither rejoicing in their defeat nor exulting in his own success[2]. 2144

'Illustriously controlling his feelings, all his senses completely enlightened, his heart impartially observing events, unpolluted by the six objects (or, fields) of sense! 2145

'Reaching to that unreached before! obtaining that which man had not obtained! with the water which he provided filling every thirsty soul! 2146

'Bestowing that which never yet was given, and providing a reward not hoped for! his peaceful, well-marked person, perfectly knowing the thoughts[3] (prayers) of all. 2147

---

[1] The streams of his virtuous qualities.

[2] This verse again is doubtful. The entire section (a hymn of praise in honour of the departed Buddha) is couched in obscure, figurative language.

[3] His well-composed and illustrious person, knowing perfectly all the reflections of men. 'Nim' is sometimes used to signify 'prayers' or 'aspirations.'

'Not greatly moved either by loving or disliking! overcoming all enemies by the force (of his love)! the welcome physician for all diseases, the one destroyer of impermanency! 2148

'All living things rejoicing in religion, fully satisfied[1]! obtaining all they need (seek), their every wish (vow) fulfilled! 2149

'The great master of holy wisdom once gone returns no more! even as the fire gone out for want of fuel! 2150

'(Declaring) the eight rules (noble truths?) without taint[2]; overcoming the five[3] (senses), difficult to compose! with the three[4] (powers of sight) seeing the three (precious ones); removing the three (robbers, i. e. lust, anger, ignorance); perfecting the three (the three grades of a holy life). 2151

'Concealing[5] the one (himself) and obtaining the one (saintship)—leaping over the seven (bodhyaṅgas?) and (obtaining) the long sleep; the end of all, the quiet, peaceful way; the highest prize of sages and of saints! 2152

---

[1] Each one satisfied; the sense seems to be that through him, i. e. Buddha, all things obtained the completion of their religious desires.

[2] Or it may be by way of exclamation, 'those eight rules which admit of no pollution!' referring perhaps to the name 'the noble rules.'

[3] I suppose 'the five' are the five senses. The expression 'difficult to compose' might be also rendered 'the difficult to compose group.'

[4] Using (i) 'the three,' and yet seeing the 'three.' The next line is, 'removing the three,' and yet perfecting 'the three.'

[5] Or it may be 'treasuring the one,' where 'the one' may be the one duty of a religious life; but it is difficult to interpret these paradoxes.

'Having himself severed the barriers of sorrow, now he is able to save his followers, and to provide the draught of immortality (sweet dew) for all who are parched with thirst! 2153

'Armed with the heavy cuirass of patience, he has overcome all enemies! (now) by the subtle principles of his excellent law (able to) satisfy every heart. 2154

'Planting a sacred seed (seed of holiness) in the hearts of those practising virtue (worldly virtue[1]); impartially directing and not casting off those who are right or not right (in their views)! 2155

'Turning the wheel of the superlative law! received with gladness through the world by those (the elect) who have in former conditions implanted in themselves a love for religion, these all saved by his preaching! 2156

'Going forth[2] among men converting those not yet converted; those who had not seen (learned) the truth, causing them to see the truth! 2157

'All those practising a false method (heretical) of religion, delivering to them deep principles (of his religion)! preaching the doctrines of birth and death and impermanency; (declaring that) without a master[3] (teacher) there can be no happiness! 2158

'Erecting the standard of his great renown, overcoming and destroying the armies of Mâra (all the Mâras)! advancing to the point of indifference to

[1] The sense seems to be, that in the case of those leading a virtuous life, i. e. a moral life, the seeds of holiness take root.

[2] All these verses might be introduced with some such exclamation as this, 'See! how he went forth!' &c.

[3] Perhaps the word '*k*u' might be rendered 'a ruling principle,' viz. of religion.

pleasure or pain, caring not for life, desiring only rest (Nirvâna)! 2159.

'Causing those not yet converted to obtain conversion! those not yet saved to be saved! those not yet at rest to find rest! those not yet enlightened to be enlightened! 2160

'(Thus) the Muni (taught) the way of rest for the direction of all living things! alas! that any transgressing the way of holiness should practise impure (not right) works. 2161

'Even as at the end of the great kalpa, those holding the law who die (or, are dead[1]), (when) the rolling sound of the mysterious thunder-cloud severs the forests, upon these there shall fall the rain of sweet dew (immortality). 2162

'The little elephant breaks down the prickly forest, and by cherishing it we know that it can profit men[2]; but the cloud that removes the sorrow of the elephant old-age[3], this none can bear[3]. 2163

'He by destroying systems of religion (sights, i. e. modes of seeing, darsanas) has perfected his

---

[1] The literal translation of this passage is curious: 'Even as at the end of the great kalpa, those holding the law, asleep; the mysterious cloud rolling forth its cracking (thunder), riving the forests, there descends as rain sweet dew.' The end of the great kalpa is the consummation of all things: 'the religious who sleep' would mean the good who are dead; 'the cracking thunder and riven forests' would point to a general overthrow; 'the rain of sweet dew' seems to refer to the good who sleep, receiving immortality, or perfection of life.

[2] 'The little elephant' may mean 'the young elephant' in its literal sense; or it may refer to 'the young disciple.' 'By cherishing it we know' may also be rendered 'knowledge-cherishing' is able, &c.

[3] 'The cloud removing the elephant old and sorrowful;' but what is 'the cloud' and who 'the elephant?'

system, in saving the world and yet saving! he has destroyed the teaching of heresy, in order to reach his independent (self-sufficient) mode (way) [of doctrine]. 2164

'And now he enters the great quiet (place)! no longer has the world a protector or saviour! the great army host of Mâra-râ*g*a, rousing their warrior (spirits), shaking the great earth, 2165

'Desired to injure the honour'd Muni! but they could not move him, whom in a moment now the Mâra "inconstancy" destroys. 2166

'The heavenly occupants (Devas) everywhere assemble as a cloud! they fill the space of heaven, fearing the endless (mastery of) birth and death! their hearts are full of (give birth to) grief and dread! 2167

'His Deva eyes clearly behold, without the limitations of near or distant, the fruits of works discerned throughout, as an image perceived in a mirror! 2168

'His Deva ears perfect and discriminating throughout, hear all, though far away (not near), mounting through space he teaches all the Devas, surpassing his method (limit) of converting men! 2169

'He divides his body still one in substance, crosses the water as if it were not weak (to bear)[1]! remembers all his former births, through countless kalpas none forgotten! 2170

---

[1] This sentence may perhaps be rendered thus, 'dividing his body yet one in substance, wading through water and yet not weak,' but the allusion is obscure. [It refers, probably, to Buddha's miraculous powers.]

'His senses (roots) wandering through the fields of sense (limits)[1], all these distinctly remembered; knowing the wisdom learned in every (state of) mind, all this perfectly understood! 2171

'By spiritual discernment and pure mysterious wisdom equally (impartially) surveying all (things)! every vestige of imperfection (leak) removed! thus he has accomplished all (he had to do). 2172

'By wisdom rejecting other spheres of life, his wisdom now completely perfected, lo! he dies! let the world, hard and unyielding, still, beholding it, relent! 2173

'All living things though blunt in sense, beholding him, receive the enlightenment of wisdom! their endless evil deeds long past, as they behold, are cancelled and completely cleansed! 2174

'In a moment gone! who shall again exhibit qualities like his? no saviour now in all the world— our hope cut off, our very breath (life) is stopped and gone! 2175

'Who now shall give us life again with the cool water (of his doctrine)? his own great work accomplished, his great compassion now has ceased to work for long (has long ceased or stopped)! 2176

'The world ensnared in the toils of folly, who shall destroy the net? who shall, by his teaching, cause the stream of birth and death to turn again? 2177

'Who shall declare the way of rest (to instruct)

---

[1] The meaning is, all his births, in which his senses or material body took every kind of shape; all these he knew. The figurative style of this 'hymn' may be gathered from this one instance, where instead of saying 'all his previous births' it is said 'his senses wandering through the field (limits or boundaries) of sense.'

the heart of all that lives, deceived by ignorance? Who will point out the quiet place, or who make known the one true doctrine (system of doctrine)? 2178

'All flesh suffering (receiving) great sorrow, who shall deliver, like a loving father? Like the horse changing his master loses all gracefulness, as he forgets his many words of guidance (so are we)! 2179

'As a king without a kingdom, such is the world without a Buddha! as a disciple (a *S*râvaka, a "much hearer") with no power of dialectic (distinguishing powers) left, or like a physician without wisdom, 2180

'As men whose king has lost the marks of royalty (bright or glorious marks), so, Buddha dead, the world has lost its glory! the gentle horses left without a charioteer, the boat without a pilot left! 2181

'The three divisions[1] of an army left without a general! the merchantmen without a guide! the suffering and diseased without a physician! a holy king (*k*akravartin) without his seven insignia (jewels, ratnâni)! 2182

'The stars without the moon! the loving years (the planet Jupiter?) without the power of life!—such is the world now that Buddha, the great teacher, dies!' 2183

Thus (spake) the Arhat[2], all done that should be done, all imperfections quite removed, knowing the meed of gratitude, he was grateful therefore (spake gratefully of his master); 2184

Thus thinking of his master's love he spake!

---

[1] Infantry, cavalry, and chariots.

[2] That is, as it seems, Anuruddha.

setting forth the world's great sorrow; whilst those, not yet freed from the power of passion, wept with many tears, unable to control themselves. 2185

Yet even those who had put away all faults, sighed as they thought of the pain of birth and death. And now the Malla host[1] hearing that Buddha had attained Nirvâ*n*a, 2186

With cries confused, wept piteously, greatly moved, as when a flight of herons meet a hawk (kite). In a body now they reach the twin (*S*âla) trees, and as they gaze upon Tathâgata dead (entered on his long sleep), 2187

Those features never again to awake to consciousness, they smote their breasts and sighed to heaven; as when a lion seizing on a calf, the whole herd rushes on with mingled sounds. 2188

In the midst there was one Malla, his mind enamoured of the righteous law, who gazed with steadfastness upon the holy[2] law-king, now entered on the mighty calm, 2189

And said: 'The world was everywhere asleep, when Buddha setting forth his law caused it to awake; but now he has entered on the mighty calm, and all is finished in an unending sleep. 2190

'For man's sake he had raised the standard of his law, and now, in a moment, it has fallen; the sun of Tathâgata's wisdom spreading abroad the lustre of its "great awakening[3]," 2191

[1] The Mallas (wrestlers) are termed 'lih-sse,' strong-masters, in Chinese. They dwelt at Ku*s*inagara and Pâvâ. The Li*kkh*avis are also called lih-sse.

[2] The holy law-king, dharmarâ*g*a.

[3] The 'great awakening' refers, of course, to Buddha as 'the awakened.'

'Increasing ever more and more in glory, spreading abroad the thousand rays of highest knowledge, scattering and destroying all the gloom (of earth), why has the darkness great come back again? 2192

'His unequalled wisdom lightening the three worlds, giving eyes that all the world might see, now suddenly (the world is) blind again, bewildered, ignorant of the way; 2193

'In a moment fallen the bridge of truth (that spanned) the rolling stream of birth and death, the swelling flood of lust and rage and doubt, and all flesh overwhelmed therein, for ever lost.' 2194

Thus all that Malla host wept piteously and lamented; whilst some concealed their grief nor spoke a word; others sank prostrate on the earth; 2195

Others stood silent, lost in meditation; others, with sorrowful heart, groaned deeply. Then on a gold and silver gem-decked couch[1], richly adorned with flowers and scents, 2196

They placed the body of Tathâgata; a jewelled canopy they raised above, and round it flags and streamers and embroidered banners; then using every kind of dance and music[2], 2197

The lords and ladies of the Mallas followed

---

[1] The 'gem-decked couch' or palanquin is probably represented in plate lxiv, fig. 1 (Tree and Serpent Worship, first edition). This is the procession of the couch through Ku*s*inagara. The curly-haired men bearing it would indicate that the Mallas and Li*kkh*avis of Vai*s*âlî were the same race.

[2] The use of 'dance and music' at funerals is an old and well-understood custom. Compare Sacred Books of the East, vol. xi, pp. 122, 123.

along the road presenting offerings, whilst all the Devas scattered scents and flowers, and raised the sound of drums and music in the heavens. 2198

Thus men and Devas shared one common sorrow, their cries united as they grieved together. Entering the city, there the men and women, old and young, completed their religious offerings. 2199

Leaving the city, then, and passing through the Lung-tsiang gate[1], and crossing over the Hiranyavatî river, they repaired to where the former Buddhas having died, had Kaityas raised to them[2]. 2200

There collecting ox-head sandal wood and every famous scented wood, they placed the whole above the Buddha's body, pouring various scented oils upon the pyre; 2201

Then placing fire beneath to kindle it, three times they walked around; but yet it burned not. At this time the great Kâsyapa had taken his abode at Râgagriha[3], 2202

And knowing Buddha was about to die was coming thence with all his followers; his pure mind, deeply moved, desired to see the body of the lord; 2203

And so, because of that his sincere wish, the fire went out and would not kindle. Then Kâsyapa and his followers coming, with piteous sighs looked on the sight 2204

---

[1] The Nâga or Nâga-Elephant gate.

[2] Had their Nirvâna-kaityas erected. The account in the text does not agree with the Southern account; but the popular Chinese record of the Nirvâna is the same as the Pâli.

[3] He was between Pâvâ and Kusinagara, according to the common account.

And reverenced at the master's feet; and then, forthwith, the fire burst out. Quenched the fire of grief within; without, the fire has little power to burn. 2205

Or though it burn the outside skin and flesh, the diamond true-bone still remains. The scented oil consumed, the fire declines, the bones they place within a golden pitcher; 2206

For as the mystic world[1] (dharma-dhâtu) is not destroyed, neither can these, the bones (of Buddha), perish; the consequence (fruit) of diamond[2] wisdom, difficult to move as Sumeru. 2207

The relics which the mighty golden-pinioned bird cannot remove or change, they place within the precious vase; to remain until the world shall pass away; 2208

And wonderful! the power of men (the world) can thus fulfil Nirvâ*n*a's laws, the illustrious name of one far spread, is sounded thus throughout the universe; 2209

And as the ages roll, the long Nirvâ*n*a, by these, the sacred relics (bones), sheds through the world its glorious light, and brightens up the abodes of life. 2210

He perished (quenched his splendour) in a moment! but these relics, placed within the vase, the imperishable signs of wisdom, can overturn the mount of sorrow; 2211

---

[1] The dharma-dhâtu (fă kai) is the mystic or ideal world of the Northern Buddhists. Literally it is the 'limit (ὅρος) of dharma;' dharma being the universal essence. This bears a striking resemblance to the gnostic (Valentinian) theory of limitation of the Divine essence.

[2] Diamond wisdom, indestructible wisdom.

The body of accumulated griefs[1] this imperishable mind (*k*i) can cause to rest, and banish once for ever all the miseries of life. 2212

Thus the diamond substance (body) was dealt with at the place of burning. And now those valiant Mallas, unrivalled in the world for strength, 2213

Subduing all private animosities, sought escape from sorrow in the true refuge. Finding sweet comfort in united love, they resolved to banish every complaining thought. 2214

Beholding thus the death of Tathâgata, they controlled their grieving hearts, and with full strength of manly virtue dismissing every listless thought, they submitted to the course (laws) of nature. 2215

Oppressed by thoughts of grievous sorrow, they entered the city as a deserted wild, holding the relics thus they entered, whilst from every street were offered gifts. 2216

They placed the relics then upon a tower[2], for men and Devas to adore. 2217

VARGA 28. DIVISION OF THE *S*ARÎRAS.

Thus those Mallas offered religious reverence to the relics, and used the most costly flowers and scents for their supreme act of worship. 2218

Then the kings of the seven countries[3], having heard that Buddha was dead, sent messengers to

---

[1] That is, the body subject to accumulation of sorrow.

[2] 'In their council hall with a lattice work of spears, and with a rampart of bows,' Sacred Books of the East, vol. xi, p. 131.

[3] The seven 'kings' were, the king of Magadha, the Li*kkh*avis of Vai*s*âlî, the *S*âkyas of Kapilavastu, the Bulis of Allakappa, the Koliyas of Râmagrâma, the Brahman of Ve*th*adipa, and the Mallas of Pâvâ; Sacred Books of the East, vol. xi, pp. 131, 132.

the Mallas asking to share the sacred relics (of Buddha). 2219

Then the Mallas reverencing the body of Tathâgata, trusting to their martial renown, conceived a haughty mind: 2220

'They would rather part with life itself (they said), than with the relics of the Buddha;' so those messengers returned from the futile embassage. Then the seven kings, highly indignant, 2221

With an army, numerous as the rain clouds, advanced on Kusinagara; the people who went from the city filled with terror soon returned 2222

And told the Mallas all, that the soldiers and the cavalry of the neighbouring countries were coming, with elephants and chariots, to surround the Kusinagara city. 2223

The gardens, lying without the town, the fountains, lakes, flower and fruit trees were now destroyed by the advancing host, and all the pleasant resting-places lay in ruins. 2224

The Mallas, mounting on the city towers, beheld the great supports of life[1] destroyed; they then prepared their warlike engines to crush the foe without; 2225

Balistas[2] and catapults and 'flying torches[3]' to

[1] The supports of life, as I take it, are the fields and fountains.

[2] It may be rendered 'bow catapults' and 'balista-stone-carriages,' or bows, catapults, balistas, and stone carriages (carrying machines?).

[3] These flying torches and other instruments were used by the Northern nations from remote antiquity. There is no indication of them, however, in the plate (xxxviii) in Tree and Serpent Worship, which, I take it, represents this scene. Asvaghosha was familiar with Kanishka and his military appliances, and these doubtless included the instruments here referred to.

hurl against the advancing host. Then the seven kings entrenched themselves around the city, each army host filled with increasing courage; 2226

Their wings of battle shining in array as the sun's seven beams of glory shine; the heavy drums[1] rolling as the thunder, the warlike breath (rising) as the full cloud mist. 2227

The Mallas, greatly incensed, opening the gates command the fray to begin; the aged men and women whose hearts had trust in Buddha's law, 2228

With deep concern breathed forth their vow, 'Oh! may the victory be a bloodless one[2]!' Those who had friends used mutual exhortations not to encourage in themselves a desire for strife. 2229

And now the warriors, clad in armour, grasping their spears and brandishing their swords 'midst the confused noise and heavy drums[1] (advanced). But ere the contest had begun, 2230

There was a certain Brahman whose name was Dro*n*a (tuh-lau-na), celebrated for penetration, honour'd for modesty and lowliness, 2231

Whose loving heart took pleasure in religion. This one addressed those kings and said: 'Regarding the unequalled strength of yonder city, one man alone would be enough (for its defence); 2232

'How much less when with determined heart (they are united), can you subdue it! In the beginning[3] mutual strife produced destruction, how now can it result in glory or renown? 2233

---

[1] Is 鍾 for 鐘? If so, it would be cymbals and drums.

[2] May they subdue those without loss or hurt to themselves.

[3] Or, from the beginning.

'The clash of swords and bloody onset done, 'tis certain one must perish! and therefore whilst you aim to vanquish those, both sides will suffer in the fray. 2234

'Then there are many chances, too, of battle, 'tis hard to measure strength by appearances; the strong, indeed, may overcome the weak, the weak may also overcome the strong; 2235

'The powerful champion may despise the snake, but how will he escape a wounded body? there are men whose natures bland and soft, seem suited for the company of women or of children, 2236

'But when enlisted in the ranks, make perfect soldiers. As fire when it is fed with oil, though reckoned weak, is not extinguished easily; so when you say that they (your enemies) are weak, 2237

'Beware of leaning overmuch on strength of body; nought can compare with strength of right (religion). There was in ancient times a *G*ina[1] king, whose name was Kârandhama (Avikshit), 2238

'His graceful (upright) presence caused such love (in others) that he could overcome all animosity; but though he ruled the world and was high renowned, and rich and prosperous, 2239

'Yet in the end he went back[2] and all was lost! So when the ox has drunk enough, he too returns. Use then the principles of righteousness, use the expedients of good will and love. 2240

'Conquer your foe by force, you increase his

---

[1] A *G*ina king, or a conquering king. Kârandhama was a name of Avikshit.

[2] Whether it means he went back 'to death,' or he lost his possessions by warfare, is not plain from the text. The phrase 'all was lost,' may also be rendered, 'he gave up all.'

enmity; conquer by love, and you will reap no after-sorrow. The present strife is but a thirst for blood, this thing cannot be endured! 2241

'If you desire to honour Buddha, follow the example of his patience and long-suffering[1]!' Thus this Brahman with confidence declared the truth; 2242

Imbued with highest principles of peace, he spake with boldness and unflinchingly. And now the kings addressed the Brahman thus: 2243

'You have chosen a fitting time for giving increase to the seed of wisdom, the essence of true friendship is (leads to) the utterance of truth. The greatest force (of reason) lies in righteous judgment. 2244

'But now in turn hear what we say: The rules of kings are framed to avoid the use of force when hatred has arisen from low desires (question of the five pleasures); 2245

'Or else to avoid the sudden use of violence in trifling questions (where some trifling matter is at stake). But we for the sake of law (religion) are about to fight. What wonder is it! 2246

'Swollen pride is a principle to be opposed, for it leads to the overthrow of society; no wonder then that Buddha preached against it, teaching men to practise lowliness and humility. 2247

'Then why should we be forbidden to pay our reverence to his body-relics? In ancient days a

---

[1] 'Hear, reverend sirs, one single word from me.
Forbearance was our Buddha wont to teach.'
Sacred Books of the East, vol. xi, p. 133.

But it is not plain how Dro*n*a could address the Mallas as 'reverend sirs,' unless indeed the brethren were going to fight, which is beyond probability.

lord of the great earth, Pih-shih-tsung[1] Nanda [or two lords, viz. Pih-shih-tsung and Nanda], 2248

'For the sake of a beautiful woman fought and destroyed each other; how much more now, for the sake of religious reverence to our master, freed from passion, gone to Nirvâ*n*a, 2249

'Without regard to self, or careful of our lives, should we contend and assert our rights! A former king Kaurava (or belonging to the Kauravas) fought with a Pâ*nd*ava (king), 2250

'And the more they increased in strength the more they struggled, all for some temporary gain; how much more for our not-coveting[2] master (should we contend), coveting to get his living (relics)? 2251

'The son of Râma, too, the *Ri*shi (or Râma-*ri*shiputra), angry with king Da*s*aratha, destroyed his country, slew the people, because of the rage he felt; 2252

'How much less for our master, freed from anger, should we be niggard of our lives! Râma, for Sîta's sake, killed all the demon-spirits; 2253

'How much more for our lord, heaven[3]-received, should we not sacrifice our lives! The two demons A-lai (Alaka) and Po-ku were ever drawn into contention; 2254

'In the first place, because of their folly and ignorance, causing wide ruin among men; how

---

[1] The character 'tsung' in this name is uncertain, I have not therefore attempted to restore it.

[2] Not-covetous; here there is a double-entendre, contrasting the absence of covetousness in Buddha with the presence of it in the Pâ*nd*avas and Kauravas.

[3] 天攝受 heaven-taken-up-received.

much less for our all-wise master should we begrudge our lives! 2255

'Wherefore if from these examples we find others ready to die for no real principle, how shall we for our teacher of gods (Devas) and men, reverenced by the universe, 2256

'Spare our bodies or begrudge our lives, and not be earnest in desire to make our offerings! Now then, if you desire to stay the strife, go, and for us demand within the city 2257

'That they open wide (distribute) the relics, and so cause our prayer to be fulfilled. But because your words are right ones, we hold our anger for a while; 2258

'Even as the great, angry snake, by the power of charms is quieted.' And now the Brahman[1], having received the king's instruction, 2259

Entering the city, went to the Mallas, and saluting them, spoke these true words: 'Without the city those who are kings among men[2] grasp with their hands their martial weapons, 2260

'And with their bodies clad in weighty armour wait eagerly (to fight); glorious as the sun's rays; bristling with rage as the roused lion. These united are, to overthrow this city. 2261

'But whilst they wage this religious war, they fear lest they may act irreligiously, and so they have sent me here to say what they require. 2262

'"We[3] have come, not for the sake of territory,

---

[1] There is nothing like this in the Southern account.

[2] 'Kings among men,' ἄνακτες ἀνδρῶν.

[3] This is the only way to take the translation, although the pronoun 'ngo standing alone would signify 'I' have come; but

much less for money's sake, nor on account of any insolent feeling, nor yet from any thought of hatred; 2263

'"But because we venerate the great *Ri*shi, we have come on this account. You, noble sirs! know well our mind! Why should there be such sorrowful contention! 2264

'"You honour what we honour, both alike, then we are brothers as concerns religion. We both with equal heart revere the bequeathed spiritual relics of the lord. 2265

'"To be miserly in (hoarding) wealth, this is an unreasonable fault; how much more to grudge religion, of which there is so little knowledge in the world! 2266

'"The exclusive and the selfishly-inclined, should practise laws of hospitality (civility)[1]; but if ye have not rules of honour[2] such as these, then shut your gates and guard yourselves." 2267

'This is the tenor of the words, be they good or bad, spoken by them. But now for myself and my own feelings, let me add these true and sincere words. 2268

'Let there be no contention either way; reason ought to minister for peace, the lord when dwelling in the world ever employed the force of patience. 2269

'Not to obey his holy teaching, and yet to offer gifts to him, is contradiction. Men of the world

---

perhaps the singular implies that Dro*n*a used the words of the chief of the kings.

[1] Should practise 'waiting for guest laws,' civil conduct. I have given here the sense of the passage.

[2] Kshatriya rules, rules or laws of chivalry.

for some indulgence, some wealth or land, contend and fight, 2270

'But those who believe the righteous law, should obediently conform their lives to it; to believe and yet to harbour enmity, this is to oppose "religious principle" to "conduct." 2271

'Buddha himself at rest, and full of love, desired to bestow the rest he enjoyed, on all. To adore with worship the great merciful, and yet to gender wide destruction, 2272

'(How is this possible?) Divide the relics, then, that all may worship them alike; obeying thus the law, the fame thereof wide-spread, then righteous principles will be diffused; 2273

'But if others walk not righteously, we ought by righteous dealing to appease them, in this way showing the advantage (pleasure) of religion, we cause religion everywhere to take deep hold and abide. 2274

'Buddha has told us that of all charity "religious charity" is the highest; men easily bestow their wealth in charity, but hard is the charity that works for righteousness.' 2275

The Mallas hearing the Brahman's words with inward shame gazed at one another; and answered the Brahma*k*ârin thus: 'We thank you much for purposing to come to us, 2276

'And for your friendly and religious counsel—speaking so well, and reasonably. Yours are words which a Brahman ought to use, in keeping with his holy character[1]; 2277

'Words full of reconciliation, pointing out the

---

[1] 功德 merit, or religious merit.

proper road; like one recovering a wandering horse brings him back by the path which he had lost. 2278

'We then ought to adopt the plan of reconciliation such as you have shown us; to hear the truth and not obey it brings afterwards regretful sorrow.' 2279

Then they opened out the master's relics and in eight parts equally divided them. Themselves paid reverence to one part, the other seven they handed to the Brahman; 2280

The seven kings having accepted these, rejoiced and placed them on their heads[1]; and thus with them returned to their own country, and erected Dâgobas for worship over them. 2281

The Brahma*k*ârin then besought the Mallas to bestow on him the relic-pitcher as his portion, and from the seven kings he requested a fragment of their relics, as an eighth share. 2282

Taking this, he returned and raised a *K*aitya, which still is named 'the Golden Pitcher Dâgoba.' Then the men of Ku*s*inagara collecting all the ashes of the burning, 2283

Raised over them a *K*aitya, and called it 'the Ashes Dâgoba.' The eight Stûpas of the eight kings, 'the Golden Pitcher' and 'the Ashes Stûpa[2],' 2284

Thus throughout *G*ambudvîpa there first were raised ten Dâgobas. Then all the lords and ladies

---

[1] Placing relics on the head was a token of reverence. Compare plate xxxviii (Tree and Serpent Worship).

[2] In reference to these *K*aityas or towers, compare the account given in the Pâli (Sacred Books of the East, vol. xi, p. 135), and also Fă-hien, cap. xxiii.

of the country holding gem-embroidered canopies, 2285

Paid their offerings at the various shrines, adorning them as any golden mountain[1]. And so with music and with dancing through the day and night they made merry, and sang. 2286

And now the Arhats numbering five hundred, having for ever lost their master's presence, reflecting there was now no ground of certainty, returned to Gridhrakû*t*a mount; 2287

Assembling in king *S*akra's cavern[2], they collected there the Sûtra Pi*t*aka; all the assembly agreeing that the venerable Ânanda 2288

Should say (recite), for the sake of the congregation, the sermons of Tathâgata from first to last, 'Great and small, whatever you have heard from the mouth of the deceased Muni.' 2289

Then Ânanda in the great assembly ascending the lion throne, declared in order what the lord had preached, uttering the words 'Thus have I heard.' 2290

The whole assembly, bathed in tears, were deeply moved as he pronounced the words 'I heard;' and so he announced the law as to the time, as to the place, as to the person; 2291

As he spoke, so was it written down from first to last, the complete Sûtra Pi*t*aka[3]. By diligent

---

[1] Or, as the Golden Mountain, i. e. Sumeru.

[2] Indra *s*ilag*ri*ha.

[3] Here we have a short account of the first Buddhist Council, called the Council of the 500. It forms no part of the Mahâ-parinibbâna-Sutta, although it is found in the Vinaya Pi*t*aka. Compare Oldenberg, Vinaya Pi*t*akam, Introduction.

attention in the use of means, practising (the way of) wisdom, (all these) (Arhats) obtained Nirvâ*n*a; 2292

Those now able so to do, or hereafter able, shall attain Nirvâ*n*a, in the same way. King A*s*oka[1] born in the world when strong, caused much sorrow; 2293

When feeble[2], then he banished sorrow; as the A*s*oka-flower tree, ruling over *G*ambudvîpa, his heart for ever put an end to sorrow, 2294

When brought to entire faith in the true law; therefore he was called 'the King who frees from sorrow.' A descendant of the Mayûra family, receiving from heaven a righteous disposition, 2295

He ruled equally over the world; he raised everywhere towers and shrines, his private name the 'violent A*s*oka,' now called the 'righteous A*s*oka.' 2296

Opening the Dâgobas raised by those seven kings to take the *S*arîras thence, he spread them everywhere, and raised in one day eighty-four thousand towers[3]; 2297

Only with regard to the eighth pagoda in Râmagrama, which the Nâga spirit protected[4], the king was unable to obtain those relics; 2298

---

[1] This episode about A*s*oka is a curious one. It would seem from it that A*s*vaghosha knew only of one king of that name, called first 'the fierce,' afterwards 'the righteous.'

[2] There are one or two Avadânas to be met with in Chinese Buddhist literature, relating to A*s*oka's sickness, and how he then desired to redeem his character by making offerings to Buddha. But the accounts are too uncertain to be admitted as conclusive evidence in the question of his conversion.

[3] This is a story everywhere received in Northern books. These eighty-four thousand towers are supposed to represent the number of sections, or perhaps letters, in the Pi*t*akas.

[4] See Fă-hien's account, cap. xxiii.

But though he obtained them not, knowing they were spiritually bequeathed relics of Buddha which the Nâga worshipped and adored, his faith was increased and his reverent disposition. 2299

Although the king was ruler of the world, yet was he able to obtain the first holy fruit[1]; and thus induced the entire empire to honour and revere the shrines of Tathâgata. 2300

In the past and present, thus there has been deliverance for all. Tathâgata, when in the world; and now his relics—after his Nirvâ*n*a; 2301

Those who worship and revere these, gain equal merit; so also those who raise themselves by wisdom, and reverence the virtues of the Tathâgata, 2302

Cherishing religion, fostering a spirit of almsgiving, they gain great merit also. The noble and superlative law of Buddha ought to receive the adoration of the world. 2303

Gone to that undying place (Am*ri*ta), those who believe (his law) shall follow him there; therefore let all the Devas and men, without exception, worship and adore 2304

The one great loving and compassionate, who mastered thoroughly the highest truth, in order to deliver all that lives. Who that hears of him, but yearns with love! 2305

The pains of birth, old age, disease, and death, the endless sorrows of the world, the countless miseries of 'hereafter,' dreaded by all the Devas, 2306

He has removed all these accumulated sorrows;

[1] That is, the first step in the Buddhist profession of sanctity (Srotâpanna).

say, who would not revere him? to escape the joys of after life, this is the world's chief joy! 2307

To add the pain of other births, this is the world's worst sorrow! Buddha, escaped from pain of birth, shall have no joy of the 'hereafter[1]!' 2308

And having shown the way to all the world, who would not reverence and adore him? To sing the praises of the lordly monk, and (declare) his acts from first to last, 2309

Without self-seeking or self-honour, without desire for personal renown, but following what the scriptures say, to benefit the world, (has been my aim.) 2310

[1] The joy of the 'hereafter,' is the joy, as men count it, of future sentient happiness. This, according to the text, it is the happiness of Buddha to have escaped.

NOTES.

I. Comparative List of 17 Chapters of the Sanskrit and Chinese Copies of the Buddhakarita.

II. Example of the Style of the Expanded Sûtras, as translated into Chinese.

III. The same Title given to different Works.

NOTE I.

LIST OF THE TITLES OF 17 CHAPTERS OF THE SANSKRIT TEXT OF THE BUDDHA*K*ARITA-KÂVYA, BY A*S*VAGHOSHA.

॥ इति श्रीबुद्धचरिते महाकाव्ये

1 भगवत्प्रसूतिर्नाम प्रथमः सर्गः ॥
Birth of the Bhagavat.

2 अंतःपुरविहारो नाम द्वितीयः सर्गः ॥
Life in the Palace.

3 संवेगोत्पत्तिर्नाम तृतीयः सर्गः ॥
Beginning of Inward Trouble.

4 स्त्रीविघातनो नाम चतुर्थः सर्गः ॥
Separation from his Wife, &c.

5 अभिनिष्क्रमणो नाम पंचमः सर्गः ॥
Departure.

6 छंदकनिवर्तनं नाम षष्ठः सर्गः ॥
Return of *Kh*andaka.

7 तपोवनप्रवेशो नाम सप्तमः सर्गः ॥
Entering the Forest of Penance.

8 अंतःपुरविलापो नामाष्टमः सर्गः ॥
Lamentation in the Palace.

9 कुमारान्वेषणो नाम नवमः सर्गः ॥
Search after the Crown Prince.

10 अश्वघोषकृते श्रेण्यभिगमनो नाम दशमः सर्गः ॥
The arrival of *S*re*n*i.

NOTE I.

Chinese Translation by Dharmaraksha.

佛 所 行 讚 經
Lit. 'Buddha's practice-praise-sûtra.'

1 生 品 第 一
Birth.

2 處 宮 品 第 二
Living in the Palace.

3 厭 患 品 第 三
Disgust at Sorrow.

4 離 欲 品 第 四
Gives up a Life of Pleasure.

5 出 城 品 第 五
Leaves the City.

6 車 匿 還 品 第 六
Return of *Kh*andaka.

7 入 苦 行 林 品 第 七
Enters the Forest of Penance.

8 合 宮 憂 悲 品 第 八
The general Grief of the Palace.

9 推 求 太 子 品 第 九
Mission despatched to search for the Royal Prince.

10 缾 沙 王 詣 太 子 品 第 十
Bimbisâra Râ*g*a goes to visit the Royal Prince.

11 अश्वघोषकृते कामविगर्हणो नामैकादशः सर्गः ॥
Renouncing Pleasure.

12 अश्वघोषकृतेऽराडदर्शनो नाम द्वादशः सर्गः ॥
Interview with Arâ*d*a.

13 अश्वघोषकृते मारविजयो नाम त्रयोदशः सर्गः ॥
Conquest of Mâra.

14 अश्वघोषकृतेऽभिसंबोधनसंस्तवो नाम चतुर्दशः सर्गः ॥
Praise of Enlightenment.

15 अश्वघोषकृते धर्मचक्रप्रवर्तनाध्येषणं नाम पंचदशः सर्गः॥
Request to turn the Wheel of the Law.

16 अश्वघोषकृते धर्मचक्रप्रवर्तनं नाम षोडशः सर्गः ॥
Turning the Wheel of the Law.

17 अश्वघोषकृते लुंबिनीयाजादिकं (यात्रिका?) नाम सप्तदशः सर्गः ॥
Going to Lumbinî, &c.

11 答缾沙王品第十一
The Prince's Reply to Bimbisâra.

12 見阿羅藍鬱頭藍品第十二
Interview with Arâ*d*a and Udrarâma.

13 破魔品第十三
Defeats Mâra.

14 阿惟三菩提品第十四
Abhisambodhi.

15 轉法輪品第十五
Turns the Wheel of the Law.

16 缾沙王諸弟子品第十六
Bimbisâra Râ*g*a becomes a Disciple.

17 大弟子出家品第十七
The Great Disciple quits his Home.

NOTE II.

EXAMPLE OF THE STYLE OF THE EXPANDED SÛTRAS, AS TRANSLATED INTO CHINESE.

PHÛ YAU KING.

KIOUEN II, § 1.

On the thirty-two miraculous signs which appeared on the eve of the Birth of Bodhisattva.

Buddha addressed all the Bhikshus and said: Ten months having been fulfilled, Bodhisattva being on the point of birth, at this time there were manifested thirty-two miraculous signs. The first was this: (1) In the after-garden all the trees spontaneously bore fruit. (2) The solid earth produced blue lotus flowers as large as a chariot-wheel. (3) All the decayed trees of the earth produced flowers and leaves. (4) The heavenly spirits drawing the chariots adorned with curtains of seven gems, arrived at the spot. (5) In the middle of the earth (or, in the earth) 20,000 treasures of precious substances appeared of themselves. (6) On every side, far and near, was perceived the agreeable fragrance of celebrated perfumes (ming hiang 名香). (7) From the snowy mountains there came forth 500 white lions, and arranging themselves in front by the gates of the city, stood there without doing harm to any one. (8) Five hundred white elephants, arranging themselves in front of the palace, stood there. (9) The Devas caused a soft and perfumed rain to fall on every hand (the four quarters, i.e. through the world). (10) There appeared in the palace of the king spontaneously a water fountain possessed of the hundred qualities of taste, fit to satisfy the wants of all who were athirst. (11) The Nâga women appearing in the air with half their body visible, remained thus. (12) Ten thousand Devîs, holding in their hands peacock-feather fans, remained thus above the palace-walls. (13) All the Devîs, holding in their hands 10,000 golden pitchers full of sweet-dew (nectar), remained fixed in space. (14) Ten thousand Devîs, holding in their hands 10,000 vases full of scented water, proceeded and stopped in the air [中 I suppose to be omitted]. (15) Ten thousand Devîs, holding in their hands standards and parasols, stood at attention. (16) All the Devîs arranging themselves in order stood still, whilst every kind of responsive music sounded spontaneously through space. (17) The four great river-drains (the four rivers flowing from the Anavatapta Lake?) remaining at rest, ceased to flow. (18) The sun and moon (the palaces of the sun and moon Devas) ceased to move. (19) The constellation Pushya descending, waited in the rear of all the other stars (or, star-concourse). (20) A net-like precious canopy entirely covered the palace of the king. (21) The divine pearl of the bright moon hanging over the palace hall, shed abroad a brilliant effulgence. (22) The lamps and fires of the palace were (by the superior light without) no longer visible. (23) Baskets and articles of dress appeared placed on their stands. (24) Articles of jewelry and treasures of every kind of precious stone appeared of themselves. (25) The five kinds of poisonous insects suddenly disappeared, whilst the fortunate bird (or bird of good omen) soaring aloft poured forth pleasant songs. (26) The pains inflicted in the different hells were allayed. (27) The earth through a great movement became perfectly level and smooth. (28) The four great highways and the narrower streets appeared perfectly smooth and ornamented with flowers. (29) All valleys and cavernous places were raised and became even. (30) The cruel designs of those who fished in the waters or hunted on the land gave way in a moment to a loving and merciful heart. (31) All the diseases to which children newly born, such as blindness, deafness, &c., are liable, were averted. (32) The tree-Devas, with half their bodies visible, appeared to all beholders, their heads reverently inclined. Such were the thirty-two miraculous signs which appeared on every side of the (palace) enclosures, sufficient to cause wonder and admiration (in those who beheld them), as indications of the approaching period. At this time the queen being about to give birth (to Bodhisattva), he, i.e. Bodhisattva, by exciting the thought in her mind by his own spiritual energy, caused her to arise at the first watch of the night, and having robed herself to go with her attendants to the place where the king was—(when she addressed him as follows):—'Listen to my words! for a long time have I thought of entering the garden for the purpose of religious meditation—supposing in every case, O Mahârâ*g*a! the idea is not displeasing or troublesome to you; in which case I would at once resort thither to reflect silently on the words of the sacred books.' The king thereupon answered, 'Willingly do I consent, saintly lady, that you should go forth to contemplate the flowers of the trees now in full bloom—for at this season, around the palace and its lovely dwellings, are countless kinds of trees, whose fruit and fragrant blossoms cannot but afford unmixed delight (to all beholders).' The queen, hearing these words, was filled with joy. Then the king commanded the precious chariot known as the 'cloud-mother' to be prepared and decorated; followed by a retinue of servants, and surrounded by attendant[1] women, thus the queen went forth to behold the trees in the Lumbinî[2] garden. The conductors of the inferior chariots were all similar in appearance and colour, distinguished for their splendour as they rode, dazzling the eyes of men. Two hundred white elephants followed and preceded the cortége, all decorated with gems and pearls. The elephants were furnished with six tusks. The king of the elephants, in the midst, was covered with a golden network, to which bells were attached that sounded melodiously[3] as the wind blew them one against the other; in other respects also they were fully caparisoned and armed. At this time there was concord and goodwill in the world, an absence of a contentious spirit. Thus surrounded, the queen wandered

[1] The expression is 'tsae' 婇.

[2] The Chinese is 'Lin-ping' for 'Lumbinî;' in the glossary the sound 'ping' is given as equal to p(ing)-(m)i, i.e. 'pi.'

[3] The sounds produced by gems striking one another. See glossary.

forth and reposed beneath the trees of the Lumbinî garden. Then *S*akra-deva and Brahma-râ*g*a and the four heavenly kings descending (flying) from their respective abodes, and scattering flowers, hastily proceeded to the palace to ascertain the state of the case, and entering the different apartments, caused the servants and attendants to receive instructions (i. e. put the thought into their minds) to sweep and prepare the way for the approach of the king on the queen's departure. This being done and reported, the king was filled with joy, and entering the palace of the female attendants, he spoke thus: 'You who desire to give me satisfaction, and to impart joy, will do as I request; let there be no differences among you, but let each one be ready to sit quietly and reflect (on what I say). Decorate yourselves in your most dazzling attire; and anoint yourselves (or, your garments) with the choicest perfumes, pure and sweet; let your bodies be covered with countless ornaments and gems whose sound is delightful to the ear and joy-giving to the beholder, prepare for yourselves every kind of musical instrument, cymbals and pipes and lutes and drums, of every sort, which may accord in producing sweet music, so that the Devîs themselves hearing it may have joy. Thus provided, attend the queen as she mounts the lovely chariot; let male and female attendants alike, and the elephants composing the cortége, be decorated in one way, and let no ill sound or discordant note be heard to discompose the mind of the queen.' And now the elephants and horses and the military attendants of every kind, decorated as aforesaid, stood by the gate, and as the queen passed through on her departure there was heard the sound as it were of a great ocean, and the shouts of those who desired her ten thousand years, whilst the ornaments which decorated the chariot, as it moved along, gave forth propitious music. The lion throne, like that of the gods, was composed of (the wood of) the four precious (gem) trees, covered with (carved?) leaves and flowers of every possible description so as to perfect it. And now the ducks and geese and the peacocks raised their piteous notes in unison, whilst banners and flags decorated with the seven precious substances were placed as a canopy over the chariot.

Then the Devas who dwell in space, surrounding the chariot as it advanced, likewise sang together in melodious strains. As soon as the queen sat down upon the lion throne the great universe (chiliocosm) was six times (or in six manners) shaken, and all the Devas scattered flowers (as they cried): 'The holy one to-day is about to be born even here beneath a tree of the Lumbinî (garden), it is he who is a god among gods.' The four heavenly kings conduct the chariot, the divine *S*akra purifies and prepares the way, whilst Brahma Devarâ*g*a leads on before, attended by a hundred thousand Devas, who ever turn towards the chariot and adore (the queen) with heads inclined.

And now the king, the father, seeing all this, was filled with joy in his heart, and reflecting with himself he exclaimed: 'This (child) must be in truth the king of gods and men, whom all the Devas, the four heavenly kings, *S*akra and Brahma, attending, agree to honour; he must indeed be one who shall attain to the condition of Buddha; for never yet in the three worlds has one received such adoration, whether Deva or Nâga or divine *S*akra or Brahma, and yet escaped with life (unsplit head). Such a one then receiving these honours must of necessity in the end prove himself a holy person (divine).' Thus the queen (advanced), escorted by 84,000 chariots drawn by horses, the same number drawn by elephants, and by the same number of chariot drivers, fully adorned, and surrounded by soldiers, spearmen and halbard bearers of approved courage and strength on the right hand and on the left, and by others in front and rear, whilst before and behind was a surrounding concourse of 60,000 attendant women accompanied by 40,000 nobles all of the family of king *S*uddhodana, whilst others, the attendants of 64,000 kings, took part in the cortége that surrounded the mother of Bodhisattva. Moreover, there were 84,000 female attendants of the Devas, the Nâgas, the Gandharvas, the Kinnaras, Mahoragas, Asuras, all sumptuously decorated with jewels and ornaments, provided with drums and musical instruments, producing harmonious sounds although differing in character, whilst with their voices they sang of the perfections (virtues) of Bodhisattva's mother. Thus surrounded and attended they approach the Lumbinî grove, the road prepared carefully and the ground perfumed with scented water and covered with divine flowers, whilst the trees themselves budded forth and blossomed and the scented oil of choicest sandal-wood was produced on every side. This, indeed, was by the express interference of the gods. And now the queen having arrived, descended[1] from her precious chariot, and accompanied by Devas and Devîs she proceeded onwards through the garden, whilst the trees in honour of her presence shed abroad their brilliant hues and their fragrant scent. The queen now observed one tree of conspicuous beauty, made perfect by every kind of pearl and precious ornament. The stalks and twigs, the branches and leaves of this tree were all in truth full of fragrance, whilst its lovely verdure spread around on every side drooped to the ground, pliant and pure as silky grass. Like a vestment of some heavenly being it covered the earth—even as had been the case from old time with respect to the laws (relating to the birth) of all the Buddhas. And now all the Devas and men, at once, strike their drums, and from innumerable instruments the followers of the queen join in the strain, as she goes forward and arrives beneath the tree. By the influence of Bodhisattva the spirit inhabiting the tree bending down a branch of its own accord rendered assistance to the queen. All the Devas who inhabit space bending down their heads did obeisance, the sun and moon shed abroad a pure unsullied light, whilst the Devas and their female attendants, filled with admiration, gathered round to render meritorious service (to the queen as she stood) beneath the tree. Meantime the tree Deva was filled with joy in considering the reason of the presence of all this vast multitude, and reasoned thus: 'Now may we all well endure to bear these bodies of ours, whilst we employ them in rendering service and obedience, for from the lowest hell[2] to the highest heavens of the Trâyastri*ms*as all sorrow must cease, all darkness disappear, whilst now the holy one is about to be

[1] I have substituted 下 for 上 in the text.

[2] I have been obliged here to substitute 間 for 擇.

born. So it is the trees are covered with flowers and foliage, whilst innumerable Devas gathered around do homage, and the great earth is shaken in six ways. The sun and moon shed abroad a pure and serene light, and music from innumerable instruments is heard around; yea, moreover, all impure desire is put away, and all the Devas are filled with joy; for to-day the holy one is to show his pity for all creatures, and therefore Brahma and *S*akra and all the gods rejoice and worship; this is the honourable one among men, whose merits surpass the sun and moon. It is he, now dwelling in the womb, who shines forth like gold with a brightness eclipsing the light of heaven; all the Devas, Brahma, *S*akra and the rest, and all the denizens of the countless worlds of space, putting away evil ways and thoughts, are now at peace, without remnant of sorrow or grief; and therefore the Devas, countless in number, offer the sacrifice of scattered flowers and music, and by their indomitable might cause the very ground to produce of itself flowers composed of the seven precious substances.' And now as Bodhisattva was born from the right side of his mother, suddenly there appeared a precious lotus flower on which he stood, and then taking seven steps he declared in words of the Fan language (or, with the voice of Brahma;—Brahmaghosha) the character of impermanency in accordance with his (subsequent) teaching (and added): 'I am now about to save and deliver all those in heaven and earth (above the heaven and below the heaven), as the lord of Devas and men to deliver (detach) them from the misery of (repeated) birth and death, as the highest in the universe (the three worlds) to cause all creatures to arrive at the condition of non-individuality (wu-wei) and thus obtain enduring rest.' Then *S*akra-*r*â*g*a and Brahma caused every kind of scented water to descend suddenly for the purpose of washing (the person of) Bodhisattva, whilst the nine dragons who dwelt in space above, caused other scented streams to descend for the purification of the holy master. The washing being finished (he stood) perfectly pure in body and soul (heart), raised far above the position which for the present he occupied as wayfarer, born of a noble parentage, like a perfect and true gem uniting in itself every rare quality and excellency: about to turn the wheel of the law, or as a wheel king (*K*akravartin) (if he continue in the world (the three worlds)) to bring all the quarters (the ten regions) under one overshadowing government. And there arose in the heart of *S*uddhodana-râ*g*a a rapturous exultation. At this time there were born children of 5000 attendants (blue-clad), who were presented to the king to become his personal guards (lih-sse, the words used generally for vri*gg*i); 800 young nurses also were delivered of sons; 100,000 elephants likewise produced their young; (as many) white mares produced their foals, their colour white as snow, their coats glossy and smooth; (as many) yellow sheep produced their lambs. At the same time there appeared two myriads of curtained precious chariots[1] for the holy one's use, (whilst those who brought them), bending their heads, desired to know whither he would go; and beyond all this the Devas caused innumerable apparitional forms to present themselves, to offer various services, and caused a glorious radiance to fill the place: 5000 Apsarases, their persons breathing fragrance, each holding a jar of scented unguents, came to the place where stood the mother of Bodhisattva, 5000 others came to escort her to the city, having flowers and heavenly garments, whilst many youths and others came with jewels and ornaments for her person. Bodhisattva arriving at the condition 'free from fear' must complete the way of Buddha[2]. Then Buddha addressed the Bhikshus: 'At the time of Bodhisattva's birth, his mother was perfectly at ease, no disagreeable malady or accompanying inconvenience disturbed her; but she was in the condition which most became her. At the same time, both in front and behind her, were 5000 female attendants providing divine incense and holding scented oil as an offering to the mother of Bodhisattva, whilst without intermission they paid her lowest reverence: there were, moreover, 5000 female attendants who offered her divine medicaments, 5000 others who presented her with

[1] Before the word for 'precious,' the text has an expression kiau-lu, which is said to mean curtain.

[2] This clause comes in without any apparent connection with the context.

jewels and necklets (or, precious necklaces), 5000 others who offered her divine robes for her person, 5000 others who offered her (or, attended her with) divine music, all these paid to her constant and reverent attention.'

And now it came to pass that there were five *Ri*shis with supernatural powers passing over this country through the air who suddenly appeared in the presence of *S*uddhodana-râ*g*a[1]. Buddha, moreover, addressed the Bhikshus and said: 'At the time of Bodhisattva's birth, during seven days from morning till evening, there was continual music, whilst all the assembly offered a hundred different sorts of food beneath the Lumbinî tree, presenting to the mother of Bodhisattva the fruits of merit resulting from the exercise of the paramitâs of charity, morality, patience, and perseverance. At this time 32,000 Brahma*k*ârins from day to day, without intermission, offered their gifts without stint, whatever (the mother of Bodhisattva) desired; *S*akra-deva and Brahma, assuming the appearance of young Brahmans (students), having taken conspicuous places amongst the assembled Brahma*k*ârins, repeated these Gâthâs:

"Having put an end to all evil ways of birth (in himself)
He has now sent universal peace among men;
All creatures enjoying concord and rest
Are free from sorrow everywhere.
As the brightness of the sun scatters darkness,
So the glory of all the Devas withers,
His glorious merit scatters all their brightness,
And causes it to decay and disappear.
(We do) not (now) consider the time when he shall have exhausted karman (i.e. be born as a Buddha),
Nor shall we hear again of such a time,
For now the glory of Buddha has appeared,
And he has become the great saint of the world;
No more for him of labour or the ills of sense (dust),
His loving heart compassionates all living creatures,
And so innumerable Devas of the Brahma heaven (or, innumerable Brahma devas)
Have come to offer him boundless sacrifice.
And therefore also the trees covered with flowers
Rest in quiet upon the peaceful (or level) earth,
(In proof that) all the world will come to him for refuge (salvation),
And that all will fully rely on him.

[1] These parenthetical clauses appear to have crept into the text, and remained there without any immediate connection.

Just as in this lower world
The lotus springs from the midst of the mire,
Thus is Prabhâpâla[1] now born in the world,
About to nourish and govern all that lives.
For like as a pliant delicate robe
Is redolent with heavenly perfume,
So if there be a man diseased or sick
He will for his sake become 'the chief physician.'
And as by his presence he has caused an absence of all lustful desire,
And peace and goodwill dwell in the world of form,
(And as) with hands clasped (all these) render him worship,
He is surely worthy to be called the 'protector of all,'
And as the Devas, and their followers,
All with compliant hearts
Mix freely with men in their common worship,
He will be in truth the 'great master of all.'
And as the pure unsullied water (rain)
Is universally diffused and causes luxuriant vegetation,
So by the right apprehension (samyakd*ri*sh*t*i) of the truth of this one's doctrine,
There shall ever be both rest and quiet."'

Buddha, moreover, addressed the Bhikshus and said: 'Seven days after the birth of Bodhisattva his mother died.' On this the thought occurred to the Bhikshus, it must have been on account of some fault on the part of Bodhisattva that such an event occurred; on which Buddha resumed: Let not such a thought present itself; and why? Because her destiny was even so, that the birth of Bodhisattva should be the term of her life; and hence at her birth, when she came down for the purpose of bearing Bodhisattva in her womb, all the Devas attended her and provided her with heavenly clothing and food. And it has ever been thus. The mothers of all the Buddhas have always died seven days after their birth; and so because at the time of Bodhisattva's birth the bodily functions of his mother were all in perfect condition, she was born as the result of her previous merit in the Trâyastri*m*s*a*s heaven. And before this, Bodhisattva not yet born, she had gone up thither, on which occasion all the Devas attending her offered her a palace to dwell in, and awaiting her in the great preaching hall they offered the queen 5000 pitchers containing the rarest scented waters; 5000 Apsarases presented her with thrones

[1] In Chinese 'hu-ming:' this was the name of Bodhisattva whilst resident in the Tusita heaven.

to sit on; 5000 others, holding caps of state in their hands, sprinkled before her on the ground perfumed water; 50,000 Brahma devas, holding golden pitchers, saluted her with expressions that she might live 10,000 years; 20,000 Nâgas with necklaced bodies, 20,000 white elephants with pearl-covered bodies, 20,000 chariots with flags and jewelled canopies surrounded her, and behind these 40,000 armed attendants, heroes of marked courage, and Bodhisattva himself in the rear. Moreover, on this occasion there were countless thousand Devas, who caused to appear in space in a moment yellow golden parapets, along which they offered worship to the mother of Bodhisattva. On that night Bodhisattva was conceived in the womb, on which occasion 20,000 damsels attendants on Mâra, proceeding from the great and superbly-adorned palace of the Kâmaloka heavens, and holding in their hands precious silken tissues, came to the place to wait on the mother of Bodhisattva; and so likewise 20,000 men (male Devas?) with highly decorated bodies, to do honour to the occasion. On that night between every two attendant women was one Apsaras[1]; the attendant women beholding the beauty of her face felt the risings of desire. And now by the power of the divine merit of Bodhisattva in the midst of this great city of Kapilavastu, 500 nobles, all of the *S*âkya race, each laid the foundation of a palace for residence, 500 in all, so that when he entered the gates of the city, they addressed him as they paid him reverence and said, 'Oh! would that Sarvârthasiddha would condescend to enter this divine abode (place[2]), this perfectly pure abode. Oh! thou whose eye beholds all things (samanta*k*akshus), thou hast come down into this world (yeou = bhava), (condescend to enter) this great palace called "Hu-tsing-fa" (defend-pure-flower), a fitting residence for Bodhisattva.'

Then the great Brahma*k*ârins and the principle princes of

[1] I take this from the French translation of the Lalita Vistara; the Chinese expression is 婇女.

[2] *K*u-tien-*k*ü; the French translation from the Tibetan renders this 'God above gods,' and so in the next phrase, tsing-tsing-*k*ü, 'perfectly pure abode or place,' the Tibetan refers this also to Bodhisattva, and translates it, 'Oh! thou pure being.' I do not see how to bring the Chinese text into harmony with the Tibetan in this passage.

the *S*âkya tribe addressing *S*uddhodana said, 'It would be perhaps convenient if the prince would condescend to agree to enter these abodes and remain in them (use them).' Bodhisattva therefore entered the 500 abodes. (Moreover they said, 'Who is there[1]) of conspicuous merit, and of complacent disposition, who can protect and order (Bodhisattva) aright?' Then 500 *Kh*andakas[2], each one said, 'We can nourish and cherish the prince.' But others replied, 'It is a difficult task to train aright and lead into obedience one possessed of such saintlike wisdom as the prince, especially such as are in the prime of their beauty and youth, for when he begins to grow up who then will be able to attend on him and direct him aright?' Then they all agreed that Mahâpra*g*âpatî alone was able to nourish (the child), and with loving heart to protect him from the heats and damps of his abode, and to feed him with child's food (pap) by which he might grow to maturity. Mahâpra*g*âpatî, the prince's maternal aunt, pure and faultless, she, they said, is the one to protect and cherish, and ever be near the person of the prince. Then *S*uddhodana-râ*g*a and the *S*âkya princes, being all agreed on this point, went together to the abode of Mahâpra*g*âpatî and expressed their wishes on the point: 'The prince's mother being dead, we beg you, his maternal aunt, to take charge of him and bring him up, that he may grow up (to manhood).' So Mahâpra*g*âpatî undertook the office.

The king now called an assembly of the *S*âkyas, wishing to find out, by enquiring of them, whether the prince was to be the lord of the kingdom, or if he was to become a recluse; desiring to solve this doubt (he called them together). Then the *S*âkyas all replied and said, 'We have heard that in the snowy mountains there is a *Ri*shi, a Brahma*k*ârin, called Asita (A-i-to), of advanced age, and possessed of much wisdom, and thoroughly understanding all qualities and substances[3] (i. e. the nature of all things).'

---

[1] I have been obliged to supply this, the text being evidently corrupt.

[2] Ku-nih. This is the transcription for *Kh*andaka, the coachman of Bodhisattva. It is possible it may here represent 'a personal attendant' only, whether male or female. In the Lalita Vistara we read *S*âkyabadhû, the wives of the *S*âkyas.

[3] I take siang here in its usual (Buddhist) sense as equal to 'lakshana,' and fă as equal to 'dharma' in the sense of 'substance.'

The king on hearing this was filled with joy, and caused a white elephant to be sumptuously equipped for the purpose of bringing to the place this learned man[1]. Then all the Devas and Nâgas and spirits assembled in countless numbers and in various shapes accompanied the cortége as it left the city. Then Asita, seeing the transformed appearances of the Devas, knew that *S*uddhodana-râ*g*a had a holy son, whose spiritual (divine) glory outshone that of all the Devas and men, and so his heart was rejoiced, and he desired to go to behold him. On this the world-honoured one (i. e. Buddha) again, for the sake of the assembly, repeated these Gâthâs:

'The Brahman *R*ishi Asita
Beholding the Devas flying thro' space,
Their forms beautiful and of golden colour,
Seeing them, was filled with joy.
Devas, Asuras, and Garu*d*as (golden-wings)
Chanting[2] their praises in honour of Buddha,
Hearing these verses, how great his joy.
Then looking by his divine sight thro' the world,
And considering the various examples of men of renown,
Whose excellences were as the mountain tops,
Or like the well-set and glossy flowers of the tree,
Wherever dwelt the lord of the three worlds,
There the wide-spreading earth would be level as the palm of the hand,
There would be heavenly and unmixed joy,
There would be abundance as the treasures of the sea king.
Regarding thus the declarations ("reason," or "way") of the law,
That one should come who would destroy evil and put an end to sorrow,
Whilst he saw the Devas flying thro' space,
And listened to their melodious songs (sounds),
Regarding these fortunate and rare occurrences,
Asita looked through the world,
And narrowly scanning (the territory of) Kapila (and the family of) *S*uddhodana-râga[3],
He saw that a child had there been born with fortunate signs.

[1] Taou *g*in, this is another instance of the use of this expression not for a Buddhist, but for a religious man generally.

[2] *K*un-to, which I can only restore to *Kh*andas, in the sense of a verse or singing a verse.

[3] The sentence is elliptical and difficult; literally rendered it would be 'scanning Ka-i-pih-wang,' where I take Ka-i to be a form for Kapi(la) (just as the expression Kiu-i, so commonly met with as the name of Bodhisattva's wife, may be restored to Gopî) and pih-wang (the white king) to be a contracted form of *S*uddh(odana)-râga.

Seeing this, rejoicing he set out,
And (arriving) stood at the king's palace gate;
He beheld there an innumerable concourse of people,
When spying out a servant (grey-clothes), he asked and said:
"All hail! where dwells the king?
I desire to have an audience with the lord of the kingdom;"
The servant seeing the *Ri*shi venerable for age,
With joy elated, entered the palace and delivered the message.
The king then ordered him to cause the *Ri*shi to appear before him,
And spreading a seat he went forthwith to meet him.
Asita, hearing (the message), was glad at heart,
And filled with a yearning desire[1],
He asked where dwelt the lord, the holy one,
For he was failing now in years and had but few to live.
The king, commanding him to be seated,
Asked him wherefore he had come[2]?
Because (he said) of the many signs he had seen, he had come,
Hearing of the excellency (superiority) of the son he had,
The thirty-two signs on his body,
He wished to behold him and inspect the fortunate indications,
Therefore (he said again) have I come.
"Welcome! (said the king) I rejoice (to see you) [or, I rejoice (to hear it)].
Now for a moment the child sleeps in peaceful rest,
But wait for a little while until he wakes,
And you shall see him beautiful as the moon at full."'

On this the mind of Asita being much perplexed, he replied to the king in the following Gâthâs and said:

'From endless Kalpas
With perseverance[3] accumulating meritorious conduct,
From time long past inspired with wisdom,
How is it possible that such a one can again take his rest in sleep?
Thro' ages past exercising the virtue of charity,
Feeling deep compassion for the poor,
Grudging nothing which he possessed,
How can such a one again seek rest in sleep?
Reverencing the rules of pure conduct (*s*îla),
Observing the moral law without transgression,
Desiring to relieve and save all that lives,
How can such a one still find rest in sleep?
Always practising patience and equanimity,
His mind harbouring no resentment,
Controlling his heart (firm) like the solid earth,
How can such a one still repose in sleep?
Persevering steadily, as the moon from its first appearance,

---

[1] Literally, 'in his heart harbouring-hungry-void.'
[2] Why himself invited, or condescended to come.
[3] Vîrya.

His eye ever looking onward without a moment's hesitation,
Regarding the example of the Buddhas of the ten regions (the universe),
How can such a one again repose in sleep?
With equal mind[1] ever lost in contemplation (dhyâna),
Without at any time disturbance or confusion,
The mind fixed as a great mountain,
How can such a one again repose in sleep?
Possessed of wisdom (prâg*ñ*â) without limit,
With divine penetration like the sun's brightness,
Able to open out and explain every subject of enquiry,
How can such a one again repose in sleep?
Always cherishing the fourfold qualities[2],
Practising love and pity, joy and equanimity
Ceaselessly and without neglect as Brahma[3] himself,
How can such a one again repose in sleep?
Reverently practising the four gracious acts[4]—
Benevolence, charity, humanity, and love—
Doing all for the good of men and that they again may profit others,
How can such a one again repose in sleep?
Reverently performing the thirty-seven divisions[5],
How can such a one again repose in sleep?
Always exercising the cross-method of indirect means (upâya),
Taking advantage of the occasion to open out and convert (explain and so convert),
Aiming in every turn to save the whole creation,
How can such a one again repose in sleep?
His heart always at perfect rest,
His mind fixed with no approach to indifference,
Entering thus on the deep and impenetrable samâdhi,
How can such a one again repose in sleep?
Seeing clearly the beginning and ending (of the history) of that and this (i. e. of all),
Beholding as though present all the Buddhas,
Explaining that they (i. e. the Buddhas) are essentially without beginning,
How can such a one again repose in sleep?
Ever practising (or using) the three gates of salvation,
(Viz.) (the gate of) perfect void, without qualities, incessant effort (prayer or vow),
(Teaching) that the ideas of real existence (bhava),
And the absence of such existence, are without solid foundation,
How can such a one again repose in sleep?
Great in love, of unfailing compassion,

[1] Yih-sin generally corresponds to the Sanskrit samyak; it denotes the condition enjoyed during samâdhi.

[2] Viz. the four qualities of heart named in the next line.

[3] Fan.

[4] Yan-hing, these four are named in the line following.

[5] The thirty-seven perfections necessary to the attainment of Bodhi. I have not thought it necessary to name these in the text.

As a boat of the law (vessel of religion) passing through the three worlds,
To save and deliver the living and the dead,
How can such a one again repose in sleep?
His religious merit (virtue) vast as space,
Himself born in this lower world for the sake of all creatures,
Under a vow to deliver these by means of the three vehicles[1],
How can such a one again repose in sleep?
Able to pass thro' the vastness of space,
Knowing the hidden depths of the wide sea,
Able to count the number of every tree and shrub,
How can such a one again repose in sleep?
Let the king hear my words,
The virtues (excellences) of his son are without compare,
His wisdom infinite (beyond the number of the dust),
How can such a one again repose in sleep?
Descending as a god into his mother's womb,
So as to save countless beings,
Not omitting even the least in his intention,
How can such a one again repose in sleep?'

And now Bodhisattva having awoke from his sleep and arisen, Mahâpra*g*âpatî, enfolding him in a white and silk-like robe, came with him to the place where the king was. The king then offered to the *Ri*shi (man of reason) a purse of gold and one of silver (yellow gold, white silver), which he declined to receive. Then unfolding the robe in which he was wrapped, (Asita) proceeded to observe the distinctive marks on the person of the prince. Of these he perceived thirty-two, viz. his entire body of a golden colour, on the summit of his head a fleshy excrescence, his hair of a purplish dark colour[2]; between the eyebrows a white soft hairy circle, from the top of his head a bright light like that of the sun, the iris of the eye of a deep blue, moving the eyes up and down with ease, forty teeth in the mouth, the teeth white and even and square, the jawbones wide and long, the tongue long and full, his breast and shoulder broad and square like a lion's, his fingers long, his heels full and round, the fingers and toes connected by a thin filament, the wheel with a thousand spokes under the feet, that which ought to be hidden[3] concealed,

[1] That is, the three degrees of *S*râvaka, Pratyeka Buddha, and Bodhisattva.

[2] This colour seems to correspond with the Greek *κύανος*; compare *κυανοχαίτης* as applied to Poseidon.

[3] Concealed, as in the horse; but the whole of this part of the text is involved. This refers to the thirteenth laksha*n*a, Koshopagatavastiguhyatâ.

his leg (calf of leg) like the stag's[1], the hair of the head curling to the right, every hair with a distinct opening, the hair or the skin soft and pliant, free from perspiration[2], on his breast the figure 卍. Asita beholding these signs was overcome with emotion, the tears fell from his eyes, and he was unable to speak. On this, the king and Mahâpra*g*â-patî were moved at heart, and with reverence (closed hands) addressed him thus: 'Is there then something unlucky? oh! tell us then its purport.' With closed hands, and raised in reverence, he replied: 'Fortunate and without the least ill omen. Let me venture to felicitate the king on the birth of this divine being (spiritual man). Undoubtedly it was on this account that the heavens and earth were greatly shaken on the evening of yesterday; and now as I understand the meaning of these signs, I will tell the king. The child possesses the thirty-two marks of a great man; if he remains in the world (i.e. a secular man) he will be a holy wheel-king (*k*akravartin) to whom the seven precious things will of themselves arrive, and his thousand sons will rule the world in righteousness; but if he leaves the world (i.e. becomes a recluse) he will of himself become a Buddha (perfectly enlightened), and be the saviour of all living things. And now because I am old, I shall assuredly not in after days behold the Buddha, nor hear his sacred instructions (sûtras), and therefore I give way to grief.' Then the king, perfectly understanding his ability in interpreting signs, caused a palace to be erected with three halls fit for the three seasons—each in a different place—one for the cool season, and this he called the Autumn Hall; one for the warm season, and this was the Cool Hall; one for the winter season, and this was the Warm Hall: and then he selected 500 dancing women of rare beauty, neither too stout nor too thin, neither too tall nor too short, neither too fair nor too dark, skilful in all feminine arts and blandishments, all of them provided with pearl and other famous

[1] There is a phrase here used 鉤鎖 hook-lock, which may possibly refer to the hooked form of the leg of the stag, though this would hardly be a sign of beauty in a human being. [It is explained in the glossary as denoting the bones well knit together.]

[2] Dust-water.

jewelled necklaces for their persons. A hundred men, each in turn, guarded the place by night. Before the several palaces were every kind of sweet fruit trees, and between the trees tanks of water, in which were every kind of aquatic flower, whilst an innumerable number (or a large number)[1] of birds with shining plumage and of different species (sounded their joyful notes on every side). The king hoped thus to amuse and please the prince, so as to prevent the rising of any desire to awaken reason (to become Buddha). The palace windows were all well secured, and the gates on opening and shutting could be heard at a distance of forty lis.

And now Buddha addressed the Bhikshus: 'When Bodhisattva was born, the great-spirit illustrious Deva (i.e. Mahe*s*vara) addressed all the pure-abode (Devas) [i.e. the Suddhâvâsakâyikas] (and said), "Bodhisattva Mahâsattva (ta-sse) through countless ages having heaped up merit and acquired (tied as in a string) virtuous conduct, by his purity which has been to him a sacred enclosure[2], by his charity which has been everywhere celebrated, by his moral conduct (*s*îla) purifying himself throughout, diligently practising right conduct, his great love and pity leading him willingly to undertake the protection of all creatures and to lay a foundation of great rest (peace) in the world, Bodhisattva thus persevering with unflagging determination to fulfil the great vow he made in ages gone by before the Buddha then living (i.e. Dîpaṅkara) to plant the root of all virtues in himself, to be distinguished by possessing the glorious and holy substance of a hundred (sources) of merit, by which to cause peace and agreement amongst all creatures, and to cause them to rise above perverse thoughts (disagreements), and by perfect purity and rejection of all that is vile, in this way to lay the foundation

[1] 千百, which is a phrase often used for 'a great number;' see Notices on Chinese Grammar [part i, by Philo-Sinensis, Batavia, 1842], p. 70; and compare Fă-hien, p. 161 (English edition), where M. Stanislas Julien has suggested another reading.

[2] Taou-*k*ang, reason enclosure; this is the usual phrase for the Bodhi ma*nd*ala, or enclosure round the Bodhi tree; it is difficult to translate in the text.

in himself for arriving at perfect wisdom, and (unfurl) the infinitely high standard of religion for the rescue of those who profess only natural powers (for their salvation), of himself to subdue (the evil powers that govern) the great universe, to become the leader and guide of gods and men, to perform fully that great sacrifice which directs men in the way from ignorance, and leads them to accumulate the excellent qualities of wisdom, to cut off the very source of repeated birth and death, to put in motion and make manifest the great vehicle—this one has just been born on the lower earth, and dwells in the king's palace—; oh then! let all living things—putting aside all private feelings (or intentions), those who have arrived at wisdom and those not yet arrived—go straightway and adore with bowed heads, let them admire his merit and virtue, let them offer their sacrifice and bestow their gifts; and as for the rest, those Devas who are not subject to religion, but are puffed up in their own estimation, not knowing that the chief true one is manifested to point out the great way, whose destiny is of infinite worth, surpassing that of Bodhisattvas unknown in number,—let all these too come and adore, let them behold this land of the king of the country of *S*râvastî [1], let [2] them acquire merit by declaring the wisdom and majesty of Sarvârthasiddha, who has been born there, let them examine his true wisdom, and thus attain to the highest method of salvation;" and then they chanted thus:

"The merits (virtues) of Siddhârtha [3] are as the sea (for extent),
And so declares Mahesvara with propriety,
Through ages too numerous to mention,
Preparing to be accepted as the honourable among men.
And now the countless host of the Devas of the pure abodes,
With glorious bodies resplendent as gems,
Are come with dignity and decorum in a body,

[1] Tsang-yeh, increase and augment. Used for *S*râvastî. Perhaps it should be Kapilavastu.

[2] In the original it is 'let them &c. of born-time.' I take born-time to be a form of Bodhisattva's name, 'Sarvârthasiddha,' because when this name was given him, the king said, 'At the time of his birth all was prosperous.' But it is obscure.

[3] Sing-shi.

To offer to the most honourable one, in person, their respectful worship.
These Devas, secure from the sufferings of the long night[1],
Fixed (or safe) in the pure gate[2] of all virtue,
Glorious with (or like) precious jewels,
Beautiful in appearance as the full moon,
Shining with radiance, but not equal to the holy one,
In reputation not to be compared with him,
They dare not pass over the royal precinct,
(Denizens of) the three worlds are unable to take so great responsibility,
Though from their persons issued such pure effulgence,
Though their words were harmonious (sweet) beyond rivalry,
Though richly (deeply) endowed with moral excellence
Beyond all other Devas,
Yet they could but offer to him their incomparable perfumes,
(They could but) reverence and adore
The Prince, unequalled for dignity,
And sacrifice to him as a god among gods.
Asita now informed (sent to) *S*uddhodana
(This message), 'The sign-interpreter desires to be admitted to see
The incomparably-beautiful divine holy one.'
The king, hearing the message, rejoiced exceedingly;
The gate-keeper respectfully announces, 'the king (desires you) to enter.'
The (sage), honoured by men, hearing this,
His hand holding a flower, was glad,
And like a divine person entered the holy abode.
And now the king beholding him enter,
Immediately rose with hands clasped together,
And arranged for him a gilded jewelled couch,
With the request that his excellency would sit on this (prepared) couch;
Immediately sitting, he examined carefully the four (quarters).
The king then desired to know wherefore he had come.
The child just born, his body replete with excellent tokens,
His conduct true, this one I am come to see;
Provided with marks and signs (indicating) his holy intelligence,
Not knowing any cause to return quickly,
Therefore do I wait here on the chair,
Expecting to be permitted to behold the glorious marks and signs.
And[3] now this attendant company (of Devas) arriving,
Quietly and joyfully they took their places above the Royal Prince,
And with reverence they behold him;
Lost in wonder, they reported to those without his unequalled (beauty)
And now, at length, (when) the exceedingly excellent lord and master,
Resplendent as gold, awaking, holy and graceful,
Raised himself, and showed his countenance,

---

[1] *K*ang-ye, viz. the long night of pain.

[2] The expression 'gate,' e.g. 'gate of the law,' means generally a 'mode' or 'method' (of salvation); hence the Devas are here said to be safe in the 'pure mode' or 'method,' i.e. to be *S*uddhâvâsikas.

[3] Here the arrival of the Devas is again referred to.

They bowed their heads to hide their eclipsed glory.
The old man (Asita), beholding him, rejoiced,
His incalculable (top unseen) excellences and endowments,
The white hair, unknown[1] among the Devas,
(A sign) that he would reach the condition of a Buddha and conquer all the hosts of Mâra,—
(Seeing these) he sighed in astonishment at the very perfect (true) excellences (virtues, adornments),
Which were a sign that he would bring down and destroy the enticements of the senses,
And that the renowned (precious) Lion had come into the world,
Who would destroy (curse) the pollutions of birth and death.
Throughout the three worlds the fire of the three impurities (rages),
From the act of thought springs up the pollution of the poisons,
The rain of the law falling on the chiliocosm,
As the water of life (am*ri*ta), destroys the fire of the senses;
Armed with the cuirass of love, beholding
(These sorrows) the workings (aroma) of pity (arises),
And with his pliant, sweet voice of Brahma,
He instructs fully the three thousand worlds;
His mouth resounds the news of the great law as a drum;
It is he who is able to destroy the teaching (sûtras) of the heretical schools,
And the complications (bands) of all evil practices,
His teaching, not being heard without avail,
Shall mightily prevail for the reformation of the age,
Like the shadow of a mighty tree,
His powerful teaching shall overshadow the world;
His wisdom able to survey the condition of all men,
His knowledge by its brightness able to scatter all darkness,
The only illustrious benefactor of Devas,
The only source of purity and truth,
Able to empty (the way of) wickedness and profit the way of heaven,
The faultless treasure found amongst men.
Then the assembled Devas, showering down flowers,
Worshipped and turned round him to the right,
After which, felicitating Buddha and the land of his birth,
Ascending into the air, they returned to heaven."'

END OF KIOUEN II.

[1] 跱 a character of uncertain signification.

NOTE III.

The same Title given to different Works.

The Chinese translators in making new translations of foreign texts, often give as their reason for doing so that the former translation or translators could not be understood or relied on. But in explanation of this we must remember that the originals themselves in the hands of successive translators, though bearing the same name, were not always copies of the same works. For instance, in the case of the work Fo-pan-ni-pan-king, that is, the Parinirvâ*n*a Sûtra, translated into Chinese by Pih-fă-tsu, between 290 and 306 A. D. We cannot doubt that the text used by this translator was another form of the Mahâ-parinibbâna-Sutta embodied in the Southern Canon[1].

But how widely another work bearing the same title, viz. Mahâparinirvâ*n*a Sûtra, and translated into Chinese by Dharmaraksha, the same priest who turned the Buddha-*k*arita into that language, differs from the simple Sûtra just named, the following brief extract will show. We will select the incident of *K*unda's offering, which is thus expanded in the last work:

MAHÂPARINIRVÂ*N*A SÛTRA,

Translated by Dharmaraksha.

Kiouen II, § 1.

'At this time, in the midst of the congregation, there was a certain Upâsaka (lay-disciple) of the city of Ku*s*inagara, the son of a blacksmith, whose name was *K*unda; this man, with his whole family, fifteen persons in all, had devoted himself to a religious life. At this juncture then it was that *K*unda, rising from his seat, addressed Buddha

[1] See some remarks on this point in the eleventh volume of the Sacred Books of the East, p. xxxvi.

in the orthodox way and said: "Oh that the world-honoured (Tathâgata) and the members of this great assembly would receive our poor offering, the very last to be presented, for the sake of bringing the benefit thereof to innumerable creatures! World-honoured one! from this time we are without a master, without a friend, with no means of advance, no helper, no refuge. Oh that Tathâgata would of his great compassion deign to receive this offering of ours before he enters Nirvâ*n*a. World-honoured! it is as though a Kshatriya, or a Brahman, or a Vai*s*ya, or *S*ûdra were to be reduced by poverty so far as to be compelled to go to another land, and there by industry prepare a piece of ground for cultivation. He procures a serviceable ox for the plough, and carefully roots up all the noxious weeds, and removes all stones and broken vessels from the ground, and then only awaits the grateful rain from heaven to crown his endeavours—so it is with me, the ox yoked to the plough is this body of mine, the cleared land (is the work of) supreme wisdom, the impediments and weeds removed are all the sources of sorrow which I have put away, and now we only await the rain of the sweet dew of the law! Look upon us, we are poor and perishing from want, without a friend, no help, no refuge; oh that Tathâgata would pity us even as he had compassion on his son Rahula!"

'Then Tathâgata replied: "Well said! well said! *K*unda. For your sake I will relieve the poverty of the world, and cause the rain of the insurpassable law to descend upon the field, and bring forth abundant fruit. Whatever your request, it shall be granted and I receive your offering. For as I accepted the gift of the shepherd girls before arriving at supreme wisdom, so now will I accept your corresponding gift before entering Nirvâ*n*a, and thus enable you to accomplish fully the Pâramitâ of charity." *K*unda replied: "Let not Tathâgata say that the merit of these two gifts is the same, for surely when the shepherd girls offered their food, the world-honoured one had not entirely got rid of all the sources of sorrow, or completed every growth of the seeds of wisdom; nor was he able at that time to cause others to complete the Pâramitâ of charity by accepting their gifts; but this last offering is like a God in the midst of gods.

The first offering was made for the support of the body of Tathâgata still suffering from human wants: this last offering is made to Tathâgata possessing an eternal, sorrowless, and unchangeable (vagra) body, the body of the law; everlasting, boundless. In these (and other) respects, then, it seems to me the two offerings differ in character and in merit." Tathâgata answered: "Illustrious youth! for ages innumerable (countless asaṅkhyeyas of kalpas) Tathâgata has possessed no such body as that you named, as suffering from human wants or necessities—nor is there such an after-body as that you describe as eternal, illimitable, indestructible. To those who as yet have no knowledge of the nature of Buddha, to these the body of Tathâgata seems capable of suffering, liable to want (but to others it is not so). At the time when Bodhisattva received the offering of food and drink at the hands of the shepherd girls, he entered into the Samâdhi known as vagra, and beheld the nature of Buddha, and so obtained the highest and most complete enlightenment (and thus was supposed to have eaten the food); so now as he receives your offering he enters the same condition; in this (and other respects) the offerings differ not in character. But principally for this reason, that as he then began to declare his law and preach it for the good of men, but did not completely exhaust the twelve portions of it, so now, having received your offering, he will preach the law in its entire form (i. e. including the Vaipulya, or last section) for the good of the assembly. But still, as in the former case, he ate not, so neither does he now eat."

'At this time the congregation having heard that the world-honoured would preach the law in its fulness after receiving the offering of *K*unda, rejoiced with exceeding joy, and opened their mouths with one accord in these words of praise: "Well done! well done! exceedingly fortunate *K*unda! Thy name is now established (in meaning), well art thou called *K*unda, for thou hast established a most excellent method of deliverance, and, therefore, thou art well named. Now shall your name be much honoured among men. Well done, *K*unda! it is indeed seldom that a Buddha appears in the world, and to be born when he is born is exceedingly difficult; to believe in him and listen to his law is difficult; but how much more so to have the privilege of offering to him the last gift before he enters Nirvâ*n*a. Glory to *K*unda! Glory to *K*unda! Like the autumn moon on the 15th day of the month, your merit is full, and as all men look up to the cloudless moon with admiration and reverence, so do we reverence thee. Glory to *K*unda! Now then Buddha has received from you his very last offering! thus have you completed the Pâramitâ of charity! Glory to *K*unda!" &c. Then the assembly uttered these verses:

"Although born in the rôle of men,
Already hast thou overleapt the six heavens,
And therefore this united congregation
With supreme reverence make this request (of thee);
The most adorable amongst men
Is now about to enter Nirvâ*n*a!
You then, we pray, to pity us,
And respectfully entreat Buddha (on our behalf)
For a longer period to remain in the world,
To bring profit and advantage to countless assemblies;
And to declare fully the treasures of wisdom,
The sweet dew of the most exalted law.
If you consent not to make this request,
Our destiny will be yet incomplete;
We therefore, on this account, and with this view,
Respectfully entreat thee as our leader."

'At this time *K*unda, overjoyed as a man whose father or mother, after having been conveyed to the tomb, suddenly re-appears alive, again prostrated himself before Buddha and repeated the following verses:

"Oh! fortunate one that I am—to have gained such distinction,
To have been born thus happily as a man!
To have cast away covetousness and folly,
To have got rid for ever of the three evil ways of life,—
Oh! fortunate one that I am, to have gained this!
To have found such a treasure of gold and gems,
To have met with such a distinguished teacher,
To have rescued myself from birth as a beast[1].
The appearance of Buddha in the world is like that of the Udumbara flower;
It is difficult to have faith in him when born,

[1] That is, in any inferior position in the animal creation.

And having met with him, to sow the seeds of virtue,
Whereby for ever to escape the sorrows of hell (Pretas),
And to destroy and put to rout
The combined power of all the Asuras (this also is difficult).
Truly to attain this when Buddha is born
Is as difficult as to cast a mustard seed on the point of a spear.
But now having completed (the Pâramitâ) of charity,
It is my happy privilege to deliver both Devas and men from life an death.
The law of Buddha is an uncontaminated law,
Like the pure flower on the surface of the water,
Able to deliver to the utmost (those highest in existence),
Able to rescue eternally from the waters of birth and death.
It is difficult when born to be born as a man,
To meet with Buddha in the world is difficult,
Even as it is hard for a blind turtle
To find the hole in a piece of wood floating on the great ocean.
And now on the ground of this offering of food,
I aspire to attain the highest recompense,
Deliverance from the whole concourse of sorrows,
To destroy them and be held by them no more.
I desire not as my aim in this
To be born as a man or a Deva,
Like others who look only for this recompense:
And when obtained find no real delight.
But now Tathâgata, by receiving my offering,
Has inspired me with true and lasting joy,
Even as the Hira*n*ya (golden?) flower
Placed on (or in a setting of) scented sandal-wood,—
So my body, like that flower,
Is now filled with joy in consequence of Tathâgata;
Like that sandal-wood (setting), having received my gift,
Such is the delight that now fills my soul.
And my present reward is equally great,
Beyond any other in point of excellence,
For *S*akra, and Brahma, and all the gods
Here present, adore and reverence (bring their offerings to) me.
But alas! all the world
Is filled with unutterable sorrow,
In the knowledge that the world-honoured Buddha
Is about to enter Nirvâ*n*a.
And the cry is heard on every hand,
'The world is left without a ruler.'
But it is not well thus to leave mankind,
They should rather be looked on as an only son,
And Tathâgata dwelling in their midst
Should completely expound the supreme law—
That law, grand as the precious Sumeru,
Planted firmly in the midst of the great sea.
The wisdom of Buddha is able completely to dissipate
The dark gloom of our ignorance,

Even as when in the midst of space
A rising cloud is suddenly dispersed.
Tathâgata is able to destroy for ever
The entire concourse of sorrows,
Even as the sun, when he bursts forth,
Disperses with his brightness the blackness of the cloud.
So it is that now the entire world
Laments and weeps with affliction
On account of the torrents of suffering
Which fall heavily upon all in their passage thro' birth and death.
On this account, therefore, the world-honoured
Ought to strengthen and increase the faith of men,
That they may escape these sorrows,
And to remain a longer while in the world."

'Then Buddha replied to *K*unda: "Even so! even so! it is as you say—the birth of a Buddha in the world is rare as the appearance of the Udumbara flower, and to be able to believe in him is also a matter of extreme difficulty; but infinitely more difficult is it to be selected as the one to present a last offering to him before he enters Nirvâ*n*a. What room, then, O *K*unda, is there for sorrowful thoughts? your heart should rather dance for joy! for you are the one thus selected to offer the last offering, and so complete your work of charity. Make not, then, such a request that Buddha should remain longer in the world, for you should now be able to realise (kwan°) even the highest truth [the province or domain (keng kiai) of all the Buddhas], the impermanency of all things, that all systems of religion (or, elements of being)—(hing°) both as to their nature and attributes—are also impermanent. And then for the sake of *K*unda he repeated these Gâthâs:

"All things in the present world
Being produced, must return to destruction;
Although the term of life were immeasurably long,
Yet it must in the end come to a close.
Prosperity gives place to adversity,
Plenty is succeeded by want,
Youth before long yields to decay,
The ruddy colour of health is paled by disease,
Life, also, is followed by death,
There is no such thing as permanency.
The most absolute monarchs,
Whose might none can dispute,
These also come to naught and change,
The years of their life are just the same,

Involved in the wheel of transmigration.
The rolling stream of life goes on,
And there is no continuing place for any.
There is no real joy to be found in the world,
For the mark set upon all these things
Is that they are all empty and unreal,
Liable to destruction and change,
Ever accompanied by sorrow,
Tinctured with fears and regrets,
And the bitterness of old age, disease, and death,
Even as an insect born in filth.
What wise man would desire
To continue in the midst of such things as these (or find his joy therein)?
So the sorrows to which the body is joined,
Are even like this impure substance.
Surrounded, as it were, with these, man lives
Without any reasonable hope of escape.
And so even the bodies of the Devas
Are likewise perishable and impure;
All things liable to desire are unreal,
And, therefore, I have cast off this cloak of covetousness.
I have discarded the very thought of desire,
And so I have arrived at the only truth,
And passed beyond the boundary of Being.
To-day I shall reach Nirvâ*n*a—
To-day I shall cross to that shore;
I have for ever got rid of sorrow,
And therefore it is to-day
I shall be (or am) ravished with unutterable joy.
In this way and by these means it is
I have arrived at the one reality:
For ever free from the bonds of grief,
To-day I shall reach Nirvâ*n*a.
No more disease, old age, or death,
The days of my life interminable, inexhaustible.
Now shall I enter Nirvâ*n*a!
Just as a great fire which is extinguished.
*K*unda! you ought not therefore
To think of measuring the truth of Tathâgata,
You should rather contemplate his true nature.
As the great Mount Sumeru,
So am I resting on Nirvâ*n*a,
Receiving and keeping in me the only joy.
This is the law of all the Buddhas.
Weep, then, and lament no more!"'

INDEX.

Abhisambodhi, the condition that stands face to face with wisdom, page 156.
Aga, king, 92.
Agastya, a *Ri*shi, 43.
Agitavatî, name of a river, meaning invincible, 1.
Âg*ñ*âta kau*nd*inya, he who knows, name of a disciple, 178.
Agnidatta Kâ*s*yapa, same as Eggidatta, description of, 197.
Aila, grandchild of Soma, 149.
Ala, mount, 244.
Alava, a demon, 244.
Ambrosia, 'sweet dew,' 15.
Âmra, garden of, 257.
Anâthapi*nd*ada, friend of the orphan, conversion of, 201.
Aṅgiras, name of a *Ri*shi, 95.
A*ñk*avari, town of, 243.
Anomâ, a river, 111.
Antideva râga, an old king, 12.
Ârâ*d*a, abode of, 137.
Ârâ*d*a Kâlâma, name of *Ri*shi, 130.
Ârâ*d*a Râma, a *Ri*shi, 131.
Ârâ*d*a Udrarâma, 131.
Asidaka, a demon, 244.
Asita, a *Ri*shi, 12.
A*s*okarâga, temple of, xiii.
Â*s*ravas, extinction of the, 187 n.
Atri, an old king, 111.
Avalokite*s*vara, the god who looks down, 207.
Ayodhyâ, country of, 245.

Barahut, Cunningham's, 231.
Bara*n*â, river in India, 171.
Bhârgavides, hermitage of, 59.
Bh*ri*gu, *Ri*shi, 10.
Bigandet, story of Eggidatta (Legend, p. 180), 197.
Bimbisâra râga, becomes a disciple, 180.
— prince's reply to, 119.
— visits the prince, 111.
Bird, double-headed, 89.
Bodhi, capable of receiving, 145.
— tree, 146.
Bodhisattva, addressed as 'Kshatriya' by Mâra, 149.
— birth of, 2.
Bournouf's Introduction to Indian Buddhism, 138.
Brahma, voice of. See Childers, sub voce, 196.
Brahmadeva, an ascetic, 12.
Brahmaloka heavens, 138.
Brahman, a soothsayer, 7, 137.
B*ri*haspati, Devas pay worship to, 78.
Buddha, ascended to the heavens of the thirty-three gods, 240.
— birth of, 4.
— death of, 307.
— first instance of mendicant life of, 169.
— Romantic History of, 72.
— the eye of. See Childers' Pâli Dict., sub voce, 165.
— the Lady Âmrâ sees, 249.
— wonders wrought by. See Spence Hardy's Manual and Beal's Romantic Legend, 185.
Buddha's foot worshipped, 258.
Buddhaghosha's Parables, by Captain Rogers, 275.
Buddhiques, Études (Leon Féer), 168.
Buddhism, Manual of (Spence Hardy), 193.
Buddhist Birth Stories, 111.
— literature, 117.
— sculptures, 112.
Buddhists' denial of 'soul' (by Northern Buddhists), 204.
Burgess, Western Caves, 247.

Catena of Buddhist Scriptures, 39.
Childers' Pâli Dict., 4.
Colebrooke, Essays, 132.

Conversion of supporter of orphans, 201.
Cunningham, General, Archæological Report, 171.

Davids, Dr. Rhys, xxxvi, 170, 176, 201, 203.
Death, the prince hearing the name of, 37.
Desire, putting away, 38.
Devadatta, son of Suprabuddha, 246 n.
Devaputra, the sun or the moon, 72.
Deva-râga, of the pure abode, 32.
Dharmaraksha, an Indian priest, i, xxv.
Dhyânas, first state, condition of ecstasy, 138.
— second state, tasting of great joy, 138.
— third state, wishing no further excellence, 138.
— fourth state, all joys and sorrow done away, 138.
Dîpava*m*sa, statement made in, xii.
Disgust at sorrow, 29.

East Market, slaughter post of the, 124.
Eitel, Handbook, sub Mûrddhâbhishikta, 4.
Elephant-dragon, 41.
Elephant, escaping the drunken, 241.
Erythrina fulgens (see Bournouf's Lotus, p. 306), 164.

Fa-hien, 58, 112, 193, 198.
Fan-fu, philosophers or students, 132.
Fang-kwang-tai-*k*wang-yan-king, Life of Buddha, xxviii.
Five outward marks of dignity, 94.
Fo-pen-hing, Life of Buddha, xxviii.
Fo-pen-hing-king, xvi.
Fo-pen-hing-tsih-king, Life of Buddha, xxix.
Fo-shwo-*k*ung-hu-mo-ho-ti-king, Life of Buddha, xxx.

Gaga mount, 244.
Gandhâra, king of, 242.
Gandharvas, heavenly musicians, 25.
Ganges, river, 111, 171.
Gautama, fall of, 39.
— ford, near Patna, 252.
— gate of, 252.
Gautamas *G*âtisruna and Dakâtili, 245.
Godama, a demon, 244.
Golden mount, 51.
Great-age, a Brahman, 245.
G*r*idhrakû*t*a mount, 246.

*G*aigîshavya, a *R*ishi, 139.
*G*ambu tree, 48.
*G*ambudvîpa, continent of, 241.
*G*ambunada gold, 23.
*G*anaka, a *R*ishi, 11.
*G*anta, description of, xxvii.
*G*ayanta, a Brahman, 92.
*G*eta, the heir-apparent, 216.
*G*etavana, the monastery at *S*râvastî, 230.
*G*etavana Vihâra, receiving of, 230.

Hama kinkhava, 244.
Haug, Parsis, 167 n.
Heaven of the thirty-three gods, 23.
Hermit, the great disciple becomes a, 192.
Hetuvidyâ *s*âstra, 209.
Hin-tsing, heaven, 138.
Hira*n*yavatî, golden river, 286.

'I,' the soul, 191.
Îkshvâku, family of, 1, 72.
Î*s*vara, banner of, 112.

Kalamasa, village of, 245.
Kalpa-fire, 237.
Kamo, the Yaksha, 244.
Ka*ñ*gana, a demon, 244.
Kapila, a *R*ishi, 244.
Kapilavastu, the people of, 64.
Kârandhama, a *G*ina king, 328.
Kashâya, coloured robe, 68.
Kâ*s*yapa, a hermit, 183.
— Shi-ming-teng, a sage, 197.
Kau*nd*inya, tribe of, 172.
Kau*s*âmbî, country of, 245.
Kava*ñ*gara, a *R*ishi, 44.
Kia-*k'ba*, a king, 3.
Kilas (Kailâsa), palace of mount, 231.
Kimbila, country of, 245.
Kin-pu râga, 234.
Ko*nd*inya (see Kau*nd*inya), family of, 178.
Ko*s*ala, country of, 230, 245.
Ku'i, town of, 180.
Ku*s*i, a *R*ishi, 11.
Ku*s*i, town of, 286.
Ku*s*inagara, a city of, 326.
Kwong-yin heaven, 138.

*K*aitya, tower, 334.
*K*andradevaputra, a *R*ishi, 44.
*Kh*andaka, return of, 59.
*K*u*n*d*adana, of the *S*âkya family, 226.
*K*ung-pen-k'i-king, Life of Buddha, xxiv.

Lay Sermons, Huxley, 204.
Leaving the city, 47.
Li*kkh*avi lions, 282.
Li*kkh*avis, residents of Vai*s*âlî, 250.
Lo-me-po-ti, royal prince, 98.
Lord *S*akra, 51.
Lumbinî, garden of, 2, 6, 17.
Lung-tsiang, gate of, 323 n.

Magadha, king of, 250.
— town of, 250.
Mahâ Kâ*s*yapa, a great sage, 199.
Mahâpra*g*âpatî Gotamî, foster-mother of Bodhisattva, 84.
Mahâvatî, country of, 244.
Makara fish, 281.
Ma-kia-ka-li, aunt attendant on Mâra, 153.
Mandâra flowers, 5.
Manto, king, 2.
Mâra, the heavenly king, 6.
Mâra Devarâ*g*a, enemy of religion, 147.
Max Müller, Professor, 10, 19, 275.
Mâyâ, mother of Buddha, 1, 23, 87.
Mi-tsang-yau, miraculous, 7.
Monkey tank, 267.
Mu*ñg*a grass, 139.
Muni, virtues of a, 146.

Naira*ñg*anâ, river, 142, 144, 267.
Nalakûvara, the son of Vai*s*rava*n*a, 20.
Na-lo-sha-po-lo, a king, 97.
Neng-yueh-*g*in, daughter of Mâra râ*g*a, 147.
Ngai-loh, daughter of Mâra râ*g*a, 148.
Nirvâ*n*a, idea of, 51.
Nung-sha, 122.

On-tai-tieh, a Brahman, 108.
O-wei-san-pou-li, 156.

Padatti, village of, 243.
Pa-lin-fo, town of, 249.
Pa*ñk*a*s*ikha, a heavenly being, 242.
Pao-yun, companion of Fa-hien, xxvii.
Parâ*s*ara, a *R*ishi, 44.
Patali, 243.
Pâ*t*aligrâma, town of, 250.
Pâ*t*aliputra, town of, 249.
Paviggi, village of, 243.
Phû-yau-king, Life of Buddha, xxv.
Pi*nd*apâla, a demon, 245.
Pi-po-lo-'an-ti, king, 97.
Pi-sha, Regent of the North, 245.
Pi*s*una, name of Mâra, 267.
Pi-ti-ho-fu-li, town of, 243.
Pi-ti-o-*k*e-na, king, 97.
Po-*k*e-lo-po-yau, king, 97.
Po-lo-na, a demon 244.
Po-lo-sa, son of Sârasvata, 10.
Po-sha-na, a mountain, 242.
Po-sun-tau, brother of Asura, 125.
Potala, a demon, 243.
Potalagâma, a demon, 244.
Potalaka, a demon, 244.
Pou-na, a star, 96.
Pushya, a star, 96.

Râ*g*ag*r*iha, town of, 131.

*R*ishya*s*ri*n*ga, son of a Muni, 39.

Saddharma, minister of religion, 111.
Saketa bird, 93.
Samâdhi, condition of religious ecstasy, 48.
Sammata, condition of ecstasy, 205 n.
Sa*m*skâra, i.e. the five skandhas, 163.
Samyak-Sambodhi, state of, 8.
Sanatkumâra, son of Brahma deva, 24.
Săng-kia-lo-c'ha-sho-tsih-fo-hing-king, Life of Buddha, xxviii.
Satavaka, name of place, 245.
Savasasin, a convert, 245.
Sâvatthi, country of, 245.
Shin-t'ung-yaou-hi-king, last version of the Lalita Vistara, xxx.
Siau-pen-k'i-king, Life of Buddha, xxiii.
Siddhârtha, name for Bodhisattva, 23.
Siu-hing-pen-k'i-king, a work translated into Chinese by two *S*rama*n*as from India, xvii.
Study of h retical books, 263.
Sumeru, mount, 9.
Sûryadeva, the sun deva, 72.
Sûtra Pi*t*aka, 335.

*S*akradevendra, palace of, 171.
*S*akra-putra, 51.
*S*âkya lion, 258.
— Muni, 198.
— tribe, 226.
*S*âriputra, disciple of Kapila, 194.
*S*ubhakr*i*tsna heaven, 138.

Ta-tseu-sui-ying-pen-k'i-king, Life of Buddha, xxiii.
Teou-lau-ma, king, 97.
Topes of the eight kings, 334.
To-tsin, tower, 198.
Trâyastri*ms*as, name of the thirty-three heavens, 68.
Triple staff, 197.

Udâyi, a Brahmaputra, 38.
Udra, a *Ri*shi, 142.
Udraka Râmaputra, 167.
Upâdâna, cleaving to existence, 161.
Upaka, a young Brahman, 168.
Upâli, son of Atalî, 227.
Upatissa, twice-born, 195.
U-pi-lo Kâ*s*yapa, 185.
Uvari, companion to Goshira, 245.

Vaggi, country of, 245.
Vai*s*âlî, a town, 244.
Vai*s*rava*n*a, the heavenly king, 20.
Vâshpa, a disciple, 180.
Vasish*th*a, priest, 12.
Vasu Devas, one of the eight, 72.
Vessels of the seven precious substances, 20.
Vimala, a *Ri*shi, 149.
Vinaya Pi*t*aka, xxvi.
Vi*s*vâmitra, a *Ri*shi, 39.
V*ri*ddha Parâ*s*ara, a *Ri*shi, 139.
V*ri*hatphala heaven, 138.
Vulture Peak, 111.

Yasa, a noble's son, 180.
Ya*s*odharâ, a lovely maiden, 24, 86.
Yen-tsz' cave, fabulous hiding-place of the sun, 313.
Yuh-yen, daughter of Mâra râga, 147.

CORRECTIONS.

Page 228, verse 1598, for 'reigns' read 'reins.'

In the spelling of Chinese words, the Canton form has sometimes been used inadvertently, as in 'Fo-sho' for 'Fo-so.'

TRANSLITERATION OF ORIENTAL ALPHABETS ADOPTED FOR THE TRANSLATIONS OF THE SACRED BOOKS OF THE EAST.

CONSONANTS.	MISSIONARY ALPHABET. I Class.	II Class.	III Class.	Sanskrit.	Zend.	Pehlevi.	Persian.	Arabic.	Hebrew.	Chinese.
Gutturales.										
1 Tenuis	k	...	....	क	𐬐	[illegible]	ک	ك	כּ	k
2 „ aspirata	kh	...	....	ख	𐬑	[illegible]	...	...	כ	kh
3 Media	g	...	....	ग	𐬔	[illegible]	گ	...	גּ	...
4 „ aspirata	gh	...	....	घ	𐬖	[illegible]	...	...	ג	...
5 Gutturo-labialis	q	...	....	...	....	...	ق	ق	ק	...
6 Nasalis	ṅ (ng)	...	....	ङ	{𐬢 (ng) / 𐬣 (N)}	...	...	...	...	...
7 Spiritus asper	h	...	....	ह	𐬵 (𐬓 hv)	[illegible]	ه	ه	ה	h, hs
8 „ lenis	'	...	....	...	....	...	ا	ا	א	...
9 „ asper faucalis	‘h	...	....	...	....	...	ح	ح	ח	...
10 „ lenis faucalis	’h	...	....	...	....	...	ع	ع	ע	...
11 „ asper fricatus	...	*‘h*	....	...	....	...	خ	خ	ח	...
12 „ lenis fricatus	...	*’h*	....	...	....	...	غ	غ	...	...
Gutturales modificatae (palatales, &c.)										
13 Tenuis	...	*k*	....	च	𐬗	[illegible]	چ	...	...	*k*
14 „ aspirata	...	*kh*	....	छ	....	...	...	...	...	*kh*
15 Media	...	*g*	....	ज	𐬘	[illegible]	ج	ج	...	...
16 „ aspirata	...	*gh*	....	झ	....	...	ژ	غ	...	...
17 „ Nasalis	...	*ñ*	....	ञ	....	...	...	...	...	...

CONSONANTS (continued).	MISSIONARY ALPHABET. I Class.	II Class.	III Class.	Sanskrit.	Zend.	Pehlevi.	Persian.	Arabic.	Hebrew.	Chinese.
18 Semivocalis	y	. . .	. . . .	य	[illegible] [illegible] init.	[illegible]	ي	ي	י	y
19 Spiritus asper	. . .	(ẏ)	. . . .	. . .	. . . .	. . .	. . .	. . .	. . .	. . .
20 „ lenis	. . .	(ẏ)	. . . .	. . .	. . . .	. . .	. . .	. . .	. . .	. . .
21 „ asper assibilatus . .	. . .	*s*	. . . .	श	[illegible]	[illegible]	ش	ش	. . .	. . .
22 „ lenis assibilatus . .	. . .	*z*	. . . .	. . .	[illegible]	[illegible]	ژ	. . .	. . .	*z*
Dentales.										
23 Tenuis	t	. . .	. . . .	त	[illegible]	[illegible]	ت	ت	תּ	t
24 „ aspirata	th	. . .	. . . .	थ	[illegible]	. . .	. . .	. . .	ת	th
25 „ assibilata	. . .	. . .	TH	. . .	. . . .	. . .	ث	ث	. . .	. . .
26 Media	d	. . .	. . . .	द	[illegible]	[illegible]	د	د	דּ	. . .
27 „ aspirata	dh	. . .	. . . .	ध	[illegible]	. . .	. . .	. . .	ד	. . .
28 „ assibilata	. . .	. . .	DH	. . .	. . . .	. . .	ذ	ذ	. . .	. . .
29 Nasalis	n	. . .	. . . .	न	[illegible]	[illegible]	ن	ن	נ	n
30 Semivocalis	l	. . .	. . . .	ल	. . . .	[illegible]	ل	ل	ל	l
31 „ mollis 1	. . .	*l*	. . . .	ळ	. . . .	. . .	. . .	. . .	. . .	. . .
32 „ mollis 2	. . .	. . .	L	. . .	. . . .	. . .	. . .	. . .	. . .	. . .
33 Spiritus asper 1	s	. . .	. . . .	स	[illegible]	[illegible]	س (ث)	س	שׂ	s
34 „ asper 2	. . .	. . .	s (ʃ)	. . .	. . . .	. . .	. . .	. . .	ס	. . .
35 „ lenis	z	. . .	. . . .	. . .	[illegible]	[illegible]	ز (ذ)	ز	ז	z
36 „ asperrimus 1	. . .	. . .	z (ʒ)	. . .	. . . .	. . .	ص	ص	צ	ʒ, ʒh
37 „ asperrimus 2	. . .	. . .	ẓ (ʒ)	. . .	. . . .	. . .	ض	. . .	. . .	. . .

	I	II	III	Sanskrit	Zend	Pehlevi	Persian	Arabic	Hebrew	Chinese
Dentales modificatae (linguales, &c.)										
38 Tenuis	...	*t*	...	ट	...	...	ط	ط	ט	...
39 „ aspirata	...	*th*	...	ठ	...	...	ظ	ظ	...	...
40 Media	...	*d*	...	ड	𐬛	[illegible]	...	...	...	...
41 „ aspirata	...	*dh*	...	ढ	...	...	...	ض	...	...
42 Nasalis	...	*n*	...	ण	𐬣	...	...	...	...	...
43 Semivocalis	r	...	...	र	𐬭	[illegible]	ر	ر	ר	...
44 „ fricata	...	*r*	...	...	...	...	...	...	...	*r*
45 „ diacritica	...	...	R	...	...	...	...	...	...	...
46 Spiritus asper	sh	...	...	ष	𐬴	[illegible]	...	...	...	sh
47 „ lenis	zh	...	...	...	...	...	...	...	...	...
Labiales.										
48 Tenuis	p	...	...	प	𐬞	[illegible]	پ	...	פּ	p
49 „ aspirata	ph	...	...	फ	...	...	...	...	פ	ph
50 Media	b	...	...	ब	𐬠	[illegible]	ب	ب	בּ	...
51 „ aspirata	bh	...	...	भ	...	...	...	...	ב	...
52 Tenuissima	...	*p*	...	...	...	...	...	...	...	...
53 Nasalis	m	...	...	म	𐬨	[illegible]	م	م	מ	m
54 Semivocalis	w	...	...	...	𐬰	...	...	...	...	w
55 „ aspirata	hw	...	...	...	...	...	...	...	...	...
56 Spiritus asper	f	...	...	...	𐬟	[illegible]	ف	ف	...	f
57 „ lenis	v	...	...	व	»	[illegible]	و	و	ו	...
58 Anusvâra	...	*m*	...	अं	[illegible]	...	...	...	...	...
59 Visarga	...	*h*	...	अः	...	...	...	...	...	...

VOWELS.	MISSIONARY ALPHABET. I Class.	II Class.	III Class.	Sanskrit.	Zend.	Pehlevi.	Persian.	Arabic.	Hebrew.	Chinese.
1 Neutralis	0	...	....	...	....	...	...	...	ְ	ă
2 Laryngo-palatalis	ĕ	...	....	...	....	...	...	...	...	...
3 „ labialis	ŏ	...	....	...	....	ا fin.	...	...	...	...
4 Gutturalis brevis	a	...	....	अ	𐬀	[illegible] init.	ـَ	ـَ	ַ	a
5 „ longa	â	(a)	....	आ	𐬁	[illegible]	ـَا	ـَا	ָ	â
6 Palatalis brevis	i	...	....	इ	𐬌	...	ـِ	ـِ	ִ	i
7 „ longa	î	(i)	....	ई	𐬍	ی	ـِي	ـِي	ִי	î
8 Dentalis brevis	*li*	...	....	ऌ	....	...	...	...	...	...
9 „ longa	*lî*	...	....	ॡ	....	...	...	...	...	...
10 Lingualis brevis	*ri*	...	....	ऋ	....	...	...	...	...	...
11 „ longa	*rî*	...	....	ॠ	....	...	...	...	...	...
12 Labialis brevis	u	...	....	उ	𐬎	...	ـُ	ـُ	ֻ	u
13 „ longa	û	(u)	....	ऊ	𐬏	ا	ـُو	ـُو	וּ	û
14 Gutturo-palatalis brevis	e	...	....	...	𐬈 (e) 𐬆 (e)	...	...	...	ֶ	e
15 „ longa	ê (ai)	(e)	....	ए	𐬉, 𐬇	ی	ـِيْ	ـِيْ	ֵ	ê
16 Diphthongus gutturo-palatalis	âi	(ai)	....	ऐ	....	...	ـَيْ	ـَيْ	...	âi
17 „ „	ei (ĕi)	...	....	...	....	...	...	...	...	ei, êi
18 „ „	oi (ŏu)	...	....	...	....	...	...	...	...	...
19 Gutturo-labialis brevis	o	...	....	...	𐬊	...	...	...	ָ	o
20 „ longa	ô (au)	(o)	....	ओ	𐬋	ا	ـُوْ	ـُوْ	וֹ	...
21 Diphthongus gutturo-labialis	âu	(au)	....	औ	𐬃 (*au*)	...	ـَوْ	ـَوْ	...	âu
22 „ „	eu (ĕu)	...	....	...	....	...	...	...	...	...
23 „ „	ou (ŏu)	...	....	...	....	...	...	...	...	...
24 Gutturalis fracta	ä	...	....	...	....	...	...	...	...	...
25 Palatalis fracta	ï	...	....	...	....	...	...	...	...	...
26 Labialis fracta	ü	...	....	...	....	...	...	...	...	ü
27 Gutturo-labialis fracta	ö	...	....	...	....	...	...	...	...	...

March, 1883.

Clarendon Press, Oxford

A SELECTION OF

BOOKS

PUBLISHED FOR THE UNIVERSITY BY

HENRY FROWDE,

AT THE OXFORD UNIVERSITY PRESS WAREHOUSE,

7 PATERNOSTER ROW, LONDON.

ALSO TO BE HAD AT THE

CLARENDON PRESS DEPOSITORY, OXFORD.

LEXICONS, GRAMMARS, &c.

(See also Clarendon Press Series, pp. 22, 25, 26.)

A Greek-English Lexicon, by Henry George Liddell, D.D., and Robert Scott, D.D. Seventh Edition, Revised and Augmented throughout. 1883. 4to. cloth, 1*l*. 16*s*.

A copious Greek-English Vocabulary, compiled from the best authorities. 1850. 24mo. bound, 3*s*.

A Practical Introduction to Greek Accentuation, by H. W. Chandler, M.A. Second Edition. 1881. 8vo. cloth, 10*s*. 6*d*.

A Latin Dictionary, founded on Andrews' edition of Freund's Latin Dictionary, revised, enlarged, and in great part rewritten by Charlton T. Lewis, Ph.D., and Charles Short, LL.D., Professor of Latin in Columbia College, New York. 1879. 4to. cloth, 1*l*. 5*s*.

The Book of Hebrew Roots, by Abu 'l-Walîd Marwân ibn Janâh, otherwise called Rabbî Yônâh. Now first edited, with an Appendix, by Ad. Neubauer. 1875. 4to. cloth, 2*l*. 7*s*. 6*d*.

A Treatise on the use of the Tenses in Hebrew. By S. R. Driver, M.A. Second Edition, Revised and Enlarged. 1881. Extra fcap. 8vo. cloth, 7*s.* 6*d.*

Hebrew Accentuation of Psalms, Proverbs, and Job. By William Wickes, D.D. 1881. Demy 8vo. stiff cover, 5*s.*

Thesaurus Syriacus: collegerunt Quatremère, Bernstein, Lorsbach, Arnoldi, Field: edidit R. Payne Smith, S.T.P.

Fasc. I-VI. 1868-83. sm. fol. each, 1*l.* 1*s.*
Vol. I, containing Fasc. I-V. sm. fol. cloth, 5*l.* 5*s.*

A Practical Grammar of the Sanskrit Language, arranged with reference to the Classical Languages of Europe, for the use of English Students, by Monier Williams, M.A., Boden Professor of Sanskrit. Fourth Edition, 1877. 8vo. cloth, 15*s.*

A Sanskrit-English Dictionary, Etymologically and Philologically arranged, with special reference to Greek, Latin, German, Anglo-Saxon, English, and other cognate Indo European Languages. By Monier Williams, M.A., Boden Professor of Sanskrit. 1872. 4to. cloth, 4*l.* 14*s.* 6*d.*

Nalopákhyánam. Story of Nala, an Episode of the Mahá-Bhárata: the Sanskrit text, with a copious Vocabulary, and an improved version of Dean Milman's Translation, by Monier Williams, M.A. Second Edition, Revised and Improved. 1879. 8vo. cloth, 15*s.*

Sakuntalā. A Sanskrit Drama, in seven Acts. Edited by Monier Williams, M.A. Second Edition, 1876. 8vo. cloth, 21*s.*

An Anglo-Saxon Dictionary, based on the MS. Collections of the late Joseph Bosworth, D.D., Professor of Anglo-Saxon, Oxford. Edited and enlarged by Prof. T. N. Toller, M.A., Owens College, Manchester. (To be completed in four parts). Parts I and II. 1882. 4to. 15*s.* each.

An Icelandic-English Dictionary, based on the MS. collections of the late Richard Cleasby. Enlarged and completed by G. Vigfússon, M.A. With an Introduction, and Life of Richard Cleasby, by G. Webbe Dasent, D.C.L. 1874. 4to. cloth, 3*l.* 7*s.*

A List of English Words the Etymology of which is illustrated by comparison with Icelandic. Prepared in the form of an Appendix to the above. By W. W. Skeat, M.A., 1876. stitched, 2s.

A Handbook of the Chinese Language. Parts I and II, Grammar and Chrestomathy. By James Summers. 1863. 8vo. half bound, 1*l*. 8*s*.

An Etymological Dictionary of the English Language, arranged on an Historical Basis. By W. W. Skeat, M.A., Elrington and Bosworth Professor of Anglo-Saxon in the University of Cambridge. 1882. 4to. cloth, 2*l*. 4*s*.

A Concise Etymological Dictionary of the English Language. By W. W. Skeat, M.A. 1882. Crown 8vo. cloth, 5*s*. 6*d*.

GREEK CLASSICS, &c.

Heracliti Ephesii Reliquiae. Recensuit I. Bywater, M.A. Appendicis loco additae sunt Diogenis Laertii Vita Heracliti, Particulae Hippocratei De Diaeta Libri Primi, Epistolae Heracliteae. 1877. 8vo. cloth, price 6*s*.

Homer: A Complete Concordance to the Odyssey and Hymns of Homer; to which is added a Concordance to the Parallel Passages in the Iliad, Odyssey, and Hymns. By Henry Dunbar, M.D., Member of the General Council, University of Edinburgh. 1880. 4to. cloth, 1*l*. 1*s*.

Plato: The Apology, with a revised Text and English Notes, and a Digest of Platonic Idioms, by James Riddell, M.A. 1878. 8vo. cloth, 8*s*. 6*d*.

Plato: Philebus, with a revised Text and English Notes, by Edward Poste, M.A. 1860. 8vo. cloth, 7*s*. 6*d*.

Plato: Sophistes and Politicus, with a revised Text and English Notes, by L. Campbell, M.A. 1867. 8vo. cloth, 18*s*.

Plato: Theaetetus, with a revised Text and English Notes, by L. Campbell, M.A. Second Edition. 8vo. cloth, 10*s*. 6*d*. *Just Published.*

Plato: The Dialogues, translated into English, with Analyses and Introductions, by B. Jowett, M.A., Regius Professor of Greek. A new Edition in 5 volumes, medium 8vo. 1875. cloth, 3*l.* 10*s.*

Plato: The Republic, translated into English, with an Analysis and Introduction, by B. Jowett, M.A. Medium 8vo. cloth, 12*s.* 6*d.*

Plato: Index to. Compiled for the Second Edition of Professor Jowett's Translation of the Dialogues. By Evelyn Abbott, M.A. 1875. 8vo. paper covers, 2*s.* 6*d.*

Thucydides: Translated into English, with Introduction, Marginal Analysis, Notes, and Indices. By B. Jowett, M.A., Regius Professor of Greek. 2 vols. 1881. Medium 8vo. cloth, 1*l.* 12*s.*

THE HOLY SCRIPTURES, &c.

The Holy Bible in the earliest English Versions, made from the Latin Vulgate by John Wycliffe and his followers: edited by the Rev. J. Forshall and Sir F. Madden. 4 vols. 1850. Royal 4to. cloth, 3*l.* 3*s.*

Also reprinted from the above, with Introduction and Glossary by W. W. Skeat, M.A.

The New Testament in English, according to the Version by John Wycliffe, about A.D. 1380, and Revised by John Purvey, about A.D. 1388. Extra fcap. 8vo. cloth, 6*s.*

The Books of Job, Psalms, Proverbs, Ecclesiastes, and the Song of Solomon: according to the Wycliffite Version made by Nicholas de Hereford, about A.D. 1381, and Revised by John Purvey, about A.D. 1388. Extra fcap. 8vo. cloth, 3*s.* 6*d.*

The Holy Bible: an exact reprint, page for page, of the Authorized Version published in the year 1611. Demy 4to. half bound, 1*l.* 1*s.*

Vetus Testamentum ex Versione Septuaginta Interpretum secundum exemplar Vaticanum Romae editum. Accedit potior varietas Codicis Alexandrini. Tomi III. Editio Altera. 18mo. cloth, 18*s.*

Origenis Hexaplorum quae supersunt; sive, Veterum Interpretum Graecorum in totum Vetus Testamentum Fragmenta. Edidit Fridericus Field, A.M. 2 vols. 1875. 4to. cloth, 5*l.* 5*s.*

Libri Psalmorum Versio antiqua Latina, cum Paraphrasi Anglo-Saxonica. Edidit B. Thorpe, F.A.S. 1835. 8vo. cloth, 10*s.* 6*d.*

Libri Psalmorum Versio antiqua Gallica e Cod. MS. in Bibl. Bodleiana adservato, una cum Versione Metrica aliisque Monumentis pervetustis. Nunc primum descripsit et edidit Franciscus Michel, Phil. Doct. 1860. 8vo. cloth, 10*s.* 6*d.*

The Psalms in Hebrew without points. 1879. Crown 8vo. cloth, 3*s.* 6*d.*

The Book of Wisdom: the Greek Text, the Latin Vulgate, and the Authorised English Version; with an Introduction, Critical Apparatus, and a Commentary. By William J. Deane, M.A., Oriel College, Oxford; Rector of Ashen, Essex. Small 4to. cloth, 12*s.* 6*d.*

The Book of Tobit. A Chaldee Text, from a unique MS. in the Bodleian Library; with other Rabbinical Texts, English Translations, and the Itala. Edited by Ad. Neubauer, M.A. 1878. Crown 8vo. cloth, 6*s.*

A Commentary on the Book of Proverbs. Attributed to Abraham Ibn Ezra. Edited from a Manuscript in the Bodleian Library by S. R. Driver, M.A. Crown 8vo. paper cover, 3*s.* 6*d.*

Horae Hebraicae et Talmudicae, a J. Lightfoot. A new Edition, by R. Gandell, M.A. 4 vols. 1859. 8vo. cloth, 1*l.* 1*s.*

Novum Testamentum Graece. Antiquissimorum Codicum Textus in ordine parallelo dispositi. Accedit collatio Codicis Sinaitici. Edidit E. H. Hansell, S.T.B. Tomi III. 1864. 8vo. half morocco, 2*l.* 12*s.* 6*d.*

Novum Testamentum Graece. Accedunt parallela S. Scripturae loca, necnon vetus capitulorum notatio et canones Eusebii. Edidit Carolus Lloyd, S.T.P.R., necnon Episcopus Oxoniensis. 18mo. cloth, 3*s.*

The same on writing paper, with large margin, cloth, 10*s.*

Novum Testamentum Graece juxta Exemplar Millianum. 18mo. cloth, 2*s*. 6*d*.

The same on writing paper, with large margin, cloth, 9*s*.

Evangelia Sacra Graece. fcap. 8vo. limp, 1*s*. 6*d*.

The Greek Testament, with the Readings adopted by the Revisers of the Authorised Version:—

(1) Pica type. Second Edition, with Marginal References. Demy 8vo. cloth, 10*s*. 6*d*.

(2) Long Primer type. Fcap. 8vo. cloth, 4*s*. 6*d*.

(3) The same, on writing paper, with wide margin, cloth, 15*s*.

The Parallel New Testament, Greek and English; being the Authorised Version, 1611; the Revised Version, 1881; and the Greek Text followed in the Revised Version. 8vo. cloth, 12*s*. 6*d*.

The Revised Version is the joint property of the Universities of Oxford and Cambridge.

The Gospel of St. Mark in Gothic, according to the translation made by Wulfila in the Fourth Century. Edited with a Grammatical Introduction and Glossarial Index by W. W. Skeat, M.A. Extra fcap. 8vo. cloth, 4*s*.

Canon Muratorianus: the earliest Catalogue of the Books of the New Testament. Edited with Notes and a Facsimile of the MS. in the Ambrosian Library at Milan, by S. P. Tregelles, LL.D. 1867. 4to. cloth, 10*s*. 6*d*.

FATHERS OF THE CHURCH, &c.

St. Athanasius: Orations against the Arians. With an Account of his Life by William Bright, D.D. 1873. Crown 8vo. cloth, 9*s*.

St. Athanasius: Historical Writings, according to the Benedictine Text. With an Introduction by William Bright, D.D. 1881. Crown 8vo. cloth, 10*s*. 6*d*.

St. Augustine: Select Anti-Pelagian Treatises, and the Acts of the Second Council of Orange. With an Introduction by William Bright, D.D. Crown 8vo. cloth, 9*s*.

The Canons of the First Four General Councils of Nicaea, Constantinople, Ephesus, and Chalcedon. 1877. Crown 8vo. cloth, 2s. 6*d*.

Notes on the Canons of the First Four General Councils. By William Bright, D.D. 1882. Crown 8vo. cloth, 5s. 6*d*.

Cyrilli Archiepiscopi Alexandrini in XII Prophetas. Edidit P. E. Pusey, A.M. Tomi II. 1868. 8vo. cloth, 2*l*. 2s.

Cyrilli Archiepiscopi Alexandrini in D. Joannis Evangelium. Accedunt Fragmenta Varia necnon Tractatus ad Tiberium Diaconum Duo. Edidit post Aubertum P. E. Pusey, A.M. Tomi III. 1872. 8vo. 2*l*. 5s.

Cyrilli Archiepiscopi Alexandrini Commentarii in Lucae Evangelium quae supersunt Syriace. E MSS. apud Mus. Britan. edidit R. Payne Smith, A.M. 1858. 4to. cloth, 1*l*. 2s.

The same, translated by R. Payne Smith, M.A. 2 vols. 1859. 8vo. cloth, 14s.

Ephraemi Syri, Rabulae Episcopi Edesseni, Balaei, aliorumque Opera Selecta. E Codd. Syriacis MSS in Museo Britannico et Bibliotheca Bodleiana asservatis primus edidit J. J. Overbeck. 1865. 8vo. cloth, 1*l*. 1s.

Eusebius' Ecclesiastical History, according to the text of Burton, with an Introduction by William Bright, D.D. 1881. Crown 8vo. cloth, 8s. 6*d*.

Irenaeus: The Third Book of St. Irenaeus, Bishop of Lyons, against Heresies. With short Notes and a Glossary by H. Deane, B.D., Fellow of St. John's College, Oxford. 1874. Crown 8vo. cloth, 5s. 6*d*.

Patrum Apostolicorum, S. Clementis Romani, S. Ignatii, S. Polycarpi, quae supersunt. Edidit Guil. Jacobson, S.T.P.R. Tomi II. Fourth Edition, 1863. 8vo. cloth, 1*l*. 1s.

Socrates' Ecclesiastical History, according to the Text of Hussey, with an Introduction by William Bright, D.D. 1878. Crown 8vo. cloth, 7s 6*d*.

ECCLESIASTICAL HISTORY, BIOGRAPHY, &c.

Baedae Historia Ecclesiastica. Edited, with English Notes, by G. H. Moberly, M.A. 1881. Crown 8vo. cloth, 10*s.* 6*d.*

Bright (W., D.D.). Chapters of Early English Church History. 1878. 8vo. cloth, 12*s.*

Burnet's History of the Reformation of the Church of England. A new Edition. Carefully revised, and the Records collated with the originals, by N. Pocock, M.A. 7 vols. 1865. 8vo. *Price reduced to* 1*l.* 10*s.*

Councils and Ecclesiastical Documents relating to Great Britain and Ireland. Edited, after Spelman and Wilkins, by A. W. Haddan, B.D., and W. Stubbs, M.A., Regius Professor of Modern History, Oxford. Vols. I. and III. 1869–71. Medium 8vo. cloth, each 1*l.* 1*s.*

Vol. II. Part I. 1873. Medium 8vo. cloth, 10*s.* 6*d.*

Vol. II. Part II. 1878. Church of Ireland; Memorials of St. Patrick. Stiff covers, 3*s.* 6*d.*

Hammond (C. E.). Liturgies, Eastern and Western. Edited, with Introduction, Notes, and a Liturgical Glossary. 1878. Crown 8vo. cloth, 10*s.* 6*d.*

An Appendix to the above. 1879. Crown 8vo. paper covers, 1*s.* 6*d.*

John, Bishop of Ephesus. The Third Part of his Ecclesiastical History. [In Syriac.] Now first edited by William Cureton, M.A. 1853. 4to. cloth, 1*l.* 12*s.*

The same, translated by R. Payne Smith, M.A. 1860. 8vo. cloth, 10*s.*

Monumenta Ritualia Ecclesiae Anglicanae. The occasional Offices of the Church of England according to the old use of Salisbury the Prymer in English, and other prayers and forms, with dissertations and notes. By William Maskell, M.A. Second Edition. 1882. 3 vols. 8vo. cloth, 2*l.* 10*s.*

The Ancient Liturgy of the Church of England, according to the uses of Sarum, York, Hereford, and Bangor, and the Roman Liturgy arranged in parallel columns, with preface and notes. By William Maskell, M A. Third Edition. 1882. 8vo. cloth, 15*s.*

The Liturgy and Ritual of the Celtic Church. By F. E. Warren, B.D., Fellow of St. John's College, Oxford. 1881. 8vo. cloth, 14*s.*

The Leofric Missal. By the same Editor. In the Press.

Records of the Reformation. The Divorce, 1527–1533. Mostly now for the first time printed from MSS. in the British Museum and other libraries. Collected and arranged by N. Pocock, M.A. 1870. 2 vols. 8vo. cloth, 1*l.* 16*s.*

Shirley (W. W.). Some Account of the Church in the Apostolic Age. Second Edition, 1874. fcap. 8vo. cloth, 3*s.* 6*d.*

Stubbs (W.). Registrum Sacrum Anglicanum. An attempt to exhibit the course of Episcopal Succession in England. 1858. small 4to. cloth, 8*s.* 6*d.*

ENGLISH THEOLOGY.

Butler's Works, with an Index to the Analogy. 2 vols. 1874. 8vo. cloth, 11*s.*

Butler's Sermons. 8vo. cloth, 5*s.* 6*d.*

Butler's Analogy of Religion. 8vo. cloth, 5*s.* 6*d.*

Heurtley's Harmonia Symbolica: Creeds of the Western Church. 1858. 8vo. cloth, 6*s.* 6*d.*

Homilies appointed to be read in Churches. Edited by J. Griffiths, M.A. 1859. 8vo. cloth, 7*s.* 6*d.*

Hooker's Works, with his Life by Walton, arranged by John Keble, M.A. Sixth Edition, 1874. 3 vols. 8vo. cloth, 1*l.* 11*s.* 6*d.*

Hooker's Works; the text as arranged by John Keble, M.A. 2 vols. 1875. 8vo. cloth, 11*s.*

Pearson's Exposition of the Creed. Revised and corrected by E. Burton, D.D. Sixth Edition, 1877. 8vo. cloth, 10*s.* 6*d.*

Waterland's Review of the Doctrine of the Eucharist, with a Preface by the present Bishop of London. 1880. Crown 8vo. cloth, 6*s.* 6*d.*

Wheatly's Illustration of the Book of Common Prayer. A new Edition, 1846. 8vo. cloth, 5*s.*

Wyclif. A Catalogue of the Original Works of John Wyclif, by W. W. Shirley, D.D. 1865. 8vo. cloth, 3*s.* 6*d.*

Wyclif. Select English Works. By T. Arnold, M.A. 3 vols. 1869–1871. 8vo. cloth. *Price reduced to* 1*l.* 1*s.*

Wyclif. Trialogus. With the Supplement now first edited. By Gotthard Lechler. 1869. 8vo. cloth. *Price reduced to* 7*s.*

HISTORICAL AND DOCUMENTARY WORKS.

British Barrows, a Record of the Examination of Sepulchral Mounds in various parts of England. By William Greenwell, M.A., F.S.A. Together with Description of Figures of Skulls, General Remarks on Prehistoric Crania, and an Appendix by George Rolleston, M.D., F.R.S. 1877. Medium 8vo. cloth, 25*s.*

Britton. A Treatise upon the Common Law of England, composed by order of King Edward I. The French Text carefully revised, with an English Translation, Introduction, and Notes, by F. M. Nichols, M.A. 2 vols. 1865. Royal 8vo. cloth, 1*l.* 16*s.*

Clarendon's (Edw. Earl of) History of the Rebellion and Civil Wars in England. 7 vols. 1839. 18mo. cloth, 1*l.* 1*s.*

Clarendon's (Edw. Earl of) History of the Rebellion and Civil Wars in England. Also his Life, written by himself, in which is included a Continuation of his History of the Grand Rebellion. With copious Indexes. In one volume, royal 8vo. 1842. cloth, 1*l.* 2*s.*

Clinton's Epitome of the Fasti Hellenici. 1851. 8vo. cloth, 6*s.* 6*d.*

Clinton's Epitome of the Fasti Romani. 1854. 8vo. cloth, 7*s.*

Freeman's (E. A.) History of the Norman Conquest of England; its Causes and Results. In Six Volumes. 8vo. cloth, 5*l.* 9*s.* 6*d.*

Vols. I–II together, 3rd edition, 1877. 1*l.* 16*s.*
Vol. III, 2nd edition, 1874. 1*l.* 1*s.*
Vol. IV, 2nd edition, 1875. 1*l.* 1*s.*
Vol. V, 1876. 1*l.* 1*s.*
Vol. VI. Index. 1879. 8vo. cloth, 10*s.* 6*d.*

Freeman (E. A.). The Reign of William Rufus and the Accession of Henry the First. 2 vols. 8vo. cloth, 1*l.* 16*s.*

Gascoigne's Theological Dictionary ("Liber Veritatum"): Selected Passages, illustrating the condition of Church and State, 1403–1458. With an Introduction by James E. Thorold Rogers, M.P. Small 4to. cloth, 10*s.* 6*d.*

Magna Carta, a careful Reprint. Edited by W. Stubbs, M.A., Regius Professor of Modern History. 1879. 4to. stitched, 1*s.*

Olaf. Passio et Miracula Beati Olavi. Edited from a Twelfth-Century MS. in the Library of Corpus Christi College, Oxford, with an Introduction and Notes, by Frederick Metcalfe, M.A. Small 4to. stiff cover, 6*s.*

Protests of the Lords, including those which have been expunged, from 1624 to 1874; with Historical Introductions. Edited by James E. Thorold Rogers, M.A. 1875. 3 vols. 8vo. cloth, 2*l.* 2*s.*

Rogers's History of Agriculture and Prices in England, A.D. 1259–1793.

Vols. I and II (1259–1400). 1866. 8vo. cloth, 2*l.* 2*s.*
Vols. III and IV (1401–1582). 1882. 8vo. cloth, 2*l.* 10*s.*

Sturlunga Saga, including the Islendinga Saga of Lawman Sturla Thordsson and other works. Edited by Dr. Gudbrand Vigfússon. In 2 vols. 1878. 8vo. cloth, 2*l*. 2*s*.

Two of the Saxon Chronicles parallel, with Supplementary Extracts from the Others. Edited, with Introduction, Notes, and a Glossarial Index, by J. Earle, M.A. 1865. 8vo. cloth, 16*s*.

Statutes made for the University of Oxford, and for the Colleges and Halls therein, by the University of Oxford Commissioners. 1882. 8vo. cloth, 12s. 6d.

Also separately,

Statutes made for the University of Oxford. 2*s*.

Statutes made for the Colleges of Oxford. 1*s*. each.

Statuta Universitatis Oxoniensis. 1882. 8vo. cloth, 5*s*.

The Student's Handbook to the University and Colleges of Oxford. Sixth Edition. 1881. Extra fcap. 8vo. cloth, 2*s*. 6*d*.

MATHEMATICS, PHYSICAL SCIENCE, &c.

Astronomical Observations made at the University Observatory, Oxford, under the direction of C. Pritchard, M.A., Savilian Professor of Astronomy. No. 1. 1878. Royal 8vo. paper covers, 3*s*. 6*d*.

Treatise on Infinitesimal Calculus. By Bartholomew Price, M.A., F.R.S., Professor of Natural Philosophy, Oxford.

Vol. I. Differential Calculus. Second Edition, 8vo. cloth, 14*s*. 6*d*.

Vol. II. Integral Calculus, Calculus of Variations, and Differential Equations. Second Edition, 1865. 8vo. cloth, 18*s*.

Vol. III. Statics, including Attractions; Dynamics of a Material Particle. Second Edition, 1868. 8vo. cloth, 16*s*.

Vol. IV. Dynamics of Material Systems; together with a chapter on Theoretical Dynamics, by W. F. Donkin, M.A., F.R.S. 1862. 8vo. cloth, 16*s*.

Rigaud's Correspondence of Scientific Men of the 17th Century, with Table of Contents by A. de Morgan, and Index by the Rev. J. Rigaud, M.A., Fellow of Magdalen College, Oxford. 2 vols. 1841–1862. 8vo. cloth, 18*s*. 6*d*.

Vesuvius. By John Phillips, M.A., F.R.S., Professor of Geology, Oxford. 1869. Crown 8vo. cloth, 10*s*. 6*d*.

Geology of Oxford and the Valley of the Thames. By the same Author. 1871. 8vo. cloth, 21*s*.

Synopsis of the Pathological Series in the Oxford Museum. By H. W. Acland, M.D., F.R.S., 1867. 8vo. cloth, 2*s*. 6*d*.

Thesaurus Entomologicus Hopeianus, or a Description of the rarest Insects in the Collection given to the University by the Rev. William Hope. By J. O. Westwood, M.A., F.L.S. With 40 Plates. 1874. Small folio, half morocco, 7*l*. 10*s*.

Text-Book of Botany, Morphological and Physiological. By Dr. Julius Sachs, Professor of Botany in the University of Würzburg. *A New Edition.* Translated by S. H. Vines, M.A. 1882. Royal 8vo. 1*l*. 11*s*. 6*d*.

Johannes Müller on Certain Variations in the Vocal Organs of the Passeres that have hitherto escaped notice. Translated by F. J. Bell. B.A., and edited with an Appendix, by A. H. Garrod, M.A., F.R.S. With Plates. 1878. 4to. paper covers, 7*s*. 6*d*.

MISCELLANEOUS.

Bacon's Novum Organum. Edited, with English notes, by G. W. Kitchin, M.A. 1855. 8vo. cloth, 9*s*. 6*d*.

Bacon's Novum Organum. Translated by G. W. Kitchin, M.A. 1855. 8vo. cloth, 9*s*. 6*d*. (See also p. 38.)

The Works of George Berkeley, D.D., formerly Bishop of Cloyne; including many of his writings hitherto unpublished. With Prefaces, Annotations, and an Account of his Life and Philosophy, by Alexander Campbell Fraser, M.A. 4 vols. 1871. 8vo. cloth, 2*l*. 18*s*.

The Life, Letters, &c. 1 vol. cloth, 16*s*. (See also p. 38.)

The Logic of Hegel; translated from the Encyclopaedia of the Philosophical Sciences. With Prolegomena by William Wallace, M.A. 1874. 8vo. cloth, 14s.

Smith's Wealth of Nations. A new Edition, with Notes, by J. E. Thorold Rogers, M.A. 2 vols. 1880. cloth, 21s.

A Course of Lectures on Art, delivered before the University of Oxford in Hilary Term, 1870, by John Ruskin, M.A., Slade Professor of Fine Art. 8vo. cloth, 6s.

Aspects of Poetry; being Lectures delivered at Oxford by John Campbell Shairp, LL.D., Professor of Poetry, Oxford. Crown 8vo. cloth, 10s. 6*d.*

A Critical Account of the Drawings by Michel Angelo and Raffaello in the University Galleries, Oxford. By J. C. Robinson, F.S.A. 1870. Crown 8vo. cloth, 4s.

Catalogue of the Castellani Collection of Antiquities in the University Galleries, Oxford. By W. S. W. Vaux, M.A., F.R.S. Crown 8vo. stiff cover, 1s.

The Sacred Books of the East.

TRANSLATED BY VARIOUS ORIENTAL SCHOLARS, AND EDITED BY F. MAX MÜLLER.

Vol. I. *The Upanishads.* [Translated by F. Max Müller.] Part I. The *Kh*ândogya-upanishad, The Talavakâra-upanishad, The Aitareya-âra*n*yaka, The Kaushîtaki-brâhma*n*a-upanishad, and The Vâ*g*asaneyi-sa*m*hitâ-upanishad. 8vo. cloth, 10s. 6*d.*

Vol. II. *The Sacred Laws of the Âryas,* as taught in the Schools of Âpastamba, Gautama, Vâsish*th*a, and Baudhâyana. [Translated by Prof. Georg Bühler.] Part I, Âpastamba and Gautama. 8vo. cloth, 10s. 6*d.*

Vol. III. *The Sacred Books of China.* The Texts of Confucianism. [Translated by James Legge.] Part I. The Shû King, The Religious portions of the Shih King, and The Hsiâo King. 8vo. cloth, 12s. 6*d.*

Vol. IV. *The Vendîdâd.* Translated by James Darmesteter. 8vo. cloth, 10s. 6*d*.

Vol. V. *The Bundahis, Bahman Yast, and Shâyast-lâ-Shâyast.* Pahlavi Texts, Part I. Translated by E. W. West. 8vo. cloth, 12*s*. 6*d*.

Vols. VI and IX. *The Qur'ân.* Parts I and II. Translated by Professor E. H. Palmer. 8vo. cloth, 21*s*.

Vol. VII. *The Institutes of Vishnu.* Translated by Professor Julius Jolly. 8vo. cloth, 10*s*. 6*d*.

Vol. VIII. *The Bhagavadgîtâ, Sanatsugâtîya, and Anugîtâ.* Translated by Kâshinâth Trimbak Telang. 8vo. cloth, 10*s*. 6*d*.

Vol. X. *The Dhammapada*, translated by Professor F. Max Müller; and *The Sutta Nipâta*, translated by Professor Fausböll; being Canonical Books of the Buddhists. 8vo. cloth, 10*s*. 6*d*.

Vol. XI. *The Mahâparinibbâna Sutta, The Tevigga Sutta, The Mahâsudassana Sutta, The Dhamma-Kakkappavattana Sutta.* Translated by T. W. Rhys Davids. 8vo. cloth, 10*s*. 6*d*.

Vol. XII. *The Satapatha-Brâhmana.* Translated by Professor Eggeling. Vol. I. 8vo. cloth, 12*s*. 6*d*.

Vol. XIII. *The Pâtimokkha.* Translated by T. W. Rhys Davids. *The Mahâvagga*, Part I. Translated by Dr. H. Oldenberg. 8vo. cloth, 10*s*. 6*d*.

Vol. XIV. *The Sacred Laws of the Âryas*, as taught in the Schools of Vâsishtha and Baudhâyana. Translated by Professor Georg Bühler. 8vo. cloth, 10*s*. 6*d*.

Vol. XVI. *The Yî King*, with an Appendix on the Philosophy of the Scholars of the Sung dynasty, professedly derived from the Yî. Translated by James Legge. 8vo. cloth, 10*s*. 6*d*.

Vol. XVII. *The Mahâvagga, and Kullavagga.* Part II. Translated by T. W. Rhys Davids and Dr. H. Oldenberg. 8vo. cloth, 10*s*. 6*d*.

Vol. XVIII. *The Dâdistân-î Dînîk, and Epistles of Mânûskihar.* Pahlavi Texts, Part II. Translated by E. W. West. 8vo. cloth, 12*s*. 6*d*.

Vol. XIX. *The Fo-sho-hing-tsan-king.* Translated by Samuel Beal. 8vo. cloth, 10*s*. 6*d*.

Vol. XXIII. *The Zend-Avesta.* Part. II. *The Sîrôzahs, Yasts, and Nyâyis.* 8vo. cloth, 10*s.* 6*d.*

The following Volumes are in the Press:—

Vol. XV. *The Upanishads.* Part II. Translated by F. Max Müller.

Vol. XX. *The Vâyu-Purâna.* Translated by Professor Bhandarkar, of Elphinstone College, Bombay.

Vol. XXI. *The Saddharma-pundarîka.* Translated by Professor Kern.

Vol. XXII. *The Âkârâṅga-Sûtra.* Translated by Professor Jacobi.

Anecdota Oxoniensia:

Classical Series. Vol. I. Part I. *The English Manuscripts of the Nicomachean Ethics,* described in relation to Bekker's Manuscripts and other Sources. By J. A. Stewart, M.A., Classical Lecturer, Christ Church. Small 4to. 3*s.* 6*d.*

Classical Series. Vol. I. Part II. *Nonius Marcellus,* de Compendiosa Doctrina, Harleian MS. 2719. Collated by J. H. Onions, M.A., Senior Student of Christ Church. Small 4to. 3*s.* 6*d.*

Classical Series. Vol. I. Part III. *Aristotle's Physics.* Book VII. Collation of various MSS.; with an Introduction by R. Shute, M.A. Small 4to. 2*s.*

Semitic Series. Vol. I. Part I. *Commentary on Ezra and Nehemiah.* By Rabbi Saadiah. Edited by H. J. Mathews, M.A., Exeter College, Oxford. Small 4to. 3*s.* 6*d.*

Aryan Series. Vol. I. Part I. *Buddhist Texts from Japan.* Edited by F. Max Müller. Small 4to. 3*s.* 6*d.*

Mediaeval and Modern Series. Vol. I. Part I. *Sinonoma Bartholomei;* A Glossary from a Fourteenth-Century MS. in the Library of Pembroke College, Oxford. Edited by J. L. G. Mowat, M.A., Fellow of Pembroke College. Small 4to. 3*s.* 6*d.*

Clarendon Press Series

The Delegates of the Clarendon Press having undertaken the publication of a series of works, chiefly educational, and entitled the Clarendon Press Series, have published, or have in preparation, the following.

Those to which prices are attached are already published; the others are in preparation.

I. ENGLISH.

A First Reading Book. By Marie Eichens of Berlin; and edited by Anne J. Clough. Extra fcap. 8vo. stiff covers, 4*d.*

Oxford Reading Book, Part I. For Little Children. Extra fcap. 8vo. stiff covers, 6*d.*

Oxford Reading Book, Part II. For Junior Classes. Extra fcap. 8vo. stiff covers, 6*d.*

An Elementary English Grammar and Exercise Book. By O. W. Tancock, M.A., Head Master of Norwich School. Second Edition. Extra fcap. 8vo. cloth, 1*s.* 6*d.*

An English Grammar and Reading Book, for Lower Forms in Classical Schools. By O. W. Tancock, M.A., Head Master of Norwich School. Third Edition. Extra fcap. 8vo. cloth, 3*s.* 6*d.*

Typical Selections from the best English Writers, with Introductory Notices. Second Edition. In Two Volumes. Extra fcap. 8vo. cloth, 3*s.* 6*d.* each.

Vol. I. Latimer to Berkeley. Vol. II. Pope to Macaulay.

The Philology of the English Tongue. By J. Earle, M.A., formerly Fellow of Oriel College, and Professor of Anglo-Saxon, Oxford. Third Edition. Extra fcap. 8vo. cloth, 7*s.* 6*d.*

A Book for the Beginner in Anglo-Saxon. By John Earle, M.A., Professor of Anglo-Saxon, Oxford. Second Edition. Extra fcap. 8vo. cloth, 2*s*. 6*d*.

An Anglo-Saxon Reader. In Prose and Verse. With Grammatical Introduction, Notes, and Glossary. By Henry Sweet, M.A. Third Edition. Extra fcap. 8vo. cloth, 8*s*. 6*d*.

An Anglo-Saxon Primer, with Grammar, Notes, and Glossary. By the same Author. Extra fcap. 8vo. cloth, 2*s*. 6*d*.

The Ormulum; with the Notes and Glossary of Dr. R. M. White. Edited by Rev. R. Holt, M.A. 1878. 2 vols. Extra fcap. 8vo. cloth, 21*s*.

Specimens of Early English. A New and Revised Edition. With Introduction, Notes, and Glossarial Index. By R. Morris, LL.D., and W. W. Skeat, M.A.

Part I. From Old English Homilies to King Horn (A.D. 1150 to A.D. 1300). Extra fcap. 8vo. cloth, 9*s*.

Part II. From Robert of Gloucester to Gower (A.D. 1298 to A.D. 1393). Second Edition. Extra fcap. 8vo. cloth, 7*s*. 6*d*.

Specimens of English Literature, from the 'Ploughmans Crede' to the 'Shepheardes Calender' (A.D. 1394 to A.D. 1579). With Introduction, Notes, and Glossarial Index. By W. W. Skeat, M.A. Extra fcap. 8vo. cloth, 7*s*. 6*d*.

The Vision of William concerning Piers the Plowman, by William Langland. Edited, with Notes, by W. W. Skeat, M.A. Third Edition. Extra fcap. 8vo. cloth, 4*s*. 6*d*.

Chaucer. The Prioresses Tale; Sir Thopas; The Monkes Tale; The Clerkes Tale; The Squieres Tale, &c. Edited by W. W. Skeat, M.A. Second Edition. Extra fcap. 8vo. cloth, 4*s*. 6*d*.

Chaucer. The Tale of the Man of Lawe; The Pardoneres Tale; The Second Nonnes Tale; The Chanouns Yemannes Tale. By the same Editor. Second Edition. Extra fcap. 8vo. cloth, 4*s*. 6*d*. (See also p. 20.)

Old English Drama. Marlowe's Tragical History of Dr. Faustus, and Greene's Honourable History of Friar Bacon and Friar Bungay. Edited by A. W. Ward, M.A., Professor of History and English Literature in Owens College, Manchester. 1878. Extra fcap. 8vo. cloth, 5*s*. 6*d*.

Marlowe. Edward II. With Introduction, Notes, &c. By O. W. Tancock, M.A., Head Master of Norwich School. Extra fcap. 8vo. cloth, 3*s*.

Shakespeare. Hamlet. Edited by W. G. Clark, M.A., and W. Aldis Wright, M.A. Extra fcap. 8vo. stiff covers, 2*s*.

Shakespeare. Select Plays. Edited by W. Aldis Wright, M.A. Extra fcap. 8vo. stiff covers.

The Tempest, 1*s*. 6*d*.	King Lear, 1*s*. 6*d*.
As You Like It, 1*s*. 6*d*.	A Midsummer Night's Dream, 1*s*. 6*d*.
Julius Cæsar, 2*s*.	Coriolanus, 2*s*. 6*d*.
Richard the Third, 2*s*. 6*d*.	Henry the Fifth, 2*s*.

Twelfth Night. *In the Press.* (For other Plays, see p. 20.)

Milton. Areopagitica. With Introduction and Notes. By J. W. Hales, M.A., late Fellow of Christ's College, Cambridge. Second Edition. Extra fcap. 8vo. cloth, 3*s*.

Bunyan. Holy War. Edited by E. Venables, M.A. In the Press. (See also p. 21.)

Locke's Conduct of the Understanding. Edited, with Introduction, Notes, &c., by T. Fowler, M.A., Professor of Logic in the University of Oxford. Second Edition. Extra fcap. 8vo. cloth, 2*s*.

Addison. Selections from Papers in the Spectator. With Notes. By T. Arnold, M.A., University College. Extra fcap. 8vo. cloth, 4*s*. 6*d*.

Burke. Four Letters on the Proposals for Peace with the Regicide Directory of France. Edited, with Introduction and Notes, by E. J. Payne, M.A. Extra fcap. 8vo. cloth, 5*s*. (See also p. 21.)

Also the following in paper covers:—

Goldsmith. The Deserted Village. 2*d.*

Gray. Elegy and Ode on Eton College. 2*d.*

Johnson. Vanity of Human Wishes. With Notes by E. J. Payne, M.A. 4*d.*

Keats. Hyperion, Book I. With Notes by W. T. Arnold, B.A. 4*d.*

Milton. With Notes by R. C. Browne, M.A.
Lycidas, 3*d.* L'Allegro, 3*d.* Il Penseroso, 4*d.* Comus, 6*d.* Samson Agonistes, 6*d.*

Parnell. The Hermit. 2*d.*

Scott. Lay of the Last Minstrel. Introduction and Canto I, with Preface and Notes by W. Minto, M.A. 6*d.*

A SERIES OF ENGLISH CLASSICS,

Designed to meet the wants of Students in English Literature, by the late Rev. J. S. BREWER, M.A., of Queen's College, Oxford, and Professor of English Literature at King's College, London.

1. *Chaucer. The Prologue to the Canterbury* Tales; The Knightes Tale; The Nonne Prestes Tale. Edited by R. Morris, Editor of Specimens of Early English, &c., &c. Sixth Edition. Extra fcap. 8vo. cloth, 2*s.* 6*d.* (See also p. 18.)

2. *Spenser's Faery Queene.* Books I and II. Designed chiefly for the use of Schools. With Introduction, Notes, and Glossary. By G. W. Kitchin, M.A.
   Book I. Eighth Edition. Extra fcap. 8vo. cloth, 2*s.* 6*d.*
   Book II. Sixth Edition. Extra fcap. 8vo. cloth, 2*s.* 6*d.*

3. *Hooker. Ecclesiastical Polity, Book I.* Edited by R. W. Church, M.A., Dean of St. Paul's; formerly Fellow of Oriel College, Oxford. Second Edition. Extra fcap. 8vo. cloth, 2*s.*

4. *Shakespeare.* Select Plays. Edited by W. G. Clark, M.A., Fellow of Trinity College, Cambridge; and W. Aldis Wright, M.A., Trinity College, Cambridge. Extra fcap. 8vo. stiff covers.
   I. The Merchant of Venice. 1*s.*
   II. Richard the Second. 1*s.* 6*d.*
   III. Macbeth. 1*s.* 6*d.* (For other Plays, see p. 19.)

5. *Bacon.*

I. Advancement of Learning. Edited by W. Aldis Wright M.A. Second Edition. Extra fcap. 8vo. cloth, 4*s*. 6*d*.

II. The Essays. With Introduction and Notes. By J. R. Thursfield, M.A., Fellow and formerly Tutor of Jesus College, Oxford. *In Preparation.*

6. *Milton.* Poems. Edited by R. C. Browne, M.A. 2 vols. Fifth Edition. Extra fcap. 8vo. cloth, 6*s*. 6*d*.

Sold separately, Vol. I. 4*s*.; Vol. II. 3*s*. (See also p. 20.)

7. *Dryden.* Select Poems. Stanzas on the Death of Oliver Cromwell; Astræa Redux; Annus Mirabilis; Absalom and Achitophel; Religio Laici; The Hind and the Panther. Edited by W. D. Christie, M.A. Second Edition. Extra fcap. 8vo. cloth, 3*s*. 6*d*.

8. *Bunyan. The Pilgrim's Progress, Grace* Abounding, Relation of the Imprisonment of Mr. John Bunyan. Edited, with Biographical Introduction and Notes, by E. Venables, M.A. 1879. Extra fcap. 8vo. cloth, 5*s*.

9. *Pope.* With Introduction and Notes. By Mark Pattison, B.D., Rector of Lincoln College, Oxford.

I. Essay on Man. Sixth Edition. Extra fcap. 8vo. 1*s*. 6*d*.

II. Satires and Epistles. Third Edition. Extra fcap. 8vo. 2*s*.

10. *Johnson. Rasselas; Lives of Pope and* Dryden. Edited by Alfred Milnes, B.A. (London), late Scholar of Lincoln College, Oxford. Extra fcap. 8vo. cloth, 4*s*. 6*d*.

11. *Burke.* Select Works. Edited, with Introduction and Notes, by E. J. Payne, M.A., of Lincoln's Inn, Barrister-at-Law, and Fellow of University College, Oxford.

I. Thoughts on the Present Discontents; the two Speeches on America. Second Edition. Extra fcap. 8vo. cloth, 4*s*. 6*d*.

II. Reflections on the French Revolution. Second Edition. Extra fcap. 8vo. cloth, 5*s*. (See also p. 19.)

12. *Cowper.* Edited, with Life, Introductions, and Notes, by H. T. Griffith, B.A., formerly Scholar of Pembroke College, Oxford.

I. The Didactic Poems of 1782, with Selections from the Minor Pieces, A.D. 1779–1783. Extra fcap. 8vo. cloth, 3*s*.

II. The Task, with Tirocinium, and Selections from the Minor Poems, A.D. 1784–1799. Extra fcap. 8vo. cloth, 3*s*.

II. LATIN.

An Elementary Latin Grammar. By John B. Allen, M.A., Head Master of Perse Grammar School, Cambridge. Third Edition, Revised and Corrected. Extra fcap. 8vo. cloth, 2*s.* 6*d.*

A First Latin Exercise Book. By the same Author. Third Edition. Extra fcap. 8vo. cloth, 2*s.* 6*d.*

A Second Latin Exercise Book. By the same Author. *Preparing.*

Anglice Reddenda, or Easy Extracts, Latin and Greek, for Unseen Translation. By C. S. Jerram, M.A. Second Edition, Revised and Enlarged. Extra fcap. 8vo. cloth, 2*s.* 6*d.*

Passages for Translation into Latin. For the use of Passmen and others. Selected by J. Y. Sargent, M.A., Fellow and Tutor of Magdalen College, Oxford. Fifth Edition. Extra fcap. 8vo. cloth, 2*s.* 6*d.*

First Latin Reader. By T. J. Nunns, M.A. Third Edition. Extra fcap. 8vo. cloth, 2*s.*

Second Latin Reader. In Preparation.

Caesar. The Commentaries (for Schools). With Notes and Maps. By Charles E. Moberly, M.A.

Part I. *The Gallic War.* Third Edition. Extra fcap. 8vo. cloth, 4*s.* 6*d.*

Part II. *The Civil War.* Extra fcap. 8vo. cloth, 3*s.* 6*d.*

The Civil War. Book I. Extra fcap. 8vo. cloth, 2*s.*

Cicero. Selection of interesting and descriptive passages. With Notes. By Henry Walford, M.A. In three Parts. Second Edition. Extra fcap. 8vo. cloth, 4*s.* 6*d.* Each Part separately, limp, 1*s.* 6*d.*

Part I. Anecdotes from Grecian and Roman History.

Part II. Omens and Dreams: Beauties of Nature.

Part III. Rome's Rule of her Provinces.

Cicero. Selected Letters (for Schools). With Notes. By the late C. E. Prichard, M.A., and E. R. Bernard, M.A. Second Edition. Extra fcap. 8vo. cloth, 3*s.*

Cicero. Select Orations (for Schools). With Notes. By J. R. King, M.A. Extra fcap. 8vo. cloth, 2*s.* 6*d.*

Cornelius Nepos. With Notes. By Oscar Browning, M.A. Second Edition. Extra fcap. 8vo. cloth, 2*s.* 6*d.*

Livy. Selections (for Schools). With Notes and Maps. By H. Lee-Warner, M.A. Extra fcap. 8vo. In Parts, limp, each 1*s.* 6*d.*

Part I. The Caudine Disaster.
Part II. Hannibal's Campaign in Italy.
Part III. The Macedonian War.

Livy. Books V–VII. With Introduction and Notes. By A. R. Cluer, B.A. Extra fcap. 8vo. cloth, 3*s.* 6*d.*

Ovid. Selections for the use of Schools. With Introductions and Notes, and an Appendix on the Roman Calendar. By W. Ramsay, M.A. Edited by G. G. Ramsay, M.A., Professor of Humanity, Glasgow. Second Edition. Extra fcap. 8vo. cloth, 5*s.* 6*d.*

Pliny. Selected Letters (for Schools). With Notes. By the late C. E. Prichard, M.A., and E. R. Bernard, M.A. Second Edition. Extra fcap. 8vo. cloth, 3*s.*

Catulli Veronensis Liber. Iterum recognovit, apparatum criticum prolegomena appendices addidit, Robinson Ellis, A.M. 1878. Demy 8vo. cloth, 16*s.*

A Commentary on Catullus. By Robinson Ellis, M.A. 1876. Demy 8vo. cloth, 16*s.*

Catulli Veronensis Carmina Selecta, secundum recognitionem Robinson Ellis, A.M. Extra fcap. 8vo. cloth, 3*s.* 6*d.*

Cicero de Oratore. With Introduction and Notes, by A S. Wilkins, M.A., Professor of Latin, Owens College, Manchester.

Book I. 1879. 8vo. cloth, 6*s.* Book II. 1881. 8vo. cloth, 5*s.*

Cicero's Philippic Orations. With Notes. By J. R. King, M.A. Second Edition. 1879. 8vo. cloth, 10*s*. 6*d*.

Cicero. Select Letters. With English Introductions, Notes, and Appendices. By Albert Watson, M.A. Third Edition. 1881. Demy 8vo. cloth, 18*s*.

Cicero. Select Letters. Text. By the same Editor. Extra fcap. 8vo. cloth, 4*s*.

Cicero pro Cluentio. With Introduction and Notes. By W. Ramsay, M.A. Edited by G. G. Ramsay, M.A. Extra fcap. 8vo. cloth, 3*s*. 6*d*.

Horace. With a Commentary. Volume I. The Odes, Carmen Seculare, and Epodes. By Edward C. Wickham, M.A., Head Master of Wellington College. Second Edition. 1877. Demy 8vo. cloth, 12*s*.

Horace. A reprint of the above, in a size suitable for the use of Schools. Extra fcap. 8vo. cloth, 5*s*. 6*d*.

Livy, Book I. With Introduction, Historical Examination, and Notes. By J. R. Seeley, M.A., Regius Professor of Modern History, Cambridge. Third Edition. 1881. 8vo. cloth, 6*s*.

Ovid. P. Ovidii Nasonis Ibis. Ex Novis Codicibus Edidit. Scholia Vetera Commentarium cum Prolegomenis Appendice Indice addidit, R. Ellis, A.M. Demy 8vo. cloth, 10*s*. 6*d*.

Persius. The Satires. With a Translation and Commentary. By John Conington, M.A. Edited by Henry Nettleship, M.A. Second Edition. 1874. 8vo. cloth, 7*s*. 6*d*.

Virgil. With Introduction and Notes, by T. L. Papillon, M.A., Fellow of New College, Oxford. Two vols. crown 8vo. cloth, 10*s*. 6*d*.

Selections from the less known Latin Poets. By North Pinder, M.A. 1869. Demy 8vo. cloth, 15*s.*

Fragments and Specimens of Early Latin. With Introductions and Notes. 1874. By John Wordsworth, M.A. 8vo. cloth, 18*s.*

Tacitus. The Annals. With Essays and Notes. Preparing.

Vergil: Suggestions Introductory to a Study of the Aeneid. By H. Nettleship, M.A. 8vo. sewed, 1*s.* 6*d.*

Ancient Lives of Vergil; with an Essay on the Poems of Vergil, in connection with his Life and Times. By H. Nettleship, M.A. 8vo. sewed, 2*s.*

The Roman Satura: its original form in connection with its literary development. By H. Nettleship, M.A. 8vo. sewed, 1*s.*

A Manual of Comparative Philology. By T. L. Papillon, M.A., Fellow and Lecturer of New College. Third Edition. 1882. Crown 8vo. cloth, 6*s.*

The Roman Poets of the Augustan Age. By William Young Sellar, M.A., Professor of Humanity in the University of Edinburgh. VIRGIL. 1877. 8vo. cloth, 14*s.*

The Roman Poets of the Republic. By the same Author. New Edition, Revised and Enlarged. 1881. 8vo. cloth, 14*s.*

III. GREEK.

A Greek Primer, for the use of beginners in that Language. By the Right Rev. Charles Wordsworth, D.C.L., Bishop of St. Andrews. Sixth Edition, Revised and Enlarged. Extra fcap. 8vo. cloth, 1*s.* 6*d.*

Graecae Grammaticae Rudimenta in usum Scholarum. Auctore Carolo Wordsworth, D C.L. Twentieth Edition. 1882. 12mo. cloth, 4*s.*

A Greek-English Lexicon, abridged from Liddell and Scott's 4to. edition, chiefly for the use of Schools. Nineteenth Edition. Carefully Revised throughout. 1880. Square 12mo. cloth, 7*s.* 6*d.*

Greek Verbs, Irregular and Defective; their forms, meaning, and quantity; embracing all the Tenses used by Greek writers, with references to the passages in which they are found. By W. Veitch. Fourth Edition. Crown 8vo. cloth, 10*s.* 6*d.*

The Elements of Greek Accentuation (for Schools): abridged from his larger work by H. W. Chandler, M.A., Waynflete Professor of Moral and Metaphysical Philosophy, Oxford. Extra fcap. 8vo. cloth, 2*s.* 6*d.*

A Series of Graduated Greek Readers:—

First Greek Reader. By W. G. Rushbrooke, M.L., formerly Fellow of St. John's College, Cambridge, Second Classical Master at the City of London School. Second Edition. Extra fcap. 8vo. cloth, 2*s.* 6*d.*

Second Greek Reader. By A. M. Bell, M.A. Extra fcap. 8vo. cloth, 3*s.* 6*d.*

Third Greek Reader. In Preparation.

Fourth Greek Reader; being Specimens of Greek Dialects. With Introductions and Notes. By W. W. Merry, M.A., Fellow and Lecturer of Lincoln College. Extra fcap. 8vo. cloth, 4*s.* 6*d.*

Fifth Greek Reader. Part I. Selections from Greek Epic and Dramatic Poetry, with Introductions and Notes. By Evelyn Abbott, M.A., Fellow of Balliol College. Extra fcap. 8vo. cloth, 4*s.* 6*d.*

Part II. By the same Editor. In Preparation.

The Golden Treasury of Ancient Greek Poetry; being a Collection of the finest passages in the Greek Classic Poets, with Introductory Notices and Notes. By R. S. Wright, M.A., Fellow of Oriel College, Oxford. Extra fcap. 8vo. cloth, 8*s.* 6*d.*

A Golden Treasury of Greek Prose, being a collection of the finest passages in the principal Greek Prose Writers, with Introductory Notices and Notes. By R. S. Wright, M.A., and J. E. L. Shadwell, M.A. Extra fcap. 8vo. cloth, 4*s.* 6*d.*

Aeschylus. Prometheus Bound (for Schools). With Introduction and Notes, by A. O. Prickard, M.A., Fellow of New College. Extra fcap. 8vo. cloth, 2*s.*

Aeschylus. Agamemnon. With Introduction and Notes by Arthur Sidgwick, M.A., Tutor of Corpus Christi College, Oxford; late Fellow of Trinity College, Cambridge, and Assistant Master of Rugby School. Extra fcap. 8vo. cloth, 3*s.*

Aeschylus. The Choephoroe. With Introduction and Notes by the same Editor. Preparing.

Aristophanes. In Single Plays, edited, with English Notes, Introductions, &c., by W. W. Merry, M.A. Extra fcap. 8vo.

The Clouds, 2*s.* The Acharnians, 2*s.*

Other Plays will follow.

Arrian. Selections (for Schools). With Notes. By J. S. Phillpotts, B.C.L., Head Master of Bedford School.

Cebes. Tabula. With Introduction and Notes by C. S. Jerram, M.A. Extra fcap. 8vo. cloth, 2*s.* 6*d.*

Euripides. Alcestis (for Schools). By C. S. Jerram, M.A. Extra fcap. 8vo. cloth, 2*s.* 6*d.*

Euripides. Helena. Edited with Introduction, Notes, and Critical Appendix, for Upper and Middle Forms. By C. S. Jerram, M.A. Extra fcap. 8vo. cloth, 3*s.*

Herodotus. Selections from. Edited, with Introduction, Notes, and a Map, by W. W. Merry, M.A., Fellow and Lecturer of Lincoln College. Extra fcap. 8vo. cloth, 2*s.* 6*d.*

Homer. Odyssey, Books I–XII (for Schools). By W. W. Merry, M.A. Twenty-fourth Thousand. Extra fcap. 8vo. cloth, 4*s.* 6*d.*

Book II, separately, 1*s.* 6*d.*

Homer. Odyssey, Books XIII–XXIV (for Schools). By the same Editor. Extra fcap. 8vo. cloth, 5*s.*

Homer. Iliad, Book I (for Schools). By D. B. Monro, M.A. Extra fcap. 8vo. cloth, 2*s.*

Homer. Iliad, Books VI and XXI. With Introduction and Notes. By Herbert Hailstone, M.A., late Scholar of St. Peter's College, Cambridge. Extra fcap. 8vo. cloth, 1*s.* 6*d.* each.

Lucian. Vera Historia (for Schools). By C. S. Jerram, M.A. Extra fcap. 8vo. cloth, 1*s.* 6*d.*

Plato. Selections (for Schools). Edited with Notes by J. Purves, M.A., Fellow and late Lecturer of Balliol College, Oxford. Extra fcap. 8vo. cloth, 6*s.* 6*d.*

Sophocles. In Single Plays, with English Notes, &c. By Lewis Campbell, M.A., Professor of Greek in the University of St. Andrew's, and Evelyn Abbott, M.A., Balliol College, Oxford. Extra fcap. 8vo. limp.

Oedipus Tyrannus. New and Revised Edition. 2*s.*

Oedipus Coloneus, Antigone, 1*s.* 9*d.* each.

Ajax, Electra, Trachiniae, Philoctetes, 2*s.* each.

Sophocles. Oedipus Rex: Dindorf's Text, with Notes by the present Bishop of St. David's. Ext. fcap. 8vo. limp, 1*s.* 6*d.*

Theocritus (for Schools). With Notes. By H. Kynaston, M.A. (late Snow), Head Master of Cheltenham College. Third Edition. Extra fcap. 8vo. cloth, 4*s.* 6*d.*

Xenophon. Easy Selections (for Junior Classes). With a Vocabulary, Notes, and Map. By J. S. Phillpotts, B.C.L., and C. S. Jerram, M.A. Third Edition. Extra fcap. 8vo. cloth, 3*s.* 6*d.*

Xenophon. Selections (for Schools). With Notes and Maps. By J. S. Phillpotts, B.C.L., Head Master of Bedford School. Fourth Edition. Extra fcap. 8vo. cloth, 3*s.* 6*d.*

Xenophon. Anabasis, Book II. With Notes and Map. By C. S. Jerram, M.A. Extra fcap. 8vo. cloth, 2*s.*

Aristotle's Politics. By W. L. Newman, M.A., Fellow of Balliol College, Oxford.

Aristotelian Studies. I. On the Structure of the Seventh Book of the Nicomachean Ethics. By. J. C. Wilson, M.A., Fellow of Oriel College, Oxford. 1879. Medium 8vo. stiff, 5*s.*

Demosthenes and Aeschines. The Orations of Demosthenes and Æschines on the Crown. With Introductory Essays and Notes. By G. A. Simcox, M.A., and W. H. Simcox, M.A. 1872. 8vo. cloth, 12*s.*

Homer. Odyssey, Books I–XII. Edited with English Notes, Appendices, etc. By W. W. Merry, M.A., and the late James Riddell, M.A. 1876. Demy 8vo. cloth, 16*s.*

Homer. Iliad. With Introduction and Notes. By D. B. Monro, M.A., Provost of Oriel College, Oxford. Preparing.

A Grammar of the Homeric Dialect. By D. B. Monro, M.A., Provost of Oriel College. Demy 8vo. cloth, 10*s.* 6*d.*

Sophocles. The Plays and Fragments. With English Notes and Introductions, by Lewis Campbell, M.A., Professor of Greek, St. Andrews, formerly Fellow of Queen's College, Oxford. 2 vols.

Vol. I. Oedipus Tyrannus. Oedipus Coloneus. Antigone. Second Edition. 1879. 8vo. cloth, 16*s.*

Vol. II. Ajax. Electra. Trachiniae. Philoctetes. Fragments. 1881. 8vo. cloth, 16*s.*

Sophocles. The Text of the Seven Plays. By the same Editor. Extra fcap. 8vo. cloth, 4*s.* 6*d.*

A Manual of Greek Historical Inscriptions. By E. L. Hicks, M.A., formerly Fellow and Tutor of Corpus Christi College, Oxford. Demy 8vo. cloth, 10*s.* 6*d.*

IV. FRENCH.

An Etymological Dictionary of the French Language, with a Preface on the Principles of French Etymology. By A. Brachet. Translated into English by G. W. Kitchin, M.A. Second Edition. Crown 8vo. cloth, 7*s*. 6*d*.

Brachet's Historical Grammar of the French Language. Translated into English by G. W. Kitchin, M.A. Fourth Edition. Extra fcap. 8vo. cloth, 3*s*. 6*d*.

A Short History of French Literature. By George Saintsbury, M.A. Crown 8vo. cloth, 10*s*. 6*d*.

Specimens of French Literature, from Villon to Hugo. Selected and arranged by the same Editor. *Preparing*.

A Primer of French Literature. By the same Author. Extra fcap. 8vo. cloth, 2*s*.

Corneille's Horace. Edited with Introduction and Notes by George Saintsbury. Extra fcap. 8vo. cloth, 2*s*. 6*d*.

French Classics, Edited by GUSTAVE MASSON, B.A.

Corneille's Cinna, and Molière's Les Femmes Savantes. With Introduction and Notes. Extra fcap. 8vo. cloth, 2*s*. 6*d*.

Racine's Andromaque, and Corneille's Le Menteur. With Louis Racine's Life of his Father. Extra fcap. 8vo. cloth, 2*s*. 6*d*.

Molière's Les Fourberies de Scapin, and Racine's Athalie. With Voltaire's Life of Molière. Extra fcap. 8vo. cloth, 2*s*. 6*d*.

Selections from the Correspondence of Madame de Sévigné and her chief Contemporaries. Intended more especially for Girls' Schools. Extra fcap. 8vo. cloth, 3*s*.

Voyage autour de ma Chambre, by Xavier de Maistre; Ourika, by *Madame de Duras*; La Dot de Suzette, by *Fievée*; Les Jumeaux de l'Hôtel Corneille, by *Edmond About*; Mésaventures d'un Écolier, by *Rodolphe Töpffer*. Extra fcap. 8vo cloth, 2*s*. 6*d*.

Regnard's Le Joueur and Brueys and Palaprat's Le Grondeur. Extra fcap. 8vo. cloth, *2s. 6d.*

Louis XIV and his Contemporaries; as described in Extracts from the best Memoirs of the Seventeenth Century. With English Notes, Genealogical Tables, &c. Extra fcap. 8vo. cloth, *2s. 6d.*

V. GERMAN.

LANGE'S German Course. By HERMANN LANGE, Teacher of Modern Languages, Manchester:

The Germans at Home; a Practical Introduction to German Conversation, with an Appendix containing the Essentials of German Grammar. Second Edition. 8vo. cloth, *2s. 6d.*

The German Manual; a German Grammar, a Reading Book, and a Handbook of German Conversation. 8vo. cloth, *7s. 6d.*

A Grammar of the German Language. 8vo. cloth, *3s. 6d.*

This 'Grammar' is a reprint of the Grammar contained in 'The German Manual,' and, in this separate form, is intended for the use of Students who wish to make themselves acquainted with German Grammar chiefly for the purpose of being able to read German books.

German Composition; Extracts from English and American writers for Translation into German, with Hints for Translation in footnotes. In the Press.

Lessing's Laokoon. With Introduction, English Notes, etc. By A. Hamann, Phil. Doc., M.A. Extra fcap. 8vo. cloth, *4s. 6d.*

Wilhelm Tell. A Drama. By Schiller. Translated into English Verse by E. Massie, M.A. Extra fcap. 8vo. cloth, *5s.*

Also, Edited by C. A. BUCHHEIM, Phil. Doc., Professor in King's College, London:

Goethe's Egmont. With a Life of Goethe, &c. Third Edition. Extra fcap. 8vo. cloth, 3*s.*

Schiller's Wilhelm Tell. With a Life of Schiller; an historical and critical Introduction, Arguments, and a complete Commentary. Fourth Edition. Extra fcap. 8vo. cloth, 3*s.* 6*d.*

Lessing's Minna von Barnhelm. A Comedy. With a Life of Lessing, Critical Analysis, Complete Commentary, &c. Fourth Edition. Extra fcap. 8vo. cloth, 3*s.* 6*d.*

Schiller's Historische Skizzen; Egmonts Leben und Tod, and Belagerung von Antwerpen. Second Edition. Extra fcap. 8vo. cloth, 2*s.* 6*d.*

Goethe's Iphigenie auf Tauris. A Drama. With a Critical Introduction and Notes. Extra fcap. 8vo. cloth, 3*s.*

Modern German Reader. A Graduated Collection of Prose Extracts from Modern German writers:—

Part I. With English Notes, a Grammatical Appendix, and a complete Vocabulary. Second Edition. Extra fcap. 8vo. cloth, 2*s.* 6*d.*

Parts II and III in Preparation.

Lessing's Nathan der Weise. With Introduction, Notes, etc. Extra fcap. 8vo. cloth, 4*s.* 6*d.*

In Preparation.

Becker's (K. F.) Friedrich der Grosse.

Schiller's Maria Stuart. With Notes, Introduction, &c.

Schiller's Jungfrau von Orleans. With Notes, Introduction, &c.

Selections from the Poems of *Schiller* and *Goethe.*

VI. MATHEMATICS, &c.

Figures Made Easy: a first Arithmetic Book. (Introductory to 'The Scholar's Arithmetic.') By Lewis Hensley, M.A., formerly Fellow and Assistant Tutor of Trinity College, Cambridge. Crown 8vo. cloth, 6*d.*

Answers to the Examples in Figures made Easy, together with two thousand additional Examples formed from the Tables in the same, with Answers. By the same Author. Crown 8vo. cloth, 1*s.*

The Scholar's Arithmetic; with Answers to the Examples. By the same Author. Crown 8vo. cloth, 4*s.* 6*d.*

The Scholar's Algebra. An Introductory work on Algebra. By the same Author. Crown 8vo. cloth, 4*s.* 6*d.*

Book-keeping. By R. G. C. Hamilton, Financial Assistant Secretary to the Board of Trade, and John Ball (of the Firm of Quilter, Ball, and Co.), Co-Examiners in Book-keeping for the Society of Arts. New and enlarged Edition. Extra fcap. 8vo. limp cloth, 2*s.*

A Course of Lectures on Pure Geometry. By Henry J. Stephen Smith, M.A., F.R.S., Fellow of Corpus Christi College, and Savilian Professor of Geometry in the University of Oxford.

Acoustics. By W. F. Donkin, M.A., F.R.S., Savilian Professor of Astronomy, Oxford. 1870. Crown 8vo. cloth, 7*s.* 6*d.*

A Treatise on Electricity and Magnetism. By J. Clerk Maxwell, M.A., F.R.S., Professor of Experimental Physics in the University of Cambridge. Second Edition. 2 vols. Demy 8vo. cloth, 1*l.* 11*s.* 6*d.*

An Elementary Treatise on Electricity. By the same Author. Edited by William Garnett, M.A. Demy 8vo. cloth, 7*s.* 6*d.*

A Treatise on Statics. By G. M. Minchin, M.A., Professor of Applied Mathematics in the Indian Engineering College, Cooper's Hill. Second Edition, Revised and Enlarged. 1879. 8vo. cloth, 14*s.*

Uniplanar Kinematics of Solids and Fluids. By G. M. Minchin, M.A. Crown 8vo. cloth, 7s. 6d.

A Treatise on the Kinetic Theory of Gases. By Henry William Watson, M.A., formerly Fellow of Trinity College, Cambridge. 1876. 8vo. cloth, 3s. 6d.

A Treatise on the Application of Generalised Coordinates to the Kinetics of a Material System. By H. W. Watson, M.A., and S. H. Burbury, M.A. 1879. 8vo. cloth, 6s.

Geodesy. By Colonel Alexander Ross Clarke, C.B., R.E. 1880. 8vo. cloth, 12s. 6d.

VII. PHYSICAL SCIENCE.

A Handbook of Descriptive Astronomy. By G. F. Chambers, F.R.A.S. Third Edition. 1877. Demy 8vo. cloth, 28s.

A Cycle of Celestial Objects. Observed, Reduced, and Discussed by Admiral W. H. Smyth, R.N. Revised, condensed, and greatly enlarged by G. F. Chambers, F.R.A.S. 1881. 8vo. cloth, 21s.

Chemistry for Students. By A. W. Williamson, Phil. Doc., F.R.S., Professor of Chemistry, University College, London. A new Edition, with Solutions. 1873. Extra fcap. 8vo. cloth, 8s. 6d.

A Treatise on Heat, with numerous Woodcuts and Diagrams. By Balfour Stewart, LL.D., F.R.S., Professor of Natural Philosophy in Owens College, Manchester. Fourth Edition. 1881. Extra fcap. 8vo. cloth, 7s. 6d.

Lessons on Thermodynamics. By R. E. Baynes, M.A., Senior Student of Christ Church, Oxford, and Lee's Reader in Physics. 1878. Crown 8vo. cloth, 7s. 6d.

Forms of Animal Life. By G. Rolleston, M.D., F.R.S., Linacre Professor of Physiology, Oxford. Illustrated by Descriptions and Drawings of Dissections. A New Edition in the Press.

Exercises in Practical Chemistry. Vol. I. Elementary Exercises. By A. G. Vernon Harcourt, M.A.; and H. G. Madan, M.A. Third Edition. Revised by H. G. Madan, M.A. Crown 8vo. cloth, 9*s*.

Tables of Qualitative Analysis. Arranged by H. G. Madan, M.A. Large 4to. paper covers, 4*s*. 6*d*.

Crystallography. By M. H. N. Story-Maskelyne, M.A., Professor of Mineralogy, Oxford; and Deputy Keeper in the Department of Minerals, British Museum. In the Press.

VIII. HISTORY.

The Constitutional History of England, in its Origin and Development. By William Stubbs, D.D., Regius Professor of Modern History. Library Edition. Three vols. demy 8vo. cloth, 2*l*. 8*s*.

Also in 3 vols. crown 8vo. price 12*s*. each.

Select Charters and other Illustrations of English Constitutional History, from the Earliest Times to the Reign of Edward I. Arranged and Edited by W. Stubbs, M.A. Fourth Edition. 1881. Crown 8vo. cloth, 8*s*. 6*d*.

A History of England, principally in the Seventeenth Century. By Leopold Von Ranke. Translated by Resident Members of the University of Oxford, under the superintendence of G. W. Kitchin, M.A., and C. W. Boase, M.A. 1875. 6 vols. 8vo. cloth, 3*l*. 3*s*.

A Short History of the Norman Conquest of England. By E. A. Freeman, M.A. Extra fcap. 8vo. cloth, 2*s*. 6*d*.

Genealogical Tables illustrative of Modern History. By H. B. George, M.A. Second Edition. Small 4to. cloth, 12*s*.

A History of France. With numerous Maps, Plans, and Tables. By G. W. Kitchin, M.A. In Three Volumes. 1873–77. Crown 8vo. cloth, each 10*s*. 6*d*.

Vol. 1. Second Edition. Down to the Year 1453.

Vol. 2. From 1453–1624.

Vol. 3. From 1624–1793.

A History of Germany and of the Empire, down to the close of the Middle Ages. By J. Bryce, D.C.L., Regius Professor of Civil Law in the University of Oxford.

A History of British India. By S. J. Owen, M.A., Reader in Indian History in the University of Oxford.

A Selection from the Despatches, Treaties, and other Papers of the Marquess Wellesley, K.G., during his Government of India. Edited by S. J. Owen, M.A., formerly Professor of History in the Elphinstone College, Bombay. 1877. 8vo. cloth, 1*l*. 4*s*.

A Selection from the Despatches, Treaties, and other Papers relating to India of Field-Marshal the Duke of Wellington, K.G. By the same Editor. 1880. 8vo. cloth, 24*s*.

A History of the United States of America. By E. J Payne, M.A., Barrister-at-Law, and Fellow of University College, Oxford. In the Press.

A History of Greece from its Conquest by the Romans to the present time, B.C. 146 to A.D. 1864. By George Finlay, LL.D. A new Edition, revised throughout, and in part re-written, with considerable additions, by the Author, and Edited by H. F. Tozer, M.A., Tutor and late Fellow of Exeter College, Oxford. 1877. 7 vols. 8vo. cloth, 3*l*. 10*s*.

A Manual of Ancient History. By George Rawlinson, M.A., Camden Professor of Ancient History, formerly Fellow of Exeter College, Oxford. Second Edition. Demy 8vo. cloth, 14*s*.

A History of Greece. By E. A. Freeman, M.A., formerly Fellow of Trinity College, Oxford.

Italy and her Invaders, A.D. 376–476. By T. Hodgkin, Fellow of University College, London. Illustrated with Plates and Maps. 2 vols. 8vo. cloth, 1*l*. 12*s*.

IX. LAW.

The Elements of Jurisprudence. By Thomas Erskine Holland, D.C.L., Chichele Professor of International Law and Diplomacy, and Fellow of All Souls College, Oxford. Second Edition. Demy 8vo. cloth, 10*s*. 6*d*.

The Institutes of Justinian, edited as a recension of the Institutes of Gaius. By the same Editor. Second Edition, 1881. Extra fcap. 8vo. cloth, 5*s*.

Select Titles from the Digest of Justinian. By T. E. Holland, D.C.L., Chichele Professor of International Law and Diplomacy, and Fellow of All Souls' College, Oxford, and C. L. Shadwell, B.C.L., Fellow of Oriel College, Oxford. 8vo. cloth, 14*s*.

Also sold in Parts, in paper covers, as follows :—

Part I. Introductory Titles. 2*s*. 6*d*.
Part II. Family Law. 1*s*.
Part III. Property Law. 2*s*. 6*d*.
Part IV. Law of Obligations (No. 1). 3*s*. 6*d*.
Part IV. Law of Obligations (No. 2). 4*s*. 6*d*.

Imperatoris Iustiniani Institutionum Libri Quattuor; with Introductions, Commentary, Excursus and Translation. By J. B. Moyle, B.C.L., M.A., of Lincoln's Inn, Barrister-at-Law, and Fellow and Tutor of New College, Oxford. 2 vols. 8vo. cloth, 21*s*.

Gaii Institutionum Juris Civilis Commentarii Quatuor; or, Elements of Roman Law by Gaius. With a Translation and Commentary by Edward Poste, M.A., Barrister-at-Law, and Fellow of Oriel College, Oxford. Second Edition. 1875. 8vo. cloth, 18*s*.

An Introduction to the Principles of Morals and Legislation. By Jeremy Bentham. Crown 8vo. cloth, 6*s*. 6*d*.

Elements of Law considered with reference to Principles of General Jurisprudence. By William Markby, M.A., Judge of the High Court of Judicature, Calcutta. Second Edition, with Supplement. 1874. Crown 8vo. cloth, 7*s*. 6*d*. Supplement separately, 2*s*.

Alberici Gentilis, I.C.D., I.C. Professoris Regii, De Iure Belli Libri Tres. Edidit Thomas Erskine Holland I.C.D., Iuris Gentium Professor Chicheleianus, Coll. Omn. Anim. Socius. necnon in Univ. Perusin. Iuris Professor Honorarius. 1877. Small 4to. half morocco, 21*s*.

International Law. By William Edward Hall, M.A., Barrister-at Law. Demy 8vo. cloth, 21*s*.

An Introduction to the History of the Law of Real Property, with original Authorities. By Kenelm E. Digby, M.A., of Lincoln's Inn, Barrister-at-Law. Second Edition. 1876. Crown 8vo. cloth, 7*s.* 6*d.*

Principles of the English Law of Contract, and of Agency in its Relation to Contract. By Sir William R. Anson, Bart., D.C.L., Warden of All Souls College, Oxford. Second Edition. Demy 8vo. cloth, 10*s.* 6*d.*

X. MENTAL AND MORAL PHILOSOPHY.

Bacon. Novum Organum. Edited, with Introduction, Notes, &c., by T. Fowler, M.A., Professor of Logic in the University of Oxford. 1878. 8vo. cloth, 14*s.*

Locke's Conduct of the Understanding. Edited, with Introduction, Notes, &c., by T. Fowler, M.A., Professor of Logic in the University of Oxford. Second Edition. Extra fcap. 8vo. cloth, 2*s.*

Selections from Berkeley, with an Introduction and Notes. For the use of Students in the Universities. By Alexander Campbell Fraser, LL.D. Second Edition. Crown 8vo. cloth, 7*s.* 6*d.* (See also p. 13.)

The Elements of Deductive Logic, designed mainly for the use of Junior Students in the Universities. By T. Fowler, M.A., Professor of Logic in the University of Oxford. Seventh Edition, with a Collection of Examples. Extra fcap. 8vo. cloth, 3*s.* 6*d.*

The Elements of Inductive Logic, designed mainly for the use of Students in the Universities. By the same Author. Third Edition. Extra fcap. 8vo. cloth, 6*s.*

A Manual of Political Economy, for the use of Schools. By J. E. Thorold Rogers, M.A., formerly Professor of Political Economy, Oxford. Third Edition. Extra fcap. 8vo. cloth, 4*s.* 6*d.*

XI. ART, &c.

A Handbook of Pictorial Art. By R. St. J. Tyrwhitt, M.A., formerly Student and Tutor of Christ Church, Oxford. With coloured Illustrations, Photographs, and a chapter on Perspective by A. Macdonald. Second Edition. 1875. 8vo. half morocco, 18*s.*

A Music Primer for Schools. By J. Troutbeck, M.A., Music Master in Westminster School, and R. F. Dale, M.A., B. Mus., Assistant Master in Westminster School. Crown 8vo. cloth, 1*s*. 6*d*.

A Treatise on Harmony. By Sir F. A. Gore Ouseley, Bart., Professor of Music in the University of Oxford. Second Edition. 4to. cloth, 10*s*.

A Treatise on Counterpoint, Canon, and Fugue, based upon that of Cherubini. By the same Author. Second Edition. 4to. cloth, 16*s*.

A Treatise on Musical Form and General Composition. By the same Author. 4to. cloth, 10*s*.

The Cultivation of the Speaking Voice. By John Hullah. Second Edition. Extra fcap. 8vo. cloth, 2*s*. 6*d*.

XII. MISCELLANEOUS.

The Construction of Healthy Dwellings; namely Houses, Hospitals, Barracks, Asylums, &c. By Douglas Galton, late Royal Engineers, C.B., F.R.S., &c. Demy 8vo. cloth, 10*s*. 6*d*.

A Treatise on Rivers and Canals, relating to the Control and Improvement of Rivers, and the Design, Construction, and Development of Canals. By Leveson Francis Vernon-Harcourt, M.A., Balliol College, Oxford, Member of the Institution of Civil Engineers. 2 vols. (Vol. I, Text. Vol. II, Plates.) 8vo. cloth, 21*s*.

A System of Physical Education: Theoretical and Practical. By Archibald Maclaren. Extra fcap. 8vo. cloth, 7*s*. 6*d*.

Specimens of Lowland Scotch and Northern English. By Dr. J. A. H. Murray. Preparing.

English Plant Names from the Tenth to the Fifteenth Century. By J. Earle, M.A. Small fcap. 8vo. cloth, 5*s*.

An Icelandic Prose Reader, with Notes, Grammar, and Glossary by Dr. Gudbrand Vigfússon and F. York Powell, M.A. 1879. Extra fcap. 8vo. cloth, 10s. 6*d*.

Dante. Selections from the Inferno. With Introduction and Notes. By H. B. Cotterill, B.A. Extra fcap. 8vo. cloth, 4*s*. 6*d*.

Tasso. La Gerusalemme Liberata. Cantos i, ii. With Introduction and Notes. By the same Editor. Extra fcap. 8vo. cloth, 2*s*. 6*d*.

The Modern Greek Language in its relation to Ancient Greek. By E. M. Geldart, B.A. Extra fcap. 8vo. cloth, 4*s*. 6*d*.

Outlines of Textual Criticism applied to the New Testament. By C. E. Hammond, M.A., Fellow and Tutor of Exeter College, Oxford. Third Edition. Extra fcap. 8vo. cloth, 3*s*. 6*d*.

A Handbook of Phonetics, including a Popular Exposition of the Principles of Spelling Reform. By Henry Sweet, M.A. Extra fcap. 8vo. cloth, 4*s*. 6*d*.

LONDON: HENRY FROWDE,

OXFORD UNIVERSITY PRESS WAREHOUSE, 7 PATERNOSTER ROW,

OXFORD: CLARENDON PRESS DEPOSITORY,

116 HIGH STREET.

The DELEGATES OF THE PRESS *invite suggestions and advice from all persons interested in education; and will be thankful for hints, &c. addressed to the* SECRETARY TO THE DELEGATES, *Clarendon Press, Oxford.*